THE *ENEADOS*

SCOTTISH TEXT SOCIETY

THE SCOTTISH TEXT SOCIETY

FIFTH SERIES

NO. 19

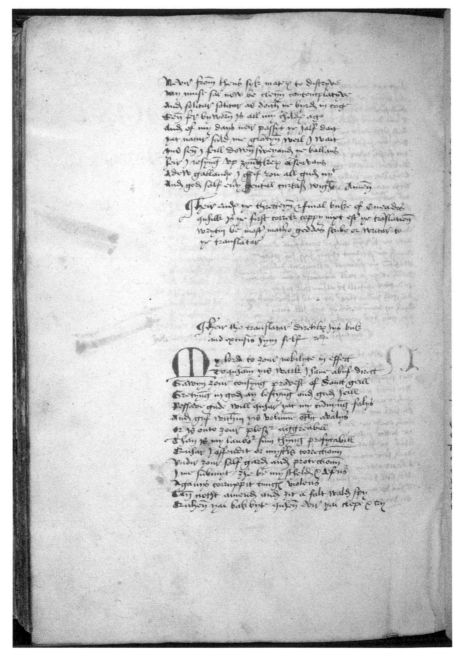

Cambridge, Trinity College Library, MS O.3.12, fol. 326v: conclusion of Book XIII with scribal colophon by Matthew Geddes. Reproduced by kind permission of the Master and Fellows of Trinity College, Cambridge.

THE *ENEADOS*

Gavin Douglas's Translation of Virgil's *Aeneid*

Volume III
Books VIII–XIII

Edited by
Priscilla Bawcutt
with Ian Cunningham

The Scottish Text Society
2022

First published 2022 by The Scottish Text Society, Edinburgh

ISBN 978-1-89797-644-9

A Scottish Text Society publication
Published by The Boydell Press
an imprint of Boydell & Brewer Ltd
PO Box 9, Woodbridge, Suffolk IP12 3DF, UK
and of Boydell & Brewer Inc.
668 Mt Hope Avenue, Rochester, NY 14620–2731, USA
website: www.boydellandbrewer.com

The publisher has no responsibility for the continued existence or accuracy of URLs for
external or third-party internet websites referred to in this book, and does not guarantee
that any content on such websites is, or will remain, accurate or appropriate

A CIP catalogue record for this book is available
from the British Library

This publication is printed on acid-free paper

Printed and bound in Great Britain by TJ Books Limited, Padstow, Cornwall

Contents

[The Proloug of the Aucht Buke]

Off dreflyng and dremys quhat dow it to endyte? f. 155ʳ
For, as I lenyt in a ley in Lent this last nycht,
I slaid on a swevynnyng, slummyrrand a lite,
And sone a selcouth seg I saw to my sycht,
Swownand as he swelt wald, sowpyt in syte   5
(Was nevir wrocht in this warld mair wofull a wycht),
Ramand, "Resson and rycht is rent be fals ryte,
Frendschip flemyt is in Frans, and faith hes the flycht,
Leys, lurdanry and lust ar our laid starn,
Peax is put owt of play,   10
Welth and weilfar away,
Luf and lawte baith tway
Lurkis ful darn.

"Langour lent is in land, all lychtnes is lost,   f. 155ᵛ
Sturtyn study hes the steir, distroyand our sport,   15
Musyng marris our myrth half mangit al most;
So thochtis threthis in thra our brestis ourthwort,
Bailfull bessynes baith blyß and blithnes can bost.
Thar is na sege for na schame that schrynkis at schort,
May he cum to hys cast be clokyng, but cost,   20
He rakkis nowder the rycht nor rakles report;
All is weill done, God wate, weild he hys will.
That bern is best can nocht blyn
Wrangwyß gudis to wyn;
Quhy suld he spair, for ony syn,   25
Hys lust to fulfyll?

"All ledis langis in land to laucht quhat thame leif is:
Lufferis langis only to lok in thar lace
Thir ladeis lufly, and louk but let or releifis,
Quha sportis thame on the spray sparis for na space;   30
The gallyart groym grunschis at grammys hym grevis,
The fillok hyr deformyt fax wald haue a fair face,
To mak hir maikles of hir man at myster myscheif is;
The gudwif grulyng befor God gretis efter grace,
The lard langis efter land to leif to his ayr;   35
The preist for a personage,
The seruand efter his wage,
The thral tobe of thrillage,
Langis ful sair.

"The myllar mythis the multyr with a met skant,   40
For droucht had drunkyn vp his dam in the dry ȝeir;
The cadgyar callis furth his capill with crakkis wail cant,

1

Calland the colȝar a knafe and culron ful qweir;
Sum schippart slais the lardis scheip and says he is a sanct,
Sum grenys quhil the gyrß grow for his gray meir, 45
Sum sparis nowder spiritual, spousyt wife nor ant,
Sum sellis folkis sustynance, as God sendis the feir,
Sum glasteris and thai gang at, and all for gait woll,
Sum spendis on the ald vse,
Sum makkis a tvme ruyß, 50
Sum grenys efter a guse
To fars his wame full.

"The wrach walis and wryngis for this warldis wrak, f. 156^r
The mukkyrrar murnys in his muyd the meill gaue na pryce,
The pyrat pressys to peill the peddar hys pak, 55
The hasartouris haldis thame hereyt hant he nocht the dyce,
The burgeß byngis in hys boith, the brovne and the blak
Byand bessely, and bane, buge, bevir and byce,
Sum ledys langis on the land, for love or for lak,
To sembyll with thar schaftis and set apon syß, 60
The schipman schrenkis the schour and settis to schor,
The hyne crynys the corn,
The broustar the beir schorn,
A fest the fedlar to morn
Covatis full ȝor. 65

"The ralȝear raknys na wordis, bot ratlis furth ranys,
Full rude and royt ressons baith roundalis and ryme;
Swengeouris and scurryvagis, swankeis and swanys,
Gevis na cur to cun craft, nor comptis for na cryme,
With berdis as beggaris, thocht byg be thar banys, 70
Na laubour list thai luk till, thar luffis ar byrd lyme;
Get ane bysmer a barn, than all hir blyß gane is,
Scho will nocht wirk thocht scho want, bot wastis hir tyme
In thiggyn, as it thrift war, and other vayn thewis,
And slepis quhen scho suld spyn, 75
With na will the warld to wyn;
This cuntre is full of Caymis kyn,
And sik schire schrewis.

"Quhat wikkytnes, quhat wanthrift now in warld walkis!
Baill hes banyst blythnes, bost gret brag blawys, 80
Prattis ar reput polycy and peralus pawkis,
Dignyte is laid dovn, darth to the dur drawis.
Of tratlys and tragedyis the text of all talk is:
Lordis ar left landles be onleill lawys,
Burgessis bryngis hame the boche to breid in thar bawkis, 85
Knychtis ar kowhubeis and commonys plukkyt crawis,

2

Clerkis for oncunnandnes mysknawis ilk wight,
Wifis wald haue all thar will,
Enewch is nocht halff fyll,
Is nowder resson nor skill   90
In erd haldin rycht.

"Sum latyt latton, but lay, lepys in lawyd lyt,
Sum penys furth a pan boddum to prent falß plakkis;
Sum gowkis quhill the glaß pyg grow full of gold 3it,
Throu cury of the quynt essens, thocht clay muggis crakkis;   95
Sum wernour for this warldis wrak wendis by hys wyt;
Sum crachour crynys the cun3e, and kepys corn stakkis;
Sum prygpenny, sum pyke thank with prevy promyt,
Sum iarris with a Ied staf to iag throu blak iakkis.
Quhat fen3eit fair, quhat flattry and quhat fals talys!   100
Quhat mysery is now in land!
Quhou mony crakkyt cunnand!
For nowther athis, nor band,
Nor selis avalis.

"Prestis, suldbe patterraris and for the pepill pray,   105
Tobe papis of patermon and prelaceis pretendis;
Ten tendis ar a trump, bot gif he tak ma
Ane kynryk of parroch kyrkis cuppillit with commendis!
Quha ar wyrkaris of this weir, quha walkynnaris of wa,
Bot incompetabill clergy, that Cristyndome offendis?   110
Quha revis, quha ar ryotus, quha rakles, bot tha?
Quha quellys the puyr commonys bot kyrkmen, weil kend is?
Thar is na stait of thar stile that standis content,
Knycht, clerk, nor common,
Burgeß, nor barroun –   115
All wald haue vp that is dovn,
Weltrit the went."

And as this leyd at the last lyggand me seys,
With a luke onlufsum he lent me sic wordis:
"Quhat bern be thou in bed, with hed full of beys,   120
Grathit lyke sum gnappar, and, as thi greis gurdis,
Lurkand lyke a longeour?" Quod I: "Lovn, thou leys.
Ha, wald thou feght?" Quod the freik: "We haue bot few
swordis.
Thar is sic haist in thi hed, I hop thou wald neyß,
That brawlys thus with thi bost quhen bernys with the   125
bourdis."
Quod I: "Churle, ga chat the, and chyde with ane other."
"Move the nocht," said he than,
"Gyf thou be a gentill man,

3

Or ony curtasy can,
Myne awyn leif brother.   130

"I spek to the into sport; spell me this thyng,
Quhat lykis ledis in land? quhat maste langis thou?"
Quod I: "Smake, lat me sleip, Sym Skynnar the hyng:
I weyn thou byddis na better bot I brek thi brow,   f. 157^r
To me is myrk myrrour ilk mannys menyng;   135
Sum waldbe cowrt man, sum clerk and sum a cachkow,
Sum knycht and sum capitane, sum Caser, sum kyng,
Sum wald haue welth at thar will, and sum thar wame fow,
Sum langis for the luffyr ill to lyk of a quart,
Sum for thar bontay or boyn,   140
Sum to se the new moyn –
I lang to haue our buke done,
I tell the my part."

"Thy buke is bot brybry," said the bern than,
"Bot I sal leir the lesson to lyß all thi pane."   145
With that he racht me a roll: to reid I began
The roytast ane ragment with mony rat rane,
Of all the mowys in this mold sen God merkyt man –
The moving of the mapamond, and how the moyn schane,
The Pleuch, and the polys, the planettis began,   150
The son, the Sevyn Starnys, and the Charl Wayn,
The Elwand, the elementis, and Arthuris Hufe,
The Horn and the Hand Staf,
Prater Iohne and Port Iaf,
Quhy the corn hes the caf,   155
And kow weris clufe.

"Thys romans ar bot rydlys," quod I to that ray,
"Leyd, lern me ane other lesson, this I ne like."
"I persaue, schir parson, thi purpoß perfay,"
Quod he, and drew me doun dern in dolf by a dyke,   160
Had me hard be the hand quhar a hurd lay,
Than prevely the pennyß begouth vp to pike –
Bot, quhen I walknyt, all that welth was wiskyt away,
I fand nocht in all that feild, in faith, a be byke;
For as I grunschit at this grome and glifnyt abowt,   165
I grapyt graithly the gyll,
Every modywarp hyll,
Bot I mycht pyke thar my fyll
Or penny come owt.

Than wolx I teyn at I tuke to sic trufis tent,   170
For swevynnys ar for swengeouris that slummyrris nocht weill;

4

Mony mervellus mater nevir merkit nor ment
Will seggis se in thar sleip, and sentens but seill:
War all sic sawys suythfast, with schame we war schent.　　　　f. 157ᵛ
Thys was bot faynt fantasy, in faith, that I feill,　　　　175
Nevir word of verite, bot all in waist went,
Throw roytnes and ravyng, that maid myne eyn reill,
Thus lysnyt I, as losanger, syk lewydnes to luke;
Bot, quhen I saw nane other bute,
I sprent spedely on fute,　　　　180
And vndre a tre rute
Begouth this aucht buke.

Heir endis the proloug of the viii buke of Ene-
ados and begynnys the aucht buke of the sammyn

Quhou Tiberinus, god of the ryver,
Till Eneas in visioun gan appeir.　　　　C. i

As thys convyne and ordinance was maid
　　Of Latyum throw owt the boundis braid,
Quhilk, euery poynt, this Troiane lord onon,
Cummyn of the howß of Kyng Laomedon,
In hevy curis flowand all on flocht,　　　　5
Avysys weill, how all this thing was wrocht,
And hastely in mynd on euery sydis
Now for this purpoß, now for that, providis,
Now heir, now thar, ryvest in syndry partis,
And sersys, turnand to and fra all artis –　　　　10
Lyke as the radyus sonnys bemys brycht,
Or than the glymerand monys schaddo lycht,
Reflexit from the brasyn veschell, we se,
Fillyt with watir to the cirkyll on hie,
Our all the howß reboundis and doys spreid　　　　15
Schynand, and sersys euery sted on breid,
Quhil in the ayr vpgoys the twynkland lycht,
Glitterand on euery spar and ruf on hyght.
The nycht come, and al thing levand sessit;
Wery of wark baith byrd and brutal best　　　　20
Our all the landis war at rest ilkane,
The profund swouch of sleip had thame ourtane;
Quhen this ilk prince, Eneas, all on flocht,
With mynd sowpyt in cuyr and hevy thocht,
And for this sorofull batale richt onglaid,　　　　25
Apon the ryver bank hym self dovn laid
Vndre the cald firmament for the nanys,　　　　f. 158ʳ
And gave schort rest onto his wery banys.
Quham to the god of that sted dyd appeir,

5

Tyberynus, furth of the still ryver,   30
Amyd the branchis of the popill treys,
As agyt man semyng hym self vpheis;
A lenȝe watry garmond dyd hym vaill,
Of cullour fawch, schaip lyke a hempyn saill,
And leiffy redis dekkis weill hys haris.   35
To meyß Eneas thochtis and hys sarys,
Thus he begouth to speke, and sayd, but dyn:
"O gentill get, cummyn of hie goddis kyn,
Quhilk from thy fays to ws with mekill ioy
Hes hyddir brocht the gret cite of Troy,   40
And Pergama, the Troiane wallys wight,
Eternaly conservis throu thy myght;
Desyrit maist of lang tyme, now welcum
Onto the grond and soill of Lawrentum,
And all the feildis eik of Latyn land.   45
Heir is thy sikkir duellyng place at hand,
Ane sovir ferm habitatioun for ay;
Withdraw the not fra hyne, paß nocht away,
Nor dreid na thing the bost of this batell.
The rancour all of goddis, I the tell,   50
And boldynnand wreth, appesyt ar almaste.
And so thow weyn not at my wordis be waist,
Nor fenȝeit dremys do to the appeir,
Vndyr sawch treis by thir bankis neir
Onon thou sall do fynd a mekill swyne,   55
With thretty hed ferreyt of grysys fyne,
Of cullour quhite, thar lugyng on the grond,
Hyr quhite brodmell abowt hyr pappis wond.
That is the place to set vp thy cite,
Quhilk of ȝour laubour sovir rest salbe;   60
Quhar that, as thretty ȝheris byrun and gane is,
Ascanyus sal do beld of lyme and stanys
The cite hait fair Alba of delyte,
Berand hys name fra the fair cullour quhite.
Thus I declar the nane oncertane thing,   65
Bot verray suythfast takynnys and warnyng.
Now harkis bot a litill, I the pray,   f. 158ᵛ
I sall the lern in quhat wordis, quhat way
Thow may cum speid, and haue the haill ourhand
Twichand this instant mater now at hand.   70
Thar bene pepill of Arcad from the ryng
Cummyn in this land, discend of Pallas kyng,
Quhilk, with Evandir kyng in cumpany,
Followand the syngnys schaw, heß fast heir by
Chosyn a sted and beldit a cite   75
Amang the knollis round or motis hie,

6

Efter thar forfader of nobill fame,
Pallas, clepyt Pallanteum to name.
Contynualy thir folkis euery ʒeir
Agane the Latyn pepyll ledis weir;   80
Adione to thir thyne ost in falloschip,
Do mak with thame a lyge, and bynd frendschip.
I sall my self convoy the the rycht way
Betwix thir brays vp the fludis gray,
So that agane the streme, throu help of me,   85
By ayris rowth thydder careit sall thou be.
Haue done, get vp, thou son of the goddeß;
First as the starris declynys, the addreß,
I meyn into the dawyng rycht ayrly,
Dewly to Iuno se thou sacryfy,   90
Hyr wreth and all sik mannans to ourset
With devoyt supplications maid of det:
And, quhen thou has optenyt victory,
To me thou sall do wirschip by and by.
I am God Tybris, watry hewyt and haw,   95
Quhilk, as thou seys, with mony iawp and iaw
Bettis thir brays, schawyng the bankis dovn,
And with full flude flowand fra tovn to tovn,
Throw fertill feildis scheryng thar and heir,
Vnder the lift the maste gentill ryver.   100
Heir is myne habitatioun huge grete,
Of mychty citeis cheif and souerane sete."
This beand sayd, this ilk god of the flude
Vnder the deip can dowk dovn quhar he stude,
And socht onto the watir grond onone,   105
So darnly hyd nane wist quhar he was gone.

The sow with grysis, as Tiberinus said,
Eneas fand, and sacrifice haß maid.

The nycht fled, and the sleip left Ene.
    On fut he startis, and onon can he se
Furth of the orient in the brycht mornyng
The sonnys hevynly bemys newly spryng,
And in the holl lufis of his hand quhar he stude   5
Dewly the water hynt he fra the flude,
Syne to the hevyn thus wyß his prayeris maid:
"O nymphys all of fludis blith and glaid,
And O ʒe haly nymphys of Lawrentum land,
Quham fra this fresch ryveris, and euery strand   10
That flowys rynnyng as we se sa cleir,
Heß thar begynnyng furth of sowrssys seir;
And O thou haly fader Tiberyne,

7

With Tybris eyk, thy blissyt flude dyvyne,
Ressaue Eneas to ȝow onbekend, 15
And now at last from all perrellys defend.
And, gif thou takis rewth of our gret skathis,
Heir I awow and promittis with aithys,
Quhar evir thy lowch or fontane may be fund,
Quhar evyr so thy spryng is, in quhat grund, 20
O flud mast plesand, the sall I our all quhar
Hallow with honorabill offerandis euermar.
Hornyt ryver, ryngand as lord and kyng
Our all the fludis in to Itall ryng,
Be in our help, now at last, I requer; 25
Eftyr sa feill dangeris and perellis seir,
Conferm thy promys and orakill in hy."
Quhen this was said, furth of all his navy
Twa galeis dyd he cheiß the ilk tyd,
With dowbill raw of ayris on athir syde, 30
And for the rowyng weil grathit thaim heß he,
Syne for the weir instrukkit his menȝe.
Bot lo, in haist befor hys eyn he saw
A mervalus and wondrus thyng to knaw –
A mylk quhite sow within the woddis lay 35
Apon the grene watris bank in hys way,
With hir lyttar new ferreit in that sted,
All of a cullour, grysys thretty hed,
Quham the devoyt Eneas on hys gyß f. 159ᵛ
Onto the, gretast Iuno, in sacryfyß 40
Brytnys, and, with hyr flok and followaris,
Hes set and offerit vp on thy altaris.
Tybyr his swelland fludis all that nycht,
Quhow lang at evir it was quhil days lycht,
Stabillys and cawmys at hys awin will; 45
The streme bakwartis vpflowys soft and still;
On syk wyß mesand his watir, that he
Ane standand stank semyt for tobe,
Or than a smoith puyl, or dub lovn and fair,
So that the ayris mycht fyndyn na contrar. 50
Tharfor Eneas can hys tyme aspy,
And hastis on hys vayage bissely;
With prosper curß and sobyr quhisperyng
The pikkyt bargis of fyr fast can thryng,
And slydis throw the schaldis stil and cleir; 55
The watir ferleys of thar fard and beir;
The forest, nocht accustummyt to se
Sik thingis, wondris quhat at this mycht be,
As to behald schynand scheldis on far
On mennys schuldris ay cumand nar and nar, 60

8

The pantit carvellis fletyng throu the flude.
Baith nycht and day ilk man, as thai war wod,
Can spend in rowth with irksum lauboryng,
The lang stremys and welys rovnd sworlyng
Our slydyng fast vpwartis the ryver,   65
Hyd and ourheldit with mony treys seir;
Endlang the still fludis calm and beyn
Thai seik and schar throu owt the woddis greyn.

Quhou Eneas with Kyng Evander met,
And bandis of kyndnes haß betwix thame knet.   C. iii

T he fyry son be this ascendit evin
   The myddill ward and regioun of the hevyn;
That is to knaw, be than it was myd day,
Quhen that on far the cite wallis se thai,
With towris and the howß hedis on raw   5
Skatterit disperß, and bot a few to knaw;
Quhilk now the mychty power of Rome tovn
Hes onto hevyn maid equal of renovn.
The kyng Evander, of moblys nocht mychty,
Held for that tyme bot sobyr sen3eory.   10   f. 160ʳ
In haist thyddir thar stevynnys can do steir
Eneas sort, and to the tovn drew neyr.
Thys Kyng Evander, born was of Arcad,
Percace the self day a gret honour mayd,
Solempnyt fest, and full hie sacryfyß,   15
Onto the gret Hercules on thar gyß,
That fostyr son was till Amphitrion,
And to the other goddis euery one,
Befor the cite in a hallowit schaw.
Pallas, hys son, was thydder alsso draw,   20
Togiddir with the principalis of 3onkeris,
The sobir senatouris, and puyr officeris,
All sammyn kest ensens; and with a stew
Besyde the altar blude sched and scalit new,
Beand lew warm, thar full fast dyd reik.   25
Bot 3it als swyth as thai persauyt eyk
The gret bargis slydand thus on raw,
And throw the dern woddis fast thydder draw,
So stilly bendand vp thar ayris ilk wight;
Thai worth affrayt of the suddand syght,   30
And euery man thai left the burdis in hy,
On fut gan starting from the mangeory.
Quham hardy Pallas dyd forbyd and diffend
Thar sacrifyß tobrek, quhill it war end:
He hynt a wapyn, with a few men3e   35

9

Thame to recontyr onon furth haldis he,
And ʒit weill far from a hill or a know
To thame he callys: "Standis, ʒyng men, howe!
Quhat cauß hes movit ʒou apon sik way
Thir strangis wentis onknawin to assay?   40
Quhiddir ettill ʒe, or quhat kynrent ʒe be?
Schaw quhens ʒe com, and quhilk is ʒour cuntre.
Quhidder do ʒe bryng onto our boundis heir
Bodword of peax, or cumis in feir of wer?"
Eneas tho, the fader of wirschip,   45
Maid answer from the pulpyt of the schip,
And in hys hand straucht furth, at he mycht se,
In takyn of peax a branch of olyve tre:
"My frend," quod he, "thou seys pepill of Troy,
To Latyn folkis ennemyß, man and boy;   50
Quhilk, flemyt of our realm, newly agane
Thai ilk Latynys heß socht with prowd bargane.   f. 160ᵛ
Onto the kyng Evander all seik we,
Hym to requir of succurß and supple.
Bair hym this message, and declar hym plane,   55
That chosyn men discend from Kyng Dardane
Beyn hyddir cummyn, besekyng hys frendschip,
To knyt vp band in armys and falloschip."
Pallas, estonyst of sa hie a name
As Dardanus, abasyt worth for schame: 60
"Cum furth," quod he, "quhat evir thou be, bern bald,
And say befor my fader quhat thou wald,
And entyr in our lugyngis the to rest,
Quhar thou salbe ressauyt welcum gest."
And furth onone he hynt hym by the hand,   65
A weil lang quhile hys rycht arm embrasand;
Syne furth togiddir rakyt thai on raw,
The flud thai leif, and entris in the schaw.
Eneas tho, with frendly commonyng,
Spak curtasly, thus sayand to the kyng: 70
"O thow maste curtaß prynce, and best in neid
That evir was byget of Grekis seyd,
Quhamto fortoun wald I suld cummyn heir,
The lawly to besekyng and requir,
And wald alsso I suld furth reke to the   75
Wippyt with bendis the branch of olyve tre,
In takyn that of thy supple I neid;
Forsuyth, I caucht na maner feir ne dreid,
Thocht thou a capitane of the Grekis be,
Yborn alsso of Arcad the cuntre,   80
Of blude coniunct to the Atrides tway,
I meyn onto Agamenon and Menelay:

10

Bot myne awin vertu, and haly oracleis
Of the goddis be devyn miracleis,
And our forbearis all of a kynred,   85
Thy fame dyuulgat into euery sted,
Heß me fermly adionyt onto the;
The fatis eik tharto inducis me,
That wilfully I obey thar command.
Schir Dardanus, the kyng first in our land   90
That belt the cite Troy or Ilion,
Our cheif fader, as Grekis grantis ilkone,
Born of Electra, Atlas douchter ȝyng,
Careit be schip come first to Troys ryng;   f. 161ʳ
And this Electra gret Atlas begat,   95
That on hys schuldyr baris the hevynnys plat.
Mercur is fader of ȝour clan alssua,
Quham the schene madyn, the fair fresch Maya,
Apon the frosty hillys top all bair,
Quhilk Cillenus is hait, in Arcad bair;   100
And this ilk Maya suythly, gif that we
Ony credens to it we heir or se
May geif, Atlas bygat, that sam Atlas
That rollys the hevynly starrit speir cumpas;
So baith our kynrentis, schortlie to conclud,   105
Devidit ar furth of a stok and blude.
Quharfor, havand confidens in thir thyngis,
Nothir by ambassat, message nor writingis,
Nor other craft, thy frendschip first socht I;
Bot myne awin self in person com in hy,   110
That onto the submittit has my hed,
And the to pray socht lawly to this sted.
For the ilk pepill vnder Dawnus kyng,
That the Rutilianys has in governyng,
Quhilk ledis weir aganys thi cuntre,   115
With cruell batal now persewis me;
And gif thai mycht expell ws of this land,
Thai weyn tharby that nocht may thame ganestand,
Bot at thai sall vnder thar senȝeory
Subdew alhaill in thraldom Italy,   120
And occupy thai boundis oriental
Quhar as the ovir see flowys alhaill,
And eik thai westir partis, trastis me,
Quhilkis ar bedyit with the neddir see.
Ressaue and knyt vp faith and ferm cunnand,   125
Tak our promyt and geif ws treuth and band;
Strang bodeis til abyde bargane haue we,
With hardy myndis in batal or melle,
Exercit in weir, and expert at sik nedis,

11

In lusty 30uth likly to do our dedis." 130
Thus said Eneas, and Evander than,
Fra tyme that he first forto speke began,
Hys eyn, hys mowth, and all hys body rycht f. 161ᵛ
Gan to behald, espying with hys syght,
Syne schortly maid hys ansuer thus agane: 135
"O quhou glaidly the, mast forcy Troiane,
I do ressaue as tendir frend and feir!
Quhou blythly now I knaw and weil may heir
The voce, the wordis and the speche, but leß,
Of thy fader, the gretast Anchises! 140
And full perfytly now I draw to mynd
The vissage of that worthy knycht maste kynd.
For weill I do ramembir, lang tyme gone,
Quhou Priamus, son of Laomedon,
To vissy hys sisteris land Hesiona, 145
Socht to the cite hait Salamyna,
And at the sammyn rayß hys vayage maid
Throu the cald frosty boundis of Arcaid.
My grene 30uth that tyme with pilis 3yng
First cled my chyn, or berd begouth to spryng; 150
I ioyt to se the Troian dukis ilkone,
And on the son of Kyng Laomedone,
That is to say, this ilk 3ong Priamus,
Forto behald was mervel gloryus;
Bot thy fader Anchises, quhar he went, 155
Was hyar far than all the remanent.
My mynd brynt, of 30uthed throu desire,
To speke and common with that lordly syre,
Tobe acquentit, and ioyn hand intil hand,
Cunnand to knyt, and bynd fordwert or band. 160
To hym I went desyrus of frendschip,
And sped that sammyn so in falloschip,
Within the wallys of Pheneß I hym led,
And quhen he dyd depart, or thens hym sped,
Ane courtly quavir full curyusly wrocht, 165
With arowis, maid in Lycia, wantand nocht,
Ane garmond he me gaue, or knychtly weid,
Prynnyt and wovyn full of fyne gold threid,
Twa goldyn bridillis eik, as he dyd paß,
Quhilk now my son occupyis, 3ong Pallas. 170
Quharfor our allyance, faith and richt hand, f. 162ʳ
As 3e desire, ar ellys adionyt in band –
We bene of ald confideratis, perfay:
Quharfor to morn, alssone as the brycht day
Begynnys allycht the landis and the sky, 175
With succurß and suppovell blythly I

12

Sal 30u fra hyne hame to 30ur army send,
And with my gudis and my mobillis amend.
And in the meyn tyme, sen, my frendis deir,
Onto our sacrefyis 3e be cummyn heir,   180
Quhilk 3eirly vsyng we as anniuersary,
That bene onlefull to defer or tary:
Tharfor with ws do hallow our hie fest,
And with glaid semlant blythly maste and lest
Accustom 30u from thens, and now instant   185
Our tabillis as 30ur frendly burdis hant."
Quhen this was said, mesis and cowpis ilkane,
Quhilk war away tak, bad he bring agane,
And he hym self the Troiane men fut het
On sonkis of gresy scheraldis hes doun set.   190
Thar pryncipal capitane syne, Ene,
Beside hym self on deß ressauys he;
The benk, ybeldyt of the grene holyne,
With lokkyrrit lyoun skyn ourspred was syne.
Than 30ng men walit bissy heir and thar,   195
And eik prestis of Hercules altar,
The rostit bullys flesch set by and by,
The bakyn breid of baskettis temys in hy,
And wynys byrlys into gret plente.
Eneas, sammyn with hys Troiane men3e,   200
Dyd of perpetual oxin fillettis eyt,
And purgit entralis, clepit clengyng meit.

Evander tellith till Eneas, but baid,
The verray cauß quhy this sacerfice was maid. C. iv

Eftir that stanchit was the hungris rage,
And appetit of meit begouth asswage,
Said Kyng Evander: "Na superstitioun vayn,
Nor mysknawlage of goddis ancyane,
Thys hie fest and gret solempnyte,   5   f. 162ᵛ
Nor this bankat and mesys, as 3e se,
Hes institut to ws, and this alter
Of sa excelland maieste standyng heir;
Bot, my deir frend and nobill gest Troiane,
We, preservit from cruel peralus pane,   10
Hantis this seruys apon sik maner,
As proper det and observans ilk 3er.
First, do behald 30ne schorand hewchis brow,
Quhar all 30n craggy rochis hyngis now,
Quhou the huge weghty brays bene dovn cast,   15
The holkit fows in the mont syde left waste,
Quhar as the craggy quhynnys, dovn declyne,

13

Has drawyn of the hill a huge rewyne.
3on was a cavern or cove in ald days,
With gousty entray far furth of all ways,   20
A grisly den and ane forworthyn gap
Of Cacus, that na mar had bot the schap
Of mannys form, for skant half man was he
Throw cruel dedis of iniquyte,
That in 3one fendlich hole dwelt hym allane –   25
A hellis byke, quhar sonnys beme nevir schane,
Quhar the vile flur evir lew warm was spred
With recent slauchter of blud newly sched.
Befor that tyrrandis 3et of men that ded is
Affixit stud mony dolorus hedis,   30
With vissage blaknyt, blude byrun, and bla,
The laithly ordur or filth stilland thar fra.
Onto this hutyt monstre, this Cacus,
The god of fyre was fader, Wlcanus;
And at hys mouth, a wondir thing to se,   35
Hys faderis reky flambe furth 3iskyt he.
As to hys body, quhar so evir he passit,
Of bustuus statur lyke nane other was it.
Proces of tyme at last heß ws inspirit,
And send ws help, as we full lang desyrit,   40
Be cummyng of the mychtful goddis presens;
For the danter of monstreis, our defens,
The maste redoutit Hercules, com at hand
Be aventour onto this ilke land,   f. 163ʳ
New from the slauchter into stern melle   45
Of Geryon, the quhilk had bodeis thre.
With prowd spul3e arryving triumphal,
This conquerour maid thyddir dryve and call
Hys bullys and hys oxin huge gret,
And eik hys ky, to pastur and to eyt   50
Endland 3one valle that is large and wyde,
And tuk thar lugyng on this ryver syde.
Bot the ondantit fury mynd of this theif,
Schrewit Cacus, all way ful of myscheif,
By his frawart engyne and sle consait   55
So that no maner wikkytnes nor dissait
Mycht be, that he ne durst nocht tak on hand,
Ne onassayt leif, out from thar stand
Four semly oxin of body gret and squar,
Als mony tendir quyis excedand fair,   60
Of all tha catal away with hym drave.
And, that thar tred suld na way be persaue,
Onto hys cave ay bakwartis by the talys
To turn thar futsteppis he thame harlys and tralys;

14

And thus his spreith he had ontil his in,   65
And with a queym stane closyt hes the gyn.
Sik way he wrocht that, quha thar tred list goif,
Na takynnys suld convoy thame to his coif.
In the meyn quhile, as all the bestis war
Repatyrit weil efter thar nychtis layr,   70
At morow ayrly first as thai removit,
For Hercules depart from thens behuffit,
The catal gan to rowtyng, cry and rar;
The woddis rang of thar sound our alquhar,
And with thar noys dynnyt hillis and knowys,   75
Quhil in the caif as that a quyok lowis,
With lowd voce squeland in that gousty hald,
All Cacus trast reuelit scho and tald.
Bot tho in greif this worthy Hercules,
Alceus nevo, the douchty Alcides,   80
That so oft syß was clepit commonly,
Within hys skyn begouth to byrn and fry
In brym fury of his bitter gall;   f. 163ᵛ
Hys wapynnys and his armour hynt withall,
Hys weghty burdon, or his knorry mayß,   85
And to the hillys hycht held in a rayß.
Than was the first tyme that ony in this erd
Of our pepill persavyt Cacus efferd,
Within his hed trublit his eyn tway.
Swyft as the wynd he fled and gat away,   90
And to his cave hym sped with ery spreit –
The dreid adionyt weyngis to his feyt.
And fra he had hym self sesyt tharin,
A stane of huge weght for to cloß the gyn
He leyt do fall, and with sic haist doun thrang,   95
The chenȝeis brak quharwith it festnyt hang,
That forgit war by hys fadris engyne;
With gret irne slottis schet the entre syne.
Bot lo, in haist Hercules come at hand
With furyus mynd careyng our the land,   100
Passage and entre sekyng bissely,
Now heir his eyn, now thar, rollyng in hy,
Graslyng hys teith and byrnand full of ire.
Of Aventynus hill thryß all the swyre
He sersys our, and thryß assays he   105
To brek and rent that craggy stone entre,
Bot all for nocht, thocht he was nevir sa wight;
So, thryß irkyt, doun from the hillys hyght
To rest hym is he to the valle gone.
Thar stude a pynnakill of quhyn or flynt stone,   110
Apon the baksyde of this cavern cald,

15

That rayß on end rycht hie fortobehald,
For wild fowlys of reif a ganand sted,
That rent raw flesch of bestis bonys ded;
The craggis all about this rolk war worn,   115
With wedderis blast to holkyt and to torn:
And as it stud on schor sweyand that tyde,
Down with the bank towart the watir syde,
Hercules it smytis with a mychty towk
Apon the rycht half, forto mak it iowke,   120
Inforsyng hym to welt it our the bra;   f. 164ʳ
And sa rudly it branglys to and fra,
That from the rutis he it lowsyt and rent,
And tumlyt dovn fra thyne, or he wald stent.
The large ayr dyd reirding with the rusch,   125
The brays dyndlit, and all dovn can dusch;
The ryver wolx effrayt with the rak,
And demmyt with the rokis, ran abak.
Than this gret cove, of Cacus sail ryall,
Was discoverit; hys inwart cavernys all,   130
Wont tobe dyrk, worth patent now and knaw –
Non otherwyß than quhen the erd ourthraw
By fors of thundyr, or erdquake with a clap,
Ryvys vp a terribill sewch or grisly gap,
Oppynnand the hellis mansioun infernall,   135
And onclosys that dyrk regioun paill
Quhilk of the goddis al abufe is hayt;
Or thocht the hellis bysme in sik estait
War oppynnyt, that his bodum se men mycht,
And dampnyt sawlys effrayt of new lycht.   140
Quharfor this worthy stalwart Hercules,
That on this wyß had Cacus set in preß,
And fund onwarnyst by this lycht suddane,
Quhar he was closyt in a cave of stane,
Fast rumesand apon a strange maner;   145
This campyoun with dartis fell of weir
Gan down tobet, and in his wod fury
Eftir all kynd of wapynnys can do cry,
With branchis rent of treis, and querral stanys
Of huge weght dovn warpand all at anys.   150
Bot this ilk Cacus, quhen that he dyd se
Fra this danger thar was na way to fle,
Furth of his throt, a wondruß thing to tell,
A laithly smok he ӡiskis blak as hell,
And all the houß involuyt with dyrk myst,   155
That sone the syght vanyst, or ony wist,
And reky nycht within a litill thraw
Gan thikkyn our al the cavern and ourblaw,

16

And with the myrknes mydlit sparkis of fyre.
The hie curage of Hercules, lordly syre, 160
Mycht this no langar suffir, bot in the gap
With hasty stert amyd the fyre he lap,
And thar as maist habundyt smokis dyrk,
With huge sop of reyk and flambis myrk,
So that the caif dyd glevyn of the heyt, 165
Thar haß he hynt Cacus, that wikkyt spreit,
That all invane hys hait kyndlyng furth gaspyt;
For as a ball he hym in armys claspyt,
And so strenȝeis hys throt, furth chirt hys eyn,
Hys hals worth dry of blud. Than mycht be seyn 170
This myrk dungeoun and onsemly hald:
The entre oppynnyt Hercules the bald,
Bet doun the closeris, and syne brocht to the lycht
Hys oxin fra him reft by subtel slycht;
And by the feyt furth harlyt was onon 175
Of Cacus the deformyt carion.
The hartis than and myndis of our menȝe
Mycht nocht be satisfyit on him to luke and se,
As to behald hys vgly eyn twane,
Hys terribil vissage, and hys grisly gane, 180
The rouch byrsys on the breist and creste
Of that monstruoß half deil wilde beste,
And in his gorge stikkand the sloknyt fyre.
Evir sen that tyme, to Hercules the gret syre
We haue this honour mayd and sacrifice; 185
Al our ofspring and ȝong men on this wyß
This day kepis solempnyte, as ȝe se.
Potitius first master heir with me,
And the famyll of Pynaria the bald,
The cheif keparis of Hercules hallowyt hald, 190
Ȝon altar in this cuthyll dyd vpbeild,
That onto ws in euery tyme of eild
Is clepyt maist solempnyt and hie altar,
And salbe reput gretast euermar.
Tharfor haue done, ȝong gallandis; now in hy 195
In wirschip of this fest and mangeory,
Of greyn branschis plet for ȝour hed garlandis,
Do waucht and drynk, bryng cowpys full in handis,
Call on our patron common god dyvyne is,
And with gud will do skynk and birl the wynys." 200
Thus sayand, the party popill grayn
Heldit his hed with skug Herculyane,
The levis from the plettis dovn hyngand,
Ane haly cowp fillit in hys rycht hand.

Than ilk man smertly tastis the wyne at tabill, 205
Prayand thar goddis fortobe aggreabill.

In lovyng of the douchty Hercules
The pepill syngis hys warkis mar and leß.

In the meyn sesson Hesperus drew neir,
Throw the declynyng of the hevynly speir:
Tharwith the prestis of the sacryfyis,
Gyrdyt in skynnys, eftir thar auld gyß,
Gan trasyng furth togidder in a rowt, 5
And formest went Potityus the stowt,
All do thai beir the byrnand hait fyre brandis,
And, to renew the bankat, with thar handis
Ful delicat danteis for the secund mete
Thai dreß onone, and furth of platis gret 10
With paysit flesch plenyst the altaris large,
Tharon bestowyng in hepis mony a charge.
Syne the menstralis, syngaris and danseris,
To syng and play with soundis, as afferis,
Abowt the kyndlit altaris, quhil thai brynt, 15
Assemblit ar ful swyth, and wald nocht stynt,
With poppil tre hattis buklyt on thar hed.
The ʒonkeris ʒonder in ane other sted
Led rowndis, dansys and fresch caralyng;
Other agit persons thame addressit to syng 20
In ympnys, ballettis and lays, throu the preß,
The lovabill gestis of mychty Hercules:
Quhou the first monstreis of his stepmoder sle,
Lugyng a bab in creddill, stranglit he;
That is to knaw, twa gret serpentis perfay, 25
The quhilk he wyrreit with hys handis tway;
And how this ilke Hercules of renovn
The ryall citeis assegis and bet dovn,
Of Troy, and eik the strang Echalia, f. 165ᵛ
A thousand hard iourneis sufferyng alssua, 30
Vndre the kyng clepit Euristeus,
By Iunoys frawart will mast envyus.
And thus thai syng: "Invyncybill weriour,
That bair of strenth and hardyment the flour,
The stern Centawres thou slew and dovn bet, 35
Dowbill of form, and on the clowd byget;
Thow brytnys eik and with thi hand heß slane
Pholus and Helyus, stalwart gyantis twane;
Of Creit the monstreis dantis thou at full,
The savage bestis, as wild bair and bull; 40
Vndre a roik, Nemee forest within,

18

Thou slew and rent the hydwyß lyoun skyn.
The laik off Stix trymlyt for dreid of the;
The grisly portar of the hellys see,
Lugyng in caif on ded banys half gnaw,   45
Dyd quaik for feir, quhen he thy vissage saw.
Na kynd of bysnyng figour dyd the gryß,
Nor byg Typheus, that agane Iove oftsyß
Movyt batell, with wapynnys fell in hand
Mycht the effray, nor thy gret strenth ganestand;   50
Nor the serpent of Lern, thou put to ded,
Fand the want nowder wysdom nor manhed,
Thocht scho, of hedis with hir mekil rowt,
The dyd assail and ombeset about.
Hail, verray child of Iove; hail, honour hie   55
Adionyt to the goddis in maieste!
Baith ws and eik thi sacrifyce infeir
We pray the wissy, at thou may cum heir
With prosper presens and ful happy fut,
In our helpyng fortobe our bute."   60
In sic sangis thar fest thai sanctify,
And Hercules hie lovyng syng and cry.
Bot principaly, and last of the laif,
Thai maid mensioun of Cacus slane in caif,
And quhou that he the flambis furth dyd blaw.   65
The wod resoundis schill, and euery schaw
Schowtis agane of thar clamour and dyn,
The hillys rerdis, quhil dyndlis roik and quhyn.   f. 166ʳ
Syne, quhen dyvyne seruys was at end,
To the cite bownys ilk man to wend.   70
Furth held the kyng onweldy in ald ȝeris,
Fast by hym haldand, as his frendis and feris,
The prynce Eneas and his ȝong son Pallas,
And, quhil thai thus towart the cite paß,
With syndry sermondis schortis he the way.   75
Eneas awondris of that he dyd say,
And kest his eyn about delyuerly,
Thai stedis all to serchyn and espy;
Sa fair placis to se and vissy tyte
This strange knycht caucht plesance and delyte,   80
And glaidly can inquiryng euery thing,
And hard the answer of the agit kyng,
Quhilk teching him perordour to him tald
Memorialis of seir forfaderis auld.

19

Quhou Kyng Evander rehersis til Enee
In eldris days the rewle of that cuntre.

Thys kyng Evandrus than, the first foundar
Of Romys burgh or palyce, can declar
And dyd reherß ontil his gest Enee:
"Thir woddis and thir schawis all," quod he,
"Sum tyme inhabyt war and occupyit 5
With nymphis and fawnys apon euery syde,
Quhilk fairfolkis, or than elvys, clepyng we,
That war engendryt in this sam cuntre,
That with ane kynd of men yborn, but leys,
Furth of ald stokkis and hard runtis of treis; 10
Quhilkis nowder maneris had nor polecy,
Ne couth thai eir the ground, nor occupy
The plewis, nor the oxin 3ok infeir,
Nor 3it had craft to conquyß nor wyn geir,
Nor kepe thar moblis quhen it gadderit was; 15
Bot, as thir bestis, or the doillit aß,
Thar fude of treis dyd in woddis fet,
Or of the wild veneson scharp to get.
First from the hie hevynnys into this land
Saturnus com, fleand gret Iovis brand, 20
Hys realmys reft, and banyst eik was he;
Bot tha ontaucht pepill of this cuntre,
That skatterit dwelt in hie hillis greyn,
He maid forgadder togidder and conveyn,
Gaue thame lawys and statutis thame to lede, 25
And wald also this regioun euery sted
War callit Latium, and clepit to hyß name,
For that he surly lurkyt in the same.
And as thai tel, and redis in mony ryme,
Of gold the warld was in that kyngis tyme; 30
Sa lykandly, in paix and liberte,
At eyß his common pepill governyt he;
Quhil, peiß and peiß, the elde syne war and war
Begouth to wolx, that cullour fading far,
As, in the sted of paix, the rage of wer 35
Begouth succeid, and covatyß of geyr.
Syne the pissance com of Ausonya,
And the pepill Sycany hecht alsswa,
By quham the land of Saturn, war and wyß,
Hes left and changit his ald name oftsyß. 40
Syne kyngis com, amangis quham for the nonys
Stern Tybrys rygnyt, a man byg of bonys,
Fra quham, ay syne, all the Italiane blude
Thar gret ryver heß clepit Tibrys flude;

20

Thus Albula hys auld trew name hes lost.   45
And me also to duel within this cost,
Banyst and flemyt of my natyve land,
Strang destany, quhilk may nocht be gaynstand,
And fortoun eik, clepit omnipotent,
Throu all extremys of sey hes hydder sent.   50
The reuerend alß and dreidfull monysyngis
Of Carmentes my moder, in mony thingis
Expert as nymphe and prophetes dyvyne,
And the autorite of god Appollyne,
Hes me constrenyt to dwel in this hald."   55
Scarß hes Evandrus all thir wordis tald,
Quhen, walkyng thens furth bot a litil space,
He can do schaw the altar and the place   f. 167ʳ
Quhilk in the langage Romane ȝit, sans faill,
Is to this day clepit port Carmentaill,   60
Quharby ramemmorit is in the ilk tovn
This ald Carmentes wirschip and renovn,
Quhilk was baith nymphe and fatale prophetes,
That first declarit, in hir sawys expreß
The gret pryncis fortocum of Ene,   65
And of Pallanteum the nobilite.
The kyng syne schew him to the haly schaw,
Quhilk strang Romulus dyd reduce and draw
In maner of franches or of sanctuary.
He schew him eik, but ony langar tary,   70
Vnder the frosty bra, the coif, was call
Ful mony ȝeris in thar leid Lupercall,
Efter thar gyß of Arcaid and estait,
To Pan the god of Lyce consecrait.
He schew alsso the wod hait Argilete,   75
That to the man of Arge, thar lost the swete,
Was dedicat, and drew to witnes that sted
That he was nevir culpabill of his ded,
And can to him declar the mater plane,
Quhat wyß his gest, this man of Arge, weß slane.   80
Fra thyne, to mont Tarpeya he him kend,
And beknyt to that sted, fra end to end,
Quhar now standis the goldin Capitoll,
Vmquhil of wild buskis rowch skroggy knoll,
Thocht, the ilk tyme, ȝit of that dreidfull place   85
Ane feirfull reuerent religioun, per cace,
The ery rural pepill dyd affray,
So that this crag and scroggis wirschippit thai.
"In ȝon schaw, on this woddy hillis top
That skowgit is with mony buskis crop,"   90
Quod Evander, "tharon a god dois dwell,

21

Bot quhat god at he be can na man tell:
My pepill that bene cummyn from Arcaid
Wenys thai saw 3onder, as thai me said,
Gret Ioue hym self, as he ful oft at large   95   f. 167ᵛ
Dyd schake his tawbart, or his beknyt targe,
And with his rycht hand dyd assembill and steir
The watry clowdis, that makis thundris beir."
And forthir eik he said ontill Enee,
"3on twa town stedis thou behaldis," quod he,   100
"With barmkyn down bet and euery wall,
Of forfaderis thai bene memoriall:
This cite beldit our ald fader Ianus,
And 3onder cite fundit Saturnus:
Ianiculum this hecht, myne awin leif brother,   105
And Saturnya clepit was that other."
Amangis thame with sic carpyng and talk,
Towart Evandrus pur lugyng thai stalk:
The catal eik behald thai raik on raw,
And in that sted thar pasturand thai saw,   110
Quhar now in Rome is the cheif merkat platis,
Baith squeil and low in thai ilk plentuus gatis
Quhilk sum tyme hecht Caryne, fair and large,
Quhar the howsis war like a turnyt barge.
And quhen thai cummyn to the palice wer,   115
Quod Evander, "At thir ilk 3ettis heir
The conquerour entrit, douchty Hercules;
This sobir manß ressauyt hym, but leß.
My gentil gest, enforß the and addreß
To lern to dar contemp welth and richeß,   120
And do thi self compone, and schaw in deid
In goddis steid worthy to succeid,
With thame equal ressauyt in sic herbry;
Amang smal geir now entris bowsumly."
And sayand this, the myghty gret Ene   125
Within his narrow chymmys ledis he,
And maid him sytting doun apon a bed,
That stuffit was with levys, and ourspred
With the rouch skyn of a bustuus wild beir
In Affrik bred befor mony a 3er.   130

Ontil Eneas Venus armour requiris
Fra Wlcanus, quhilk grantis hir desiris.   C. vii

The nycht approchis, with hir weyngis gray   f. 168ʳ
Ourspred the erd and put all lycht away,
Quhen Venus moder till Ene efferd,
And not but cauß, seand the felloun rerd,

22

The dreidfull bost and assemly attanys   5
Aganys hir son of pepill Laurentanys,
To Wlcanus, hir husband and gud man,
Within hys goldyn chalmyr scho began
Thus forto spek, and with hir wordis the fyre
Of dyvyne luf can towartis hym inspire.   10
Quod sche: "Quhil that the kyngis of Grece and Arge
Down bet the Troiane wallys wyde and large,
That destinat war, bath towr, town and wall,
Of ennemyß be flambys to down fall,
Na help onto thai wrachit folkis I socht,   15
Nane armour axit, nor thy craft besocht,
Nor the, my derrest spowß, exerß bad I
Thy craft, nor wark invane wald occupy,
Albeit that to the childring of Pryam kyng
I was bedettit into mekill thing,   20
And the ontollerabill laubour of Ene
Bewalit oft wepand ful sair," quod sche,
"Quhilk now by Iovys power stad remanys
Within the boundys of Rutilyanys.
Quharfor this tyme I, thy ilk spowß and wyve,   25
Thy blissyt godhed, derrest to me on lyve,
Cummys lawly tobeseik and requer
For wapynnys, harneß, armour and sic ger.
For my deir son I, moder, prays the,
Sen Nereus douchter, Thetys, mycht," quod sche,   30
"Induce the till enarm hir son Achill,
And eik Tythonus spouß, at hir awin will,
Aurora, with hir terys so the brak
Fortill enarm hir child Menon the blak.
Behald quhat pepill, lo, assemblit bene,   35
Quhat wallit townys with ʒettis closyt in teyn
Gryndys thar wapynnys aganys me and myne,
To bring ws to distructioun and rewyne."
Thus said the goddeß, and in hir milk quhite armys   f. 168ᵛ
Ful tendirly belappys him and warmys,   40
Quhil that he musys so, that hait fyre sle
Of luf bekend onon ressauyt he;
The natural heit into the merch dyd glyde,
Persand the banys maid soft on every syde:
Nane other wyß than as, sum tyme, we se   45
The schynand brokkyn thundris lychtnyng fle
Wyth subtel fyry stremys throu a ryft,
Persand the watry clowdis in the lift.
Venus hys spowß, confiding in hir bewte,
Ful glaid persavys that hym caucht had sche.   50
The fader than Vlcanus, god abuf,

Lokkyt in the eternal cheyn of luf,
Answerd and said: "Quharfor, myne awin hart deir,
Sa far about thou glosys thy mater?
Why axis thou nocht planely thy desire?   55
Quhiddir is becum of me, thy lord and syre,
The ferm confidence, thou suld haue, goddeß?
Quhat nedyt mor bot schaw thy mynd expreß?
Gyf siclike curis and desire had bene
Into thy mynd that sam tyme, I meyn   60
Duryng the subuertioun of Troys ryng,
To ws it had bene bot a lesum thing
Troianys til haue enarmyt at thy request:
Nowder the fader almychty at the lest,
Ne ʒit the fatis contrary dyd ganestand,   65
Bot Troys cite mycht haue langar stand,
So that Kyng Priamus ryng, by our power,
Mycht haue remanyt fully othir ten ʒeir.
And now, gif thou the grathis forto fecht,
And tharto be thy mynd set, I the hecht   70
All maner thing, with solist diligens,
That may be wrocht in my craft or sciens,
Or ʒit may be forgit in irne or steill,
Or moltyn mettal graif and burnyst weill,
Sa far as fyre and wynd and hie engyne   75
Into our art may cumpaß or dyvyne.
Tharfor desist of thi strenth to haue dreid,   f. 169ʳ
Or me to pray in ocht at thou heß neyd,
For in sic cacis thar nedis na request.
Am I nocht reddy to fulfill thy behest?"   80
Thir wordis beyng said, this hait syre
Gan hir enbrasyng al at his desyre,
And, lappit to hys spowsys breist in armys,
The plesand natural sleip, to beit his harmys,
And eyß hys wery membris, can he tak.   85
Syne as he had slummyrrit bot a snak,
Quhen the first silence of the quyet nycht
Hys myddil curß and cirkill run had rycht,
Provokyng folk of the first sleip awaik;
Lyke as the puyr wife, quhilk at evin had raik   90
Hyr ingill, rysys fortobeit hir fyre,
As scho that heß nane other rent nor hyre
Bot with hir rok and spynnyng forto thryve,
And tharwithall sustene hir enty lyve;
Hir day wark to encreß, or scho may se,   95
Thartill a part of the nycht ekis sche,
And at the candill lycht hir handys tway,
And eik hir pur damysellis, as scho may,

24

Natly exercis forto wirk the lyne,
To snoif the spyndill, and lang thredis twyne, 100
Quharby scho mycht sustene hir powerte,
Kepe chaist hir spowsys bed in honeste,
And tharwith eik foster hir childer lyte –
The mychty god of fyre this tyme als tyte,
And no slawar, bot on the sam maner, 105
Furth of hys bed startis, and hynt his geir,
And to hys smyddy craft and forge hym spedis.
Thar standis ane ile, with reky stanys as gledis,
Vpstrekyng hie betwix the cost Sycille
And Lyparen, god Eolus wyndis ille; 110
Vndre the quhilk byg iland in the see
Ane coif thar is, and hyrnys feill thar be,
Lyke till Ethna holkyt in the mont
By the Ciclopes fornace worn or bront,
That makis rumlyng, as quha dyd thunder heir, 115   f. 169ᵛ
The bustuus dyntis on the styddeys seir;
Ane huge dyn and noys the strake doyth mak.
The irne lumpys in tha cavys blak
Can byß and quhissill, and the hait fyre
Doith fuf and blaw in blesys byrnand schire; 120
Quhilk forges bene Wlcanus duellyng call,
And efter Wlcan that cuntre nemmyt all.
The mychty god of fyre dovn from the hevin
Into this forsaid ile discendit evin,
Quhar as, intill hys large and gowsty caif, 125
The hydduus Ciclopes forgit furth and draif,
Brontes, Storopes, and nakyt Pyracmon,
The glowand irne to well and peyn onon.
The fyreflaucht, 3yt nocht formyt perfitely,
Quhilk the fader of goddis oft throw the sky 130
From euery art dovn in the erth doys cast,
Thai had into thar handys wirkand fast;
That ane part polist, burnyst weill and dycht,
Thar other party not perfytit rycht.
Thre rawys wel tha of the frosyn hail schour, 135
Thre of the watry clowd, to eik the stowr,
Thre blesys of the byrnand fyris brycht,
With thre blastis of the south wyndis lyght,
Syne to thar wark, in maner of gun powder,
Thai myddillyt and thai myxit this feirful sowder, 140
A grysly sound, gret dreid, and goddis ire,
Quham followys ay the fel flambys of fyre.
Ane other sort ful bissely to Mart
The rynnyng quhelys forgis, and weir cart,
Quharwith the men to batale doys he steir, 145

25

And movys citeis to rayß mortal weir.
Thai dycht and polyß egirly alssua
The horribill terget, bustuus Egyda,
Quhilk is the grevyt Pallas grysly scheild,
With serpent scalys puldrit in goldyn feild,   150
Togidder lynkyng lowpyt eddris twa
And in the breist of the goddeß graif thai
Gorgones hed, that monstre of gret wondir,   f. 170^r
With eyn wawland, and nek bane hak in sondyr.
"Away with this, 3he Ethna Ciclopes,"   155
Quod Wlcanus, "and all sic warkis seß,
And at I say enprentis in 3our thocht.
Ontill a forcy man ar tobe wrocht
Harneß and armour; now nedys it," quod he,
"3our strenth exerß and pythis schaw; lat se   160
Quha nymlyast can cum and turn thar handis;
Now on all master poynt of craft it standis.
Do put away in haist all maner delay."
Na mar he said, bot wondir frakly thai
Onto thar laubour can thame all addreß,   165
Assignand euery man hys part expreß:
The irne the mettal throw thir cundyttis flowys,
The moltyn gold and weirlyk steil hait glowys,
And furth of gousty furnace fundyt ran.
Maste craftely to forgyng thai began   170
A hug gret semly target, or a scheild,
Quhilk only mycht resistyng into feild
Agane the dynt of Latyn wapynnys all;
In euery place sevin ply thai well and call.
Sum can ressaue the glowand heyt, sum wynd   175
With blawand bellys bet the fyre behynd;
Sum of the trowch apon the sparkand gledis
The byssand watir strynklys and ourspredis.
The huge coif and all the mont within,
For strak of styddeys, can resound and dyn.   180
Amangis thame self thai grisly smythys gret
With mekill forß dyd forge, peyn and bet,
And can thar armys hesyng vp and dovn
In nowmyr and in dew proportioun,
And with the grippand turcaß oft alsso   185
The glowand lump thai turnyt to and fro.

Evander telland Eneas thingis seir,
Vlcanus armour dyd in the sky appeir.

Quhil that the fader of Lemnos, Wlcanus,
Within the boundis of wyndy Eolus
To wyrk this geir hastis on euery syde,   f. 170ᵛ
The blisfull lycht ayrly at morrow tyde,
And myrthfull sangis of the byrdis bay,   5
The swallow, syngis on the ruf hir lay,
Awalknyt Kyng Evander, and maid ryß
Within his sobir chymmys quhar he lyis.
Vpstart the ald, and cled hym in hys cote,
Apon his feyt hys meit schoys hote   10
War buklyt on the gyß of Tuscany;
Syne our hys schuldris, down hys myddill by,
Hyngis buklyt hys trasty swerd Arcaid;
From hys left arm, about the rycht syde layd,
Ywymplyt was the spottit pantheris skyn;   15
Hys twa keparis can furth by hym ryn
From the hie palyce, bustuus hundis two,
That haldis thar lordis payß quhar evir he go.
Furth held this heir the secret prevy way
Towart the sted quhar as Eneas lay,   20
Hys Troiane gest, ramembring al at rycht
Hys help and promys grantit ȝister nyght.
On the sam wyß, at morow ful ayrly,
Eneas hastis vp, and mycht nocht ly.
The kyng only bot with his son Pallas,   25
Achates with Eneas accumpaneit was.
Thai ionyt handis sone as thai war met,
And syne amyd the chalmer doun thame set,
Quhar, finaly, thai fel in commonyng
Of secret materis and attentik thing.   30
The kyng begouth, and said first til Ene:
"Maist souerane ledar of Troiane cumpane,
Quha beand on lyfe nevir grant I sall
Troy is distroyt, nor castyn doun the wall,
Nor ȝit the Troiane power put at vnder;   35
We haue bot sobir pissance, and no wonder,
To help in batale, and to mak supple
Onto so hie excellent maieste:
On this half closyt with the Tuscane flude,
On ȝonder syde ar the Rutylianys rude,   40
Nyddris our boundis, as full oft befallis,
With thar harnes clatteryng about our wallis.
Bot I purpoß adione to the onon   f. 171ʳ
A huge pepill, and landis mony one,

27

Ostis of fertill realmys neir fast by.   45
O fortoun, or we wyst, so happely
Thou schawist the in our help and supple!
And O maste douchty campioun Ene,
Desyrit of the destany and fatis,
Heir ȝe be weill arryvit many gatis!   50
Fundyt of ald stanys, not far hyne,
Inhabyt stand the cite Agyllyne,
Quhar that the worthy pepill Lydyane,
Vailȝeant in batale, duellis and dois remane
Apon the egge of the Hetruscan hillys.   55
Thir folkis all in lykyng at thar willis
This land inhabyt, vale, mont and swyre,
Quhil fynaly, ful prowd in his empyre,
Meȝentyus begouth thar tobe kyng,
And in gret forß of armys tharon ryng.   60
Suld I reherß the ontellabil myscheif,
The cruel dedis, slauchter and huge greif,
Of that tyrant, quhilk ȝit the goddis dyng
Apon hys hed reseruys and ofspring!
For he, besyde his othir wikkyt deyd,   65
The quyk bodeis, speldit furth on breid,
Adionyt to the corps and caryoun ded,
Layd hand to hand, baith face to face and hed,
Quhil quyk mowthis dyd ded mowthis kyß –
O, quhat maner of torment call ȝe this!   70
Droppand in worsum and filth laithly to se,
So miserabilly enbrasyng, thus wyß he
By lang proceß of ded can thame sla.
Quhil, at the last, of this ennoy and wa
Hys citesanys irkyt, syne in a rowt   75
Enarmyt ombeset his manß abowt.
Hym al enragit on his wild maner
Besegit thai, and of his complicis seir
Hes slane onon, and all in pecis hakkit,
And fyre blesis on his hie biggingis swakkit.   80
Amyd the slauchter, on cace, eschapit he,
And to the feildis Rutilyane can fle,   f. 171ᵛ
Quhar intill armys, be Turnus hys ost,
He hym begouth defend apon that cost.
Quharfor Hetrurya all, full iustly   85
Aggrevyt, rayß in armys by and by,
Onto punytioun and all tormentis seir
Thar kyng to ask, and seik in feir of weir.
To thir mony thousand pepill," quod he,
"Souerane ledar I sal the ione, Ene.   90
For now thar schippys ful thik reddy standis,

Brayand endlang the costis of thir landis.
Thai byd display thar baneris owt of faldis,
Bot ane ancyent dyvynour thame withhaldis,
Schawand the fatale godly destyne: 95
'O ʒe mast valʒeand ʒong gallandis,' quod he,
'And pepill cummyn from Meonya,
ʒhe that bene flour of chevalry alssua,
The vertu and the strenth of vassallage
Of ancistry and men of ʒour lynnage, 100
Quham iust dolour steris on this wyß,
Baldly aganys ʒour ennemyß to ryß:
All thocht Meʒentyus, to hys myscheif,
Heß weil deservit aganys hym ʒour greif
Thus in commotioun forto rayß and steyr, 105
ʒyt neuertheleß belevys, owt of weir,
So gret a pepill, as vnder Turnus kyng
And Latynus leyndis, forto down thryng
Onlesum is till ony Italyane –
ʒow behuffis to seik a strange chiftane.' 110
Of Hetrurya the ostis vnder scheild
With that word stoppit in the sammyn feild,
Of the goddis admonysyng all effrayt.
Tarchon hym self, thar duke, lyst not delay it,
Bot to me send ambassatouris all bovn, 115
Offerand to me the ceptre and the crovn
Of al thar realm, and thar ensenʒeis brocht,
Requyryng me that I refusyt nocht
Tocum and be chiftane of thar army,
The realm Tyrrheyn eik to ressaue in hy. 120
Bot my febill and slaw onweldy age, f. 172ʳ
The dasyt blude gane far by the hait rage,
Or than the owtworn dait and mony ʒeris,
With forß falʒeit to hant the strange weris,
Envyis that I suld ioys or bruke empyre. 125
My son Pallas, this ʒong lusty syre,
Exhort I wald to tak the steir on hand,
Ne war that of the blude of this ilk land
Admixit standis he, takand sum strynd,
Apon hyß moderis syde, of Sabyne kynd. 130
Bot thou, quham baith thi ʒeris and thy blude
The fatis favouris, and is so conclude
By the goddis abufe as, owt of weir,
Tobe callyt and schaip for this mater,
Go to the batal, campyoun maste forcy, 135
The Troianys baith and Italyanys to gy.
And forthir eik, this sammyn ʒyng Pallas,
Our son, our hop, our comfort and solace,

29

I sal adione in falloschip," quod he,
"As his master, to exerß vndre the,   140
And lern the fayt of knychtly chevalry,
Hard marcyall dedis hantyng by and by,
Tobe accustummyt and behald thy feris,
For wondyr followyng thy warkis in ʒyng ʒeris.
Twa hundreth walyt horß men, wight and stern,   145
Of Arcaid, sal I geif onto that bern,
And of hys awin behalf, in thy supple,
Alß mony Pallas sal promyt to the,
Quhilk in the hail may weill four hundreth bene."
Skant this was said, quhen castyng dovn his eyn,   150
Trast Achates, and Anchyß son Ene,
Sat starrand on the grond, baith he and he,
And in thar hartis dyd full oft compaß
Ful mony hard aduersyte and cace,
With drery cheir and myndis sad bath twa,   155
Ne war Venus, lady Citherea,
Dovn from the hevin of comfort to thame sent
Ane oppyn takyn, cleir and evident.
For suddanly thai se, or thai be war,   f. 172ᵛ
The fyreslaucht betyng from the lyft on far,   160
Cum with the thundris hydduus rumlyng blast,
Semyng the hevyn suld fall and all doun cast;
The ayr onon can dynnyng vp and doun
With brag of weir and Tyrreyn trumpys sovn.
Thai lysnyng to persaue and heir the dyn,   165
Ay mar and mar agane it dyd begyn
To rerd and rattill apon a feirfull wyß,
Quhill at the last thai se and al espyiß
Throw the cleir sky and regioun of the hevyn,
Amang the clowdis, brycht as fyry levyn,   170
The glitterand armour burnyst lemand schene,
And, as thai schuke, thar rayß thunder bedene.
Abasyt in thar myndis worth the laif,
Bot this lord Troiane knew and dyd persave
Full weil the sound and all the cace expreß   175
Be promyß of hys moder the goddes;
Syne can rehers it plane, and thus gaitis said:
"Forsuyth, forsuyth, my gentill ost, be glaid,
The nedis not to ask, ne ʒit speir
Quhat signyfyis thir wondris dyd appeir;   180
For I am callyt to the hevin," quod he.
"The haly moder, my genitryce, schew me
That sic a takyn suldbe send, scho said,
Gyf ony wald with batale ws invaid,
And, in my helpyng, hecht doun throu the ayr   185

30

To send Wlcanus armour, gude and fair.
Allace, how feill slauchter now apperis
To wrachit Latynys in thir mortal weris!
By me, Turnus, quhat panys salt thou dre!
O Tybir fair that rynnys in the se,   190
Quhou mony scheldis, helmys and stern body
Vndre thy fludis warpyt law sall ly!
Lat thame array thar ostis now lat se,
And baldly brek thar frendschip maid with me."

Evander sendis hys son, the ȝong Pallas, With hys army in help of Eneas.

Fra this was sayd, from his hie set he start;   f. 173ʳ
    And first the sloknyt fyris hes he gart,
The rakyt harthis and ingill ȝister nycht,
On Hercules altar beyt and kyndill bryght,
And glaidly went to wirschip and to call   5
Sobir Penates, goddis domesticall;
And walyt twynteris, efter the auld gyß,
He slew and brytnyt onto sacryfyß,
With hym Evander eik, and all hys feris
Of Troiane menȝe, lusty fresch ȝonkeris.   10
Syne doun in haist he went onto hys schippys,
Hys folkis he visseyt and his falloschippys,
Of quhais nowmyr heß he walyt owt
Ane certane, the mast lykly, bald and stowt,
Quhilk suld hym follow into euery place.   15
The remanent tuk byssely thar rayß
Down by the watyr, on the followand flude
Discendand slawly, to beir message gude
Sone efter this ontill Ascanyus ȝyng,
Twychand hys fader and of euery thing.   20
The horssys syne war gevin and furth brocht
To the Troianys that onto Tuscane socht;
And till Eneas led onon thai gaue
A gentill steyd excedand all the laif,
On quham at all partis was ourspred and fold   25
A dun lyonys skyn with nalys of gold.
Than throu the litil cite all on raw
The fame onon dywlgat swyftly flaw,
Quhou that the horsmen spedis thame bedene
To go onto the land and cost Tyrrene.   30
The wyssys and avowys than, for feir,
By woman and the matronys dowblet wer;
Mor grew the dreid the narrar drew dangar,
Now Martis ymage semys walxin mair.

31

The fader than Evander, as thai depart,   35
By the rycht hand thame gryppyt with sair hart,
Hys son enbrasyng, and full tenderly
Apon hym hyngis, wepand ontellabilly,
And thus he sayd: "O sen omnipotent
Hie Iupiter my ȝyng ȝheris by went   40   f. 173ᵛ
Wald me restor! in sic strenthis and eild,
So as I was quhen first in batal feild
The armys of the ostis down I dang
Of Preneste vndir the wallis strang,
And victor of myne ennemyß, as prowd syre,   45
Hail hepys of thar scheildis brynt in fyre;
Quhar, with this sammyn rycht hand quellyt and slane,
Vndre the hellys grond Tartareane
Kyng Herylus was sent to dwell for ay,
Quhamtill hys moder Feronya the gay,   50
Into the tyme of hys natiuite,
Grisly to say, had gevyn sawlys thre,
And that he suld beir armour thryß in fyght,
And thryß behwyt to the ded be dicht;
Fra quham that tyme this rycht hand, not the leß,   55
Tha sawlys all bereft, and thar expreß
Of alsmony enarmouris spulȝeit clene.
Gyf so war now with me as than heß bene,
Ne suld I nevir depart, myne awyn child deir,
From thyne maste sweit enbrasyng, for na weir;   60
Nor our nychtbour Meȝentyus in hys fed
Suld na wyß, mokkand at this hasard hed,
By swerd haue killyt so feill corpß as slane is,
Nor thys burgh of samony citesanys
Left desolat and denudyt," quod he,   65
"Bot O ȝe goddis abuf, and Iove mast hie,
The governour of hevynly wyghtis all,
On ȝou I cry, on ȝou I clepe and call;
Begyn to haue compaciens and piete
Of ȝour awin wofull kyng of Arcadye;   70
Oppyn and inclyne ȝour dyvyne godly erys,
To heir and ressaue the faderis meik prayeris.
Gyf it be so ȝour godhed and gret myghtis
Be presciens provyd heß, and forsychtis,
Pallas my son in salfty hail and feir,   75
Gyf the fatis preservys hym of danger,
Sa onys in my lyfe I may hym se,
Agane togidder assemblyt I and he;   f. 174ʳ
I ȝow beseik my febill lyfe to respyte,
That I mycht lyf, and endur ȝyt a lyte   80
All pane and laubour that ȝou list me send.

32

Bot, O faynt fortoun, gyf thou doys pretend
And mannancis ony myschewoß cace,
Now, now furthwith, into this sammyn place
Suffir me swelt, and end this cruel lyfe,   85
Quhill dowtsum is 3yt all sic sturt and stryfe,
Quhil hope oncertane is of thing tocum,
And quhil I thus, my deir child, all and sum
My lustis plesance, and my last weilfair,
The in myne armys enbrasis but dispar;   90
So that, eftir, na sorowfull messynger
With smert ennoy hurt nevir myne agit cyr."
The fader Evander with full sory hart,
At lattir poynt quhen thai war to depart,
Thir wordis spak, syne fel in swoun rycht thar: 95
Hys men hym hynt and to hys chalmyr bar.
Be this, the rowt of horsmen strang in fyght
War ischit at the portis euery wight;
Amangis the formast the duk Eneas,
And eik the trast Achates, furth can paß,   100
Syne other nobillis of the Troianys stowt;
The 3yng Pallas rydyng amyd the rowt,
So farrand and so lusty personage,
Cled in a mantill in hys tender age,
Quhilk dyd ourheld hys burnyst armour brycht –   105
On hym to luke was a mor gudly syght
Than on the day stern, quhilk at morn ayrly
Baithit in the occeane rysys in the sky,
Quhois fyry bemys Venus in speciall
Chosys abuf all starnys gret and small,   110
Heich in the hevin liftyng hys vissage schene,
To chayß away the myrknes with hys eyn.
The wofull moderis, quakand for cald dreid,
Stude on the wall behaldand quhar thai 3eid,
And dyd convoy or follow with thar sight   115
The dusty sop, quharso the rak went rycht,   f. 174^v
Govand apon thar bryght armour at schane,
So fer as that thar luke mycht thame attane.
The cumpany al sammyn held array
Throw scroggy bussys furth the narrest way,   120
Enarmyt rydyng thyddir as thai wald.
The brute and dyn from thame vpsprang thik fald,
The horny hovyt horß with four feyt
Stampand and trottand on the dusty streyt.

Quhou that Venus ontill Eneas brocht
The godly armour be Wlcanus wrocht.   C. x

Thar growys a gret schaw, neir the chil ryver
  Quhilk that flowys with hys frosty stremys cleir
Down by the cite of Agillyna,
That other wyß is clepyt Cereta,
Quhilk is in wirschip haldyn and in dreid   5
By faderis ald, the large boundis onbreid,
As sanctuar; and with deip clewchis wyde
Thys schaw is closyt apon euery syde –
Ane thyk ayk wod of skowgy fyrris stowt
Belappys all the said cuthill abowt.   10
The fame is that the Grekis ancyane,
Quhilk clepyt bene to surname Pelasgane,
That quhilum lang tyme in the formast eildis
The Latyn boundis occupeyt and feildis,
To Syluanus fyrst dedicat this schaw,   15
The god of bestis and of feildis faw,
And constitut to hym solempnyt fest.
Duke Tharcon, and the Tuscanys maste and lest,
Not fer from thens, intyll a strenthy place
Thar palȝeonys all had plantyt apon cace,   20
That from the top of the hillys hyght,
The army all thai mycht se at a syght,
With tentis stentit strekand to the plane.
Thyddyr held Eneas, the souerane Troiane,
And all the bernys of hys ryall rowt   25
Chosyn for the batall, lusty, stern and stowt,
And, wery of thar travale, thocht thai best
Thar self and horssis to refresch and rest.
Bot than Venus, the fresch goddes, bedene   f. 175ʳ
Amang the hevynly skyis brycht and schene,   30
Berand with hir the dyvyne armour cleir,
To mak tharof a presand, can draw neir,
And as on far hir son scho dyd behald,
Secret allone by the chill ryver cald,
Amyd ane holl cleuch, or a dern valle,   35
Of hir fre will tyll hym apperis sche,
And with sic wordis to hym spak, sayng:
"Lo, my reward heir, and my promysyng
Fulfillyt iustly by my husbandis wark;
So that, my son, now art thou sovyr and stark,   40
That the not nedis to haue ony feir
Fortill resist the prowd Latynnys in weir,
Nor ȝit the strang Turnus to assaill,
Hym to provok, or challance for batale."

34

Thus said the scheyn Citherea fair of face,   45
And, with that word, can hyr deyr child enbrace,
And thar the schynand armour forgane his sycht
Vndre a bowand aik layd dovn full rycht.
Seand sic gyftis of this trast goddeß,
This gentill knycht reiosyt wolx, I geß,   50
Glaid that so gret honour ressauyt he,
That scarsly kowth he satisfyit be
Forto behald thir armour bryght and schene;
On euery peyß to vissy kest hys eyn,
Tharon wondrand; betwix hys handis two   55
And byg armys thame turnys to and fro.
The grysly crystit helm he can behald
On feirfull wyß spowtand the fyre thik fald,
The fatale swerd, dedly to mony ane,
The styf hawbryk of steill yburnyst schane,   60
Of huge weght and bludy sangwyne hew,
That sic a glanß or variant cullour schew,
As quhen the byrnand sonnys bemys brycht
The watry clowd persand with hys lyght,
Schynand on far, forgane the skyis how   65
Schapys the figour of the quent rayn bowe.   f. 175ᵛ
The lyght legharnes on that other syde,
Witht gold and burnyst laton puryfyde,
Grathit and polyst weill he dyd aspy,
The speir, and eik the scheild so subtelly   70
Forgyt that it was ane ontellabill thyng.
For Vlcanus, of fyre the lord and kyng,
Knawand full weill the art of prophecy,
And syndry thingis tocum eik by and by,
The valȝeand dedis of Italyanys,   75
The gret triumphys als of the Romanys,
And of Ascanyus stok all nobil knyghtis,
Thar batalys all per ordour, weir and fyghtis,
Had tharin porturat properly and grave,
Amang al otheris, in Martis gresy cave   80
The sukkyn wolf furthstrekand breste and vdyr;
Abowt hir pappys, but feir, as thar moder,
The twa twynnys, smal men childer ȝyng,
Sportand ful tayt gan to wrabill and hyng;
And scho hir lang rovnd nek bane bowand raith   85
To geif thame sowke, and can thame culȝe baith,
Semyng scho suld thar bodeis by and by
Lyk with hir tong, and clenge full tenderly.
Not fer from thens Rome cite eikyt he,
Quhar by ane new inuentioun wonder sle,   90
Sittand into ane holl valle or slak,

35

Within the lystis for the triumphe mak,
War Sabyne virgynys revyst by Romanys,
As that thai war assemblyt for the nanys
The gret gammys Circenses forto se,   95
Quhilk iustyng or than turnament cleip we.
With hasty sterage thar most thou behald
The werys rasyt aganys Romanys bald
By agyt Tatyus and fell Curitanys:
Syne the ilk princis, and the said Romanys,   100
The weris sessyt sammyn all infeir,
Enarmyt stad befor Iovys alter,
With cowpys full in hand for sacryfyß.   f. 176ʳ
Thar mycht thou se thame, efter the ald gyß,
The swyne stekit brytnyt sone and slane,   105
Conferm thar trewys and mak paix agane.

Quhou that Wlcanus thar, amang the laif,
Storys tocum dyd in the armour graif.   C. xi

Fra thyne not far the chariot thou mycht knaw,
Metus Suffytius in seir pecis draw;
Albeit thou thocht thys cruelte, Kyng Albane,
Quhy wald thou not at thy promyß remane?
Quhy list thou not thy faith obserue and saw?   5
Thys faithles wightis entralys war outdraw,
By command of Tullus Hostilyus,
And throw the woddis harlyt, euery buß,
Quhil that the tharmys and the bowellys rent
Scroggis and breris all with blude bysprent.   10
Thar mycht thou se Tarquynus in exile
Furth cast of Rome, and syne, within schort quhile,
By Kyng Porsenna into batale plane
Commandit fortobe ressauyt agane;
With that a felloun sege al Rome about   15
Dyd ombeset, and closyt with hys rowt;
The Romanys than discendit from Enee
Rusch onto wapynnys for thar liberte.
Thou mycht behaldin eik this ilk Porsen
Lyke as he had dyspite, and bostand men;   20
For that the hardy Cocles, darf and bald,
Durst brek the bryg that he purposit to hald,
And eik the virgyn Chelya, quhar scho stude,
Hyr bandis brast, and swam our Tibir flude.
Manlyus the knycht abufe into the scheild,   25
In the defens for Iovys tempil beild,
Kepand the strenth and castell Tarpeia
And haldand the heich Capitoll alssua,

36

Stud porturat, neir the chymmys calendar,
Quhais ruffis laitly ful rouch thekit war   30
With stra or gloy by Romulus the wight.
Thar was alsso engravyt all at ryght   f. 176ᵛ
The siluyr ganer, flyghterand with lowd scry,
Warnand all reddy the gilt entre by,
Quhou the Franchmen dyd the ȝet assaill: 35
Thar mycht thou se the Franch army alhaill
Haist throu the bussys to the Capitoll,
Sum vndermyndand the grond with a hoill,
So that almaist thai wan the fortereß;
Gret help thame maid the cloß nychtis myrknes;   40
Thar haris schane as doith the brycht gold wyre,
And all of gold wrocht was thar rich attyre,
Thar purpour robbys bygareit schynand brycht,
And in thar hand withhaldand euery knycht
Twa iavillyng speris, or than gyssarn stavis,   45
Forgit in the montanys al sik maner glavys,
Thar bodeis all with lang tergis ourheild.
Syne ȝonder mar was schapin in the feld
The dansand prestis, clepit Salii,
Hoppand and syngand wonder merely,   50
And Panos prestis, nakit Lupercanys,
The toppyt hattis quhar the woll threid remanys,
And bowyt buklaris falland from the sky.
Thar mycht besene, forgyt maste craftely,
The chaist matronys throw the cite all   55
In soft charis thar gemmys festual
Ledand, and playand with myrthis and solace.
A far way thens ful weill engravit was
The vgly hellis set Tartareane,
The deip dungioun quhar Pluto dois remane,   60
And of the wikkyt pepill all the pyne;
Thar was thou markyt, cursyt Catylyne,
Hyngand out our ane schorand hewch or bra,
And trymland for the feirfull dreid and wa,
To se the furyus grysly sisteris facis,   65
That with thar scurgis wikkit pepill chacis;
The rychtwyß folkis, at levit deuotly,
Fra thame war partit in a place far by,
And the wyß man Censorius Cato
Gevand thar iust rewardis till all tho.   70
Myd way betwix the other storeis seir,
The swelland seys fygour of gold cleir   f. 177ʳ
Went flowand, bot the lippyrrand wallys quhyte
War pulderit full of fomy froith mylk quhite;
The delphyn fyschys, wrocht of siluer schene,   75

37

In cirkill swepand fast throu fludis grene,
Sewchand swyftly salt stremys; quhar thai far,
Vpstrake thar talys the stour heir and thar.

Eneas mervellys of the storeys seir
Wrocht be Wlcanus in hys armour cleir.

C. xii

A myd the seys mycht be persauyt weill
The weirly schippis with thar snowtis of steill,
The Actiane batalys, semyng as quha dyd se
The mont Lewcata, standand by the seye,
For ostis arrayt glowand as the gleyd;   5
Of glitterand gold schane all the flude on breid.
On that a party, thar myght thou behald
Cesar August Octauyan the bald,
Movand to batale the Italyanys,
With hym senatouris and worthy pepill Romanys,   10
And goddis domestik, quhilk Penates hait,
With all the gret goddis of mair estait;
Heich in the forstam stand he mycht be sene,
From hys blyth browys brent and athir eyn
The fyre twynklyng, and hys faderis star   15
Schew from hys helmys top schynand on far.
The byg and stowt Agrippa, hys frend deir,
Hys navy led at hand weil by neir,
As he that in hys help and succurß fyndis
The prosper favouris baith of goddis and wyndis: 20
Quhais forhed schane of ane prowd syng of weris,
A crown with stammys sic as schippis beris.
Marcus Antonyus cummys thame aganys
With hail suppovel of barbaryanys,
As nobill victour and cheif conquerour,   25
Careand with hym of Orient the flour;
Diuerß armyis and pepillys for melle,
From Perß, Egipt and costis of the Red See,
The power all assemblit in hys flote,
Ane huge rowt and multitude, God wote,   30   f. 177ᵛ
The ʒondermast pepill, clepit Bractanys,
Quhilk neir the est part of the warld remanys.
Hym followys to the feild, ane schame to say,
Hys spowß Egiptiane, Queyn Cleopatra.
Thai semyt sammyn ruschand all togidder,   35
Quhill all the sey vpstowris with a quhidder;
Ourweltit with the bensell of the ayris,
Fast fra forstammys the flude swowchis and raris,
As thai togiddir matchyt on the depe.
Thou suld haue wenyt, quha tharto tuke kepe,   40

38

The gret ilandys, Ciclades, hail vprent,
Apon the sey fletand quhar thai went,
Or huge hie hillys, concurrand all atanys,
Togiddir rusch and meyt with other montanys;
On athir hand with sa gret forß and weght   45
The men assalys in schip of towr to feght.
Thai warp at other brycht blesys of fyre,
The kyndillyt lynt and hardis byrnand schire;
The castyng dartis fra hand to hand dyd fle,
Slang gaddis of irne, and stane cast gret plente: 50
Neptunus feildis, all the large flude,
For new slauchter wolx blandit red of blude.
Amyd the ostis Cleopatra queyn
The rowtis dyd assembill to feght bedene,
With tympane sound, in gyß of hir cuntre,   55
Prouocand thame to move in the melle:
Nor ȝit beheld scho not the eddris twane
Behynd hir bak, that efter hes hir slane.
The monstruus goddis figuris, of al kynd
That honorit ar in Egipt or in Inde,   60
And eik the barkand statw, Anubis,
Agane Neptune, agane Venus, I wyß,
And als agane Mynerva, porturat standis
In that bargane, with wapynnys in thar handis.
Amyd the feld stude Mars, that felloun syre,   65
In plait and mail, wod brym and ful of ire;
The sorofull Fureys from the firmament   f. 178ʳ
By the goddys to tak vengeans war sent;
In went Discord, ioyus of that iourne,
With mantill rent and schorn men mycht hir se;   70
Quham followit Bellona of batell,
With hir kynd cosyng, the scharp scurgis fell.
Actyus Appollo, seand in the sky
Of this melle the dowtsum victory,
Hys bow abufe thar hedis hes he bent,   75
Lyke forto schote hys dartis and down sent;
For dreid of quham all the Egiptianys,
All thai of Ind, and the Arabyanys,
And thai of Sabey, turnyt bak to fle.
Cleopatra the queyn thar mycht thou se   80
Wynd sayll about, and gang befor the wynd,
Ay mar and mair dredand persute behynd,
Sclakand schetis, and haldand rowme at large,
With purpour saill abufe hir payntit barge.
The mychty god of fyre hir wrocht and maid   85
Ful pail of hew, sorowfull and not glaid,
In syng tocum of hir smert hasty ded,

39

Amangis ded corpsis new of slauchter red,
And, with the west wynd and the wallys haw,
Frawart the flude of Nyle our stremys blaw;⁣ 90
Quhilk Nylus ryver, murnand for thar diseyß,
Hys large skyrt onbrede spred thame to pleß,
With all his habyt oppynnyt thame to call,
As thocht hym list ressaue the venquyst all
Within hys watry bosum, large and rude, 95
And hyde in secret cundyte of his flude.
Within the wallis syne of Romys cite,
Cesar, ressauyt with triumphis thre,
Thou mycht behald, thar offerand on his gyß
Till Itale goddis immortal sacryfyce; 100
Our all the cite, in maist singular ioy,
The blysfull fest thai makyng man and boy,
So that thre hundreth ryall tempillys dyng
Of ryot, ryppet and of revellyng f. 178ᵛ
Ryngis, and of the myrthful sportis seir 105
The stretis soundyng on solacius maner;
At euery sanctuary and altar vpstent
In caralyng the lusty ladeis went;
Befor the altaris eik, in cirkyll round,
The brytnyt bestis strowyt all the ground. 110
Cesar hym self, seysit in sete ryall,
Within the snaw quhite statly merbill wall
Of God Phebus tempill, thar as he sat
Visseand the pepillis gyftis, this and that,
And on the prowd pillaris, in takynnyng 115
Of hys triumphe, maid thar be vp hyng.
The pepill by hym venquyst mycht thou knaw,
Befor hym passand per ordour, all on raw,
In langsum tryne; and how feil kyndis seir
Of tungis and of langage men mycht heir, 120
Alß mony diuerß habyttis wor thai strange,
Alß feil sortis of armouris dyd thai change.
Vlcanus heir the beltles Numydanys,
And thai folkis that in Affrik remanys,
Had gravyn weill; and ȝonder porturat was 125
The Leleganys, and the pepill Carras,
And Gelones, tha pepill of Sythia,
In archery the quhilk ar wonder thra.
The mekill flude Eufrates, fast by,
With streym now semyt flow mair sobirly; 130
The Moryn pepill eik, fast by the see,
Of men reput the last extremite,
The forkyt flude of Reyn eik pantit was,
And the ondantit Danys thar dyd paß,

40

The flude Arax of Armeny alsso,   135
Havand disdene a bryg our it suld go.
Eneas, of hys moderis gyft wondryng,
Our al Vlcanus scheild samony a syng
Wrocht on sic wyß, nocht knawand the mater,
To se the figouris of thir storeis seir   140
Reiosyt wolx, and syne deliuerly   f. 179ʳ
Apon hys schulder hyntis vp in hy
The famus honour, and hie renownye,
Or gloryus iestis of hys posthcryte. etc.

Explicit liber octauus Eneados
Incipit prologus noni libri eiusdem

Sequitur prologus

[The Proloug of the Nynth Buke]

Thir lusty warkis of hie nobilyte
   Agilyte dyd wryte of worthy clerkis,
And tharin merkis wysdome, vtilyte,
Na vilyte, nor sic onthryſty sperkis;
Scurilyte is bot for doggis at barkis,   5
Quha tharto harkis fallys in fragilyte.

Honeste is the way to worthyneß,
Vertu, doutleß, the perfyte gait to blyß;
Thou do na myß, and eschew idilneß,
Persew prowes, hald na thing at is hys;   10
Be nocht rakleß to say sone ȝa, I wyß,
And syne of this the contrar wyrk expreß.

Do tyll ilk wight as thou done to waldbe;
Be nevir sle and doubill, nor ȝit our lyght;
Oyß not thy mycht abufe thyne awin degre,   15
Clym nevir our hie, nor ȝit to law thou lycht;
Wirk na malgre, thocht thou be nevir sa wyght,
Hald with the rycht, and preß the nevir to le.

Eneuch of this, ws nedis prech na mor,
Bot, accordyng the purpoß said tofor,   20
The ryall style, clepyt heroycall,   f. 179ᵛ
Full of wirschip and nobilnes our all,
Suldbe compilit but thewhes or voyd word,
Kepand honest wyß sportis quhar thai bourd,
All lowuß langage and lychtneß lattand be,   25

41

Observand bewte, sentens and grauyte.
The sayar eik suld weil considir thys,
Hys mater, and quhamto it entitilit is:
Eftir myne authouris wordis, we aucht tak tent
That baith accord, and bene conuenient,   30
The man, the sentens, and the knychtlyke stile,
Sen we mon carp of vassalage a quhile.
"Gyf we discryve the woddis, the treis," quod he,
"Suld conform to that manis dignyte
Quhamto our wark we direct and endyte."   35
Quhat helpis it? Full litill it wald delyte
To write of scroggis, broym, haddir or rammale;
The lawrer, cedyr or the palm triumphale
Ar mar ganand for nobillis of estait:
The muse suld with the person aggre algait.   40
Stra forto spek of gayt to gentill wight;
A hund, a steid, mar langis for a knyght,
Quhamto efferis hant na rebald daill –
Thar suld na knycht reid bot a knychtly taill.
Quhat forsis hym the bussart on the brer,   45
Set weil hym semys the falcon heroner?
He comptis na mair the gled than the fewlume,
Thocht weil hym lykis the goshalk glaid of plume.
The cur, or mastys, he haldis at smal availl,
And culȝeis spanȝellis, to chace pertryk or quaill.   50
Ne byd I not into my stile for thy
To speke of trufis, nor nane harlotry;
Sen that myne author with sic eloquens
Hys buke illumnyt hes, and hie sentens,
Sa fresch endyte, and sang poeticall,   55
That it is clepyt the wark imperiall,
Endyt onto the gret Octauyane,
The emperour excellent and maste souerane;   f. 180ʳ
By quham, the gospell makis mensioun,
The hail warld put was to discriptioun   60
To numbir all the pepill tharin suldbe,
So, but rebellioun, al quhar obeyit was he.
Bot, sen that Virgill standis but compar,
Thocht in our leid hys sayngis to declar
I haue in ryme thus far furth tane the cur,   65
Now war me laith my lang laubour mysfur:
All thocht my termys be nocht polist alway,
Hys sentence sall I hald, as that I may.
Gyf ocht be weill, thank Virgil and nocht me;
Quhar ocht is bad, gays myß, or owt of gre,   70
My lewytnes, I grant, heß all the wyte,
Kouth not ensew hys ornat fresch endyte,

42

Bot, with fuylhardy curage malapert,
Schupe to enterprit, and dyd perchance pervert,
Thys maist renownyt prynce of poetry –   75
Quhar I sa dyd, mea culpa I cry.
ʒit, by my self, I fynd this proverb perfyte,
"The blak craw thinkis hyr awin byrdis quhite:"
Sa faris with me, bew schirris, wil ʒe hark,
Can nocht persave a falt in all my wark,   80
Affectioun sa far my rayson blyndis.
Quhar I mysknaw myne errour, quha it fyndis
For cheryte amendis it, gentil wight,
Syne pardon me, sat sa far in my lycht,
And I sal help to smor ʒour falt, leif broder;   85
Thus, vail que vail, ilk gude deid helpis other.
And for I haue my wark addressyt and dycht,
I dar sa, baith to gentil barroun and knycht,
Quhais name abufe I haue done notyfy,
And now of prowes and hie chevelry   90
Behuffis me to write and carp a quhile;
The mar glaidly I sal enfors my stile,
And for hys saik do scharp my pen all new,
My maste renownyt author to ensew,
That thar salbe, wyll God, litill offens,   95   f. 180ᵛ
Salvand owr bustuus wlgar differens.
Na mar as now in preambill me list expone,
The nynt buke thus begouth Eneadon. etc.

Explicit prologus
Incipit liber nonus Eneados

Iuno to Turnus in message Iris sent,
To sege the Troianys, Eneas tho absent.   C. i

Quhyll on this wyß, as I haue said or this,
Sik materis and ordinancis wirkand is
In diuerß placis set full fer ytwyn,
Saturnus get, Iuno, that list not blyn
Of hir auld malyce and iniquyte,   5
Hir madyn Iris from hevin sendys sche
To the bald Turnus malapert and stowt,
Quhilk for the tyme was with all his rowt
Amyd ane valle wondyr lovn and law,
Sittand at eys within the hallowyt schaw   10
Of god Pilumnus, hys progenitor.
Thamantis douchtir knelys hym befor,
I meyn Iris, this ilk fornamyt maid,
And with hir rosy lippys thus hym said:

43

"Turnus, behald on cace reuoluyt the day,   15
And of hys fre will sendys the, perfay,
Sik avantage and oportunyte,
That set thou wald haue axit it," quod sche,
"Thar was nevir ane of all the goddis dyng
Quhilk durst haue the promittit sic a thing.   20
Eneas, desolat levand hys cite,
Hys navy eik, hys ferys and hail menʒe,
Is till Evander socht, and Palatyne,
That burgh. But not eneuch, for farther syne
To the extreme citeis of Tuscany   25
In mont Corythus haldys he in hy,
And doys assembill the wild lauboreris,   f. 181ʳ
That quhilum com fra Lyd, till armys in weris.
Quhat dredis thou? Now tyme is to prik horß,
Now tyme fortill assay ʒour cartis and forß.   30
Haue done, mak na mar tary nor delay,
Set on thar strenthis sone, gif thame affray."
Quod sche, and tharwith, in hys presens evin,
With equale weyngis flaw vp in the hevin,
Vndre the clowdis schapand, quhar scho went,   35
A gret rane bowe of diuerß hewys ment.
The ʒong man knew hir weill, and hastely
Vp baith hys handis hevis to the sky,
With sic wordis followand, as scho dyd fle:
"Iris, thou bewte of the hevynnys hie,   40
Throw all the clowdis and thir skyis brovn,
Quha heß the send to me in erth a dovn?
Quhow is becummyn on this wyß," quod he,
"Sa brycht weddir and cleir serenyte?
I se the hevynnys oppynnyt and devyde   45
And movand sternys in the lyftis syde:
So gret takynnys and reuelacions schaw
I sal persew, and follow quhat befaw;
Quhat evir thou be that callys to the weris,
Thy command sal I obey, as efferis."   50
And thar withall, with wordis augurall,
Eftir thar spayng cerymonys diuynal,
Onto the flude onon furth steppis he,
And of the stremys crop a litill we,
The watir lyftis vp intill his handis,   55
Full gretumly the goddys, quhar he standis,
Besekand till attend to hys prayer,
The hevynnys chargeyng with feil awowis seir.
With this the ostis all in the plane feild
Held furth arrayt, schynand vnder scheld.   60
Men mycht behald full mony riall stedis,

44

Full mony pantyt targe and weirlyke wedis;
Of giltyn geir dyd glytter bank and buß.
The formast batale ledis Mesapus;
The hyndmast ostis had in governyng   65 f. 181ᵛ
Of Tyrrhyus the sonnys or childer ȝyng;
Turnus thar duke rewlys the myddill ost,
With glave in hand maid awful feir and bost,
Thame till array raid turnand to and fro,
And by the hed alhaill, quhar he dyd go,   70
Hyear than all the rowt men mycht hym se.
In sik ordour furth haldis his menȝe
Lyke as sum tyme Ganges, the flude Indane,
Sevyn swelland ryveris efter spayt of rayn
Ressauyt in hys large bosum inhy,   75
In hys deip trowch now flowys esely;
Or as vmquhile the fertill flude, Nylus,
Ourfletand all the feildis, bank and buß,
Syne, efter the gret fludis watry rage,
Returnys swagit to hys auld passage.   80

Turnus segis the Troianys in gret ire,
And all thar schippis and navy set in fyre.   C. ii

Be this the Troianys in thar new cite
A dusty sop vprysand gan do se,
Full thik of stowr vp thryngand in the ayr,
And all the feildis myrknyt mair and mair.
Caycus first cryis, as he war wod,   5
Dovn from the hie garrat quhar he stude:
"O citesanys, how gret ane ost," quod he,
"Is lappit in ȝone dusty stew I se!
Swith hynt ȝour armour, tak ȝour wapynnys all,
Bryng hydder dartis, speil vp on the wall!   10
Our ennemys cummys at hand, but dowt!"
"Hay, hay, go to!" than cry thai with a schowt,
And with a huge bruyt Troianys at schort
Thar wallys stuffyt and closyt euery port,
For sa Eneas, maste expert in armys,   15
At hys departing, dredand for thir harmys,
Gaif thame command, gif thai assalȝeit wer
Or hys returnyng, be hard fortoun of weir,
That thai ne suld in batale thame array,
Nor in the plane thar ennemys assay,   20 f. 182ʳ
Bot bad thai suld alanerly withhald
Thar strenth within thar fowseis, as he wald,
And kepe thar wallys forsely and weill,
With fowcy dichis and wapynnys styfe of steill.

45

Tharfor, all thocht baith schame and felloun ire 25
Thar breistis had enflambyt hait as fyre,
In the plane feild on thar famen to set,
3it neuertheleß thar portis haue thai schet
Fortill obey the command of Enee;
On boß turrettis and on towris hie 30
Enarmyt stude thar fays till abyde.
Turnus the chiftane on the tother syde
Come to the cite, or that ony wist,
Furth fleand swipperly, as that hym best list,
Befor the ost, quhilk went bot esy paß, 35
With hym a twenty chosyn men he haß;
Apon a sterand steid of Trace he sat,
Of cullour dapill gray and wail fat,
Full hie rysand abuf his knychtly hed
Hys goldin helm, with tymbrel al blude rede. 40
"Go to, 3yng gallandis, quha that list," quod he,
"Thar ennemyß assail3e first with me!"
And, with that word, threw a dart in the air,
As he to geif batale all redy war,
Syne in plane feild with browdyn baneris gay 45
Bargane to byde drew hym till array.
Hys feris all ressauyt the clamour hie,
And followand thar chiftane, he and he,
The bruyt rasyt with grisly sound attanys,
And gan to mervell the dolf hartit Troianys, 50
That durst nocht, as thame semyt, in plane feild
Thame self aventour, nor 3it with sper and scheld
Mach with thar fa men in patent bargane,
Bot hald thame in thar strenthis euery ane.
And all commovit, brym and full of ire, 55
Baith heir and thar Turnus the grevyt syre   f. 182ᵛ
Went on horsbak, seirsand abowt the wall
Every dern way and secret passagis all,
Gyf ony entre or tocome espy
He myght, fortill assail the cite by. 60
Lyke as we se, wachand the full scheip fald,
The wild wolf ourset with schowris cald
Of wynd and rane, at myddis of the nycht,
Abowt the bowght plet all of wandis tyght
Brays and gyrnys; tharin bletand the lammys 65
Full sovirly liggis vnder thar dammys;
He brym and felloun his rageand furour
Aganys the absentis, reddy to devour,
Rasys in ire, for the wod hungris lyst;
Hys wysnyt throt, havand of blude sic thrist, 70
Gendris of lang fast sic ane appetyte

46

That he constrenyt is in extreme syt –
Nane other wyß, the feirfull fervent ire
In Turnus breist vpkyndillis hait as fyre,
Seand thir wallys and fortressis attanys;   75
The huge ennoy byrnys hym throu the banys,
Imagynand by quhat resson or way
Hys ennemyß he mycht wyn till assay,
And on quhat wyß the Troianys fra thar strenth
He mycht expell, and in plane feild on lenth   80
Mak thame to ische in patent batale place.
And as he musand was heiron, percace,
The navy of thar schippys he dyd invaid,
That fastby ionyt to the wall was layd,
With dychys and with fowseis dern abowt,   85
In the flude watir, as neir owt of dowt;
Quham fra he had espyit, but abaid
At hys feris, quhilkis wilfull war and glaid,
Eftir the fyre and kyndillyng dyd he cry,
And in hys awin handis hyntis vp in hy   90
A blesand fyre brand of the fyrryn tre.
Than byssely Rutilyanys, he and he –
So the presens of Turnus dyd thame steir,   f. 183ʳ
That euery man the rekand schydis in feir
Rent fra the fyris and on the schippis slang;   95
The semys crakkis, the watir byssyt and sang,
The tallownyt burdis kest a pikky low,
Vpblesis owrloft, hechis, wrangis and how,
Quhill myxt with reik the fell sparkis of fyre
Heich in the air vpglydis byrnand schire.   100

Quhou the fyre was expellit fra the navye,
The schippis translait in nymphis or goddessis of see.   C. iii

Say me, O Musys, reherses and declare,
Quhilk of the goddis sa cruel flammys sayr
Held from Troianys? quha sa vehement fyre
Drave from thar schippis, thus wyß byrnand schire?
The deid is auld forto beleif or wry,   5
Bot the memor remanys perpetualy.
The first tyme quhen the Troiane Eneas
By sey to tak hys vayage schap to paß,
And gan do beld his schippis vp ilkane
In Ida forest, that mont Phrygiane,   10
The moder of goddis, Berecyntia,
Spak to hir son gret Iupiter, thai sa,
With sikkynd wordis, sayand: "My child deir,
Grant this ane axin quhilk I the requeir,

47

Grant thy belovit moder bot a thing,   15
Thou at art master of the hevynly ryng.
Apon the top of Gargarus," quod sche,
"Thar grew a fyr wod, the quhilk into dante
Full mony ȝeris held I, as is knaw.
Thys was my cuchill and my hallowit schaw,   20
Quhar that the Phrygianys maid me sacrifice;
Ful weill me lykyt thar to walk oftsyß,
With pikky treis blak skuggit abowt,
And abundans of hattyr gestis stowt,
Quhilk glaidly I haue gevin a ȝong Troiane,   25
Strang Eneas, discend from Kyng Dardane,
Fortill support the mysteris of hys navy.   f. 183ᵛ
And now the dowtsum dreid, for the ilk quhy,
Full pensyve haldis me and doith constrene:
Deliuer me of thys feir be sum meyn,   30
My deir son, suffir at thy moderis request
Be admittit this a tyme, be the leste,
So that tha schippis be nevir mair ourset
With contrar curß, nor ȝit with storm dovn bet;
Quharby thai may haue sum avale," quod sche,   35
"At thai vmquhile grew in our hillys hie."
Hyr son, the quhilk rewlys at hys lykyng
The hevyn, the starris, and all erdly thyng,
Ansuerd and said: "O moder best belovyt,
Quhou art thou thus agane the fatis amovyt?   40
Or quharto axis thou to thir," quod he,
"With mortale handis wrocht of stokkis and tre,
That is to say, thir schippis so habill to faill,
That lesum war thai suldbe immortale?
And that Enee, in dedly corps onsure,   45
Assoverit fermly throw all dangeris fuyr?
Quhat god heß to hym grantyt sik frelage?
Bot for thy saik, quhen fully thar vayage
Thai haue compleyt, and at costis of Itale
Arryvit ar, and in tha portis set sail,   50
And thar duke Troiane careit our the see
To boundis of Lawrentum, that cuntre,
Alsmony of thame as than heß eschaipe
The wally fludis sall I turn and schaip
Furth of thar mortale formys corruptabill,   55
And sall command thame fortobe mair habill
From thens forthwart, as immortale," quod he,
"In nymphes turnyt and goddessys of see,
Lyke as Nereus douchter, Clotho gay,
And Galathea, throw fomy fludis gray   60
Scheryng with braid brestis delytabill,"

Quod Iupiter, and till hald ferm and stabill,
Be Stix the flude, Pluto hys broderis see,
Hys godly aith and promyß sworn hes he;
Be that ilk pykky laik with brays blak, 65
And laithly sworlys, till kepe at he spak f. 184ʳ
He dyd afferm hys hecht, and in takynnyng
The hevynnys all maid trymmyll at hys likyng.
Tharfor the day that he by promys set
Is now at hand, and the ful tyme of det 70
By the werd sisteris schaip is now compleit,
Quhen Turnus thus in hys iniuryus heit
Admonyst heß hys pepill and commandis,
With dry schydis and with hait fyre brandis,
The moder of goddis by sik flambys fell 75
Furth of hir hallowyt schippis to expell.
At this tyme first apperis in hir syght
A new takynnyng of gret plesand lycht,
And a braid schynand clowd thai dyd aspy
Cum from the est, rynnand our all the sky; 80
The rowtis eik onone thai gan behald
Of Ideanys, tha wightis that in the hald
Ar of the moder of the goddis cloß;
Dovn throu the air eik come a feirful voce,
And fillit all the ostis baith atanys 85
Of Troiane pepill and Rutulianys,
Sayand: "Troianys, dreid na thing, haist ȝou nocht
Fortill defend my schippis, albeit ȝe mocht,
For that cauß tak na wapynnys in ȝour handis,
For rather, now as that the mater standis, 90
Sal it be lefull Turnus fyre the see,
Or that he byrn my bargis maid of tre.
O ȝe my schippys, now to ȝou I say,
Go fre at large quhar ȝou list away,
Go furth and swym as goddessis of the see; 95
The moder of goddis commandis so tobe."
And, wyth that word, als tyte furth from the bra
Ilk barge bownys, cuttand hir cabyll in twa,
Lyke delphyn fysch onon as thai tuke kepe,
Thar snowtis dowkand held vnder the deip. 100
Syne from the grond, a wonder thing to say,
With als feill virgyne facis vpsprang thai,
And throu the fludis, quhar thame list, dyd fair,
Quhou mony steill stammyt bargis that ayr f. 184ᵛ
Stude by the costis syde, or thai war fyryt. 105
Rutylianys wolx affrayit with myndis myryt;
Mesapus musyng can withdraw on dreich,
Seand hys stedis and the horssis skeich;

49

And eik the ryver brayt with hayß sovnd,
Quhill Tyberinus bakwartis dyd rebound,   110
As thocht hyß curß dyd stot and step abak.
Bot netheleß, for all the feir thai mak,
The hie curage and forcy hardyment
Baid onamovyt in Turnus stowt entent,
So that baldly with hardy wordis on hie   115
Thar spretis rasyt, and rycht fersly he
Gan thame repreve, that tuk for nocht affray.
"Thir monstruus takynnys at ȝe se, perfay,
Sekis myscheif to the Troianys," said he,
"And by this way gret Iupiter, as ȝe se,   120
Heß now byreft thar help and confidens,
Quharby thai wont war to fle for defens.
Now nowder Rutyliane fyre nor swerdis dynt
May thai withstand, for all thar fors is tynt.
Sen that thai may not eschape by the see,   125
Nor heß na maner hope away to fle,
The maist half of the Troiane help is lost;
This land is in our power, feld and cost;
So that thai sal na wyß eschape our brandis,
Quhou mony thousand douchty men of handis   130
Ar heir assemblyt, all Italyanys.
I compt na thing all thocht ȝon fant Troianys
Rakkyn thar fatis that thame hydder brocht;
All syk vayn ruyß I feir as thing of nocht,
In cace thai prowd be of the goddis answeris,   135
And thame avant tharof with felloun feris.
It may weill suffyß, and eneuch, I wyß,
Baith to thar fatis and Venus grantit is,
That evir thir Troianys in this cost fast by
Hes anys twichit the bowndis of Italy.   140
My werdis eik and fatale destane
Be the contrar is grantit onto me,
Thys cursyt pepill tobet down with my glave,   f. 185ʳ
For my deir spouß, quham byreft me thai have:
Nor this ennoy alanerly twichis nocht   145
The twa Atrydes, that Troy to rewyne brocht
(I meyn the principal chiftanys, breder twa,
That is to knaw, Agamennon and Menelay);
Ne ȝit allane this cauß to armys steris
The pepill of Myce to move batale and weris;   150
Bot principaly this querrell myne I knaw.
Gif it had bene eneuch, as that thai schaw,
At thai bot anys distroyit aucht tobe,
It war enewch and mycht suffyß, think me,
That thai haue faltit anys lang tyme befor.   155

50

Quhy dowbill thai thar trespaß mor and mor?
All thocht that wemen brocht thame to foly,
3yt hait thai not wemen aluterly.
Quhat meyn thai be this myddill mantill wall,
This litill stop of dykis and fowseis all?　　　　　　　160
Weyn thai this be a strenth that may thame save?
Thar lyfe is now in iuperte, thai raif,
Full neir thar ded thai stand: all man may knaw
Quhidder gif the wight wallys of Troy thai saw,
Belt by the hand of Neptunus, that syre,　　　　　　　165
Rent and bet down, and all the town in fyre.
Bot O 3e walyt knychtis of renown,
Quham I behald with pykkis brekand dovn
3on fortereß, and now present with me
Assal3eand this affrayt strenth we se;　　　　　　　170
Ws nedis not Wlcanus armour heir
Aganys thir maste fant Troianys in our weir,
Nor 3it we mystir not a thousand schippis.
All thocht hail Tuscany in to falloschippis
With thame adione, and cum on euery syde,　　　　　　　175
Lat thame nocht dreid that we, be nyghtis tyde,
Sall thyftuusly Palladium steill away,
Nor sla thar wachis slepand; na perfay,
Dern in ane horssis belly large or wyde,
Thame to dissave, we sall ws neuer hyde,　　　　　　　180
For we determyt haue by forß in fyght,　　　　　　　f. 185ᵛ
In plane batale, and on days lyght,
With fyre and swerd 3on wallys ombeset.
So dowchtely we schape to do our det,
That thai sall not beleif weir vndertane　　　　　　　185
Agane Grekis, nor pepill Pelasgane,
Quhilkis in thar weris previt sa spreitleß men
That Hector thame delayt 3eris ten.
Now, chosyn men and walyt weriouris,
Sen the maist part of this days howris　　　　　　　190
Is gane," said he, "I hald it for the best
Eftir this gud iournay 3e tak 3ou rest;
Do eyß 3our bodeis and 3our horß quhil day,
Bot hald 3ou reddy for the batale ay.
In the meyn tyme, of the nycht wach the cur　　　　　　　195
We geif Mesapus, the 3ettis to discur
And forto beit brycht fyris abowt the wallys."
Twyß sevin Rutilianys for al chance befallys
Was chosyn with knychtis forto wach the town;
Ilkane ane hundreth fallowys reddy bown　　　　　　　200
Of 3oung gallandis, with purpour crestis red;
Thar giltyn geir maid glitteryng euery sted

51

Quhar so thai walk and rowmys still and soft.
Thai stalk about, and wardis changis oft,
And sum tyme, on the greyn herbys down set, 205
Thai byrll the wyne, and ilk man dyd hys det
Fortil ourturn goblettis of mettell bryght.
The schynand fyris our al the land kest lycht;
And all the fornycht thir wachis sikkyn way,
But sleip, dyd spend in revale, gam and play. 210

Heir Nysus carpis to his frend Eurilly
Till vndyrtak ane aventur onsilly. C. iv

The Troianys, from thar forttreß quhar thai stude
   All thar deray beheld and vnderstude,
And baith with armour and with wapynnys brycht
The towr hedys thai stuffyt all that nyght,
And feill tymys in hasty effeir for dreid 5
The portis vissy thai, gyf ocht war neid,
And draw briggis befor the ȝettis vprasyt, f. 186ʳ
Iunct to the wallys, at thai suld nocht be trasyt;
And euery man stud reddy in hys geir
Enarmyt weill, and in his hand a speir. 10
Mnestheus stern and eik Serestus stowt
Ful bissy war to walk and go abowt,
Tyll ordinance forto put every thing,
For thame Eneas at his departyng
Had deput rewlaris to hys ȝong son deir, 15
And master capitanys of hys ost in weir,
Gyf so betyd ony aduersyte
Or aventour befor hys returne.
Ane hail legioun about the wallis large
Stude wachyng, bodyn with bow, speir and targe; 20
The danger was by cuttys sone decyde,
At euery corner quha, or quha, suld byde,
And euery man his curß abowt dyd sleip,
Quhill that his fallow had his ward to keip.
Nisus, Hirtacus son, that tyme was set, 25
As for hys stand, to byde and kepe the ȝet,
As he that was in armys bald and stowt,
Ane the maist valȝeant intill all that rowt,
Quham Ida hys moder, ane huntryce,
In falloschip send with Ene ful wyß; 30
To cast dartis nane sa expert as he,
Nor forto schoyt swyft arrowys half sa sle.
Euryalus, hys fallow, stude hym by,
Of all Eneas ost nane mair gudly,
Nor ȝit mar semly cled in Troiane armys, 35

Stowt, of hie curage, dredand for na harmys;
Hys florist ȝouth ravest hys vissage ȝyng,
Ȝit nevir schavyn, with pilis newly spryng.
To thir twa was a will in vnyte,
A lust, and mynd in vniformyte;   40
Sammyn thai ȝeid to mete, to rest or play,
And baith togidder in batale ruschit thai;
Now sammyn eik thai war in statioun set,
As baith in feir to kepe the common ȝet.
Nisus thus spekis: "O brothir myne Ewrylly,   45   f. 186ᵛ
Quhiddir gif the goddis, or sum spretis sylly,
Movys in our myndis this ardent thochtfull fyre,
Or gif that euery manis schrewit desyre
Be as his god and genyus in that place,
I wait nevir how it standis; bot this lang space   50
My mynd movys to me, heir as I stand,
Batale or sum gret thyng to tak on hand.
I knaw not to quhat purpoß is it drest,
Bot be na way may I tak eyß nor rest.
Behaldis thou not so surly, but affray,   55
Ȝon Rutylianys thame haldis glaid and gay?
Thar fyris now begynnys schyne full schire,
Sowpyt in wyne and sleip baith man and syre
At quyet lugyng ȝondyr at thar will;
Queym silens haldis the large feildis still.   60
Considir this profundly, I the pray,
Quhat suld I dreid, quhat thynkis thou, now say.
Baith common pepill and the heris bald
To bryng agane Eneas ful fane thai wald;
Langyng ful sair efter hys hame cummyng,   65
And of hys mynd to haue sur wittering,
Thai all desyre sum attentik men be send.
Gyf, as I wald, thou had licens to wend,
Sen weill I knaw thy famus nobill dedis,
In sik a cace, me think, na ma thar nedis,   70
Vndre ȝon moyte the way fund weill I se
To hald onto the wallys of Pallante."
Ewrialus, smyte with hie fervent desyre
Of new renown, quhilk brynt hym hait as fyre,
And half eschamyt of this bodword glaid,   75
Thus til hys best belovyt fallow said:
"Nisus broder, in souerane actis hie,
For ony cauß, quhou may thou refuß me
With the to go in falloschip as feir?
Suld I the send allane in sik danger?   80
My fader, Opheltes, the quhilk all hys days
The weris hantit, nevir apon that ways

53

Instrukkit me, nor tawcht sik cowardy.
Was I not lernyt to hant chevalry
Amyd the Grekis brag, and Troiane weris? 85
Haue I me born with the, at thou afferis
Off my curage? The maist douchty Enee,
And of fortoun to the last extremyte,
Haue I not followyt, refusand na pyne?
Heir is, heir is, within this corps of myne, 90
A forcy spreit that doith this life dispyß,
Quhilk reputtis fair to wissyll, apon sik wyß,
With this honour thou thus pretendis to wyn,
This mortale stait and life that we bene in."
Nisus ansueris: "Forsuyth, my broder dyng, 95
Of the, God wait, ȝit dred I nevir sic thing,
For so to think in faith onlefull wer.
So hail and feir mot salf me Iupiter,
And bryng me sowund agane with victory,
As euer ȝit sic consait of the had I. 100
To wytnes draw I that ilk god," quod he,
"With frendly eyn quhilk dois ws heir and se,
And in my mynd first movit this consait.
Bot gif that so betyde, as weill ȝe wait
In sic aventouris thar bene dangeris seir, 105
Be hard fortoun or aventour of weir,
Or goddys dispositioun happin it fall,
My will was the to salue fra perrellis all:
Thy florist ȝouth is mair worthy to leif
Than forto put in danger of myscheif. 110
I wald alsso at hame sum frend haue had
That gif at I war takyn and hard stad,
Or fra me reft the lyfe, and sa with hald,
Quhilk my body or banys ranson wald,
And lay in grave eftir our Troiane gyß; 115
Or, gyf fortoun wald suffir on na wyß
My body mycht be brocht to beriall,
Than to hys frend the seruyce funeral
With obsequeis to do for corps absent,
And in my memor vp a tumbe to stent. 120
Ne wald I not alsso that I suld be
Cauß or occasioun of sic duyll," quod he,
"To thy maist reuthfull mother, trast and kynd,
Quhilk anerly of hir maist tendir mynd,
From all the other matronys of our rowt, 125
Heß followyt the, hir luffyt child, abowt,
Ne for thy saik refusyt not the see
And gave na forß of Acestes cite."
The tother tho hym ansuerit sone agane:

54

"My frend, for nocht thou says sik wordis vane,   130
Ingirand cacis ar of nane effek;
My first entent I list not change nor brek.
Haist ws," quod he, and tharwithall baith twa
The nixt wach thai walknyt quhar thai lay,
Quhilk gat on fut and to thar rowmys went.   135
Eurialus, to fulfill hys entent,
With Nysus furth can hald hys way onon,
And to the prynce Ascanyus ar gone.

Quhou at the consal the fornamyt two
Ontill Eneas purchest leif to go.   C. v

A pon the erth the othir bestis all,
  Thar bissy thochtis sessyng, gret and small,
Ful sownd on sleip dyd cawcht thar rest be kynd,
All irksum laubour forȝet owt of mynd;
Bot the cheif ledaris of the Troiane rowt,   5
And flowr of fensabill ȝyng men stern and stowt,
In the meyn tyme sat at wyß consell
For common weill and materis hie befell,
Consideryng wisly quhat ado thar was,
Or quha suld message beir to Eneas;   10
Amyddis thar tentis, in feild quhar thai stand,
With scheildis schrowd, apon thar speris lenand.
Tho Nysus and Eurialus, baith twane
Glaid of this cast, seand thair tyme maste gane,
Besocht thai mycht be admittit to say   15
A gret mater of weght, quhais delay
Mycht harm gret deill, and eik be thar avyß
Thar erand was worth audiens and of price.
Ascanyus first, seand thar hasty way,
Admittit thar desire, and bad thame say.   20
Than this Nisus, Hirtacus son, thus said: f. 188ʳ
"Gentill Troianys, with equal myndis glaid
Ressaue my wordis, for this thing," quod he,
"Quhilk I ȝow tell may nocht considerit be
With sik as ws, nor men sa ȝong of ȝheris,   25
Bot to ȝour wisdomys till avyß efferis.
The Rutilianys, ourset with sleip and wyne,
Lyggis sowpit, fordoverit, drunk as swyne:
To set apon thame, and await with skaith,
The place surly we haue espyit baith,   30
Quhilk reddy may ful esely be get
In ȝondir forkyt way, strekis fra the ȝet
Down to the seys cost the nerrest went,
Quhar the fyris fast falȝeis, neir owt brynt,

55

So that the blak reik dyrknyß all the air.   35
Gif that ȝe suffir wald, as I said ayr,
That we mycht vse this oportunyte
Quhilk fortoun haß ws grant, sone suld ȝe se
Eneas socht by ws at Pallantyne,
And hyddir brocht in schort quhile efter syne,   40
With ryche spulȝe, and mekill slauchter maid.
We knaw the way thidder full weill," he said,
"And all the watyr of Tibyr vp and down;
In dyrk valeys oft we saw the town,
As we by custum oft the huntyng hantit."   45
Agit Alethes, that na wisdome wantit,
Bot baith was rype in consale and in ȝheris,
Onto thir wordis digestly maid ansueris:
"O kyndly goddis of our natyve landis,
Vndre quhais myghtis all tyme Troy vpstandis,   50
All thocht the weill tharof in dowt remanys,
ȝit list ȝou not distroy all the Troianys,
Ne thame so clene defait aluterly,
Sen sa stowt myndis as we heir aspy
And sa bald reddy breistis gevin haue ȝhe   55
To thir ȝongkeris." And sayand thus, can he
The rycht handis and schuldris of baith embrace,
With terys tryncland our his chekis and face.
"O manly knyghtis, quhat reward condyng
May ganandly be geif for syk a thyng,   60   f. 188ᵛ
Forsuyth I can nocht in my mynd devyß;
Bot ȝour maist cheif ganȝeld and gyft to pryß
The gret goddis mot rendyr ȝou," said he,
"And ȝour awin vertu mot be renowne;
The remanent onone ȝe sall ressaue,   65
Sa that na wyß ȝe sal ȝour medis crave,
By the handys of reuthfull Eneas;
Or, gif he sone from this lyfe happynnys paß,
Ascanyus, quhilk as ȝit is bot page,
ȝong and fordward into hys hailsum age,   70
Sall render ȝour desert, I tak on hand,
And sik thankis, quhil that he is levand,
Sal nevir be forȝet nor do away."
The sammyn word onon, as he dyd say,
Furth of hys mowth Ascanyus hes hynt: 75
"I hecht forsuyth that deid sall nevir be tynt,
For all my weil alanerly doys hyng
Apon my faderis prosper hame cummyng.
Nysus," said he, "I ȝou pray and beseik,
Be our Penates, kyndly goddis meik,   80
And be Assaracus goddis domesticall,

Quham ʒe the cheif stok of our kynrent call,
And be the secret closettis or entre
Of the venerabill auld canus Veste,
Bryng hame my fader sone, I ʒou exort: 85
All that perteynyng is to me, at schort,
Baith twychand consale and commandment,
Or aventouris of fortoun, in ʒour entent,
In ʒour willys, I put all haill," quod he,
"Bryng hame my fader that I may hym se,   90
For had we hym ressauyt, I dar say,
Is no thing suld ennoy ws nor effray.
Twa siluer cowpys, wrocht rycht curyusly
With figuris grave, and punsyt ymagery,
I sall ʒou geif (the quhilk my fader wan   95
Quhen conquest was the cite Arisban),
Twa charis rych, or trestis quently fold,
And twa gret talentis of the fynast gold,   f. 189ʳ
And eik the crafty ancyent flacconys two
Quhilkis to me gave the Sydoneß Dido.   100
And gyf, certis, as victouris ws betydis
To conquyß Ital, as the fatys provydis,
Tharin to bruke the crown and ceptre wand,
And to distribut the pray, as lord of land –
Beheld ʒe nocht quhat kyn a cursour wycht,   105
Quhou prowd armour, weil gilt and burnyst brycht,
That Turnus bair this ʒister nyght?" quod he.
"The sammyn scheld, and helm with crestis thre
Semyng of fyre all rede, and the ilk steid,
Fra this sammyn hour, Nysus, salbe thy meid;   110
I sall thame sort fra all the remanent.
And forthir eik my fader, of hys ascent,
Twelf chosyn matronys sall ʒou geif all fre,
Tobe ʒour sclavys in captiuite,
With all thar childryng and thar hail ofspryng,   115
Thar moblys, catal, rentis and armyng;
And eik that feild and pryncipal peyß of land
Quhilk Kyng Latinus heß now in hys hand.
And O thou wirschipfull ʒong child, quhais age
Is to my ʒouthed in the nerrest stage,   120
With all my hart I the ressaue evin heir,
In all cacis as tendir fallow and feir.
But the, na glorius act in my materis
Salbe exercyt, nother in paix nor weris:
In euery thing, baith into word and deid,   125
The maist trast salbe geif the for thy meid."
Ewrialus maid this answer for hys syde:
"That day sal neuer cum, nor tyme betyde,

For my defalt onworthy sall I be
Fortyll attene sa souerane dignyte.   130
Lat fortoun send ws gude luk, gif scho lest,
Or mysaventour, I sal do my best –
Lo, this is all, na mair I may promyt.
Bot, abuf all thingis, a gift grant me ȝit,
That I beseik the oft and monyfald: 135   f. 189ᵛ
Ane moder, cummyn of Priamus blude of ald,
Within this town I haue, quhilk silly wyfe,
Me forto follow not comptand hir lyfe,
The realm of Troy mycht not withhald," said he,
"Nor ȝit in Sycyll Acestes fair cite.   140
Now hir I leif onhalsyt as I ryde,
Of this danger, quhat so evir betyde,
All ignorant and wait no thyng, puyr wight;
To wytnes draw I heir this ilk gude nycht,
And thy rycht hand, my lord and prynce maste hie,   145
The wepand teris may I not suffir nor se
Of my deir moder, nor that rewthfull syght.
Bot I beseik thy gentyll hart of ryght
Forto comfort that cayrfull creatur;
That desolat wight to succur schaw thi cuyr.   150
Grant this a thyng, and suffir that of the
This a gude hop I bair of town with me;
And far the baldar, quhat so fortoun send,
Ontill all dangeris glaidly sall I wend."
The Troianys all for reuth, at speke hym heris,   155
Smyte with compassioun, brastis furth of terys,
With tender hartis menand Ewrialus.
Bot principaly lusty Ascanyvs.
The ymage of hys faderly piete,
Prent in hys mynde, hym strenys swa that he   160
Wepand answerd, and said: "My brother deir,
I promyß all thou desiris, out of weir,
For thy commancement and stowt begynnyng
Is sa douchty I may the nyte na thyng.
Forsuyth this woman, quhat so evir scho be,   165
Fra thyne fordwart sal moder be to me,
Wantyng na mar of my moder in plane
Alanerly bot Creusa, hyr name;
And thus of sik a byrth na litill blyß
Sall hyr betyde, quhou evir efter this   170
The chans turnys, owder to weill or wo.
Be this ilk hed I swer to the also,   f. 190ʳ
By quhilk my fader wont was forto swer,
All that I haue onto the promyst heir
Gyf thou returnys in prosperyte,   175

Failȝeand tharof, as Iove defend swa be,
To thy moder and onto thy kynred
Sall fully bene obseruyt, in thy sted."
Thus sayd he wepand, and tharwith alssua
Hys gyltyn swerd he hynt his schuldris fra,   180
Quham wonder craftely in the land of Creyt
Lycaon forgyt had, and wrocht it meyt
Within a burnyst scheith of evor bone;
Thame baith togiddir he gaue Ewrill onone.
Syne Mnestheus a bustuus lyon skyn,   185
That rowch and weirlyke tawbart na thing thyn,
To Nysus gave; and the traste Alethys
With hym hes helmys cosyt, and gaue hym hys.

Furth haldis Nysus and Eurillius baith tway,
And huge slauchter thai haue maid be the way.   C. vi

Onon thai held enarmyt furth thar way,
Quham all the nobillys ȝyng and ald, perfay,
Convoyt to the portis, na thyng fayn,
Prayand full oft Iove bryng thame weil agane.
Bot principaly the fresch Ascanyus ȝyng,   5
Abufe al otheris in hys commonyng
Schawand the wysdome, consait and forsyght
Of agit man, and eik the curage wight,
Gave thame feill chargis and commandmentis
To beir hys fader, twychand hys ententis;   10
Bot with the wynd tha skatterit war on raw,
And all for nocht amang the clowdis flaw.
Furth ischit thai, and by the fowcyis went is,
In silens of the dyrk nycht, amangis the tentis
And perellus pailȝeonys, to thame ennemy,   15
Thai entrit ar, and caucht gret harm tharby
(Bot netheleß, or ony skaith thai hynt,
The ded of mony was thar douchty dynt).
Apon the gyrß, ourset witht sleip and wyne,   f. 190ᵛ
Fordoverit, fallyn down als drunk as swyne,   20
The bodeys of Rutylianys heir and thar
Thai dyd persaue; and by the cost alquhar
The cartis stand with lymmowris bendyt strek,
The men lyggyng, the hamys abowt thar nek,
Or than amangis the quhelys and the thetis;   25
All sammyn lay thar armour, wyne and metys,
Baith men and cartis myddillyt all our ane.
With ane baß voce thus Nysus spak agane:
"Ewrialus, the mater now thus standis,
Fortobe stowt and forcy of our handis.   30

59

Thys is our passage, quhilk way we mon wend.
Thy part salbe to kepe and to defend
That nane onset cum on ws at the bak;
Spy far about, tharto gude tent thou tak.
I sall befor mak voyd passage and way,   35
And the convoy throu a large streit away."
Rehersand this, onon he held hym cloß,
So that na noys mycht thar be hard or voce,
And tharwith eik with drawyn swerd in preß
He can assail the pompus Rhamnetes,   40
Quhilk lay, percace, slepand soft and sownd
On prowd tapetis spred apon the grond;
A kyng he was, and a spa man, suyth to sayn,
To Turnus kyng mast trast auguriane,
Bot with hys diuinatioun nor augury   45
The trake of deth ne cowth he not put by.
Thre of hys seruandis, that fast by hym lay,
Ful raklesly he kyllyt, all thocht thai
Amang thar speris lyggyng war infeir;
And quellyt ane to Remus was squyer.   50
The cartar syne, luggyng apon the streit,
He hynt onon amang the horssis feyt,
And with hys swerd hys nek, hyngand on syde,
In twane hes hakkyt; and the sammyn tyde
Thar lordis hed, I meyn this said Rhamneyt.   55
Of smytis he, quhill all the bed wolx weyt;
Lyke a ded stok the corps wantand the hed
Lay bullerand, al besprent with sprayngis red,
And als the erth grew warm with teppet blude.   f. 191ʳ
Attour he stekit hes eik, quhar he stude,   60
Twa forcy men, Lamus and Lamyrus,
And als the lykly ȝong child, Serranus,
That all the fornycht in ryot and in play
Had spendyt as he lyst, and now he lay
With membris strekit, and plesand vissage brycht,   65
Ourset with god Bachus mekill of myght:
Ful happy and weill fortunat had he be,
In sport and gam on the sam wyß gif he
All the remanent of that nycht had spent,
Quhil the lycht day, and tyl hym self tane tent.   70
Lyke as the empty lyoun, lang onfed,
Be nychtis tyde quhen all folk sleip in bed,
Trubland the fald full of silly scheip,
The wod rage of hys hungir is so deip
That he constrenyt is sik wyß to fair;   75
He ryvis and he harlys heir and thar
The tendir bestis, that for awfull feir

Of hys presens dar nowder bleyt nor steir;
He rummysis with bludy mowth and brays –
So dyd Ewrilly, and none other ways,   80
And na leß slauchter maid he in the plane,
Of ire inflambyt in his wod brane.
A multitude of commonys of birth law,
By quhilk resson thar namys ar onknaw,
He ombeset and put to confusioun,   85
And Fadus syne with Hesebus dang he down,
And Arabys also onwarnystly,
And Rhetus eik, lay walkand hard thame by
Behaldand all thar sterage and deray,
Bot, of the stowt Ewrialus for affray,   90
Behynd a wyne bote or a pype hym hyd,
Quham Eurialus, as the cace betyd,
Keppyt on hys swerdis poynt, that all the blaid
Hyd in hys cost vp to the hyltis glaid –
To ded he duschis down bath styſ and cald,   95
And vp the purpour spreit of lyf he ȝald,
And blude and wyne mixt he can furth schaw,
At he last drank owt ȝeskis in the ded thraw.   f. 191ᵛ
And, by sik slyght full brym, thus he enforcis
To mak huge slauchtir of onweldy corpcis,   100
Etlyng wightly to the nixt stude fast by.
Thar as Mesapus feris all dyd ly,
And the last fyris almaste quynchit owt,
The horß, per ordour, tyit weill abowt,
Etand thar meit he mycht behald and se;   105
Quham schortly Nysus bad seß and lat be,
For he persauyt Eurialus by his feris
Had our gret lust to slaughter, and dangeris
Persauyt nocht quhilkis war apperand eft.
"Desist," quod he, "this mater mon be left,   110
For the day lycht, quhilk is to ws onfrend,
Approchis neir, we may na langar lend.
Gret harm is done, eneuch of blude is sched,
Throw owt our fays a patent way is red."
And sayng thus, thai sped thame on thar way: 115
Behynd thame, for vptakyng quhar it lay,
Mony brycht armour richly dyght thai left,
Cowpys and goblettis, forgyt far, and beſt
Of massy syluyr, lyand heir and thar,
Prowd tapysry, and mekill precyus war;   120
Salf that Eurialus with hym tursyt away
The rial trappouris, and myghty patrellys gay,
Quhilkis war Rhamnetes stedis harnessyng,
And, for the mair remembrance in takynnyng,

Ane rych tysche or belt hynt he syne,   125
The pendentis wrocht of burnyst gold maste fyne
(Quhilk gyrdill ane Cedicus, that was than
Duryng his tyme ane the myghtyast man,
Bereft a strang Rutiliane, as thai tell,
Quham he venquyst in singular batell,   130
And send it syne to ane Remulus hes he,
That duke was of the Tiburtyne cite,
In syng of frendschip and ferm acquentans:
Thus athir absent ionyt allyans;
Syne this ilk prynce, into hys legacy,   135   f. 192ʳ
That tyme apon hys ded bed dyd he ly,
This gyrdill left to ʒongar Remulus,
Hys tendyr nevo, that is heir slane thus);
Euryll, as said is, heß this iowell hynt,
Abowt hys sydis it brasyng, or he stynt –   140
Bot all for nocht, suppoß the gold dyd gleit.
Mesapus helm syne, for him wondir meit,
With schynand tymbret and with crystis hie,
Apon hys hed onon buklyt hes he.
Furth of the tentis with this bownyt thai,   145
And fra thar fays held the sovyr way.

Quhou capitane Volscens, cumand Turnus till, Recontrit Nysus and hys fallow Ewrill.

C. vii

In the meyn quhile, as this other army
Thus at the sege gan in the feildis ly,
From Lawrentum, Kyng Latinus cite,
War horsmen sent to Turnus, forto se
Quhat he plesyt, and the kyngis entent   5
Tyll hym to schaw; thre hundreth men furth went
With scheild on schuldir vndre capitane Volscens,
And be this cummyn war to the distens
Neir to thar ost, and, as the cace dyd fall,
Thai held fast vnder this new cite wall.   10
Quhar as on far towart the left hand thai
Turnand thar curß bakwart persauyt tway
(For the brycht helm in twynkland starny nycht
Mythis Eurilly with bemys schynand lycht,
Quhilk he, onwar, persauyt nocht, allace!),   15
And as thai scars war thus aspyit on cace,
Volscens the capitane, from amyd his rowt,
Said, "Stand, fallowis," and cryis with a schowt,
"Quhat is the cauß of ʒour cummyng," said he,
"That rydis thus enarmyt? Quhat ʒe be,   20
And quhidder ar ʒe bown, ʒe schaw ws plane."

The tother twa maid nane ansuer agane, f. 192^v
Bot in the woddis hyis at the flicht,
Assurit gretly in dirknes of the nycht.
The horsmen than prekis, and fast furth sprentis 25
To weil beknawin pethis, and turnys wentis
Baith heir and thar; sone ombeset haue thai
The owtgatis all, thai suld nocht wyn away.
The wod was large, and rowch of buskis ronk,
And of the blak ayk schaddowis dym and donk, 30
Of breris ful, and thyk thorn ronnys stent –
Scarsly a strait rod or dern narow went
Tharin mycht fundyn be that men mycht paß.
Quharthrou Eurialus gretly cummyrrit was,
Quhat for myrknes, thik buskis, branch and breir, 35
And weght also of the new spulȝeit geir.
Tharto the hasty onset and affray
Maid hym gang will in the onknawin way.
Nysus wes went, and by this chapyt cleir
Hys ennemys, onwar quhar was hys feir: 40
And as he stude at that sted, efter syne
From Alba cite clepit was Albyne,
Quhar, for the tyme, this forsaid Latyn kyng
Hys horß at pastour held in stabillyng,
He blent abowt to se hys frend so deir, 45
Bot all for nocht, thar was na man hym neir.
"Ewrill," quod he, "allace onhappely
In quhat part of this land the left haue I?
Or quhar sall I the seik? O wailaway!"
Tharwith this ilk wilsum perplexit way 50
Bakwart he held, euery futstep agane,
Throw the dern wod dissaitfull and onplane;
Quhil, at the last, amang rank buskis he
Errit by the way, becauß he mycht nocht se.
The horß stampyng and the dyn he heris, 55
The wordis and the takynnys come to his erys
Of thame quhilk at persewit hym at the bak.
A lytil space efter tent gan he tak,
And hard a scry; harknand quhat that suld be, f. 193^r
Eurilly takyn in handys dyd he se, 60
Quham the dissaitfull onbekend dern way,
The myrk nycht, and the hasty dowtsum fray,
Betrasyt had, that all the mekill rowt,
Or he was war, hym lowkyt rownd about.
Full gret debait he maid, as that he mocht; 65
Ourset he was, defens was all for nocht.
Quhat mycht than silly Nysus do or say?
Be quhat forß or wapynnys dar he assay

Forto deliuer hys tendir cousyng deir?
Suld he or not aventour hym self heir,　　　　　　　　　　70
And rusch amyd hys ennemys in that sted,
To procur in haist by wondis ane honest ded?
Vprasys he onon hys arm bakwart
To thraw a gevillyng or a castyng dart,
And, lukand vpwart towart the cleir moyn,　　　　　　　75
With afald voce thus wyß he maid hys boyn:
"O Latonya, goddes of mekill myght,
Mastres of woddis, bewte of sternys brycht,
Be thou present, and send me thy supple,
Addreß my wark, be directrix," said he:　　　　　　　　80
"Gif euer that Hirtacus, my fader deir,
Offrit for me sum gift at thy alter;
Or gif that I of my huntyng and pray
Ekyt thy honour ony maner way,
Or, at thy standart knoppit post of tre,　　　　　　　　85
Thy haly tempillys rufe, or bawkis hie,
Gif evir I hung or fixit ony thyng,
Wild bestis hed, wapynnys or armyng;
Thoil me to trubbill this gret rowt of men,
Do dreß my dartis in this wilsum den,　　　　　　　　　90
So that my schote and myssour may go rycht
Throu the dyrk ayr and silens of the nycht."
Thus sayand, with al forß of hys body
The grundyn dart he leyt do glyde in hy.
The fleand schaft the nycht schaddoys devydis,　　　　95
And rycht forgane him on the tother sydis　　　　　　　f. 193ᵛ
It smate Sulmonys scheild, hang on his bak,
Quharin the querral al in schuldir brak;
Bot with the dynt the rynde is revyn swa,
Hys hart pipis the scharp hed persyt in twa.　　　　　100
Down duschis he in ded thraw all forlost,
The warm blude furth bokkand of his cost,
And for the cald of deth hys lungis lap,
With sobbys deip blawys with mony clap.
Hys ferys lukis about on euery syde,　　　　　　　　　105
To se quharfra the grundyn dart dyd glyde.
Bot lo, as thai thus wondrit in effray,
Thys ilk Nysus, worthin provd and gay,
And baldar of this chance swa with hym gone,
Ane other takill assayt he onon,　　　　　　　　　　　110
And with a sownd smate Tagus, but remede,
Throu athir part or tymplis of his hed;
In the harn pan the schaft he hes affixt,
Quhil blude and brane al togidder mixt.
The felloun capitane, Volscens, neir wod wendis,　　　115

Seand na man quhamof to get amendis;
He mycht do stanche his ire, and syth his thocht,
For quha that threw the dartis saw he nocht.
"Thou, not the leß," quod he, "that standis by,
With thy hait blude for baith twa sal aby   120
The pane for this myscheif." And with that word,
He ran apon Euryll with drawyn sword.
Than Nisus, dredand for his fallow kynd,
Begouth to cry, all wod and owt of mynd,
Nor na langar in dern hym hyde he mycht,   125
Nor of his frend behald sa reuthfull syght:
"Me, me, ȝe sla; lo, I am heir," he said,
"That dyd the dede; turn hidder in me ȝour blaid
And swerdis all, O ȝe Rutilyanys!
All be my slycht now ȝour feris slane is;   130
That silly innocent creatour so ȝyng
Myght, nor ȝit durst, on hand tak sic a thing –
Be hevynnys he, and all the starnys, I swer,
That ws behaldis with thar bemys cleir."   f. 194ʳ
Sik wordis said he, for on sic maner,   135
And sa strangly, his frend and fallow deir,
That sa myschancy was, belovit he,
That rather for hys life him self list de.
Bot thar was na remedy nor abaid:
The swerd, wightly stokit, or than was glaid   140
Throu owt hys cost – allace, the harmys smart!
That mylk quhite breist is persyt to the hart.
Down ded ruschit Eurialus ryght thar.
The blude bruschand outour his body fair,
And on hys elbok lenand a litill on wry,   145
Hys hed and hals bowys hevely –
Lyke as the purpour flour in fur or sewch,
Hys stalk in two smyt newly with the pleuch,
Dwynys away, as it doith faid or de;
Or as the chesbo hedis oft we se   150
Bow down thar knoppis, sowpit on thar grane,
Quhen thai be chargyt with the hevy rane.
Bot Nysus than ruschit amyd the rowt,
Amangis thame all sekand Volscens the stowt,
And on Volscens alanerly arestis,   155
Thocht rownd about with ennemys he prest is,
Quhilk heir and thar onon at euery syde
Hym ombeset with warkand woundis wyde.
Bot netheleß thame stowtly he assalit,
Not amovit, as na thing him had alit,   160
And euer his schynand swerd about him swang,
Quhil at the last in Volscens mouth he thrang,

65

As he, forgane him standand, cryit and gapit.
Allace, quhat reuth was it he not eschapit!
For he deand bereft his fa the life;   165
Stekit and hurt sa oft with speir and knyfe,
Fell down abuf his frendis ded body,
Quhar best him likit ded to rest and ly.
O happy baith, O fortunat and dyng!
Gif myne endyt or stile may ony thing,   170
Nevir day nor proceß of tyme sal betyde,   f. 194ᵛ
That ȝour renown sal owt of memor slyde,
Quhil the famyl and ofspring of Enee
The stane immovabill of the Capitolie
Inhabitis, and sa lang as Romanys bald   175
The monarchy of the empyre sal hald.
The schamful victouris, thir Rutilyanys,
The pray and spreth, and other geir that ganys,
Ioysyng but obstakil, Volscens ded body
Onto the tentis wepand bair in hy.   180
And na leß murnyng hard thai in that sted
For Rhamnetes, fund hedleß, pail and ded,
Togiddir with samony capitanys,
And gret herys, so wrachitly as slane is,
Serranus ȝyng, and the gentill Numa,   185
And nobill corpsis brytnyt mony ma.
Gret preß flokkit to se the bodeis schent,
Sum men ȝit throwand half ded on the bent;
Of recent slauchter and the hait effray
The feld abowt all warmyt quhar thai lay,   190
That all with spait was blandyt and on flude
In bullyrrand stremys of the fomy blude.
The spulȝe led away was knaw full rycht,
Mesapus rich hewmet schynand brycht,
The goldin gyrdill, and trappouris prowdly wrocht, 195
With mekill swete and labour agane brocht.

Ewrillys moder hir sonnys deth bewalis,
And quhou Rutilianys the cyte first assalis.   C. viii

Be this Aurora, levand the safron bed
Of hir lord Titan, had the erth ourspred
With new cleirneß, and the son scheyn
Begouth defund hys bemys on the greyn,
That euery thing worth patent in the lyght.   5
Turnus, enarmyt as ane douchty knyght,
Till armys steris euery man abowt,
In plait and maill full mony forcy rowt
Prouocand to the bargane and assay;

Ilk capitane hys folkis settis in array,　　　　　　　10　f. 195ʳ
And gan thar curage kyndill in ire to fyght,
Be schamefull murmur of this ȝister nycht.
And forthir eik, ane miserabill thing to se,
Ewril and Nysus hedys, on speris hie
Fixit, thai rasyt haldand to the wall,　　　　　　　15
With huge clamour followyng ane and all.
The forcy and the stowt Eneadanys,
That for the tyme in this cite remanys,
The bront and fors of thar army that tyde
Endlang the wallis set on the left syde,　　　　　　20
For on the rycht hand closyt the ryver;
Thai held the forfront quhar thar was danger,
Kepand the braid fowseis and towrls hie;
And as thai stand ful dolorusly, thai se
The twa hedys stikkand on the speris,　　　　　　25
A miserabil syght, allace, onto thar feris;
Thar facis war ourweil bekend, baith twa,
The blaknyt dedly blude droppand tharfra.
In the meyn quhile, throw the drery cite
The weyngit messynger, Fame, dyd swyftly fle,　　30
And slippand come to thy moder, Ewrilly.
Than suddanly that wrachit wight onsilly
Al pail become, as na blude in hir left,
The naturale heit was from the banys reft.
Furth of hir hand the spynnyng quheil smate sche,　35
The ȝarn clewis, spyndill and broche of tre,
All swakkit our, and full onhappely
Furth fleys scho with mony schowt and cry,
With wepyng and with wifly womentyng,
Ryvand hir haris, to the wallys can thring　　　　40
All wod enragit, and with a spedy payß
Dyd occupy tharon the formaste place,
Takand nane hede, na ȝit na maner schame,
Swa amangis men to ryn, and rowp or raym;
Na maner feir of perrel seys sche,　　　　　　　45
Nor mynd of dartis cast that fast dyd fle.
And as that from the wall hyr sonnys hede　　　　　f. 195ᵛ
Behaldis sche, wofull, and will of rede,
With hir petuus rewthfull complantis sayr
The hevynnys all scho fillyt and the ayr.　　　　　50
"O my Ewryll," lamentabilly scho cryis,
"Sall I the se demanyt on syk wyß?
O thou, the lattyr quyet of myne age,
Quhou mycht thou be sa cruell in thy rage
As me to leif alyve, thus myne allane?　　　　　　55
O my maist tendir hart, quhar art thou gane?

67

Na licens grantit was, nor tyme, ne space,
To me thy wrachit moder, allace, allace,
Quhen thou thy self onto sik perrellis set,
That I with the mycht samekill laser get   60
Als forto tak my leif for evir and ay,
Thy last regrait and quethyng wordis to say.
Ichane, allace, intill ane oncouth land,
Nakyt and bair thy fair body on sand
To fowlys of reif and savage doggis wild   65
Sall ly as pray, myne awin deir only child!
Nor I, thy moder, layd not thy corps on beir,
Nor with my handis lowkyt thyne eyn so cleir,
Nor wysche thy wondis to reduce thy spreit,
Nor drest the in thy lattir clathis meyt,   70
The quhilkis I wrocht, God wayt, to mak the gay,
Full bissely spynnand baith nycht and day,
And with sic wobbis and wark, for the, my page,
I comfort me in myne onweldy age,
And irkyt not to laubour for thy sake.   75
Quhar sall I seik the now? allake, allake!
Or in quhat land lyis now, maglyt and schent,
Thy fair body, and membris tyrvit and rent?
O deir son myne, O tendir get," quod sche,
"Is this the comfort at thou dois to me,   80
Quhilk hes the followyt baith our seys and landis?
O 3e Rutilianys, steik me with 3our brandis;
Gyf thar be rewth or piete in 3our banys,   f. 196ʳ
Do swak at me 3our dartis all atanys;
With 3our wapynnys first 3e sal me sla.   85
O thou gret fader of goddis," can scho say,
"Haue reuth apon me, wrach of wrachis all,
And on my catyve hed thou lat dovn fall
Thy thundris dynt of wildfyre fra the hevin,
Law vndre hell tharwith to smyte me evin,   90
Sen that this langsum cruel life I ne may
Consume nor endyng be nane other way."
With this regrait the Troiane myndis all
War smyte with reuth; endlang the large wall
The duylfull murnyng went and womentyng;   95
Thar hie curage, to tel a wondyr thyng,
That oneffrayt was batale to sustene,
Wolx dolf and dull the petuus sycht to sene.
Bot as scho thus kyndillis sorow and wo,
Ane Ideus, and Actor, Troianys two,   100
At the command of Illyoneus past,
And 3yng Ascanyus wepand wonder fast,
And hynt hyr vp betwix thar armys squar,

Syne hamewart to hir lugyng thai hyr bair.
Bot than the trumpettis weirly blastis abundis, 105
With terribill brag of brasyn bludy soundis;
The skry, the clamour, followys the ost within,
Quhill all the hevynnys bemyt of the dyn.
The Volscenaris assemblyt in a sop
To fyll the fowseis and the wallis to slop, 110
All sammyn hastand with a pavyß of tre
Hesyt togidder abuf thar hedys hie;
Sa sairly knyt that maner embuschment
Semyt tobe a cloß volt quhar thai went.
Ane other sort pressyt to haue entre, 115
And clym the wallis with leddyrris large and hie,
Quhar as the army of the Troiane syde
Was thynnast scattyrrit on the wallis wyde,
And brycht arrayt cumpany of the men f. 196ᵛ
War diuidit or sloppit, at thai mycht ken 120
The weirmen not sa thyk in syk a place.
Bot the Troianys, that oft in sik lyke cace
Be lang vsage of weir war lernyt and kend
Quhou thai thar town and wallys suld defend,
All kynd of wapynnys and dartis at thame slyngis, 125
And dang thame down with pikkis and poyntit styngis,
Down weltyng eik of huge weght gret stanys,
Be ony way gif tharby for the nanys
Thai mycht on forß dissevyr that punʒe
Quhilk thame assalʒeit thekit with pavyß he, 130
For weill thai knew thar fays al maner of teyn
Vndir that volt of targis myght susteyn,
Sa lang as thai sammyn onsyverit war.
Bot now thai mycht thar ordour hald na mar;
For the Troianys, or evyr thai wald ceß, 135
Thar as the thikast rowt was and maist preß,
Ane huge weght or hepe of mekill stanys
Ruschys and weltis down on thame atanys,
That diuerß of Rutilianys lay thar ondyr;
The laif skalyt on brede; brok was in sondir 140
The covertouris and ordinance of thar scheldis.
Fra thens, the hardy Rutilianys in the feildis
Pressyt na mar in hydlys forto fyght,
Bot thame enforcis now with all thar mycht,
With ganʒeis, arrowys, and with dartis slyng, 145
Thar famen from the wallys forto dyng.
And at ane other syde with felloun feir
Meʒentyus the grym, apon a speir,
Or heich styng or stour of the fyr tre,
The blak fyre bleß of reik in swakkis he; 150

69

And Mesapus, the dantar of the horssys,
Neptunus son, with hys menȝe enforcis
Tyl vndermynd the dike and rent the paill –
Leddyris he axis the wallys to assaill.

Quhou Turnus set the ȝet towr into fyre, And maid gret slauchter of Troianys in his ire.

C. ix

Calliope, and O ȝe musys all,   f. 197[r]
   Inspire me til endyte! On ȝou I call
To schaw quhat slauchter and occisioun,
Quhou feill corpsis thar war brytnyt doun
By Turnus wapynnys and hys dartis fell,   5
Quham euery man kyllit and send to hell:
Help and assist to revolue heir with me
The extreme dangeris of that gret melle.
Ȝhe blissyt wightis, forsuyth, ramembris weill
Sik thyngis, and quhar ȝou lyst may reveill.   10
Thar stude a towr of tre, huge of hycht,
With batellyng and kyrnellys all at ryght,
Set in ane neidfull place neir by the ȝet,
Quham to assailȝe, ourcum and down bet,
With hail pyssance all the Italianys   15
At vtir power ombeset atanys;
And by the contrar, on the tother syde
Alkynd defencis can Troianys provyde,
Threw stanys down, and sillys heir and thar,
At euery part or oppyn fenystar   20
The grundyn dartis leyt down fle thikfald.
Turnus the prynce, at was baith darf and bald,
Ane byrnand bleiß leyt at the fortreß glyde,
And festynnyt the fyre hard to the towris syde,
Quhilk with the wyndis blast, thar as it stak,   25
Vpblesyt in the burdis and the thak,
And spreddis wide amangis the gestis gret;
The byrnand low consumyt all throu hete.
Within thai schuddrit for the fell effray,
Bot all for nocht to preß to wyn away;   30
Na laser was the danger to eschape,
For as thai ran abak, and can thame schaip
Fortill withdraw towart the tother syde
Quhar as the fyre was not ȝit ourglyde,
And hurlyt all togydder in a hepe,   35
Tho with thar swechtis, as thai reill and leipe,
The byrnand towr down rollys with a rusche,
Quhill all the hevynnys dyndlyt of the dusch.   f. 197[v]
Down weltis the men half ded with brokyn banys,

70

The huge heip thame followit all atanys,   40
On thar awyn wapynnys stikkand he and he,
Sum stekit throu the cost with spilys of tre
Lay gaspand, of thame all that scarsly tway,
Ane Helenor and Lycus, gat away;
Of quhom the formest, this ilk Helenor,   45
Now in hys florist ȝouth, was get and bor
Betwix Meonyus kyng, in prevyte,
And Lycynya the boynd wench wondir sle,
Quhilk hym to Troy had send that hendyr ȝer,
Onkend, in armour forbodyn for wer;   50
Delyver he was with drawin swerd in hand
And quhite target, onsemly and evill farrand.
Thys Helenor, seand hym self in dowt
Amyd thousandis enarmyt of Latyn rowt,
Behaldand graithly apon athir hand   55
Arrayt ostis of Latyn pepill stand;
Lyke the wild ragyt best, quham huntaris stowt
Heß ombeset with thyk range all abowt,
Scand be na meyn that scho mycht evaid,
Apon the wapynnys rynnys with a braid,   60
Slyppis hir self, and with gret forß hir beris
Apon the pantis of the huntyng speris –
Nane othir wyß, this ilk ȝong Helenor,
Thus ombeset behynd and als befor,
Amyd hys fays ruschys reddy to de,   65
Quhar thikkast was the preß thar etlys he,
Quhilkis, but abaid, alssone heß hym slane
As spark of gleid wald in the sey remane.
Bot Lycus, spedyar far on fut than he,
Throw owt the ostis and armyt men can fle,   70
And to the wallys wan, and vp on hyght
Enforcis hym to clym with all hys mycht
And forto grip sum of hys feris handis;
Quham Turnus, lanssand lychtly our the landis,
With speir in hand persewys forto spill,   75
And quhen he heß ourtane him at his will,
Thus dyd hym chyde: "O catyve wytleß knaip,   f. 198ʳ
Quhat, wenyt thou our handis to eschaip?"
And tharwith drew hym doun, quhar he dyd hyng,
And of the wal a gret part with hym bryng –   80
Lyke as the egill, Iovis squyer, straucht
Within hys bowand clukis had vp clawcht
A ȝong cygnet, or quhit swan, or a hair,
Tharwith resursyng heich vp in the ayr;
Or as a ravanus bludy wolf throu slycht   85
Hyntis in hys gowl, furth of the fald be nycht,

71

The litill tendyr kyd, or the 3ong lam,
With feill bletingis socht by the gait, hir dame.
Rutilianys for ioy than rasyt a schowt,
And fast invadys the cite all abowt; 90
With hepys of erd the fowsy do thai fyll;
Sum otheris presyt with schydis and mony a syl
The fyre blesys abowt the ruf to slyng.
Bot Ilioneus that tyme dyd doun dyng
With a gret quhyn, or roch of cragy stone, 95
Ane Lucetyus, and brak hys nek bone,
As that he dyd approche towartis the 3et,
The hait flammys of fyre tharin to set.
Liger a Troiane from the wall also
Doun bet a Rutiliane hait Emathio. 100
A Phrigiane eik, Asylas, stern and stowt,
All tofruschit Choryneus withowt,
Quhilk was in dartis castyng wonder sle;
On far to schute scharp flanys and lat fle
Nane mar expert than this Emathio. 105
Ceneus ourquhelmyt Ortygius also;
And this Ceneus, quhilk than gat the mastry,
Belyve Turnus with a dart ded gart ly;
And down dyngis alsso this ilk Turnus
Ithis, Clonyus, and eik Dioxippus, 110
Promulus als, and bustuus Sagaras,
And syne the huge byg Troiane, hait Idas,
Standand forto defend the towris hie.
Capys, a Troiane, bet doun Pryverne,
Quham Themyllus with a scharp casting dart 115 f. 198ᵛ
Had newly hurt and wondyt in sum part;
And he hys hand plat to the wound in hy,
Hys scheild besyde hym swakkand fulychly,
So that the fedderit arrow furth dyd glyde,
And nalyt hys hand plat to the left syde; 120
The schaft and hed remanyt in hys cost,
Be dedly wound the lyfe thus hes he lost.
Arcens, Arcentis son, stude on the wall,
In brycht armour ful semly schynand all,
Hys mantill of the purpour Iberyne, 125
With nedill wark brusyt rych and fyne,
Of vissage was he plesand forto se;
Hys fader Arcens send him with Enee;
Fostyrrit he was and vpbrocht tendirly
Within hys moderis hallowyt schaw, fast by 130
The flude Symethus into Sycill land,
Quhar as the plentuus fat altar dyd stand
Of the placabill goddis, Palycy hecht.

72

Ane gret staf slung byrrand with felloun weght
Hynt Meȝentius, hys scheild syne by hym lays, 135
The stryngis thryß abowt hys hed assays,
And this ilk Arcens standyng hym forgane
Hes smertly with a ledyn pellok slane;
Hys harn pan and forhed al to claif,
Quhil at the led in sondir brak and raif, 140
That he ourtumlys speldit on the sand.
Thus gret slauchtir was maid fra hand to hand.

Heir ȝyng Ascanyus the strang Numanus slew,
Quhilk wordis owtragyus to the Troianys schew. C. x

Ascanyus this ilk tyme, as is said,
That wont was with his schot bot to invaid
The wild bestis, quhilkis cowth do not bot fle,
First heir in bargane leyt swyft arrowys fle,
And by hys handis slew strang Numanus, 5
That was to surname clepit Remulus,
Had laitly Turnus ȝyngast systir wed,
As for hys spowß, and brocht ontill hys bed. f. 199ʳ
This ilk Numanus Remulus in that sted
Befor the frontis of the batell ȝeyd, 10
Furth schawand mony diuerß sawys seir,
Baith ganand and onganand forto heir,
Rycht prowd and hely in his breist and hart
That newlyngis of the kynrik was a part
To him befall. His gret estait this wyß 15
Woustand he schew with clamour and lowd cryis:
"Aschame ȝe nocht, Phrigyanys that twyß taik is,
Tobe inclosyt amyd a fald of stakis,
And be assegit agane sa oft syß
With akyn spilis and dikis on sik wyß? 20
Schame ȝe not to prolong ȝour lyvis?" said he.
"Thir venquyst cowart wightis behald and se,
That dar our spousage into batale craif!
Quhat wild dotage so maid ȝour hedis raif?
Or quhat onthrifty god in sic foly 25
Hes ȝou bywavit heir till Italy?
Heir ar not the slaw weirmen Atrydes,
Nor the fenȝear of fair speche Vlixes.
Bot we, that bene a pepill derf and dour
Cumyn of kynd, as keyn men in a stour, 30
Our ȝoung childring, the first tyme born thai ar,
Onto the nixt rynnand flude we bair
To hardyn thar bodeis and to mak thame bald
With the chil frostis and the watyr cald.

Our childir ȝyng exercis bissely   35
Huntyng with hundis, hornys, schowt and cry,
Wild deir throw owt the woddis chaiß and mait.
To dant and reyn the horssis ayr and layt,
That is thar game and sport thai hant on raw,
Or with thar bowys schute, or dartis thraw.   40
Our ȝong spryngaldis may all laubouris endur,
Content of litill fuyde, I ȝou assur,
Of ȝouth thai be accustumat tobe skant,
The erd with plewch and harrowys forto dant,
Or than in batal bettis citeis down.   45   f. 199ᵛ
In euery age with irne graith ar we bown,
And passand by the plewys, for gad wandis,
Broddis the oxin with speris in our handis;
Nor ȝit the slaw nor febill onweldy age
May waik our spreit, nor mynyß our curage,   50
Nor of our strenth to altyr ocht or pair.
The steill helmys we thrist on hedis hair;
Best likis ws all tyme to rug and reif,
To dryve away the spreth, and thar on leif.
ȝour pantit habittis dois of purpour schyne;   55
ȝour hartis lykis best, so I dyvyne,
In idilneß to rest abuf al thing,
To tak ȝour lust, and go in karellyng;
ȝour cotys heß traland slevys our ȝour handis,
ȝour foly hattis trappouris and brasyng bandis.   60
O verray Phrygiane wifis, dasyt wightis!
To call ȝou men of Troy that onrycht is;
ȝe be onworthy to sa hie style to clame.
On Dyndyma top go, and walk at hame,
Quhar as the quhissill rendris soundis seir,   65
With tympanys, tawbronys, ȝe war wont to heir,
And boß schawmys of turnyt buschboun tre
That grew in Berecyntia montane hie,
Onto the moder of Ida dedicat,
Callys efter ȝou to danß, and nocht debait: 70
ȝeld ȝou to men, and leif al ȝour armyng,
Rendir ȝour swerdis, and all wapynnys resyng."
Ascanyus ȝyng, byrnand for proper teyn,
Sa gret owtrage of wordis mycht not sustene,
Herand sa hie avant of pompus pryde,   75
And sik dispyt blawyn owt apon hys syde.
Hys bow with horß sennonys bend hes he,
Tharin a takill set of sovir tre,
And tasand vp his armys far in twyn,
Thus onto Ioue lawly dyd begyn   80
To mak hys first petitioun and prayer:

"Omnipotent hie Iupiter, me heir
Assist to this hardy commancement.
My self onto thy templis sal present
Solempnyt gyftis, maste gudly may be get,   85   f. 200ʳ
And eik befor thyne altar sall I set
A ȝoung bullok of cullour quhite as snaw,
With goldin schakaris hys forhed arrait on raw;
The best salbe full tydy, tryg and wight,
With hed equale till hys moder on hycht,   90
Can all reddy with hornys fuyn and put,
And scrape or skattyr the soft sand with his fut."
The fader of hevin exceppit hys prayer,
And, on that part quhar the lift was maist cler,
Towart the left hand maid a thundyrryng;   95
All sammyn soundyt the dedly bowys stryng.
Quhyrrand smertly furth flaw the takill tyte,
Quyte throw the hed the Remulus dyd smyte;
The grundyn steill outthrowch hys tympillys glaid.
"Hald on thy ways in haist," Ascanyus said,   100
"Thy self to loif, knak now scornfully
With prowd wordis all at standis by.
Sik boydword heir the twyß takyn Troianys
Sendis for hansell to Rutylianys."
Thus far spekis Ascanyus, and na mair.   105
Bot the Troianys rasyt a scry in the ayr
With rerd and clamour of blithnes, man and boy,
That to the starnys thar curage sprang for ioy,
Ascanyus extolland abuf the skyis.
And, as thai mak this ryot on sik wyß,   110
Down from the regioun of the hevin tho
The brycht curland haryt Appollo,
Apon a clowd sittand quhar he wald,
The ostis of Italianys can behald,
And eik new Troys cite, with cheir glaid   115
Till Iulus the victor thus he said:
"Eik and continew thy new vailȝeand dedis,
Thou ȝong child, for that is the way the ledis
Vp to the starnys and the hevynnys hie,
O thou verray goddis ofspring," quod he,   120
"That sall engendir goddis of thy seyd.
In the, be verray resson and of neid,   f. 200ᵛ
All batalys, quhilkis by werd ar destinate
Agane Assaracus howß to move debait,
Salbe appasit, and to quyet brocht.   125
This litill town of Troy, that heir is wrocht,
May nocht withhald the in sik boundis lyte."
And sayand thus, from the heich hevin als tyte

75

Discendis he, movand the hailsum ayr,
And to the child Ascanyus socht rycht thar;   130
Hys figur changit that tyme as he wald
In lykneß of ane Butes, hayr and ald,
That pursevant tofor and squyer had be
To Troiane Anchyß, fader of Enee,
And trasty kepar of hys chalmyr dur;   135
Now had Ene committ to hym the cur
For tyll attend apon Ascanyus ȝyng.
Lyke to this ancyent Butes in al thyng
Furth steppys Phebus, baith in voce and hew,
With lokkis quhite and armour na thing new,   140
Rowsty, and with a felloun sound clattring,
And sic wordis spak to Iulus ȝyng,
That otherwyß is hayt Ascanyus,
With ardent mynd of bargane desyrus:
"Eneas verray douchty son and ayr,   145
It may suffice, the nedis do na mair,
Sen, thou onhurt, with thy schote in this sted
The strang Numanus thou heß dung to ded.
This first loving and eik hie renownee
The souerane Apollo grantys the,   150
Nor na disdene at the sal haue, suthly,
Tobe hys peregall intill archery.
Leif of, my child, and of sic batale ceß;
Na mair at this tyme; draw the owt of preß."
On this wyß carpys the brycht Appollo,   155
And in the myddis of hys sermond tho
He vanyst far away, I wait neuer quhar,
Furth of this mortal sycht in the schire ayr.
The nobillys, and the Troiane capitanys trew,
Be thir takynnys the god Appollo knew,   160   f. 201ʳ
And hard hys arrowys clatterand in hys cace.
Tharfor thai haue withdraw furth of that place
Ascanyus, at brycht Phebus mychty charge,
And wald no langar thoill hym go at large;
All thocht to feght he had desyre and ioy,   165
Hame to hys innys dyd thai hym convoy;
Syne to the bargane heß thame sped agane,
In oppyn perrellys, dangeris and all pane
Thar personys and thar lyvys for thar town
Offerand, and for defens maid thame bown.   170

Quhou Pandarus and Bitias, brethir twane,
Kest vp the ȝettis, and thar was Bytias slane.   C. xi

Endlang the wallys kyrnellys euerystand,
The bruyt and clamour rayß fra hand to hand;
Thar bustuus bowys keynly do thai bend,
Scharp querrellis and castyng dartis furth send,
Quhilk thai with lyamys and thwangis lang owt threw;   5
Sa thik the ganȝeis and the flanys flew,
That of schaftis and takillys all the feildis
War strowit, and the large planys ourheldis.
In boß helmys and scheldis the weirly schote
Maid rap for rap, reboundand with ilk stot.   10
Scharp and awfull incressis the bargane,
Als violent as euer the ȝet doun rane
Furth of the west doith smyte apon the wald
In October, quhen the twa sternys cald,
That clepyt beyn the Kyddis, first vpspryngis;   15
And als thik as the hail schour hoppys and dyngis
In furdys schald, and brays heir and thar,
Quhen trublit beyn the hevynnys and the ayr
With stormy tempest and the northyn blastis,
Quhill clowdis clattris, and all the lyft ourcastis.   20
Pandarus and Bytias, twa brethir germane,
By Alcanor engendryt, that Troiane,
Quham Hybera, the wild forestereß knaw,
Bred and vpbrocht in Iovys haly schaw,   f. 201ᵛ
Sa byg ȝong men thai war, sa gret and wight,   25
That equale semyt thame tobe of hight
With fyr treis of thar landis or hillys;
And tharto eik sa egyr of thar willis
At thai the port, quhilk be Eneas charge
Was commandyt to kepe stekit, all at large   30
Has warpyt oppyn onbreid to the wall,
And baldly dyd thar fays clepe and call
To entyr, gyf thai durst, and thame assay,
Sa gret confidens in thar forß had thai.
And thai within stude by the ȝet, that tyde,   35
Quhilk oppin was on the rycht and left syde,
As thai had towris beyn baith gret and squar,
Enarmyt with thar wapynnys brycht and bair,
The hie tymbrettis of thar helmys schane –
Lyke tobehald as bustuus akis twane   40
Besyde the beyn ryver Athesys grow,
Or flowand fludis bankis of the Pow,
Vpstrekand thar byg croppys to the ayr,
And onsned branschis wavand heir and thar.

77

Alsswith as the Rutylianys dyd se 45
The ʒet oppyn, thai rusch to the entre,
Quercens formast, and Equycoly,
A lusty knycht in armys rycht semly,
Wight Tynarus, ferß myndyt to assaill,
And bald Hemon, with curage marcyall. 50
Bot thai with all thar complicis in fyght
War dung abak, and constrenyt tak flycht,
By Troiane rowtis, or than in that stryfe
Quha that abaid lost in the port thar lyfe.
Tho brymmar grew thar ferß mudis within, 55
So that the Troianys can flok and sammyn ryn
Towart that place, and maid felloun debait;
So bald thai wolx that in the plane gait,
Ischand without the portis on the land,
Thai durst recontyr thar fays hand for hand. 60
A messynger to Turnus come that tyde, f. 202ʳ
That wondir fersly at ane othir syde
The town assalʒeis; and thar he til hym schew
Quhat hait slauchter hys fays maid of new,
And sik a port had all wyde oppyn set. 65
Hys first purpoß he left, and to that ʒet,
With felloun ire movit, furth sprent he tho,
Towart the Troianys and prowd brethir two;
And fyrst hes slane byg Antyphates,
That him on cace met formest in the preß, 70
Son to the bustuus nobill Sarpedon,
In purcheß get a Thebane wench apon.
Hym smate he down with the cast of a dart;
The fleand schaft Italian to his hart
Glydand, throw owt the schire ayr duschit sone, 75
The stomok persyt, and in the cost is done.
The how cavern of his wond a flude
Furth bruschit of the blaknyt dedly blude;
So deip the grundyn steill hed owt of sycht is,
Ful hait and warm it festnyt in his lychtis. 80
Syne Meropes and Erymanthus he
And Aphydnus slew with his hand al thre;
And efter that, with a stern mynd full teyn,
Slew Bytias, for al his glowrand eyn,
Bot that was nother with dart, swerd nor knyf 85
(For na sik wapyn mycht him haue reft the lyfe),
Bot with ane hydduus byssand fyry speir,
That clepit is "phalarica" in weir,
Quhilk with sa vehement fors this Turnus threw
That as the thundris dynt at him it flew, 90
Quham nowder scheld of twa bull hydis thik,

Nor ȝit the dowbill malyt traste hawbrik,
All gilt with gold, mycht it resist nor stynt.
The bustuus body down duschit of the dynt,
Quhil all the erd to granyt with a rattill;   95
The hydduus scheild abufe him maid a brattill –
Lyke as the hie pillar of marbill stone
Standand apon the cost Euboycon,   f. 202ᵛ
Vmquhile besyde Bais, the rych cite,
With grysly swecht down duschit in the see;   100
Quhilk was of ald of massy stanys a byng,
And by the fludis sik wyß doun was dyng,
Hys fall drew down the cite quhar it stude,
And ruschit in a fer way in the flude;
The seys mixt ourran, and all ourhed   105
Blak slyke and sand vp poplit in the sted;
Quhill of the feirfull sovnd the ilandis twa
Trymlyt, Inaryme and eik Prochita;
Quhilk Inaryme, at Iupiteris command,
Full hard bed is to Typheus the gyand.   110
At this tyme Mars, the god armypotent,
Ekyt the Latynys fors and hardyment,
With felloun ire prikland so thar myndis
That as hym lyst he turnys so and wyndis;
And makis the Troianys tak the flycht gud speid,   115
On thame he kest sik feir and schamfull dreid.
The Latyn pepill flokkis on euery syde
Quhen thai beheld the port sa oppynnyt wyde,
Seand thai had a rowm to fecht at will;
The god of stryfe thar curage steris thartill.   120

Quhou Turnus the byg Pandarus smat doun,
Lyke a wod lyoun past within the town.   C. xii

Pandarus, seand hys brotheris corps at erd,
And on quhat wyß thus fortune with thame ferd,
And quhou the chance of batale ȝeid al wrang,
Full forcyly with hys braid schuldris strang
He thristis to the levys of the ȝet,   5
And closyt queym the entre, and furth schet
Without the port a gret sort of hys feris,
In hard bargane amyd the mortal weris;
And of hys ennemyß sum inclosyt he,
Ressavand all at thrang to the entre.   10
A fuyll he was and wytles in a thyng,
Persauyt not Turnus, Rutilian kyng,   f. 203ʳ
So violently thryng in at the ȝet;
Quham he onwar within the cite schet,

Lyke as ane rageand wild tygyr onstabill   15
Amang the febill bestis onfensabill.
Sone as Turnus hym heß inclusyt seyn,
A glowand new lyght brystis from hys eyn,
Hys armour ryngis or clattris horribilly;
Hys crystis trymlyt on hys hed in hy,   20
That in hys sanguane bludy scheild als straucht
Kest schynand fyry bemys lyke fyre flaucht.
All suddanly, affrayit Eneadanys
Hys face onfrendly persauyt and byg banys.
The hydduus Pandarus than hym self furth schew,   25
That wonder fervent in hys furour grew;
Hys broderis slauchter to revenge in will,
Thus austernly he spekis Turnus ontill:
"Thys is not Queyn Amatais cheif cite,
Suld the begeif into dowry," said he,   30
"Nor ȝit the myddis of Ardea cite bald,
Thi faderis burgh, Turnus, doith the withhald.
Thou seys thy fays strenth and wallys wyde;
ȝeild the for thy, thou may eschape na syde."
Turnus agane, with curage blyth and glaid,   35
Nocht abasyt, ful baldly to hym said:
"My frend, begyn, gif thou heß hardyment,
And mach with me allone apon this bent,
And hand for hand, gif at it be thy will,
Thou sal schaw Pryam heir thou hes fund Achill."   40
The tother tho a huge speir of haill tre,
With bark and knottis altogidder, leyt fle
In al his forß, bot the dynt dyd no deir;
Nocht bot the ayr was wondyt with the speir,
For wikkyt Iuno, the ald Saturnus get,   45
Choppyt by the schaft, and fixt it in the ȝet.
"Ha!" quod Turnus, "sa sal thou not astart
Thys wapyn now in faith or we depart,   f. 203ᵛ
Nor on sik wyß eschape this bytand brand,
Quhilk my gret forß thus rollys in my hand;   50
For he that aw this swerd, and wond sal wyrk,
Is not sa faynt, ne sa sone sall nocht irk."
And with that word, standand on hys typtays,
Hevyng hys swerd, heich hys hand dyd rayß;
Down with the dynt duschit the steil blaid keyn   55
Amyd hys forhed, hard betwix hys eyn,
Hys berdleß chekis or hys chaftis rownd
In sondyr schorn heß with a grysly wound:
Sa felloun sownd or clap maid this gret clasche,
That of hys huge weght, fell with a rasche,   60

The erd dyndlyt, and all the cite schuke.
So large feild hys gowsty body tuke,
That fer onbreid ourspred was all the plane,
Hys armour sparkyt with hys blude and brane.
Baith to and fra, apon hys schuldris tway,   65
Hys hed clovyn in equale halfis lay.
Of dreidfull raddour trymlyng for affray,
The Troianys fled rycht fast and brak away,
And gif Turnus had than incontinent
Ramembryt hym, and kauch in mynd to rent   70
The lokkis vp, and oppyn the ȝettis wyde,
So that hys feris without the port that tyde
Mycht haue entryt, and cumyn in the cite,
The last day of the batale that had be,
And latter finale end to the remanys   75
Of Phrigiane folkis and pepil Troianys.
Bot sic ardent hie furour marcyall,
And of slauchter desire insaciall,
Draif hym to follow thame that him gaynstandis;
And first he kyllit Phalarys with his handis,   80
And ane other, that Gyges hecht, alssua,
Of quham the howchys bath he smate in twa;
Syn speris rent and hynt vp all on raw
And at the flearis bakkis fast dyd thraw,   f. 204ʳ
That wondir was to se hym quhar he went,   85
For Iuno ekyt hys strenth and hardyment.
Syne ane Hales onto the corpsis ded
In cumpany he ekyt in that sted;
And Phegeas doun brytnys in the feld,
Spetit throw owt the body and hys scheld;   90
Alchandrus syne, and the prowd Halyus,
Nemonas eik, and keyn Prytanyus,
Quhilkis mysknew Turnus was within the wall,
And to the bargan dyd thar feris call,
Apon the grund onon al ded he layd,   95
In bargan full expert; syne dyd invaid
With schynand swerd, hard at the dykis syde,
Ane Lynceus, the quhilk the sammyn tyde
Resistys, as he myght, with fell afferis,
And efter help cryis apon hys feris;   100
Bot with a strake he smate hys nek in twa,
Baith helm and hed flaw far the body fra.
And, efter thir, ane Amycus he slew,
That bayn had beyn to wild bestis enew;
Was nane other mair happy nor expert   105
To graith and til invnct a castyng dart,

And with vennom to garnys the steil hedis.
By Turnus handis the ilk tyme done to ded is
Eolus son, hait Clytius, the heynd,
And Creteus also, was the Musys frend –   110
Creteus, poet to Musys famyliar,
That in hys mynd and breist all tymys bar
Sangis and gestis, musyk and harpyng;
Apon hys stryngis playd he mony a spryng,
Lays and rymys on the best awyß,   115
And euermar hys maner and his gyß
Was forto syng, blason and discryve,
Men and stedis, knychthed, wer and stryve.

The Troianys set on Turnus dyntis rude,
Quhill at he fled, and lap into the flude.   C. xiii

A t last Mnestheus and strang Serestus,   f. 204ᵛ
The Troiane capitanys, herand quhow that thus
Thar pepill slane war doun, dyd convene;
Thar feris fleand pail and wan haue thai sene,
And thar cheif ennemy closyt in thar wallys.   5
Mnestheus on thame clepys thus and callys:
"Quhar ettill ʒhe to fra hyne? Quhidder wald ʒhe fle?
Quhat other wallys seik ʒhe, or cite?
Quhar haue ʒe other strenth or fortereß?
O citesanys, behaldis heir expreß   10
Nane bot a man standand ʒou aganys,
Closyt within ʒour dykis and wallys of stanys,
Onrevengit, sa gret occisioun
And huge slauchter sal mak within ʒour tovn,
Or sa feill valʒeand ʒyng capitanys kend,   15
Onresistit, thus down to hell sall send!
O maste onworthy cowartis, ful of slewth,
Of ʒour onsilly cuntre haue ʒhe na rewth,
Nor piete of ʒour ancyent goddis kynd?
Think ʒhe na lak and schame into ʒour mynd,   20
To do sa gret owtrage to strang Enee,
In hys absens thus catyfly to fle?"
The Troianys by sik wordis as he said
In curage grew, and fermly all abaid,
Abowt thar fa man flokkand in a rowt.   25
Turnus a litil, thocht he was stern and stowt,
Begouth frawart the bargane to withdraw,
And sattil towartis the ryveris syde a law,
Ay peyß and peyß, to that part of the tovn,
Was closyt with the ryver, rynnand dovn.   30
Troianys, that seand, the mar apertly

Assalȝeit hym with mony schowt and cry,
And thikkyt fast abowt hym inveroin.
As quhen abowt the awfull wild lyoun,
With thar invasibill wapynnys scharp and squar, 35
Ane multitude of men bilappyt war, f. 205ʳ
And he full fers, with thrawin wlt, in the start,
Seand the scharp poyntis, recullys bakwart,
Bot forto gif the bak and fle away
Nowder hys greif nor curage suffir may; 40
And, thocht he wald, for all hys mekill mycht,
Agane samony men and wapynnys brycht
To preß fordwart may he cum na speid.
Nane other wyß Turnus, at sik a neid,
Steppys abak with huly payß full still, 45
Hys mynd scaldand in greif and egir will;
And forthir eik amyd hys fays he
Twyß ruschit in, and schuddrit the melle;
And twyß also that onrebutit knycht
Endlang the wallys put thame to the flycht. 50
Bot al togidder, intyll ane convyne,
Apon hym haill the town assemlyt syne,
Nor Saturnus get, Iuno, in that fyght
Agane thame durst him minster strenth nor mycht;
For Iupiter had from the hevynnys fair 55
Send dovn Iris, quhilk duellis in the ayr,
Onto hys spouß and sister thar at hand
Ful scharp chargis bryngis and command,
Leß than Turnus, quhou evir the chance befallis,
Withdrew hym fra the fatale Troiane wallys; 60
Quharthrow this valȝeand campioun ȝong and keyn
Nowder with his scheild sa mekil mycht sustene,
Nor sic defens mak with his hand, as ayr.
With dartis at him swakkit heir and thar
On sik wyß is he quhelmyt and confundyt, 65
That euer in ane hys boß helm rang and soundyt,
Clynkand abowt hys halfheddis with a dyn;
Hys sovir armour, strang and na thyng thyn,
Is brokkyn and byrsyt with feill stonys cast;
So thik war dyntis, and strakis smyt so fast, 70
That of his helm down bettyn war the crestis;
Sa sair the bosys of hys target prest is, f. 205ᵛ
Hys scheild na langar mycht sik rowtis sustene;
The Troianys, with this Mnestheus, in thar teyn
Dowblys thar dyntis at hym with speris cast, 75
As it had bene the hydduus thundris blast.
Our all hys body furth ȝet the swait thik,
Lyke to the trynland blak stremys of pyk;

Ne gat he laser anys hys aynd to draw –
The febillit brath ful fast can beit and blaw   80
Amyd hys wery breist and lymmys lasch.
Than at the last, al suddanly, with a plasch,
Harnes and al togiddir, quhar he stude,
Him self he swakkis and lap into the flude.
With giltyn stremys hym keppyt the ryver,   85
And bar hym vp abuf hys wallis cleir,
Syne blithly careit to hys feris bedene;
All blude and slaughter away was weschyn clene. &c

Explicit liber nonus
Sequitur prologus in decimum

Incipit prologus libri decimi

He plasmatour of thyngis vniuersall,
Thou renewar of kynd that creat all,
Incomprehensibill thy warkis ar to consave,
Quhilk grantyt heß to every wight to haue
Quhat thing mast ganys onto hys governall.   5

Quhou mervellus beyn diuisions of thy gracis,
Distribut so to ilk thing in all placis!
The son to schyne our all and schaw hys lyght,
The day to laubour, for rest thou ordanyt nycht,
For diuerß causys schupe seir sessonys and spacis,   10

Fresch veir to burgioun herbys and sweit flowris,   f. 206ʳ
The hait symmyr to nuryß corn all howris
And breid all kynd of fowlys, fysch and beste,
Hervist to rendir hys frutis maste and leste,
Wyntir to snyb the erth with frosty schowris.   15

Not at thou nedyt ocht, all thyng thou wrocht,
Bot to that fyne thou maid al thing of nocht,
Of thy gudnes tobe participant;
Thy Godhed na rychar, nor ȝit mar skant,
Nowthir now nor than, set thou ws wrocht and bocht.   20

Thy maist supreme indiuisibill substans,
In ane natur thre personys, but discrepans,
Regnand etern, ressauys nane accident;
For quhy? thou art rycht at this tyme present
It at thou was, and evir sal, but varians.   25

Set our natur God haß to hym vnyte,
Hys Godhed incommixt remanys perfyte,
The Son of God havand verray naturis twane
In a person, and thre personys all ane
In deite, natur, maieste and delyte.   30

The Son the self thing with the Fader is,
The self substans the Haly Gaist, I wyß,
Is with thame baith; thre distinct personage,
Ar, war and be sall, euer of ane age,
Omnipotent, a Lord, equale in blyß,   35

Quhilk souerane substans, in gre superlatyve,
Na cunnyng comprehend may nor discryve;
Nowther generis, generat is, nor doith proceid,
Allane begynnar of euery thing, but dreid,
And in the self remanys etern on lyve.   40

The Fader, of nane generat, creat ne boir,   f. 206ᵛ
Hys only Son engendris evirmor;
Not makis, creatis, bot engendris all way
Of hys substans; and all tyme of baith twa
Procedis the Haly Gaist, equal in glor.   45

Of baith, from ane begynnyng, procedis he;
So bene the warkis of the Trinite
Maist excellent, and wondirfull to consave –
ʒit thame to traste the mair meryte we have,
That be na manys rayson previt may thai be.   50

The Fader knawys hym self, quhilk knawlege spredis
Be generatioun etern, that evir bredis
Hys Son, his word and wysdom eternall:
Betwix thir twa is luf perpetuall,
Quhilk is the Haly Gaist, fra baith procedis.   55

Not at the Faderis natur mynyst is,
Of hys substans he generis his Son in blys;
Ne so the Son of hys kynd is ybor,
That he a part heß tharof, and na mor;
Bot all he gevys hys Son, and all is hys.   60

The ilk thing he hym gevis, that he remanys:
Thys syngill substans indifferently thus ganys
To thre in ane, and ilkane of tha thre
The sammyn thing is in a maieste,
Thocht thir personys be seuerall in thre granys: 65

85

Lyke as the sawle of man is ane, we wait,
Havand thre poweris distinct and separate,
Vndirstandyng, rayson and memor;
Intelligens consideris the thing befor,
Rayson discernys, memor kepys the consait. 70

As thai beyn in a substans knyt all thre, f. 207^r
Thre personys ryngnys in a Deite.
We may tak als ane other similytude,
Grosly the sammyn purpoß to conclud;
Flambe, lyght and heit bene in a fyre we se. 75

Quhar euer the low is, lycht and heit bene thar,
And had the fyre bene byrnand euermar,
Evyr suld the flambe engendrit haue hys lyght,
And of the byrnand low the flambys brycht
Perpetualy suld heit haue sprung alquhar. 80

So generis the Fadir the Son with hym etern,
From baith procedis the Haly Gaist coetern.
Thus rude exemplys and figuris may we geif;
Thocht, God by hys awin creaturis to preif,
War mair onlikneß than liknes to discern. 85

Frend, farly nocht, na cauß is to complene
Albeit thy wyt gret God may nocht attene,
For mycht thou comprehend be thyne engyne
The maist excellent maieste dyvyne,
He mycht be reput a pretty God and meyn. 90

Considir thy raison is so febill and lyte,
And hys knawlage profund and infynyte,
Considir quhou he is onmensurabill:
Hym, as he is, to knaw thou art not habill;
It sufficis the beleif thy creid perfyte. 95

God is, I grant, in all thing nocht includyt;
Gevis all gudneß and is of nocht denudyt;
Of hym heß all thing part, and he nocht mynyst;
Hail he is alquhar, not diuidit ne fynyst;
Without all thing he is, and nocht excludit. 100

O Lord, thy ways beyn investigabill! f. 207^v
Sweit Lord, thy self is sa inestimabill,
I can write nocht bot wondris of thy mycht,
That lawyt sa far thy maieste and hyght
Tobe born man intill ane oxis stabill. 105

Thow tuke mankynd of ane onwemmyt maid,
Inclosyt within a virginis bosum glaid,
Quham all the hevynnys mycht nevir comprehend;
Angellis, scheiphyrdis and kyngis thy Godheid kend,
Set thou in cryb betwix twa bestis was laid.   110

Quhat infynyte excellent hie bonte
Abufe thy warkis all, in wonderfull gre,
Lord, quhen thou man wrocht to thyne awyn ymage,
That tynt him self throu hys fulych dotage!
Thou man becam, and deit to mak hym fre.   115

Maid thou not man first president vnder the,
To dant the bestis, fowlys and fysch in sec,
Subdewit to him the erth and all tharin,
Syne paradice grantit hym and all his kyn,
Gave him fre will, and power nevir to dee,   120

Enarmyt him with raison and prudence,
Only bad hym kepe thyne obediens,
And to hym suld all creatouris obey?
Bittir was that fruyt for his ofspryng, and fey,
Maid deth onknawin be fund, and lyfe go hens.   125

O thyne inestimabill luf and cheryte
Becam a thrall to mak ws bondis fre,
To quykkyn thy sclavys tholyt schamfull ded maste fell!
Blissyt be thou virginal frute, that hereit hell,
And pait the pryce of the forbodin tre!   130

Thocht thou large stremys sched apon the rude,   f. 208^r
A drop had bene sufficient of thy blude
A thousand warldis to haue redemyt, I grant;
Bot thou the well of mercy wald nocht skant,
Ws to provoik to lufe the, and be gude.   135

Our all this syne, thyne infynyte Godhed,
Thy flesch and blude in form of wyne and bred,
Tobe our fuyd of grace, in plege of glor,
Thou hest ws geif, in perpetuall memor
Of thy passioun and dolorus paynfull ded.   140

Quhat thankis dew or ganзeld, Lord benyng,
May I, maist wrachit synfull catyve indyng,
Rendir for this souerane peirles hie bonte?
Sen body, saule and all I haue of the,
Thou art my pryce, mak me thy praye condyng.   145

87

My makar, my redemar and support,
Fra quham all grace and gudnes cumis at schort,
Grant me that grace my mysdedis til amend,
Of this and all my warkis to mak gud end:
Thus I beseik the, Lord, thus I exort.   150

From the, begynnyng and end be of my muse:
All other Ioue and Phebus I refuß.
Lat Virgill hald hys mawmentis to him self;
I wirschip nowder ydoll, stok nor elf,
Thocht furth I write so as myne autour dois.   155

Is nane bot thou the Fader of goddis and men,
Omnipotent eternal Ioue I ken;
Only the, helply Fader, thar is nane other:
I compt not of thir paygane goddis a fudder,
Quhais power may nocht help a haltand hen.   160

The scripture clepys the God of goddis, Lord;   f. 208ᵛ
For quha thy mandat kepys in ane accord
Bene ane with the, not in substans, bot grace,
And we our Fader the clepys in euery place:
Mak ws thy sonnys in cherite, but discord.   165

Thow haldis court our cristall hevynnys cleir,
With angellis, sanctis and hevynly spretis seir,
That, but cessyng, thy glor and lovyng syngis:
Manifest to the, and patent, bene all thyngis,
Thy spowß and queyn, maid and thy moder deir.   170

Concord for evir, myrth, rest and endles blyß,
Na feir of hell, nor dreid of ded, thar is
In thy sweit realm, nor na kynd of ennoy,
Bot all weilfair, eyß and euerlestand ioy;
Quhais hie plesance, Lord, lat ws neuer myß! Amen   175

Explicit prologus
Incipit liber decimus &c.

Quhou Iupiter the court of goddis dyd call,
And Venus makis complaynt amangis thame all.   C. i

O n breid or this was warp and maid patent
The hevynly hald of God omnipotent.
The kyng of men and fader of goddis all
Ane consale or a sessioun maid do call,
Amang the spretis abufe and goddis gret,   5

Within hys sterrit hevyn and mylky set:
Quharfra, amyd hys trone sittand full hie,
Our all the erd he mycht behald and se
The Troianys castellys and the pepill Latyne.
Down sat the goddis in thar segis dyvyne,   10 f. 209ʳ
The faldyn ȝettis baith vp warpyt braid.
First Ioue hym self begouth, and thus he said:
"O hevynly wightis, of gret power and mycht,
Quhou is betyd ȝour myndis bene sa lycht,
That ȝour decreit fatale and sentens hie   15
Retretit thus and turnyt bakwartis suldbe?
Or quhy with frawart myndis now of layt
Aganys ȝour ressonabill oraclys ȝe debait?
My will was not at the Italianys
In batale suld concur contrar Troianys.   20
Quhat maner discord be this at we se,
Expreß agane our inhibitioun?" said he,
"Quhat dreid or reuerens thame, or thame, heß movyt
To ryn till armys, and rasys weir controvit?
Or hes sic wyß persuadyt to bargane,   25
With bludy wapynnys rent, and mony slane?
Haist not the sesson to provoke nor prevene;
Of batale cum sal detfull tyme bedene,
Heirefter, quhen the ferß burgh of Cartage
To Romys boundis, in thar feirfull rage,   30
Ane huge myscheif and gret qualm send sall,
And thyrll the hie montanys lyke a wall:
Than war iust tyme in wreth to mak debait,
Than war the tyme to rug and reif thus gait.
Now of sic thingis leif and desist; with me   35
Glaidly do makis frendly amyte."
A few wordis on this wyß Iupiter said,
Bot not in quhoyn wordis him answer maid
The fresch goldyn Venus: "O thou," quod sche,
"Fader of all, O eternal powste,   40
Regnand abufe all men, and goddis eik,
To the I cum, the rewthfully beseik,
Sen thar nane other maieste bene ne glor
That in sik neid may help ws to implor.
Thow seys quhou, with bost and felloun feir,   45
The Rutilianys makis gret derray and steir,   f. 209ᵛ
And quhou Turnus, pransand on semly stedis,
Throw owt the ostis rydis in steill wedis,
And quhou orpyt and prowdly ruschis he
Amyd Troianys, be fawour of Mars," quod sche,   50
"The strenth of wallys, nor the portis schet,
May nocht salf Troianys; lo, within the ȝet,

Amyd the cloß muralʒeis and paill
And dowbill dikis, quhou thai thame assaill,
Quhill the fowceis of blude rynnys on spait; 55
Eneas absent of this na thing wait.
Quhidder gif that thou list suffir neuermar
Thar sege scalit, nor thame fre of dangar?
Behald agane abowt New Troys wall,
ʒit bot begyn to byg, and not cloß all, 60
Quhou inveroin musteris thar ennemyiß;
Ane other ost and sege abowt thame lyis,
And newly, lo, Tedeus son, not far
From Arpos cite into Calabar,
To wery Troianys movis, Diomed. 65
I feill agane my wondis newly bleid,
And I, thy blude, thi get and douchter schene,
ʒit mortale wapynnys mon thoil eik and sustene!
Gyf the Troianys, but thy benevolens,
Or repungnant to thy magnificens, 70
Heß socht onto the cost of Italy,
Lat thame be punyst and thar cryme aby,
And I sall suythly stand content for me,
Thou mak thame na kynd help nor ʒit supple.
Bot gif thai followit haue for thar behufe 75
Sa feill responsis of the goddis abufe,
With syndry admonitions, charge and redis
Of the infernal wightis and spretis that ded is,
Than wald I knaw the cauß or resson quhy
That ony mycht pervert or ʒit bewry 80
Thy commandmentis? How, or quharfor, may thai
New fatys mak and the ald do away? f. 210ʳ
Quhat nedis to reherß, quhou on the cost
Of Scycilly thar schippis brynt war lost?
Or quharto suld I dwel, to schaw ʒou thus, 85
Quhou be the god of tempest, Eolus,
The rageand wyndis send war our alquhar,
Or Iris catchit throw clowdis of the ayr?
Now movit eyk bene fendlych wightis affrayt:
Befor, only that chance was onassayt, 90
Bot now Alecto newly is furth sent
Into the ovir warld, that fell torment,
With Bacchus fury enragit by and by,
Walkand throu all citeis of Italy.
Na thyng I pauß on the empyre," quod sche, 95
"All thocht we hoip had at sic thing suld be,
Quhen fortoun schew tharof sum apperans:
Lat thame be victour quham thou lyst avans.
And gif na realm in this warld remanys,

Quhom thy stern spouß list geif to the Troianys,　　　　100
I the beseik of Troy by the rewyne,
By that subuersioun rekand, and huge pyne,
Suffyr that ȝyng Ascanyus mot be
Salf fra all wapynnys, and of perrell fre;
And, at the lest, in this ilk mortall stryve　　　　105
Suffir thy nevo to remane alyve.
As for Ene, forsuyth, I mak na cair:
Thoill hym in onkowth stremys, as he was ayr,
Be dryve and warpyt euery sey abowt,
To follow furth in danger and in dowt　　　　110
Quhat curß and went at fortoun lyst hym sent;
Most it pleß the fader omnipotent
That I may bot defend ȝon litill page,
And hym withdraw from this ferß weris rage.
I haue in Cipyr the cite Amathus,　　　　115
And the hie standand burgh that hayt Paphus,
And eik the ille yclepyt Cythera,　　　　　　　　f. 210ᵛ
The hallowyt hald als of Idalya,
Quhar, rendryt vp all armys in that stede,
Duryng hys age he sobir lyfe may led.　　　　120
And command eik with gret forß and mastry
The burgh of Cartage down thryng Italy;
Fro thyne sall na thing resist nor gaynstand
Contrar citeis of Tyre or Affrik land.
Quhat proffit haß it done, or avantage,　　　　125
Of Troys batale to haue eschape the rage,
And throw amyd the Grekis fyrys eik
Haue fled away, and throw the sey haue seik,
Sa feill dangeris bywent and ourdryve
Our streym and landis; gyf that thus belyve　　　　130
Troianys hes socht till Itaill, to vpset
New Troys wallys, tobe agane doun bet?
Had not bene bettir thame in thar natyve hauld
Have syttyn still amang the assys cauld,
And lattyr isillys of thar kynd cuntre,　　　　135
Or barrand soyll quhar Troy was wont tobe,
Than thus, fra ded to ded, from payn to payn,
Be catchit on, and euery day be slane?
Restor, I pray the, to thai wrachit wightis
Xanthus and Symoes, fludis quhilk of rychtis　　　　140
Was wont tobe thar propyr herytage.
O fader, suffir the fey Troiane barnage
To seik agane quhat hard myschance befallys
To Troy or Ilyon with thar brokyn wallys."

To Venus complaynt Iuno fra end till end
Maid hasty ansuer, hir actioun to defend.   C. ii

The queyn Iuno than, but mair abayd,
Prykkyt with felloun fury thus furthbrayd:
"Quhy doys thou," said scho, "to me sik offens,
Constrenyng me brek cloß profund sylens,
And with thy wordis, quhar ayr I was koy,   5
Prouokis to publyß and schaw myne hyd ennoy?
Quhat maner man, or quhilk of goddis, lat se,
To move batale constrenyt heß Ene,   f. 211ʳ
Or to engyre hym self to Latyn kyng
As mortal fa, within hys proper ryng?   10
I geif the cace, to Italy socht he
Of the fatys by the autoryte,
Provokyt tharto be the wyld dotage
Of wod Cassandra in hir fury rage.
Lat se, for all this, gyf that anys in sport   15
To leif hys strenthis we dyd hym exhort,
Or forto put hys lyfe in ony danger,
To sayll, or submyt hym to wyndis seir?
Lat se, gyf we hym causyt to walk at large,
And till ane bab commyt the batellys charge,   20
And governance haill of hys cite wallys?
Lat se gyf we, how evir the chance befallys,
Persuadyt hym forto commove and steir
Other quyet pepill with hym to rayß the weir,
Or till adione vp frendschip and ally   25
With Tyrrhene pepill and folk of Tuscany?
Quhat god amovit hym with sic a gawd
In hys dedis to oyß sik slyght and frawd,
Or quhilk of our hard poweris wrocht sic thyng?
Quhar was Iuno with all, this lady ȝyng?   30
Or quhar was sche also quhen, ȝistir nycht,
Irys was send down throu the clowdis brycht?
Is this a thing ful onlesum, but let,
Thocht Italianys with flambys ombeset
The new cite of Troy vprysand, lo?   35
And is it not full gret dispyt also
That, in hys natyve land and faderis ryng,
Turnus remane, or pretend tobe kyng,
Quhamto the god Pylumnus grandschir is,
And haly nymphe Venylia moder, I wyß?   40
Quhat, thinkis thou lesum is at Troianys infeir
Violens to mak with brandis of mortall weir
Agane Latynys, syk onkowth heritage
Tyll occupy and subdew in bondage,   f. 211ᵛ

92

And thar catale in spreth to dryve away?   45
Quhat, haldis thou lesum als, I pray the say,
From otheris to withdraw sa thyftuusly
Thar eldfaderis and maist tendyr ally,
Or, from betwix thar breist and armys tway,
Thar treutht plyght spowsys forto reif away?   50
Tocum and beseik trewys in strange landis,
With syng or takyn of paix born in thar handis;
And netheleß, to mak reddy for weir,
Purvay thar schippis, provide armour and geir?
To salf Ene, heß thou not power and mycht   55
From Grekis handis hym to withdraw be slycht,
And set in sted of that man, light as lynd,
Owder a clowd or a waist puft of wynd?
And eik thou may transform the schippis," quod sche,
"Intil alsmony goddessis of the see.   60
Bot, be the contrary, Rutilyanys ofspryng
We suld support, that is forbodyn thyng!
Thy son Ene, mysknawing this deray,
As thou allegis, is absent now away:
And quhat iniurys, absent mot he remane,   65
And ignorant for ay of this bargane?
Thow haß Paphos, thyne is Idalia,
And thyne mot be the ile of Cithera.
Sen thou heß all thir at command and will,
Lat other folkis in paix and rest dwell styll.   70
Quharto assalȝeis thou a strang cite,
That heß bene oft exercyt in melle,
And lyst invaid pepill with hartis kene?
I can not fynd quhat occasioun ȝe meyn.
Haue we etlyt the Phrigyane febill geir   75
Down from the grund to welt our into weir?
Quhidder was it we, or than Parys, that faltyt,
That wrachit Troianys by Grekis war assaltit?
Quhat was the cauß that Europ and Asya
To rayß the weir in armys war sa thra   80   f. 212ʳ
Aganyst otheris, and thar auld allyans
With thiftuus reif to brek on sic myschans?
Was I not governour and cheif ledar thar,
The tyme quhen that the Troiane adulterar
Ombesegyt the cite of Spartha,   85
And the queyn Heleyn reft and brocht awa?
Or quhidder gif I evir into that weir
Mynysterit dartis, wapynnys or sic geir?
Or ȝit that bargane stuffyt or bet, lat se,
With Cupydis blynd lust and subtilite?   90
Than had bene honest tyme, and ganand baith,

93

Till haue previdit for thy frendis skaith.
Now, al to layt, with thyne iniust complantis
Aganyst ws thou rysis, and attantis
Forto warp owt thy vane wordis chydyng,   95
Quhilk certis may avale the in na thing."
With siclyke wordis Iuno fra end to end
Gan hir querrell sustene and als defend,
And all the hevynly wightis dyd quhyspir and rown,
In opynyonys full diuerß, vp and down –   100
Lyke as first, or wyndis blast be persave,
The swouch is hard within the woddis waif,
With frasyng soundis quhisland, 3it onknaw
Quharof cumis this bruyt owt throw the schaw,
All thocht it be to maryneris a syng,   105
Of wyndis blast to follow sur taknyng.
The fader than omnipotent maist hie
That our all thingis heß souerane maieste,
Begouth to say, and quhen he spak, all cessyt,
The hevynly heich howß of goddis was pecyt,   110
The erthis grund schuke trymlyng for feir,
And still but movyng stud the hevynnys cleir,
The wyndis eik thar blastis lownyt sone,
The sey calmyt hys fludis playn abone.
"Ressaue," quod he, "my sawis, and tak tent,   115
And thir my wordis within 3our myndis enprent.
Sen that algatis 3it may not sufferit be   f. 212ᵛ
Latynys confidir with Troianys and Ene,
Nor 3e can nocht mak end of 3our debait,
I sal me hald indifferent, the meyn gait,   120
And as for that, put na diuersyte
Quhiddir so Italianys or Troianys thai be;
Quhow evir this day the fortoun with thame standis,
Bruke weill thar chance and werd on athir handis,
Lat ich of thame hys hoip and forton sew: 125
Quhidder so the fatys heß determyt of new
Troianys tobe assegit with Italianys
To thar myscheif, or wraik of the Troianys,
Quhilkis with frawart admonytions sa lang
Peraventour heß errit and gane wrang –   130
Nowder Troianys nor Rutilianys freith will I.
Lat athir of thame thar awin fortoun stand by,
And bruke thar wark thai haue begun; but faill,
Kyng Iupiter salbe to all equale.
The fatis sal provyd a way mair habill."   135
And with that word, fortill hald ferm and stabill
Hys godly aith and promyß, sworn heß he
Be Stix the flude, Pluto hys broderis see,

Be that ilk pykky layk with brays blak,
And laithly golf, to kepe all that he spak, 140
And, til afferm hys aith, at hys lykyng
The hevynnys all maid trymbill, for a syng.
Thus endit was the consale, and al doyn,
And Iupiter rayß fra hys goldyn troyn,
Quham hevynly wightis amyddis thame with ioy 145
Ontill hys chymmys ryall dyd convoy.

Quhou the Troianys defendis thar cyte, Eneas absent sekand mair supple.

Duryng this quhile, all the Rutilianys stowt
The cite portis lappit rownd abowt,
Forto down bet the Troianys, euery syre,
Inveroin all the wallys with hait fyre.
Eneas barnage, at myschefis huge 5 f. 213ʳ
Thus ombeset, and segyt but refuge,
Inclusyt war but hop to wyn away,
And sobyrly at defens, as thai may,
On the hie towris hedis stud on raw.
Ful thyn the cirkyllys of the wallys law 10
Thai mannyt abowt, for in the first front stude
Iasyus, Imbrasus son, and eik the gude
Tymetes, son of strang Icetoan,
And by thame alsso the Assaracus twane,
The eldar Thybrys with Castor full wroth, 15
Brethir germane to Kyng Sarpedon boith,
Quham Clarus had and Hemon, ferys twa,
Followyt from the hie realm of Lycya.
Ane Agmon of Lyrnesya fast thar by
Presys with all the forß in hys body 20
A felloun stone to welt the wallys tyll,
Quhilk semyt be a gret part of a hyll;
Na leß of statur than hys fader Clytyus
Was he, nor ellys hys brother Mnestheus.
With dartis thai assaill the cite fast, 25
And thai defend with slungis and stane cast;
Sum presys thik the wyld fyre into slyng,
The arrowys flaw spangand fra euery stryng.
The Dardane child, the ʒyng Ascanyus,
Principall thocht and cuyr of Dame Venus, 30
Amyd the rowtis, incovert quhar he ʒeid,
Thar mycht be seyn in hys fresch lustyhed,
Lyke as ane gem, with hys brycht hew schynyng,
Departis the gold set amydwart the ryng,
Or in the crownell pyght, or rych hynger, 35

95

Quhilk doys the nek array or the hed ger;
And mair semly than evor bane to se,
Craftely closyt within the box of tre,
Or than amyd the blak terebynthyn
Growys by Orycia, and as the geit dois schyne.   40
Hys curland lokkis hyngis down weill dek   f. 213ᵛ
About hys schuldris our hys mylk quhyte nek,
Ane circulet of plyabill gold so bryght
Abuf hys haris apon hys hed weil pyght.
Thow Ismarus, of magnanymyte   45
Fulfyllit, eik thar myght men the se,
Invnctand venemus schaftis the ilk tyde,
Addreß dartis, and wyrk wondis full wyde;
Cummyn of the gentill blude of Meony,
In Lyde cuntre born thou was, fast by   50
The plentuus sulȝe quhar the goldyn ryver
Pactolus warpys on grund the gold vre cleir.
Reddy at hand was Mnestheus wight,
Quham the renowne of this ȝistir nycht,
For that he Turnus our the dychys drave,   55
Full prowd maid in hys curage our the laif.
With hym was Capys thar alsso, quham by
The town Capua is namyt in Champany.
Thus athir party into hard barganyng
Stude at debait, quhill Eneas the kyng,   60
With all hys ferys, baith day and mydnycht
Slydis throw owt the salt famys lyght.
For efter that fra Kyng Evander he
Departit was, as heir abufe said we,
And entrit in amyd the Tuscane tentis,   65
The kyng he socht, and tald hym hys ententis,
Hys name to hym rehersyng and hys blude,
And hys desyre, fully to conclude,
Heß schawyn planely, twychand quhat he socht,
And quhat supple alsso with hym he brocht,   70
And tald quhat army prowd Meȝentyus
Had convenyt, and how the bald Turnus
So violent and ferß was in hys will,
Exhortyng hym to tak gude heyd heirtill,
And how instabill was all warldis chance,   75
All manis surte hyngand in ballance;
And onto this hys request and prayer   f. 214ʳ
Adionyt heß on ful gudly maner.
Thar was na mair delay, bot Tarchon kyng
All reddy was to fulfyll hys lykyng,   80
With moblys and all ryches at command,
And vp gan knyt thar fordward and cunnand

96

Of amyte and perpetuall ally.
Than of the fatys fre, in thar navy,
At command of the goddis, pepill Tuscane 85
Ar entrit in thar schyppys euerilkane,
Submytting thame ontill a strange duke.
Eneas barge than furth the vayage tuke
Befor the laif, as almeral of the flote,
And in hir stevyn kervyn full weil, God wot, 90
The lyonys that the Phrygyane armys bene,
Abufe the quhilkis porturat fair and greyn
Was Ida forest, to fugytyve Troianys
Thar best belovyt forest and natyve wanys.
In hyr was set the gret prynce Eneas, 95
That with hym self can mony thing cumpas
Twychyng the chancis of batal in that tyde.
Pallas adionyt sat by hys left syde,
And he at hym dyd wysly ask and speir
The curß and namys of the starnys cleir, 100
Quhilk in the styl hevyn schynys on the nycht;
Now speris he, franand with all hys myght,
To knaw Eneas wandryng be the see,
And quhou huge payn he had on landis dre.

Heir comptis Virgill the pepil of Tuscane,
Quhilkis with Eneas com to the bargane. C. iv

The Musys now, sweit goddessis ychone,
Oppyn and oncloß ȝour mont of Helycon,
Reveil the secretis lyand in ȝour mycht,
Entone my sang, addreß my style at rycht,
To schaw quhat pyssance, ostis and army 5
At this tyme from the boundis of Tuscany f. 214ᵛ
In falloschyp com with the prynce Ene,
And stuffyt schippys of weir set to the see.
Fyrst, Prynce Massycus cummys with hys rowt,
Into hys barge Tygrys, with stelyt snowt, 10
Sowchand throw owt the fludis quhar scho went,
A thousand stowt ȝong men of hys talent
Vndir hym ledyng, for the batale bown,
From Clusyum com vmquhile, that nobill town,
And fra the Tuscane cite of Cosa; 15
Baith castyng dartis and flanys vsyt tha,
With arrow casys and other quavyrris lycht,
And mortal bowys buklyt for the fyght.
Sammyn furth salys Abas, and hym by
Hys barnage stud enarmyt rychly; 20
Hys weirlyke schip our the fludis ilkane

97

Of god Appolloys goldyn statw schane.
The rych cyte of Populonyas,
Hys natyve cuntre, quharof born he was,
Sax hundreth men of armys in wer expert   25
With hym heß send, and the ile in that part
Illua callyt, within the Tuscane see,
Sa rych of steill it may nocht wastyt be,
Thre hundreth eik heß send with hym to paß.
The thryd capitane, worthy Asylas,   30
Of goddis eik and men interpretur,
Of euery spayng craft that knew the cuyr,
Quhat the hart pypis and bestis entralys ment,
Quhat signyfeit the starnys, quhar thai went
Thar rycht cursis abufe the hevynnys hie,   35
And euery byrdis vocis weil knew he,
And quhat betaknyt, schynyng from the hevyn,
Thyr fyry blastis or this thundris levyn;
A thousand men assemlyt with hym ledis,
With awful speris and scharp grundyn hedis;   40
Quham the Hetruscane cite, Pysa gud,
Inhabyt first from Alpheus that flude,
Send tyll obey hym as thar capitane.   f. 215ʳ
Syne followys Astur, the semlyast of ane,
Astur, maist sovyr horsman forto seik,   45
Of variant cullour was hys armour eik;
Thre hundreth walyt men with hym he led.
All of a will, furth to the batal sped
The folkis alhail dwelt in the cite sweit
Of Agelyn, otherwyß callyt Cerete,   50
And thai that dwellys in tha feldis, I wyß,
Endlang the bankis of flud Mynyonys,
Or intill ancyent Pyrgus town alssua,
Or inhabytis the cyte Grauyssa,
Ful contagius of tempest and grewß ayr.   55
Suld I the pretermyt, sen thou was thar,
I meyn the, Cygnus, of Lygurianys
The cheif ledar, amang other capitanys
Ane the maist forcy into batal sted?
Ne wil I not forȝet, suld I be ded,   60
The, strang Cupauus, with thy few menȝe,
Fra quhais tymbret rysys apon hie
The lusty swannys fedrame, brycht and scheyn
(The cryme and cawß of all ȝour woful teyn
Was luf and amouris), or pompus array   65
Schrowd in ȝour faderis connysans al to gay.
For, as thai tell, quhil dolorusly Cygnus
Maid hys complant amang the scroggy buß

Of poppill tre branschis lang and squar,
Quharin the twa systeris transformyt war, 70
And gan bewail Phaeton, hys best belovyt;
Quhil that he sang and playt, as hym behwyt,
The dolly tonys and lays lamentabill,
With sic regrate to comfort and astabill
Hys hevy amorus thochtis ennoyus, 75
In quhite canoß soft plumys ioyus
Became ourheld, in lyknes of a swan,
And led hys age na mar furth lyke a man,
Bot tuke hys flycht vp from the erd in hy
And with a swouchand voce socht in the sky. 80 f. 215ᵛ
Hys son, this tyde, havand hys falloschippys
Distribut equaly into syndry schippys,
Amang the navy and the flote at large,
With ayris rollys furth hys bustuus barge,
Clepyt Centaurus, and ithandly syne he 85
Dryvys throu fludis of the stormy see.
Byg of statur stude he lyke to feght,
Bostand the streme with ballast of huge weght,
And with hys lang and lusty ballyngar
Ourslydis the deip fludis in thar fair. 90
The nobill Ocnus from hys natyve land
A fair army assemlyt brocht at hand,
Son of god Tibris, the Tuscane ryver,
Beget apon Manthus the lady cleir,
That was baith nymphe and famus prophetes. 95
Thys Ocnus was the ilk man quhilk expreß
Of Mantua the cite dyd he wall,
And eftir hys said moderis name can call
Mantua, myghty of ald ancystry
And forfaderis. Bot hys geneology 100
Was not of ane kynrent cummyn all,
For that town had thre clannys principall,
And, vnder euery clan or trybe of tha,
War other sobyr famyllis twyß twa;
Mantua eik was cheif and principall hed 105
Till all thir pepill wonnyng in that sted,
Takand thar forß and hardyment ilkane
From the lynage and nobill blude Tuscane.
Meȝentius, throu hys auld tyrranny,
Furth of this cite aganyst hym in hy 110
Fyve hundreth men till armys maid do steir;
Quham Myncyus, the fresch rynnand ryver,
That from the lowch of Bennacus ischis down,
And is ourheldyt all with redis brovn,
Heß careit to the braid seys large 115

99

Within thar weirly schip and awfull barge.
Furth held the stowt and degest Aulestes,
Quhilk with gret strenth of rowaris in that preß,
Rasyng thame on thar thoftis for the nanys,
The fludis smate with hundreth arys at anys, 120
Quhill that the fomy stowr of stremys le
Vpweltis from the braid palmys of tre.
The mekill howke hym bair was Tryton callyt,
For in hir forstam was the monstre stallyt,
With watry trumpe fleyand the fludis gray; 125
Quhar as scho salyt, men mycht se hym ay
With byrsy body porturyt, and vissage
All rowgh of harys, semyng of cullage
In mannys form fra hys cost to hys crown,
Bot from hys belly, and thens fordwart dovn, 130
The remanent straucht lyke a fyschis tayll,
In symylitud of huddon or a quhaill;
Vndre the breist of this ilk bysnyng thyng
The sey wallys bulrand makis murnyng.
Sa mony walyt capitanys, nobill men, 135
In help of New Troy, with schippys thryß ten,
Slydis throw the salt stremys of the see
With stelyt stevynnys and bowand bylge of tre.

Eneas schippis, translait in nymphis of see,
Tald hym quhou Turnus assegit the cyte.

C. v

Be this declynyt was the days lyght;
The moyn intill hyr waverand cart of nycht
Held rollyng throw the hewynnys myddil ward,
As Eneas, the Troiane prynce and lard,
For thochtis mycht na wyß hys membris rest, 5
Samony curys in hys mynd he kest,
Bot sat in proper person, and nane other,
To steir hys carvell and to rewle the ruther,
And forto gyde the salys takand tent.
Onone, amyd hys curß, thar as he went, 10
Recontyris hym hys falloschip in hy
Of nymphis, quham of schippys and his navy
The haly moder, clepyt Cybele,
Maid to becum goddessys in the see.
All sammyn swam thai, hand in hand yfeir, 15
And throw the wallys fast dyd sewch and scheir,
Als feill in numbyr nymphys throu the flude,
Als laitly with thar stelyt stevynnys stude
Of Troiane schippys by the costis syde.
A weil far way, as our the streme thai glyde, 20

Thar kyng thai knaw, and all in carralyng
About hys schyp went circulyt in a ryng,
Amangis quham, in speche the maist expert,
Cymodocea to the wail astart,
And with hir rycht hand can the eft casteill   25
Do gryp onon, that all hir bak ilk deill
Abuf the sey watir dyd appeir;
Beneth the calmyt stremys fair and cleir
With hir left hand craftely swymmys sche;
Syne on this wyß spekis till Enee,   30
That of this wonderus mervell knew na thing:
"Walkis thou or not, thou verray goddis ofspryng,
Our prynce and master Eneas? Now awaik,
Takill thy schippys, and thy schetis sclaik.
We beyn thy navy and thy flote," quod sche,   35
"Bowyt sum tyme of fyr and bych tre,
Grew in the haly top of mont Ida,
And now, as present thou behald ws may,
Nymphes we beyn, and salbe euermor.
For, as ʒon faithles Turnus by the schor   40
Invadyt ws with glavys and with fyre,
On forß constrenyt for the flambys schire,
Thy cabillys we in sundyr brak in haist,
To seik the throw the sey, as we war chaist;
And than the moder of goddis, Cybele,   45
Havand of ws compassioun and piete,
In this figour haß ws all translait,
For euermar tobe deificat,
As goddessys, quhar so ws lykis best,   f. 217ʳ
Amangis the fludis forto leif and lest.   50
Bot thy deir child, ʒyng Ascanyus stowt,
Besegyt is, and closyt rownd abowt
With wallys, fowcy and trynschis, ather syde,
Amyd dartis or quarrellys fast doys glyde,
And dreidfull hostis of stern pepill Latyne,   55
By weir enforsyng to distroy all thyne.
Evandrus horsmen, clepyt Arcadanys,
Mydlyt sammyn with Hetrurianys,
Quham in thy help thou sendis by the land,
Thai placis now, quhar as thou gaue command,   60
Can occupy, abydand thy cummyng:
Bot Turnus heß determyt, as certane thing,
Gret garnysonys to send betwix thame sone,
That ʒour hostis sall not togidder ioyn.
Get vp, haue done, and sone in the mornyng,   65
Alsswyth as the brycht day begynnys to spryng,
Thy ferys haill thou fyrst to harnes call,

And with thy scheild invynsibill tharwithall
Thy selvyn schrowd, quham mychty god of fyre
To the, as ane maist souerane lord and syre,　　　　　　　70
Haß wrocht and gevyn, and with gold sa brycht
The bordouris haß ourgylt and forgit at rycht.
Gyf thou belevys not my sawys invayn,
The lyght of day to morn, I schaw the playn,
Huge hepys sal behald in feld dung down　　　　　　　75
Of Rutilianys by fell occisioun."
Thus said sche, and, departand with a skyp,
By hir rycht hand schowys furth the schyp
As scho that was in that craft rycht expert,
And throw the wallys on the tother part　　　　　　　80
Glydys away vndir the fomy seys,
Als swyft as ganȝe or feddyrrit arrow fleys,
That stryvys forto pyngill with the wynd:
The remanent hir followys fast behynd.　　　　　　　f. 217ᵛ
Anchises son, the gret Troiane Ene,　　　　　　　85
Awondris, onwyttyng quhat this mycht be,
And, netheleß, hys curage dyd avance
With this ilk fatale augury or chance;
Syne schortly, lukand to the hevyn abone,
On this maner can pray and maid hys boyn:　　　　　　　90
"O blyssyt moder of the goddis," quod he,
"That hallowyt art in the montane Ide,
Quhamto the toppys of mont Dyndymane,
And eik the towryt citeis mony ane,
With renyt lyonys ȝokkyt to the char,　　　　　　　95
Ful tendyr bene and hartly euermar;
Be thou in batall now my president,
Be my protectrix, dewly takand tent
At this orakyll be hastyt to our weill;
O haly goddeß, with happy fute of seill　　　　　　　100
Cum and assistis to thyne awyn Troianys."
No mor he spak, bot, with that word atanys,
In the meyn quhile vpspryngis the brycht day,
Chasand the clowdis of the nycht away.
And fyrst Eneas gan hys ferys command　　　　　　　105
Thar baneris to displayt and follow at hand,
Thar curage eik and curace to addreß,
And graith thame for the batail all expreß.
For he, be than, hys Troianys mycht behald,
And of the eft schyp into hys town and hald　　　　　　　110
Men mycht hym se and knaw, quhar at he stude,
Hys schynand new scheild from amyd the flud
Into hys left hand rasyt hie on hyght.
The Troianys from the wallys of that sycht

War sa reiosyt, vp thai rasyt a cry 115
That rerdis to the starnys in the sky.
The hoip of hys returnyng hait as fyre
Dowblyt thar curage, and vprasyt thar ire,
That with thar handis fast thai dartis slyng,
With sic a dyn of clamour and crying, 120
And trumpys blast rasyt within the town   f. 218ʳ
Sik maner bruyt, as thocht men hard the sovn
Of crannys crowplyng, fleand in the ayr
With spedy fard in randoun heir and thar;
As from the flude of Trace, hait Strymone, 125
Vndre the dyrk clowdis, oft we se,
Thai fle the weddris blast and rak of wynd,
Thar glaidsum soundis followand thame behynd.
Bot quhat mycht meyn this affeir and deray
A gret farly and wondyr was, perfay, 130
To Turnus, kyng of Rutuleis, that tyde,
And the Italiane dukis hym besyde,
Quhill thai at last beheld towart the cost,
And saw the navy cum and mekill ost,
Semand the sey of schippys all ourflet. 135
The creist or schynand tymbret that was set
Abufe Eneas helm and top on hyght
Kest byrnand flambys with a glytterand lycht,
And eyk the goldyn boyß of hys bukleir
Large fyry stremys on breid schew fair and cleir – 140
Lyke as the comete stern sanguynolent,
With hys red cullour tryst and violent,
Schynys sum tyme apon the donk nycht;
Or frawart Syrius, that fervent star brycht,
Quhilk with the scaldand heyt at hys rysyng 145
Byrnys the erth of drowth, and is the syng
Pretendand tyll all mortale folk, I geß,
Contagyus infirmyteis and seiknes,
That with hys schrewyt lyght canicular
Infekkyt all the hevynnys and the ayr. 150
Bot Turnus hardy stalwart hie curage,
For all this feir, demynyst nevir a stage,
Quhilk manfully schup thame to withstand
At the cost syde, and dyng thame of the land,
That on na wyß thar thai suld arryve; 155
And with glaid semlant gan his folk belyve
Exortyng forto rayß thar spretis on hie,   f. 218ᵛ
And with hys wordis forthirmar eik he
Gan thame repreif of thar sa hasty feir.
"Lo! now present," says he, "is cummyn heir 160
The mater quhilk ȝe lang desyrit haue;

The tyme is now to gryp in hand ȝour glaif;
The tyme of batale reddy is at hand,
Quhar strenth beis schawyn in stalwart stowr to stand.
Now euery man ramembir on his spowß, 165
Thynk on thar natyve land and dwellyng howß;
Reduce ȝe now onto ȝour mynd, ilkane
The worthy actis of ȝour eldris bygane,
Thar lovabyll fame, and ȝour awyn renowne;
And lat ws formest haist ws to the see, 170
And thar recontyr our fays, or thai land,
Quhill as thai first set fut apon the sand,
With slyde tocummyn, half deil in effray,
Or thai thar fut steppis ferm, and tak array.
Hap helpis hardy men, be myne avyß, 175
That weil dar tak on hand stowt interpryß."
Thus said he, and tharwith in hys thocht
Devisys quham maist ganandly he mocht
Led with hym, to resist and meit his fays,
Or quham he suld not from the sege vprays, 180
Bot styll remane to ferm and cloß the town,
The wallys and the trynschis enveroun.

Eneas fra the schippis landit his ost,
And Turnus thame assalit at the sey cost. C. vi

In the meyn sesson, the Troiane Ene
Begouth hys folkis from thar schippis hie
On bryggis and on plankis set on land:
Mony abaid the ebbyng of the sand,
Quhill the swarffard wallys abak dyd draw, 5
Than in the schaldis dyd thai leip on raw;
And sum with ayris into coggis small
Etlyt to land. But tho amang thame all
The prynce Tarchon can the schor behald, f. 219ʳ
Thar as hym thocht suldbe na sandis schald, 10
Nor ȝit na land bryst lyppyrryng on the wallys,
Bot quhar the flude went styll, and calmyt all is
But stowr or bullyr, murmour or movyng;
Hys stevynnys thydder steryng gan the kyng,
And on this wyß hys ferys dyd exort: 15
"Now, O ȝe walyt flour of weir, at schort,
Bend vp ȝour ayris styth, and rayß ȝour schippys.
Haist owr the flude, bair to the schoyr with skyppys,
And with ȝour stelyt stevynnys, ane and all,
Thys ground onfrendly to ws and inimicall 20
Do scheir and cleif in sundyr lyke a stok,
Lat euery barge do prent hir self a dok:

Na forß I not in sik port by this meyn
To brek the schyp, sa we the land atteyn."
Fra Tarchon had thir wordis said, but mair   25
Hys feris startis ilk man till ane ayr.
The stowrand famy bargis dyd rebound,
Inrowand fast towart the Latyn grond,
Quhyl that thar stammys tuke the bankis dry,
And thar kelys stak in the slyke fast by,   30
But ony harm or danger, euery one.
Bot sa tyd not onto thy schyp, Tarchon,
For in the schald scho stoppys, and dyd stand
Apon a dry chyngill or bed of sand,
A lang tyme all to schakyng with the flude,   35
Quhill fynaly, thar rokkand as scho stude,
To brystis scho, and ryvys all in sondyr,
Warpyt the men amyd the faym thar vndir;
The plankis, hechis and mony brokyn ayr,
That on the streym went flotand heir and thar,   40
Maid to thar landing gret impediment,
And slyddry glar so from wallys went
That oft thar feyt was smyttyn vp on loft;
Bot finaly, all drowkyt and forwrocht,
Thai salwyt war, and warpyt to the cost.   45   f. 219ᵛ
Than na delay of sleuth nor feir ne bost
Withheld Turnus, bot with hys haill armee
Aganyst Troianys by the cost of the see
He dyd array all sammyn in that stound.
The trumpettis blew thar bludy weirlyke sownd.   50
And fyrst, in syng of gud luk in the weris,
Ene the rowtis of the lauboreris,
Or rurall husbandis, invadis and ourset,
And heß the Latyn commonys haill doun bet,
By slauchter fyrst of thar chiftane, Theron,   55
Amang all otheris the biggast man of one,
Quhilk set apon Eneas or he wyst;
Bot he throw owt hys syde hys swerd hes thryst,
Persyt the stalwart platit scheild of steill,
And throw the schynand hawbrik euery deill;   60
The giltyn mailȝeis makis hym na sted,
For in the cost he tholys dynt of ded.
Syne smate he Lychas, and hym heß al to torn,
That of hys ded moderis waym was furth schorn,
And onto Phebus god was consecrait,   65
And was sa chancy in hys ȝong estait
That he the swerd eschapit by hys hap;
Bot not at this tyme so the dedis clap.
And not far thens this douchty Eneas

105

Kyllyt the dowr and stalwart Cysseas,   70
And put to deth the bustuus Gyas strang,
That with hys burdoun down haill rowtis dang:
Thar strenthy handis helpyt thame na thyng,
Nowder Hercules wapynnys nor armyng
Mycht thame defend, nor ȝit thar syre, that heght   75
Melampus, and companȝeon was in feght
To Hercules in hys sair iourneis feill,
Quhil he in erth was levand and in heill.
And lo, as Pharon cryis and dois rowst
With haltand wordis and with mekill woust,   80
Eneas threw a dart at hym that tyde,   f. 220ʳ
Quhilk, as he gapyt, in hys mowth dyd glyde.
And thou also, the fey Greyk, Cydon,
Quhilk strangly luffyt thir ȝong childer ichone,
As thou the ȝyng Clytius dyd persew,   85
Quhais ȝallow berd begouth to spryng of new,
And was alhaill thy new lust and desyre,
Be the rycht hand of this ilk Troiane syre
Thar had bene maid end of thy amouris greyn,
And wrachitly had lyin ded, I weyn,   90
War not the brethir of the clan Phorcanys
Apon Eneas assemblit all atanys;
In numbyr sevyn thai war, and dartis sevin
Alsammyn thai kest, forcy as fyry levin,
Of quham sum dyd but harm or other deir   95
Stot from hys scheild, his hewmet or hed geir,
And sum, that wald haue hyt hys corpß in hy,
Venus hys haly moder choppyt by.
Than to the traist Achates said Ene:
"Reik me dartis and castyng speris," quod he,   100
"That in the Grekis bodeis fixit stude,
Quhylum in Troys planys bedyit with blude,
And my rycht hand sall thraw thame so ilkane
On Rutulanys, that nane sal fle invane."
A bustuus schaft with that he grippyt haß,   105
And incontrar hys aduersaris gan tayß
Quhilk flaw towartis Meonyus fast by;
Owt throw the scheild platit with steill in hy
Duschyt the dynt, and throw the corslettis glydis,
Gyrd throw the cost persyng baith the sydis.   110
Onto hym startis Alcanor, hys brothir,
To beir hym vp, quhen that he saw hym schuddir,
With hys rycht arm, bot throw hys gardy sone
The grundyn hed and bludy schaft ar done,
Furth haldand the self randoun as it went;   115
The ryght arm, from the schulder al to rent,

106

Apon the mankyt sennonys hyngis by,
As impotent, quyte lamyt, and dedly.
Than Numytor furth of hys brotheris corps
Ruggis the trunschon, and with all hys forß   120
It swakkis at Ene, bot he na mycht
Had till attane ne wond the nobill knycht;
3yt with the dynt the gret Achates thee
He hurt and stren3eit haß a litill wee.
With this come Clawsus, full of vassalage,   125
Confidand in hys 3outh and florist age,
The Curytanys with hym brocht in the preß,
And with a lang styf speir ane Dryopes
Smate in the halß, vnder the chyn, sa sair
That hym byreft was in the place rycht thar   130
Baith voce and spreit of lyfe, and that na wonder,
For hys nek bayn and throte war carf in sondir,
That doun he duschys with a felloun rerd,
Quhil that hys forret raschit on the erd,
And of hys mouth, a petuus thing to se,   135
The lopprit blude in ded thraw voydis he.
Thre otheris syne this ilk Clawsus haß slane,
Born into Trace of the clan Boryane;
And thre com fra the cite of Idas,
And other thre of cite Ismaras,   140
By diuerß chancis put he al to ded.
Alesus hym recontris in that sted,
And all the barnage com from Aurunca,
That auld cite; and thame followys alssua
To that melle the son of Neptunus,   145
That is to knaw, the worthy Mesapus,
Quhilk into horsman craft was maist expert.
Now presys this syde, and now 3onderwart,
To reill abak and to expell in fyght
Thar aduersaris, and mak thame tak the flycht.   150
Thus by the cost Ausonya that tyde
Hard wolx the batale apon athir syde.
As thocht sum tyme amyd the large ayr
The contrar wyndys stryvys heir and thar,
With brethfull blastis in thar equale mychtis,   155
Nane lyst obey tyll other, all sa wight is,
Nowder thai amang thame self, nor 3it the clowdis,
Ne 3it the rageand seys, quhilkis sa lowd is;
So that the bargane lang standis in dowt,
Quha salbe victor, and quha vnderlowt,   160
Sa forcyly remanys the elementis
Contrary otheris to thar awin ententis –
Nane other wyß the Troiane hostis in feild,

And Latyn rowtis ʒokkit vnder scheild,
Metys in the melle: ionyt sammyn than   165
Thai fewtyr fut to fut, and man to man.

Quhou Pallas confortis his ost of Archadye,
Quhilkis gave the bak and tuke purpoß to fle.   C. vii

B ot quhen that Pallas at ane owtyr syde
  Persavyt hys Arcad army that tyde
In sic a place had takyn land attanys,
Quhar as a burn had warpyt rowand stanys,
And buskis with the brays down had bet,   5
That thai war in sa hard myscheif ourset,
As men nocht vsyt forto go feght on fute,
And than, constrenyt, knew nane other buyt,
For scharpneß of that sted, bot leif thar horß;
That weil persauyt he how that on forß   10
Thai gave the bak, and schupe to tak the flycht,
The Latynys followand thame in all thar mycht:
Than, quhile with prayer, now with wordis sowr,
Thar curage he enflambis to the stowr,
Quhilk maner havyngis, suyth as is the creid,   15
As vtir poynt remedy at sik a neid.
"My ferys," says he, "quhydder do ʒe fle?
I ʒou beseik, be ʒour gret renowne,
And be ʒour forcy dedis done of ald,
And by ʒour pryncis fame, Evander bald,   20
And be the ostis and mony victoryß
That ʒe in weir and batale wan feill syß,
And be my gude beleif and hoyp, that now   f. 221ᵛ
With haill confidens restis fixt in ʒow,
As to atteyn onto my faderis glor,   25
To ondertak sik dedis done befor;
Do nevir, for schame, onto ʒour self that lak,
To lyppyn in speid of fute and gyf the bak.
With swerdys dynt behuffis ws, perfay,
Throw amyddis our ennemys red owr way.   30
Quhar ʒondir sop of men thikkis in a rowt,
ʒondir is the passage quhar we moste wyn owt;
ʒondir ʒour nobill cuntre wyl ʒe paß;
ʒon way to wend exhortis ʒour duke Pallas.
Heir is na power of dyvynyte,   35
Nor goddis myght gaynstandyng ws," quod he,
"Nane other bargane haue we in thir fyghtis
Bot agane dedly and with mortale wightis:
Alsmony mortale bodeis heir haue we,
And als feill handis to debait the melle.   40

Behaldis, quhou the sey with obstakill gret
Inclusys ws, and at our bak can bet;
On land is left ws heir na place to fle.
Quhat, wald ȝhe ryn to Troy owt throw the see?"
Thus said he, and furthwith, or he wald ceß,   45
Amyd hys fays ruschit in the preß,
Quhar as the rowtis thikast war in stowr.
And first of other, to hys fatale howr,
Hym metys Lagus, a Rutilyane,
Quham fyrst ourrollyt with a mekill stane,   50
Throw gyrd hys cost syne with a castyng dart,
Persyng hys rybbys throuch, at the ilk part
Quhar beyn the cupplyng of the ryg bone,
And the ilk schaft stak in hys corß onone.
Pallas it ioggillit, and furth drew in hy;   55
Quham ane Hysbon, standand neir tharby,
Wenyt to have kawcht, bot the gryp he falyt;
For as onwar he stowpyt, and devalyt
Wod wroth for wo of this myschewß ded
Of hys deir fallow, in the ilk sted   60
Pallas hym keppyt syk wyß on hys brand   f. 222ʳ
That all the blaid, vp to the hylt and hand,
Amyd hys flaffand longis hyd haß he,
On sik maner that na man mycht it se.
Syne Pallas set apon Anchemolus   65
And Sthenelus, that of the kyng Rhetus
Prynce of Marrubyanys, ancyent pepill, beyn;
The quhilk Anchemolus was that ilk, I weyn,
Defowlyt hys faderis bed incestuusly,
And had forlayn hys awyn stepmoder by.   70
And ȝe allso, stowt gemel brether twa,
Childir and sonnys onto hym Dawcya,
Tymber, I meyn, and thy brother Laryde,
Amyd the feild Rutiliane dyd abyde;
Ȝe war sa lyke in form and symylitude   75
Nane mycht decern betwix ȝou quhar ȝe stude
(Quhilk maner errour, or sik mysknawyng,
To fader and mother is oft plesand thyng.
Seand thar childer resembill ane lykneß);
Bot at this tyme haß Pallas, as I geß,   80
Markyt ȝou swa with sic rud differens,
That by hys keill ȝe may be knaw fra thens.
For swa stud with the, Tymber, thou art ded,
Evandrus swerd heß swepyt of thy hed;
And thy rycht arm of smyttyn, O Laryd,   85
Amyd the feild lyis the besyde,
And half lyfleß thi fyngyrris war sterand,

109

Within thy neif doys gryp and faik the brand.
Than schame and dolour, mydlit baith ourane,
Baldis the pepill Arcad eueryane   90
To the bargane aganyst thar ennemyß,
For Pallas wordis maid thar curage ryß,
And eik, for thai beheld befor thar eyn
Hys dowchty dedis, thai hym love and meyn.
For Pallas than throw gyrd Rhethus the kyng,   95
As he on cace glaid by on char fleyng:
Na mair space was of tary ne delay
That Ilus deth prolongit the ilk day;
For as agane the, Ilo, with fell feir   f. 222ᵛ
Pallas addressyt had a stalwart speir,   100
Rhetheus start in betwix, and cawch the dynt,
As he on cace was fleand ferß as flynt
From thy handis, the maist forcy Teutras,
And thy brother Tyres, that by the was:
Ourweltis Rethus in ded thrawys atanys,   105
And with hys helys smayt the Rutilian planys,
Tumlyt from hys hie cart chargit quhar he sat,
And on the grund rebundis with a sqwat.
And lyke as sum tyme in the symmyris drowth,
Quhen wyndis rysys of the north or sowth,   110
In seir placis the hyrd, at hys desire,
Amang the scroggy rammell settis the fyre;
Wlcanus hostis of brym flambys red
Spredand on breid, vpblesys euery sted;
Than he that set the kyndillyng glaid and gay   115
Behaldis quhou that the low doys mak deray,
Blesand and crakand with a nyce reuery –
Non other wyß, the Archadanys in hy
All sammyn socht in feild with all thar mycht,
And maid debait to help Pallas in fyght.   120
Bot tho Alesus, keyn into batale,
Thame to recontyr etlys, and assaill,
And gan hym self weil schrowd vnder his scheild,
Syn manfully ruschit amyd the feild,
Quhar that he slew ane Lacon, and Pheres,   125
And Demodocus eftir in the preß.
As hym Strymonyus by the gorget grippyt,
With hys brycht brand hys rycht hand he of quhyppyt;
And Thoas syne sa smayt apon the hed
With a gret stane, quhil myxt of blud all red   130
The harnys poplit furth on the brayn pan.
Thys ilk Alesus fader, as witty man,
Forto eschew hys sonnys fatys strang,
Hyd hym prevely the thik woddis amang;

Bot, fra the auld Alesus lay to de,   135
And ȝeldis vp the breth with wawland e,
The fatale systeris set to hand onon,   f. 223ʳ
And can this ȝong Alesus so dispon,
That by Evandrus wapynnys, the ilk stownd,
He destinat was to caucht the dedis wond;   140
Towart quham Pallas bownyt haß ful sone,
And in hys renk on this wyß maid hys boyn:
"Now grant, thou god and fader Tyberyne,
Gude chance and forton to this hed of myne
The quhilk I tayß apon this castyng speir,   145
That it may throw Alesus body scheir;
And ȝon harneß, cote armour and spulȝe brycht,
Quhilk now sa weirly schynys on ȝon knycht,
Sall hyng apon ane ayk fast by thi bra."
The god hys askyn hard as he dyd pray,   150
For quhil Alesus onavisytly
Cled with hys scheild Imaonus, hym by,
That was to hym hys frend and fallow deir,
Hys breist stud nakyt, but armour or geir,
Quharin he Pallas dedly schaft ressauyt.   155
Bot Lawsus, wilfull hys syde to haue savyt,
As he that was a gret part of the ost,
And lyst not suffir, with sik feir na bost,
Or slauchter maid be Pallas and deray,
At his cumpanȝeis suld caucht mair affray,   160
Ruschit in the melle; and first in hys teyn
Slew Abas, that gret bargane dyd sustene.
The thikast sop or rowt of al the preß,
Thar as maist tary was, or he wald ceß,
Thys Lawsus alto sparpillyt and invadys: 165
Down bettyn war the barnage of Archadyß,
Down bettyn eik war the Hethruryanys,
And ȝhe also, feil bodeis of Troianys,
That war not put by Grekis to vtyrrans.
Than all the ostis semlyt with speir and lans,   170
The chiftanys all ionyt with hail poweris,
The hyndmast wardis swarmyt al yferis;
So thik in staill all marryt wolx the rowt,
Oneyß mycht ony turn hys hand abowt
To weild hys wapyn, or to schuyt a dart.   175   f. 223ᵛ
Full douchtely Pallas on the ta part
Inforcis hym to greif hys fays that tyde;
Lawsus resistis on that othir syde.
Thar agis was not far indifferent,
And of maist semly statur, quhar he went,   180
Thai war excellent of bewte baith tway;

Bot so it stude, at fortoun, walloway,
Wald nother suffir to hys realm resort.
And netheleß to meyt sammyn at schort,
As into feild to preif thar hardyment,   185
The governour of hevyn omnipotent
Lyst na way thoill; for, belyve eftir this,
To athir of thame thar dedly fatys, I wyß,
To ane far grettar aduersar remanys,
As heir onon doys follow vnder anys.   190

Quhou that ferß Turnus has ȝong Pallas slane,
For quham hys folkis makis gret dolour and mayn.   C. viii

Duryng this fervour of the bargane swa,
The haly nymphe, clepit Iuturna,
Hir brother Turnus dyd monyß and exhort
To succur Lawsus, and hys folk support;
The quhilk Turnus, as in hys spedy char   5
The myd rowtis went sloppand heir and thar,
Beheld hys ferys debatand with Pallas:
"Lo, now is tyme to desist, and lat paß
All sic bargane," quod he, "cessis in hy;
For I will set on Pallas anerly;   10
Only to me, and to nane other wight,
The victory pertenys of sik a knycht;
Glaidly I wald hys fader stude heirby,
This interpryß to dereyn and aspy."
Thus said he, and hys feris at command   15
Voydit the feild, and all plane left the land.
Than ȝong Pallas, seand Rutylianys
Withdraw the feild sa swith, and rovm the planys,
At the prowd byddyng of thar prynce and kyng,
Amervellit full gretly of this thing,   20   f. 224ʳ
And farly can on Turnus to behald,
Our all hys bustuus body, as he wald,
Rollyng hys eyn, and all hys corps in hy
With thrawyn luke on far begouth aspy;
Syne movyng fordwart, with sic wordis on hie,   25
To answer Turnus speche, thus carpys he:
"Owthir now", quod he, "for ay be lovyt I sall
Of rych kyngly spulȝe triumphall,
Quhilk heir I sall rent from myne aduersar,
Or than salbe renownyt evirmar   30
Of ane excellent end moist gloryus.
Do wa thy bost and mannance maid to ws,
For my fader, quhom thou desyris besyde,
Reputtis all elyke, quhou evir the chance betyde."

112

And sayand thus, amyd the plane furth startis: 35
The blude congelyt abowt Archadyane hartis.
Turnus down lepys from hys twa quhelit char,
And bownys fast towartis his aduersar.
Lyke as ane lyoun from the hillys hycht,
Amyd the valle had scharply gottin a sycht 40
Of sum prowd bull, with hys horn in the plane
Addressand hym reddy to mak bargane,
Cummys bradand on the best fast in a lyng –
On siclyke wyß was Turnus tocummyng;
And quhen that Pallas saw hym cum sa neir 45
He mycht areke to hym a casting speir,
Formast he bownys to the ionyng place,
Gyf sa betyd that forton, of hir grace,
Hys interpryß for stowt ondertakyng
Wald help, or hym support in ony thing, 50
As he that 3ong was, and of strenth all owt
Na wyß compeir to Turnus stern and stowt;
And to the gret goddis in hevyn abone
Apon this maner prayand said he sone:
"I the beseik, thou myghty Hercules, 55
Be my faderis gestnyng, and the ilk deß
Quhar thou strangear was ressauyt to herbry,
Assist to me, cum in my help in hy,   f. 224ᵛ
To perform this excellent fyrst iourne,
That Turnus in the ded thraw may me se 60
Bereif fra hym hys bludy armour red,
And 3aldand vp the breth in the ilk sted,
Mot with hys eyn behald me hym befor
In hie tryumphe, with ourhand as victor."
Gret Hercules the 3ong man hard onon, 65
And from the boddum of hys hart can gron,
Hydand hys smart for rewth of Pallas 3yng,
Seand the fatys wald haue hys endyng;
And for ennoy salt terys, all invayn,
Furth 3ettyng our hys chekis thyk as rayn. 70
Tho Iupiter, hys curage to astabill,
Thus to hys son spak wordys amyabill:
"Tyll euery mortale wofull wight, perfay,
Determyt standis the fixit lattir day;
Ane schort and onrecoverabill term is set 75
Of lyfe, quhen all most neydlyngis pay that det:
Bot, to prolong thar fame by nobill dedis,
Fra vertuus wark that cumys and procedis.
Quhou mony sonnys and deir childryn," said he,
"Of goddis kyn, vnder Troy wallys hie 80
War done to ded, and brytnyt blude and bone,

113

So that amangis all otheris Sarpedon,
My tendir get, my kyn and blude, lyis slane.
Forsuyth also, I say the into plane,
The fynale fayt awatis Turnus in feild,   85
The dait and methis approchis of hys eild."
On this wyß spak gret Iove to Hercules,
And with that word, hys eyn towart the preß
On the Rutilian feild addressis he.
And, the ilk stownd, 3ong Pallas lattis fle   90
With mekill forß at Turnus a gret speir,
And syne onon hys brycht brand burnyst cleir
Hyntis furth of the scheith to mak debait.
The schaft flaw towart Turnus, and hym smait
Apon the schulder, abuf the gardis hie   95
That rysys vmast tharapon we se,   f. 225ʳ
And throw the bordour of the scheild swa persyt
Quhill fynaly in sum deill it traversyt,
And hurt a part of Turnus byg body.
Than Turnus smyttyn, full of felony,   100
A bustuus lance with grundyn hed ful kene,
That lang quhile taysyt he in proper teyn,
Leyt gyrd at Pallas, and thus wyß said he:
"Considir 3ongkeir, gyf our lancis be
Bettir of tempyr and mair penytratyve."   105
And, with the word, the schaft flaw furth belyve,
So that the scharp poynt of the brangland speir
Throw owt amyddis of the scheild can scheir,
Persand sa mony platis of irne and steill,
And sa feill plyis of bull hydis ilk deill,   110
All sammyn cowchit in hys target strang,
The bustuus strake throw all hys armour thrang,
That styntit na thing at the fyne hawbryk,
Quhil throu the cost thyrlyt the dedly pryk.
Pallas, nocht schrynkand for the mortale dynt,   115
Invane the hait schaft of hys wond heß hynt,
For al togidder by the sammyn way
The blude and sawle passys hyne bath tway.
Apon hys wond onon he ruschis down,
Abuf hym rang hys harneß with a sovn,   120
And that onfrendly erth ennymycall
That in hys deth he suld not scryk nor call,
As was the gyß, with bludy mowth bait he.
Turnus, abufe hym standand, carpys on hie:
"O 3he pepill of Arcaid, takis tent,   125
And my wordis do reherß and present
To Kyng Evandar, sayand hym playnly,
That hys son Pallas to hym send haue I

114

In sik array as that he heß deservyt;
And, of my gentryß, wil he be preservit 130
To all estait and honour funerall,
With all solace pertenyng beryall
Of tumbe and of entyrment, as efferis.
Na lytill thyng, perfay, into thir weris f. 225ᵛ
Hes hym bycost the frendschip of Ene." 135
And sayand thus, with hys left fut hes he
Pallas ded corps ourwelt, or euer he stent,
And syne abowt hys sydis sone haß rent
Hys goldyn gyrdill, pasand a gret deill,
Quharin was gravyn craftely and weill 140
Of Danavs douchteris the iniquyte,
Quhou that the fyfty 30ng men, schame to se,
War fowlly murthuryt on the first nycht,
As thai war spowsyt to thar ladeis brycht;
The chalmeris portyrit war bysprent with blude; 145
Quhilk historeis Eurition, warkman gude,
Had carvyt weill and wroch full craftely
In weghty platis of the gold massy,
Of quhais spul3e now is Turnus glaid,
Ioyfull and blyth that he it conquest had. 150
O manis mynd, so ignorant at all
Of thingis tocum and chancis quhilkis may fall!
Vpheit sone in blynd prosperyte,
Can not be war, nor myssour hald with the!
The tyme sall cum quhen Turnus sall, perfay, 155
Hait and wary this spul3e and this day,
Desyrand he mycht by for mekill thing
That he had nevir twichit Pallas 3yng.
Abowt the corps assemblit tho his feris,
With mekill murnyng and huge plente of terys; 160
Apon a scheild Pallas body thai laid,
And bair hym of the feild, and thus thai said:
"O Pallas, quhou gret dolour and wirschyp
To thy fader, and all hys falloschip,
Sall thou rendir and bryng hame," said thai. 165
"Thys was to the in weyrfar the first day,
Quhilk first in bataill dressyt the to go;
The ilk for ay haß the bereft tharfro!
And, not the leß, thy swerd leiffis in the planys
Gret hepys ded of the Rutilianys." 170

The rich Magus na ranson mycht reskew,
And preist Hemonydes, baith Eneas slew. C. ix

Tho nane incertane rumour nor demyng, f. 226ʳ
Bot sovyr boydword cam thar, and warnyng,
Ontill Eneas of this gret myschance,
Schawand quhou that his folkis stud in ballance,
As bot in litill distans all from ded; 5
The tyme requiryt forto set remeid,
And succur Troianys quhilkis had tane the flycht.
Than, as wod lyon, ruschit he in the fight,
And all quham he arekis nerrest hand
Without reskew dovn mawis with his brand; 10
The bytand blaid abowt hym inveroum
Amyd the rowtis reddis large rovm.
Enragit and inflambit thus in ire
Throw owt the ostis Turnus, that prowd syre,
Quhilk had this new slauchtir maid, socht he, 15
Ay prentand in his mynd befor hys e
The gudly Pallas, was sa stowt and ȝyng,
And the gret gentryce of Evander kyng,
The cheir and fest hym maid bot a stranger,
Per ordour all thing, quhou and quhat maner 20
He was ressauyt and tretit thankfully,
Syne of hys band of frendschip and ally
With athis sworn and interchangit handis,
Remembryng tho his promyß and cunnandis.
Amovit in this heit, or euer he stynt, 25
Four ȝong men quyk he heß in handis hynt,
That born was of the cite hecht Sulmon;
Alsmony syne he takyn haß onon
Bred and vpbrocht besyde the flude Vfens,
Quham that he etlys forto send from thens 30
To Pallas lykewalkis and obsequeis,
To strow his funeral fyre of byrnand treis,
As was the gyß, with blude of presoneris,
Eftir the ald rytis into mortale weris.
Syne hynt Eneas a perellus lance in hand, 35
And it addressis far furth on the land
To ane Magus, that subtell was and sle,
And iowkit in vnder the speir haß he;
The schaft schakand flaw furth abufe hys hed; f. 226ᵛ
And he Eneas in that sammyn sted 40
Abowt the kneis grippyt humylly,
With petuus voce syne thus begouth to cry:
"Be thy deir faderys gost I the beseik,
And be that gud beleif quhilk thou haß eik

116

Of Ascanyvs vprysyng to estait,   45
Thys silly sawle of myne, sa faynt and mayt,
Thow salf to my a son and fader deir.
I haue a howß, rych, full of mobillis seir,
Quharin bedelvyn lyis a gret talent,
Or charge of fyne siluer, in veschell quent   50
Forgyt and punsyt wonder craftely;
Ane huge weght of fynast gold tharby,
Oncunʒeit ʒit, ne nevir put in wark:
Sa thou me salf, thy pyssans is so stark,
The Troianys glory nor thar victory   55
Sal na thyng change nor dymynew tharby,
Nor a puyr sawle, thus hyngand in ballance,
May sik diuisioun mak nor discrepans."
Thus said this silly Magus, all invane,
Quhamtill Eneas answeris thus agane: 60
"Tha mony talentis of fyne siluyr and gold,
Quhilkis thou rehersand heir befor heß told,
Do kepe onto thi small childyr and ayris;
Lat thame bruke weill, I consent it be tharis.
All interchange and ransonyng, perfay,   65
In this batale Turnus heß done away,
Now laitly slayand ʒong Pallas, allace!
That rewthfull harm, and that myschews cace,
Felys baith Ascanyus and my faderis gost,
For thai na litill thyng tharby heß lost."   70
Thus sayand, by the helm hym grippys he
With hys left hand, and fast as he mycht dre
Writh down hys nek, quharin, but mair abaid,
Hys bludy brand vp to the hyltis slaid.
Not far thens stude Hemonydes allane,   75
Prest onto Phebus and the thrynfald Dyane,
On quhais hed wympillit holy garlandis   f. 227ʳ
With thar pendentis lyke to a mytyr standis,
Hys habyt as the scheyn son lemand lycht,
And all hys armour quhite and burnyst brycht;   80
Quham Eneas assalyt myghtyly,
And gan to chayß owt throw the feld in hy,
That fleand stummyrryt and to grond went sone;
The Troiane prynce down lowtis hym abone,
And with hys brand hym brytnys at devyß,   85
In maner of ane offerand sacryfyß.
The large schaddow of Eneas in feild
Dyd haill the ded corps of this preist ourheld.
Serestus sortis vp hys armour gay,
And on hys schuldris careit heß away,   90

117

To hyng as trophe or syng victoriall
Tyll Mars the god, quhilk Gradyus is call.

Quhat douchty chiftanys of the Latyn land
That day Eneas kyllit with hys hand.

C. x

Ceculus, discendit of Wlcanus blude,
And Vmbro eyk, the stalward chiftane rude,
That cum was fra the montanys Marsyane,
The bargane stuffis, relevand in agane.
Bot Eneas, discend from Dardanus,   5
Ganstandis thame, ful brym and furyus,
And onto ane, hech Anxurus, in the feild
Of strak the left arm all dovn with the scheld;
Quhilk had maid sum gret vant, spekand prowdly,
Wenyng that in hys sawys by and by   10
Thar had bene gret effect and hardyment,
As thocht he wald extoll in hys entent
Hys manhed to the hevyn and starnys hie,
And promyß to hym self, for hys bonte,
Agit cannos hayr and lang proceß of ȝeris: 15
Lo, now he lyggis law, for all hys feris!
Syne baldly with glaid curage, as I geß,
Agane Eneas can Tarquytus dreß,
In schynand armour wonder prowd and gay,
Of Dryope born, the nymphe or schene may,   20   f. 227^v
To Fawnus wonnyng in the woddis greyn;
And, to recontyr Ene inflambyt in teyn,
Kest hym selvyn; bot the tother, but feir,
Buyr at hym mychtyly with a lang speir
Throw owt hys scheild of payß and hawbrik fyne,   25
That to the grund gan dovn hys hed declyne;
All thocht he than full humylly hym besocht,
And schupe to say mekill, all was for nocht;
Hys pallat in the dust bedowyn stude,
And the body baithit in the hait blude   30
Ene ourweltis, sayand thir wordis withall,
With trublit breist and mynd inimicall:
"Now ly thou thar, that wenyt the so wight
That thou was feirfull ontill euery wight.
Thy best belovit mother sall the not haue   35
To erd, as custum is, nor delf in grave,
Na do thy bonys honour with sik cuyr
As thame to lay in fadyrris sepultur;
Bot salbe left to the wild bestis fuyd,
Or than the spait watir of this flude   40
Sal bair the in the deip, and thar on raw

118

With empty throtis sal thy banys gnaw
Thir sey monstreys in thar wod rage,
And lape thy blude thar hungir to asswage."
Syne, but delay, Antheus and Lycas,   45
Quhilkis that of Turnus first ward ledaris was,
Persewys he, and also Numa bold,
And Camerthes, brycht schynand all of gold,
Son of the manly Volscens capitan;
In all the fertill grond Ausonyane   50
The richast man, and kyng was this Volscens
Of Amyclys the cite of silens.
And lyke as Egeon, the kyng of gyandis,
Quhilk had, thai say, ane hundreth armys and handis,
And fyfty mowthys, of quham the fyre dyd schyne,   55
As he into the batale gigantyne
Incontrar Iovis thundir and fyre flaucht
With alsmony scharp drawyn swerdis fawght,   f. 228^r
Clatterand in bargane with samony scheildis –
The sammyn wyß, enragent throw the feildis   60
Went Eneas, as victor with ourhand,
Fra tyme that anys bedyit hys burnyst brand
And wet he had in hait Rutiliane blude.
So that allso, in this ilk fury wod,
He draif at Nypheus amyd the breste bane,   65
Set in hys fourquhelit chariot allane;
Bot fra the horß on far dyd hym aspy
Sa grym of cheir stalkand sa bustuusly,
For feir thai start abak, and furth can swak
The duke Nypheus wyd oppyn on hys bak,   70
And brak away with the cart to the schor,
With stendis feill and mony bray and snor.
The self stound, amyd the preß fut hoyt
Lucagus entyris in hys chariote,
With quhyte horß drawyng wonder lustely,   75
Hys brother Lyger sittand neir hym by;
This Lyger led the renȝeis with hys hand,
Bot bald Lucagus swakkis a burnyst brand.
Eneas mycht nocht suffir nor sustene
Of thame sic fervour in thar felloun teyn,   80
Bot ruschit furth, and with a gret speir
Forganyst thame can into feght appeir;
Quhamto this Liger carpys upon hie:
"Thou seys nocht Dyomedis stedis heir," said he,
"Nor ȝit Achillis char persavis draw,   85
Thocht athir venquyst the in feild, we knaw;
Nor ȝit the Troiane planys behaldis thou.
The end of thyne age and of bargane now

Salbe maid in thir landis on this grond."
Sic wordis vayn and omsemly of sovnd   90
Furth warpys wyde this Lyger fulychly,
Bot the Troian barroun onabasitly
Na wordis pressis to rendir hym agane,
Bot at hys fa leyt fle a dart or flayn,
That hyt Lucagus, quhilk, fra he felt the dynt,   95
The schaft hyngand into hys scheild, but stynt   f. 228ᵛ
Bad dryf hys horß and char al fordwart strecht,
As he that hym addressit to the fecht,
And strekit furth hys left fut in hys char;
Bot sone Eneas speir was reddy thar,   100
Beneth hys schynand scheild reversyt law,
So that the grondyn hed the ilk thraw
At hys left flank or leisk persyt tyte,
Quhill clar owt our the charyot is he smyte,
And on the grond weltis in the ded thrawys;   105
Quham on this wyß with sowr wordis and sawys
The petuus Eneas begouth to chyd:
"Lucagus," said he, "forsuyth as at this tyde
Na slaw curß of thy horssys onweldy
Thy cart has rendryt to thyne ennemy,   110
Nor 3it na vayn wrathys nor gaistis quent
Thi char constrenyt bakwart forto went,
And malgre thyne withdraw thi fays gryppys;
Bot lo now, of thy fre will, as thou skyppys
Owtour the quhelys of thy cart, God wait,   115
Levand the renys and horß all desolat."
Thys beand said, the horß renys he hynt.
The tother fey brother, or evyr he stynt,
Lap fra the cart, and kneland petuusly,
Vphevand hys bayr handis, thus dyd cry: 120
"O Troiane prynce, I lawly the beseik,
Be thyne awyn vertuus and thy thewys meyk,
And be thy parentis maist of renowne,
That sik a child engendryt heß as the,
Thow spair this wofull sylly sawle at lest,   125
Haue rewth of me, and admyt my request."
With wordis feill as he thus can requer,
Ene at last on this wyß maid answer:
"Syk sawys war langer furth of thy mynd.
Sterve the behuffis, leß than thou war onkynd   130
As for toleif thy broder desolait
All hym allane, na follow the sam gait."
And tharwithall the hyrnys of hys gost
He rypyt with the swerd amyd hys cost,   f. 229ʳ
So tyll hys hart stoundis the pryk of deth;   135

120

He weltis our, and ȝaldis vp the breth.
Thys Dardane prynce as victor thus in weir
Samony douchty corpsis brocht on beir,
Amyd the planys reddand large gait,
As doys a rowtand ryver red on spait;   140
That for hys dyntis wolx hys fays agast,
As for the feirfull drumly thundris blast;
Quhil fynaly Ascanyus the ȝyng page,
And the remanent of Troian barnage,
Quhilk war, as said is, besegyt invane,   145
Thar strenth heß left and takyn heß the plane.

Iuno rycht quayntly causys Turnus to fle,
Ane fenȝeit figour persewand of Enee.   C. xi

The ilk stound, of hys awyn fre volunte,
Ioue callys Iuno, and thus carpys he:
"O thow my syster german and my feir,
My best beluffyt spowß, most leif and deir,
Thyne opynyon haß not dissauyt the,   5
As thou belevyt: now may thou not se
Quhow Venus doys susteyn and fortyfy
The Troiane rowtis and pyssans by and by?
Nane actyve handis, nor stowt myndis, I weyn,
Nor bodeys reddy all perrellys to sustene,   10
Haue thai, thou may se be experiens."
Quhamto Iuno, with humyl reverens,
Answeryt: "My sweit and mast gudly husband,
Quharto lyst the renew my sorow at hand,
As cayrfull wight, that lykis nocht sic bourdis?   15
All efferd of thy fatal dreidfull wordis
I am bestad; bot war I now, I weyn,
Als strangly belovyt as I sum tyme haue bene –
Thocht ȝit, God wait, accordyt so tobe
Baith to myne honour and thy dignyte –   20
I say, war I beluffyt as I was ayr,
Thou Ioue almyghty ryngand euermar
Suld not deny me sa sobyr a thyng,
Bot at I mycht withdraw, at my lykyng,   f. 229ᵛ
Furth of the feild Turnus, and hym save   25
Onto hys fader Dawnus, that our the lave
Belovyt hym, as rayson wald," quod sche.
"Now sall he perysch, and now sal he de,
And sched hys gentyll blude sa pacient,
In grewß panys be Troianys tort and rent;   30
And netheleß hys kyn orígynall
Is renownyt of godly stok ryall,

121

Discendit of our seid and hevynly clan,
Fra god Pylumnus to rekkyn the ferd man;
And eik thow wait, full oft with large hand,   35
With mony oystis and ryght fair offerand,
Thy templys and thyne altaris chargit haß he,
In wirschyp of thy myghty maieste."
The souerane kyng of hevyn imperiall
In few wordis maid answer thus at all: 40
"Gif thow askis a resput or delay,
Bot for a tyme or tyll a certane day,
Of thys evident deth of Turnus ჳyng,
Desyrand I suld grant the sik a thyng,
All thocht he mortale be rycht sone we knaw,   45
I leif the to remove hym and withdraw,
And from this instant perrellus hard fayt
Steill hym away, and gyde hym by the gait,
For so lang space ჳyt restis at will of me
To lenth hys lyfe, quhilk I the grant," quod he.   50
"Bot gif sa beys, that vndre thy request
Mair hie pardon lurkis, I wald thow cest;
For gif thou wenys that all the victory
Of the batale, and chancis by and by,
May be reducyt and alterat clar agane,   55
A mysbyleve thou fosteris all invane."
To quham Iuno on this wyß said wepyng:
"Quhat harm mycht fall, thocht be sum takyn or syng
Thow schew thy mynd, and grantit that," quod sche,
"Quhilk be thy wordis of fatale destane   60
Now grunschis thou to geif or to conceid?
That is to say, quhat forß, thocht thou in deid   f. 230ʳ
Waldyst appreif and ratyfy agane
That Turnus lyfe a lang tyme suld remane?
Bot now approchis to that innocent knycht   65
A feirfull end – he sal to ded be dicht,
Or than my sawys ar voyd of veryte.
And O, wald God at rathar sa suldbe
That I dissauyt war bot with fals dreid,
And at thou list, as thou has mycht in deid,   70
Thy fatale promyß and thy statutis strange
In bettir purpoß to translait and change!"
Fra scho thir wordis had said, the ilk tyde
Dovn from the hevyn scho leyt hir selvyn slyde,
Befor hyr dryvand a tempestuus wynd,   75
And all abowt, befor and eik behynd,
Within a clowd of myst circulyt cleyn:
So throw the air bownyt furth this queyn
Towart the Troiane hostis in the planys,

122

And to the tentis socht of Lawrentanys.   80
Thys goddes than furth of ane boyß clowd
In lyknes of Ene dyd schaip and schrowd
A voyd figur, but strenth or curage bald,
The quhilk wondyrus monstre tobehald
With Troiane wapynnys and armour grathis sche,   85
With scheild and helm and tymbret set on hie,
Be semlant lyke Eneas godly hed;
And tharto ekis scho in euery sted
Quent fenȝeit wordis, fant and contyrfait,
With voce, but mynd, or ony other consait;   90
And fenȝeis eik hys concernans and pacis
(Syklyke as that, thai say, in diuerß placis
The wraithis walkis of goistis that ar ded,
Or as the slepy dremys, fra sted to sted
Fleand in swevyn, makis illusionys,   95
Quhen mennys myndis oft in dravillyng gronys);
And all befor the forfront of the feild
Richt haltandly, as curageus vnder scheild,
Musturis this ymage, that with dartis keyn
Aggrevyt Turnus, and dyd hym chyde in teyn,   100   f. 230ᵛ
Prouocand hym to bargane and tyl ire.
And Turnus tho als hoyt as any fyre
Thys figur dyd invaid, and tharat he
In gret dispyte a quhirrand dart leyt fle;
Bot this ilk schaddo, as sum deill addred,   105
Turnyt abowt, and gaif the bak and fled.
Than Turnus, wenand Ene had tane the flycht,
And al awondryt of that selcouth syght,
Within hys mynd a vayn comfort kawch he,
And cryis lowd: "Quhydder fleys thou now, Ene?   110
Leif nevir, for schame, thus dissolait and waist
Thy new allyans promyst the in haist,
Of Lavynya the spousyng chalmyr at hand,
And all this ilk regioun and this land,
Quhilk thou sa far haß socht owt our the se: 115
My rycht hand sal the saysyng geif," quod he.
With sik wordis he schowtand dyd persew,
And ay the glymmyrand brand baith schuke and schew,
Nathyng persavand quhou this myrth and blyß
Away quyte with the wynd bewavit is.   120
On cace thar stude a mekill schip that tyde,
Hyr wail ionyt til a schor rokis syde,
With plankis and with bryggis layd on land,
The entre reddy grathit weill thai fand;
In the quhilk schyp Osynyus kyng, I wyß,   125
Come laitly from the cite of Clusys.

Thydder went this wrath or schaddo of Ene,
That semyt, all abasyt, fast to fle,
And hyd hyr dern vndre hychis tharin.
Na slawar Turnus hastis hym to ryn, 130
That but delay he spedis to this schyp,
Ran owr the bryg, and inwith burd can skyp;
And scars was entrit in the forcastell,
Quhen Saturnys douchter saw hir tyme befell;
Than soyn the cabyll in sondir smytis sche, 135
And fra the schor draif the schip throu the see.
Bot Turnus absent thus that sammyn howr
Eneas seyrssys throw amyd the stowr, f. 231ʳ
And in hys renk quham euer he met lay ded;
Full mony a man he kyllit in that sted. 140
And tharwithall hys lycht and fenȝeit gost,
Fra tyme the schip was chargyt fra the cost,
No langar sekis hyrnys hir to hyde,
Bot flaw vp in the ayr the sammyn tyde,
And al dissoluyt into a dyrk clowd. 145
The meyn sesson, can forß of wyndis lowd
Turnus far furth amyd the deip sey dryve;
He dyd behald abowt hym tho belyve,
All ignorant quhat wyß this chance was wrocht,
And of hys lyfe salvyng na thyng he rocht; 150
With handis iunct vphevit towart hevyn,
Syk wordis he furth braid with drery stevyn:
"Almychty fader of the hevynnys hie,
Haß thou me reput on sic wyß tobe
Confusyt in this schame for myn offens? 155
And will I suffyr syk torment and pennans?
Quhidder am I dryve, and from quhens am I cumyn?
Quhat maner eschewyng or fleyng haue I nummyn?
In quhat estait sall I return agane?
Sall I evir se the wallys Lawrentane, 160
Or evir eft my tentis sall I se?
Quhat may ȝon ost of men now say of me,
Quhilkis my querrell and me followit to feild,
Quham now, allace, lo, feghtand vnder scheild
Ȝondir (schame to say the harm) sa wikkytly 165
Reddy to myschews deth beleft haue I?
Lo, I behald thame fleand paill and wan,
And heris the granyng of mony douchty man
In my defalt falland fey to grond.
Quhat sal I do, allace the wofull stond, 170
Or quhilk land (thocht a thousand tymys I stervit)
May swelly me sa deip as I haue servyt?
Bot, O ȝe wyndis, rathar haue mercy,

On rowkis and on craggis by and by
Do swak this schyp, sen heir na erth I se,   175   f. 231ᵛ
And haue of wrachit Turnus sum pyete,
Quhilk of hys fre will, stad in this maner,
Besekis ȝow with all hartly prayer;
Do warp my body on the schaldis onkend,
Far furth on Syrtys at the warldis end,   180
Quhar Rutilyanys me nevir fynd agane,
Sa that na fame nor rumour may remane
Eftir my deth of this schaymfull trespaß."
And, sayand thus, in mynd dyd he cumpaß
Full mony chancis rolland to and fro,   185
Quhiddir gif he suld, for proper lak and wo,
Into this fury smyte hym with hys brand,
And thryst the bludy blaid in with hys hand
Throw owt hys rybbys and sched his hart blude,
Or than to swak hym self amyd the flude,   190
Swymmand to seik the nerrest costis bay,
In feild agane the Troianys to assay.
Athir way till assay thryß presyt hes he,
And thryß hym styntis Iuno, queyn mast hie,
Havand compassioun of this ȝong man bald,   195
And can asswage hys mynd, and hand withhald.
Furth held the schip, slydand owt our the fludis,
With prosper wynd and followand tyde sa gude is,
Quhill he is careit suyrly throw the see
Tyll Ardea, hys faderis auld cite.   200

In Turnus sted Meȝentius dyd succeid,
Killyt doun his fays, and spulȝeit of thar weid.   C. xii

Durand this quhile, in fatis marciall,
    Meȝentyus movyt with ardour bellycall,
Be instigatioun of Ioue in that neid,
Can to the batale in hys place succeid,
And the Troianys to invaid na thing sparis,   5
That semyt prowd as all the feild war tharis.
Than sammyn to recontyr hym atanys
Semlyt haill ostis of Hethrurianys,
And all assailȝeit Meȝentyus allon;
Aganyst a man thai rowtys euery one,   10
Inflambyt all in malyce, maid persutys,   f. 232ʳ
And thik as haill schour at hym schaftis schutis.
Bot he, lyke to a ferm rowk, quhilk we se
Strekyt on lenth amyd the large see,
Sytuat aganys the rageand wyndis blast,   15
And brym wallys boldynnand wondyr fast,

From all that violens doys hym self defend,
And haill the forß sustenys to the end
Baith of the hevynnys and byr of seys rage,
Remanand onremovyt ferm in hys stage: 20
Als stern standis Meȝentyus in that stound.
And first he hes fellit and laid to the grond
Hebrus, the son of ane Dolycaon,
And hym besyde Latagus slew onon,
And Palmus eik, accustumat to fle: 25
Bot with a stane Latagus brytnyt he
Quhilk of a montane semyt a gret nuke,
With quham hym on the vissage he ourtuke;
And Palmus howgh sennonys smait in tway
Maid hym sa slaw he mycht nocht fle away;   30
Thar armour syne to Lawsus gevyn heß he
To weir on hys schuldris, and crovn on hie
Thar creistis set, the quhilk sa rychly schane.
He slew also Evantus a Troiane,
And Mynas syne he kyllys in the feild,   35
Quhilum to Parys companȝeoun and evin eild;
Quham on a nycht Theana, gude and fair,
To hys fader Amycus in Troy bair,
Quhen Heccuba, douchter of Cisseus,
Dremyt scho was gret, the story tellis thus,   40
With a fyre broynd, and the self samyn nycht
Was delyver of Parys, the fey knycht,
Quhilk in hys natyve cite maid hys end:
Bot thir feildis Lawrentan ombekend
Withhaldis now the body of Mynas.   45
So brym in stowr that stond Meȝentyus was,
Lyke to the strenthy sangler or the bor,
Quham hundis quest with mony quhryne and ror
Down dryvyng from the hightis maid discend,   f. 232ᵛ
Quhilk mony wyntyr tofor had hym defend   50
In Vesulus, the cauld montane hie,
That is ourheldyt with mony fyr tre;
Or than the bustuus swyne weil fed, that bredis
Amang the buskis rank of ryspe and redis,
Besyde the layk of Lawrens, mony ȝheris,   55
Quhen that he is betrappyt fra his feris
Amyd the huntyng ralys and the nettis,
Standis at the bay, and vp his byrsys settis,
Grasland hys tuskis with astern fyry eyn,
With spaldis hard and harsk, awfull and teyn,   60
That nane of all the huntmen thar present
Hym to engreif haß strenth or hardyment,
Nor dar approchyng within hys byt neir,

126

Bot standand far on dreich with dart and speir,
Assoverit of hys reik, the beste assays,   65
With felloun schowtis, bustuus cryis, and brays.
Nane other wyß stud all the Tuscane rowt
This stalwart knycht Meʒentius abowt,
And, thocht thai iust cawß had of wreth and feyd,
Thar was nane of thame durst hym put to ded,   70
Nor curage had with drawyn swerd in hand
Hym till assaill, nor mach apon the land;
Bot with takillis and castyn dartis on far
Thai warp at hym, bot durst not ane cum nar,
And with huge clamour hym infestis that tyde;   75
He, onabasyt, abowt on euery syde
Behaldis, gyrnand full of proper teyn,
And with hys scheild choppyt by schaftis bedene.
Furth of the ancyent boundis of Coryt tho
Was cum a Greik, quhilk clepyt was Acro,   80
That fugityve into his lusty heyt
Had left hys spowsal trewth plicht oncompleit;
Quham as Meʒentius saw amyd the rowt
Hym grevand soir, as weriour stern and stowt,
And saw the plesand plomys set on hycht   85
Of hys tymrell, and eik the purpour brycht,
Quhilk of his trewthplycht lufe he bair in syng;
Than lyke a hungry lyon rumysyng,
Constrenyt by hys rageand empty maw,   f. 233ʳ
The beistis dennys circuland all on raw,   90
Gif he on cace aspyis a swyft ra,
Or the ʒyng hart with spryngand tyndis twa,
Ioyful he bradis tharon dispytuusly,
With gapand gowle, and vprasys in hy
The lokkyrris lyand in his nek rowght,   95
And all the bestis bowellis thrymlys throwght,
Hurkylland thar on, quhar he remanyt and stude,
Hys gredy gammys bedyis with the red blude –
On the sammyn wyß, Meʒentyus rycht baldly
Mydwart hys fays rowt ruschit in hy;   100
Down smytis fey Acron amyd the ost,
That in the ded thraw, ʒaldand vp the gost,
Smate with hys helys the grond in maltalent,
And brokkyn schaftis with hys blude bysprent.
This ilk Meʒentius eik dedenʒeit nocht   105
To sla Orodes, quhilk than was onflocht,
That is to knaw, quhill frawart hym he went,
And reput na wyß, as by hys entent,
Syk ane fleand to wond into the bak,
Onawarnyst, quhen he na defens mycht mak,   110

127

Bot ran abowt and met hym in hys rayß;
Than athir man assemblit face for face.
Orodes mair of prattik was all owt,
Bot the tother in dedis of armys mair stowt,
That to the erth ourthrawyn he heß his feir,   115
And possand at hym with hys stalwart speir,
Apon hym set hys fut, and thus he said:
"O now my feris, beys blyth and glaid;
Lo, a gret party of this weir, but leß,
Heir lyis at erd, the douchty Orodes."   120
Hys feris sammyn rasyt vp a cry,
With ioyus sound in syng of victory,
And blew the pryß triumphall for his deth;
Bot this Orodes, ȝaldand vp the breth,
Onto Meȝentyus carpys thus on hie: 125
"Me onrevengit, thou sal nocht victour be,
For weill I wait that sone I salbe wrokyn,   f. 233ᵛ
Na, for all thy prowd wordis thou haß spokkyn,
Thow sall nocht lang endur into sik ioy;
Bot siclyke chancis and semblant ennoy   130
Abydis the, thocht thou be nevir sa bald,
Thys sammyn feild sall thy ded corps withhald."
To quham Meȝentyus smyland said in teyn:
"Thou sall de first, quhat evyr to me forseyn
Or previdyt haß myghty Iove," quod he,   135
"Quham fader of goddis and kyng of men cleip we."
And sayand thus, the schaft the ilk thraw
Furth of hys wond and body dyd he draw.
Tho Orodes the hard rest doith oppreß,
The cauld and irny slepe of dethys streß,   140
And vp the breth he ȝald onon rycht
With eyn closyt in evir lestand nycht.
Cedicus altotrynschit Alcathous,
And Sacrator to grund laid Hydaspus;
Rapo, ane Arcaid, haß Parthenyus slane,   145
And Orses, wondir byg of blude and bane;
And Mesapus kyllyt the stowt Clonyvs,
And Erycates with Lychaonyus;
The formast lyggand at the erd he ourraucht,
That by hys hedstrang horß a fall had cawcht,   150
And Lychaonyus eik, a fut man, he
Lyghtit on fut and slew in the melle.
Aganys hym than went a man of Arge,
Hait Lycyus, bodyn with speir and targe;
Bot by the way Valerus, gude in nedis,   155
Nocht inexpert in douchty eldris dedis,
Recontryt hym, and put hym to the ded;

Salyus a Troiane in that sammyn sted
Atronyus slew; and Nealces, expert
To schut the fleand arrow or castyng dart,   160
Quhilk invadis a man or he be war,
Slew Salyus with schot, beand on far.

Quhou Eneas the ȝong Lawsus haß slane,
Quhilk fred his fader hurt in the bargane.   C. xiii

Thus awfull Mars equaly with hys brand   f. 234^r
  The sorow rasyt apon athir hand:
Huge slauchter mayd was and seir woundis wyd,
Thai kyll and ar bet down on euery syde,
That sammyn in the feild thai fall infeir,   5
Baith the victouris, and thai that venquyst weir,
And nother party wist, nother he nor he,
To salf hym self quhar away to fle:
So that the goddis in Iovys hevynly hald
Had compassioun and rewth for tobehald   10
The wroith and ire of athir in the fightis,
That sik distreß rang amang mortal wightis.
Venus towart the Troiane syde tuke tent;
Aganyst quham, all full of maltalent,
Saturnus douchter Iuno, that full bald is,   15
Towart the party aduersar behaldis;
And the pail furour of Tysiphone
Walkis wod wroth amydwart the melle.
Bot pryncipaly Meȝentyus all engrevyt,
With a gret speir, quharwith he feill myschevit,   20
Went brangland throu the feild all hym allon;
Als bustuus as the hydduus Orion,
Quhen he on fut woyd throu the mekill see,
Scherand the streym with hys schuldris hie,
Abufe the wallys of the flude apperis;   25
Or lyke ane ancyent ayk tre, mony ȝheris
That grew apon sum montane toppys hycht,
Semand so hie to euery manis sycht,
Quhilk, thocht hys rutis spred in the grond all sydis,
Hys crop vpstraucht amyd the clowdis hydis –   30
Syk lyke Meȝentius mustyrris in the feild,
With huge armour, baith speir, helm and scheild,
Aganyst quham Eneas fast hym hyis,
Fra tyme amyd the rowt he hym aspyis.
The tother, onabasyt, all reddy thar   35
The cummyng of hys douchty aduersar
Abydis stowtly, fermyt in hys forß,
And massely vpstude with bustuus corß:

129

And, mesurand with hys e als large spaiß   f. 234^v
As he mycht thraw a castyng speir, thus says: 40
"My rycht hand, and this fleand dart mot be,
Quhilk now I tayß, as verray God to me!
Assistyng to my schot I ȝou beseik;
For I awow, and heir promittys eyk,
In syng of trophe or triumphall meith,   45
My lovit son Lawsus forto cleith
With spulȝe and all harneß rent," quod he,
"Of ȝondir rubbaris body, falß Enee."
Thus said he, and fra hys hand the ilk tyde
The castyng dart fast byrrand lattis glyde,   50
That fleand sclentis on Eneas scheild,
Syne, standand far onrovm ȝond in the feild,
Smate worthy Anthores the ilk thraw,
Betwix the bowellys and the rybbys law:
Anthores, ane of gret Hercules ferys,   55
That com from Arge into hys lusty ȝheris,
Inherdand to Evander the Arcaid,
And had hys dwellyng and hys residens maid
In Palentyn, cite Italian,
Onhappely now lyggis thus down slane,   60
All of a wound and dynt quhilk in the fycht
Addressit was towart ane other knycht.
Ȝit, deand, he beheld the hevynnys large,
And can ramembir hys sweit cuntre of Arge.
Than the reuthfull Eneas kest hys sper,   65
Quhilk throu Meȝentius armour all dyd scher;
Throw gyrd hys targe platyt thryß with steill,
And throw the cowchit lynnyn euery deill,
And thrynfald plyis of the bullys hydis,
That law down in hys flank the dynt abydis;   70
Bot it byreft hym nowder lyfe ne mycht.
Eneas tho, quhilk was expert in fyght,
Ioyfull quhen that Meȝentius blude saw he,
Furth hynt hys swerd at hang law by hys thee,
And fervently towart hys fa can paß,   75
Quhilk, for the dynt, sum deill astonyst was.
Quhen Lawsus saw this aventour of weir,
He wepyt wail sair for hys fader deir;
Sa wobegone becam this lusty man   f. 235^r
That salt teris fast our hys chekis ran.   80
Forsuyth, I sall not ourslyp in this sted
Thy hard myschance, Lawsus, and fatale ded,
And thy maist dowchty actis bellycall:
O fresch ȝongker, maist dyng memoriall
I sall reherß, gyf ony faith may be   85

Gevyn to sa gret dedis of antiquyte.
With this Meȝentyus menȝeit drew abak,
Harland hys leg quharin the schaft stak,
That quhar he went he baris our the feild
Hys ennemyß lance fixit in hys scheild.   90
Betwix thame ruschys in the ȝong Lawsus,
Amyd thar wapynnys, stern and curagus,
Hym self haß set forto sustene the fyght;
Vnder Eneas rycht hand rasyt on hycht,
That reddy was to smyte a dedly wond,   95
In steppis he, and baldly the ilk stound
The bytand brand vphevyt keppyt he,
And can resist and stynt the gret Enee.
Hys feris followys with a felloun schowt,
Quhill that Meȝentius of the feild wan owt,   100
Diffend and coverit with hys sonnys scheild,
Thai cast dartis thikfald thar lord to held,
With schaftis schot, and flanys gret plente,
Perturband thar stern aduersar Ene,
That all enragyt hys sovir targe erekkit,   105
And thar vndre hym haldis closly dekkyt.
And lyke as sum tyme clowdis brystis attanys,
The schowr furthȝettand of hoppand hailstanys,
That all the plewmen and thar hynys inhy
Fleis of the croftis and feildis by and by;   110
And eik the travellour ȝond vnder the wald
Lurkand withdrawys to sum sovir hald,
Owdir vnder watyr brays and bankis dern,
Or in sum craggis clyft, or deip cavarn,
So lang as that the schour lestis on the plane,   115
That he may, when the son schynys agane,
Exers hys iourne, or hys wark alsfast –
Syk wyß Ene with schoit and dartis cast   f. 235ᵛ
Was all ourheld, and ombeset ilk syde,
Quhil he the preß of batale styntis that tyde,   120
And all thar forß sustenyt and deray;
Reprevand Lawsus, thus begouth to say,
And mannansyt hym with brand of blude all red:
"Quhidder hastis thou sa fast apon thy ded?
Or quhou dar thou ondertak into fyght   125
Syk interpryß, quhilk is abuf thy mycht?
Thou art nocht wyß; thy tendir hart," quod he,
"And rewthfull mynd all owt dissavis the."
Bot for all thys ȝong Lawsus, vail que vaill,
Wald no wyß ceß Eneas till assaill.   130
Than hyear rayß the wraith and felloun ire
Of the ilk manfull Troiane lordly syre,

And eyk the fatale sisteris tho in deid
Had wymplyt vp this Lawsus lattyr threid:
For so Eneas stokis hys styf brand   135
Throw owt this ʒongker, hard vp to hys hand,
That swerd, befor maid mannansyng and bost,
Throw gyrd that gentill body and hys cost,
Hys target persand and hys armour lycht,
And eik hys cote of goldyn thredis brycht   140
Quhilk hys moder hym span; and, to conclude,
Hys bosum all is fillyt of hait blude;
Sone efter is the spreit of lyfe furth went
Down to the goistis law with sad entent,
And left the body ded, and hyne dyd paß.   145
Bot quhen Anchises son, ferß Eneas,
Beheld hys wlt and contenans in deyng,
Hys sweit vissage sa in the ded thrawyng
Becummyn wan and paill on diuerß wyß,
He sychit profundly owder twyß or thryß,   150
And drew abak hys hand, and rewth haß hynt;
For sa into hys mynd, eftir the dynt,
The ymage of hys faderly piete
Imprentit waß, that on this wyß said he:
"O douchty ʒynglyng, worthy tobe menyt,   155
Worthy tobe bewalyt and complenyt,
Quhat sall the reuthfull compacient Ene   f. 236ʳ
For sa gret lovabill dedis rendir the?
Or quhat may he the ʒeld sufficient
For sik natural and inborn hardyment?   160
Thyne armour, quharof sumtyme thou reiosyt,
With the I leif, for ay tobeyn eniosyt;
Onto thy parentis handis and sepulcre
I the beleif tobe entyrit," quod he,
"Gyf that sic maner of triumphe and cost   165
May do thame plesour, or eyß onto thy gost.
Bot thou, onsilly child, sa will of red,
Do comfort heirwith thy lamentabill ded,
That thou ourmatchit art and thus lyis slane
By the gretast Eneas handis twane."   170
Syne he hys feris can repreif and chyde
That thai sa lang delayt hym besyde,
Makand na haist to bair hys corps away;
And he hym self betwix hys armys tway
The ded body vplyftis fra the grond,   175
That with red blude of his new grene wond
Besparklyt had hys ʒallow lokis brycht,
That ayr war kemmyt and addressyt rycht.

132

Fra Meӡentius knew ӡong Lawsus deceß,
Hym to revenge his lyfe lost in the preß.

The meyn sesson, hys fader with his feris,
Down at the fludis syde of Tyberis,
Stanschit his wondis with watyr by and by,
Weschand the blude and swait from hys body.
Hys helm of steil besyde hym hang weil ne   5
Apon a grayn or branch of a grene tre;
Hys other weghty harneß, gud in neid,
Lay on the gyrß besyde hym in the meid;
Hys trasty chosyn verlettis hym abowt;
And he ful sor wondyt, all in dowt,   10
Stude lenand with hys wery nek and bonys,
Owt our a bowand tre, with sair gronys;
Hys weil kemmyt berd, hyngand ful straucht
Apon his breist, onto hys gyrdill raucht;
And feill tymys on Lawsus menys he,   15   f. 236ᵛ
Prayand full oft he mycht hym salfly se,
And mony messyngeris onto hym heß send,
To withdraw hym the feild, and to defend
That he abyde na langar in bargane
And schaw quhat sorow for hym hys fader had tane.   20
Bot than Lawsus ded owt of the feild
Hys wofull feris careit apon a scheild,
Wepand sa gret a man was brocht to grond,
And discumfyt with sa grysly a wond.
Meӡentius mynd and consait, the ilk tyde,   25
Suspekand the harmys quhilkis war betyde,
Onfar considerit the cauß of thar murnyng,
And on hys canos hair the dust gan slyng,
With mekill powdir fyland hys hasart hed;
And baith hys handis in that sammyn sted   30
Towart the hevin vphevis in a fary,
And he the goddis and starnys fast dyd wary;
Syne, lenand on hys sonnys corps, thus cryis:
"O my deir child and tendir get heir lyis!
Had I sa gret appetit and delyte   35
Onto this wrachit lyfe, sa ful of syte,
That I the sufferit to entyr in my sted
Vndre our fays hand, and with thy ded
My lyfe is salfit? Ha, I thy fader heir,
Quhilk the begat, my only son sa deir,   40
Suld I be salf and lyfand eftir the,
Throu tha sa grisly wondis that I se?
Allace, onto me, wrachit catyve thing,
Myne exill now at last and banysyng

133

Becummyn is hard and insufferabill! 45
The stound of deth, the panys lamentabill,
Is deip engravyn in my hart onsound;
Now am I smyttyn with the mortal wond!
I, the self man was the cauß of thy ded,
With my trespaß, my child, in euery sted 50
Filyt the glor and honour of thy name,
Thy hie renovn bespottand with my schame,
As I that was, by invy and haitrent
Of my awin pepill, with thar haill assent,
Expellit from my ceptre and my ryng, 55
And was adettyt, for my mysdoyng f. 237ʳ
Onto our cuntre, till haue sufferit pane:
I aucht and worthy was to haue bene slane,
And to haue ӡald this wikkyt sawle of myne
Be all maner of turment and of pyne, 60
Fortill amend myne offencis and fed.
Ha, now I lyf, allace, and thou art ded!
Ӡit want I not off men the cumpany,
Nowder lyght of lyfe, ne cleirneß of the sky,
Bot soyn I sal thame leif and part thar fra." 65
And sayand thus, sammyn with mynd ful thra
He rasyt hym vp apon hys wondit thee,
And determyt to revenge hym or de;
For thocht the violens of hys sair smart
Maid hym onfery, ӡit hys stalwart hart 70
And curage ondekeit was gude in neid.
He bad ga fech Rhebus, hys ryall steid,
Quhilk was hys wirschip and hys comfort haill,
And hys support hys fays to assaill;
For by this horß in euery gret iourne 75
Hame fra the feild victour eschapit he.
Quhamto Meӡentyus, but mair abaid,
Seand the steid drowpand and sad, thus said:
"Rhebus, we twa heß levit lang yfeir,
Gyf that to mortal wightis in this erd heir 80
Ony tyme may be reput lang," quod he.
"Owder this day beys thou revengear with me
Of Lawsus dolorus deith, and wrek our schame,
And sall as victour with the bryngyn hame
Ӡon bludy spulӡe, and Eneas hed; 85
Or, gif na fors nor strenth into that sted
Will suffir ony way that it be so,
We sal in feild sammyn de baith two.
For, O moist forcy steid, my lovyt foill,
I can na wyß beleif at thou may thoill 90
Tobe at ony otheris commandment,

Nor that the list dedeyn, gif I war schent,
Till obey ony master or lord Troiane."
And sayand thus, ful towartly onane
The steid bekend held to hys schulder plat,   95   f. 237ᵛ
And he at eyß apon hys bak doun sat,
And baith hys fystis fillyt with dartis keyn,
With helm on hed burnyst brycht and scheyn,
Abuf the quhilk hys tymbret buklyt was,
Lyke till a lokryt mayn with mony faß.   100
And into sik array with swyft curß he
Furth steris hys steid, and draif in the melle.
Deip in hys hart boldynnys the felloun schame,
Myxit with dolour, angir and defame;
The fervent luf of hys son ȝyng of age   105
Gan catchyng hym into the furyus rage;
Tharto alsso persuadis to the fyght
Hys forß weil knawin, hys hardyment and mycht;
And, in sik poynt, throw owt the rowtis all
With mychty voce thryß dyd Eneas call.   110
Eneas hard hym cry, and weil hym knew,
And glaid tharof can towartis hym persew,
And prayand says: "The fader of goddis hie,
And eik mychty Apollo, that grant to me,
Thou wald begyn in bargan on this land   115
To mell with me, and to meyt hand for hand."
Thus carpyt he, and with stern lance, but tary,
Furth steppys forto meyt hys aduersary.
Bot Meȝentius, seand hym cumand,
Cryit to hym onon and bad hym stand: 120
"O thou maist cruell aduersar," said he,
"Quhat wenys thou so to effray and bost me,
Sen thou my son haß me bereft this day,
Quhilk was only the maner and the way
Quharby thou myght ourcum me and distroy?   125
Now, sen that I haue tynt all warldis ioy,
Nowdyr I abhor the ded, to starve in fycht,
Nor rak I ocht of ony goddis mycht.
Desist, and ceß to bost me or mannaß,
For I am cum to de in this ilk plaß;   130
Bot first I bryng the thir rewardis," quod he.
With that word, at his fa a dart leyt fle,   f. 238ʳ
And efter that ane other haß he cast,
And syne ane other haß he fixit fast,
About hym prekand in a cumpaß large: 135
Bot all thir dyntis sustenyt the goldin targe.
Thryß on the left half fast, as he war wod,
About Eneas raid he quhar he stude,

135

Thik with hys handis swakkand dartis keyn;
And thryß this Troiane prynce our all the greyn,   140
Intil hyß stalwart stelyt scheild stikand owt,
Lyke a hair wod the dartis bair abowt.
At last, as he ennoyt of this deray,
This irksum traysyng, iowkyng and delay,
And cumryt wolx samony dartis invane   145
Thus oft to draw furth and to cast agane,
As he that was matchit that tyme, but faill,
With hys fa man in bargane inequale,
Quhilk ay was at avantage and onflocht,
Full mony thing revoluyt he in thocht;   150
Syne on that weirman ruschit he in teyn;
In the forhed, betwix the horsys eyn,
He kest hys speir with all his fors and mycht.
Vpstendis than the stalwart steid on hycht,
And with his helys flang vp in the ayr;   155
Down swakkis the knycht sone with a fellon fair,
Foundris fordwart flatlyngis on hys spald,
Ourquhelmyt the man, and can hys feit onfald.
Than the Latynys, and eik pepill Troianys,
The hevynnys dyndlit with a schowt at anys.   160
Eneas gyrd abufe hym with a braid,
Hynt furth hys swerd, and forthir thus he said:
"Quhar is he now, Meȝentius, sa stern?
Quhar is the ferß stowt curage of that bern?"
Quhamto Meȝentius, this ilk prynce Tyrrheyn,   165
Fra that he mycht alyftyn vp his eyn
To se the hevynnys licht, and draw hys braith,
And hys rycht mynd agane recoverit haith,
Thus answeris: "O thou dispituus fo,
Quharto me chydis thou reprochand so,   170
And mannancis me to the ded by and by?   f. 238ᵛ
Of my slauchter I think na villany,
Nor on sik wyß heir com I not in feild,
That I stand aw to swelt vnder my scheild;
Nor, I beleif, na frendschip in thy handis,   175
Nane syk trety of sawchnyng nor cunnandis,
My son Lawsus band vp with the, perfay.
Bot of a thyng I the beseik and pray,
Gif ony plesour may be grantit or beld
Till aduersaris, that lyis venquyst in feild;   180
That is to knaw, suffir my body haue
Ane sepultur, and with erd be bygrave.
I knaw abowt me standand in this sted
My folkis byttyr haitrent and gret feid:
Defend me from thar furour, I requeir,   185

And grant my corps, besyde my sonnys infeir,
Into sum tumbe entyrit for tobe."
And sayand thus, knawand at he most de,
Befor hys eyn persavyt the burnyst brand,
That throuch hys gorge went from Eneas hand;   190
Within hys armour, schortly to conclude,
Furth bruschit the sawle with gret stremys of blude.
Be this the son declynyt was almost,
So that the Latynys and Rutilian ost,
Quhat for the absens of thar duke Turnus,   195
And new slauchter of bald Meȝentius,
Withdrew thame to thar raset in affray,
And Troianys went onto thar rest quhil day.

Explicit liber decimus Eneados
Sequitur prologus in Vndecimum eiusdem

[The Proloug of the Elevint Buke]

Thow hie renown of Martis chevalry,   f. 239ʳ
 Quhilk gladis euery gentill wight to heir,
Gif thou mycht Mars and Hercules deify,
Quharfor beyn nobillys to follow prowes swer?
Weill auchtyn eldris exemplis ws to steir   5
Tyll hie curage, all honour till ensew:
Quhen we considir quhat wirschip tharof grew,
All vyce detest, and vertu lat ws leyr.

Prowes, but vyce, is provit lefull thyng
Be haly scriptur into syndry place,   10
Be Machabeus, Iosue, Dauid kyng.
Mychael, and eyk hys angellys full of grace,
That can the dragon furth of hevynnys chace
With vailȝeand dyntis of ferm myndis contrar,
Nane other strokis nor wapynnys had thai thar,   15
Nother speir, buge, pol ax, swerd, knyfe nor mace;

In takynnyng that in chevalry or fyght
Our myndis suld haue iust ententioun,
The grond of batale fundyt apon rycht;
Not for thou lyst to mak discentioun   20
To seik occasyons of contentioun,
Bot rype thy querrell, and discuß it plane:
Wrangis to reddreß suld wer be vndertane,
For na conquest, reif, skat nor pensioun.

137

To speke of moral vertuus hardyment, 25
Or raithar of dyvyne, is myne entent;
For warldly strenth is febill and impotent
In Goddis sight, and insufficient.
The Psalmyst says that God is not content
In mannys stalwart lymmys nor strenth of corß, 30
Bot into thame that trastis in hys forß,
Askand mercy, and dredand iugement.

Strang fortitud, quhilk hardyment cleip we, f. 239ᵛ
Abuf the quhilk the vertu souerane
Accordyng pryncis, hecht magnanymyte, 35
Is a bonte set betwix vicis twane:
Of quham fuyl hardynes clepit is the tane,
That vndertakis all perrellis but avice;
The tother is namyt schamefull cowardyce,
Voyd of curage, and dolf as ony stane. 40

The first is hardy all owt by mesur,
Of tyme nor rayson gevis he na cuyr,
No dowt he castis, bot all thinkis suyr,
Nocht may he suffir, nor hys heit endur;
The tother is of all prowes sa puyr, 45
That evir he standis in feir and felloun dreid,
And nevir dar vndertake a douchty deid,
Bot doith all curage and all manheid smuyr.

The first soundis towart vertu sum deill,
Hardy he is, couth he be avyse; 50
Of hardyment the tother haß na feill:
Quhou may curage and cowardys agre?
Of fortitud to compt ʒou euery gre,
As Arestotill in hys Ethikis doith expreß,
It wald, as now, conteyn our lang proceß; 55
Quharfor of other chevalry carp will we.

Gyf Crystis faithfull knychtis lyst ws be,
So as we aucht, and promyst heß at font,
Than mon we byd baldly, and neuer fle,
Nowder be abasyt, tepyt nor ʒit blunt, 60
Nor as cowartis to eschew the first dunt.
Pawle witnessith, that nane sall wyn the crown,
Bot he quhilk dewly makis hym reddy bown
To stand wightly, and feght in the forfront.

And quha that sall nocht wyn the crown of meid, 65 f. 240ʳ
That is to say, the euerlestand blyß,

138

The fyre eternall neidlyngis most thai dreid:
For Cryst into his gospell says, I wyß,
Quha bydis nocht with me contrar me is;
And gif thou be aganyst God, but weir   70
Than art thou wageour onto Lucifer.
God salf ws all from sik a syre as this!

The armour of our chevalry, perfay,
So the Apostyll techit ws expreß,
Not corporall bot sperituall beyn thai,   75
Our conquyst haill, our vassellage and prowes,
Aganyst spretis and pryncis of myrknes;
Not agane man, owr awyn brother and mait,
Nor ȝit aganyst our makar to debait,
As rabell tyll all vertu and gudneß.   80

The flesch debatis aganys the spiritual gost,
Hys hie curage with sensual lust to law,
And, be the body victor, baith ar lost;
The spreit wald vp, the corß ay down list draw:
Thy secund fa the warld, ane other thraw,   85
Makis strang assaltis of covatyß and estait,
Aganyst quham is full perrellus debait;
Thir fays famyliar beyn full quaynt to knaw.

Lyff in thy flesch as master of thy corps,
Lyf in this warld as nocht ay to remane;   90
Resist the fendis slycht with all thy forß,
He is thy ancyent ennemy, werst of ane;
A thousand wylys he heß, and mony a trane,
He kendillis oft thy flesch in byrnand heit,
He causys wrachit plesans seym full sweit,   95
And, for nocht, of this fals warld makis the fane.

He is thy fa and aduersar principall,   f. 240ᵛ
Of promyssioun wald the expell the land,
For he the sammyn lost, and caucht a fall;
Enfors the strangly contrar hym to stand.   100
Rayß hie the targe of faith vp in thy hand,
On hed the halsum helm of hoip onlace,
In cheryte thy body all embrace,
And of devoit oryson mak thy brand.

Stand at defens, and schrynk not for a schor;   105
Thynk on the haly marthyris at ar went,
Thynk on the payn of hell, and endleß glor,
Thynk quhou thy Lord for the on rude was rent,

139

Thynk, and thou fle fra hym, than art thou schent,
Thynk all thou sufferis ontyll hys paynis nocht is,   110
Thynk with quhou precyus pryce as thi sawll bocht is,
And ay the moder of grace in mynd enprent.

Feill beyn thy fays, fers and full of slycht,
Bot be thou stalwart campioun and knycht;
In feild of grace with forsaid armour brycht   115
Thou may debait thame lyghtly in ilk fyght:
For of fre will thyne acton is sa wight
Nane may it perß, wilt thou resist and stand;
Becum thow cowart, crawdoun recryand,
And by consent cry cok, thy ded is dycht.   120

Thynk quhou that fa is waik and impotent,
May venquyß nane bot thame lyst be ourcum;
He sall the nevir ourset, but thy consent.
Eith is defens to say nay, or be dum;
And for thy weill, lo, thys is all and sum: 125
Consent nevir, and thou sall nevir be lost,
By disassent thou may venquys ane ost,
And, for anys ʒa, tyne thy meid euery crum.

Na wondir is, for by exempill we se,   f. 241ʳ
Quha servys hys souerane intill all degre   130
Full mony days, and efter syne gif he
Commyttis anys trayson, suld he nocht de,
Leß than hys prynce, of gret humanyte,
Pardoun hys falt for hys lang trew seruys,
Gyf he wald mercy craif? The sammyn wyß   135
We beyn forgevyn, so that repent will we.

Bot quhat avalys begyn a strang melle,
Syne ʒeld the to thy fa, but ony quhy,
Or cowartly to tak the bak and fle?
Na, thar sall nane optene hie victory,   140
Leß thai sustene the bargane dowchtely;
And quha so perseueris to the end
Ane conquerour and campioun euer is kend,
With palm of triumphe, honour and glory.

The maist onsilly kynd of forton is   145
To haue beyn happy; Boetius techis so;
As, to haue beyn in welth and hartis blyß,
And now tobe dekeit and in wo:
Richt so, quha vertuus was, and fallys tharfro,
Of verray rayson malewrus hait is he;   150

140

And ȝit, by grace and hys fre volunte,
He may recovir meryt agane alsso.

I say "be grace", for quhen thou art in grace,
Thou may eik grace to grace, ay mor and mor;
Bot quhen thou fallys be syn tharfra, allace,   155
Of thy meryt thou gettis hyr nevirmor;
ȝit quhen thou dewly disponys the tharfor,
Doand all that in the thar may be done,
Of hys gudnes the etern Lord alssone
Restorys the meryt, with grace in arlys of glor.   160

Haill thy meryt thou had tofor thy fall,   f. 241ᵛ
That is to say, thy warkis meritabill,
Restorit ar agane baith gret and small
And grace tharto, quhilk is sa profitabill
That thou tharby to eik meryt art habill;   165
Bot nocht ilk gre of grace thou had befor;
That gettis thou not sa soyn, quhill forthyrmor:
Be war tharfor, fall not, bot standis stabill.

For lyke as quha offendit had hys lord,
That lang tofor hys trew servand had bene,   170
And syne agane becumis at ane accord
With hys master, all thocht hys lord wald meyn
On hys ald seruyce, ȝit netheleß, I weyn
He sall nocht soyn be tendir, as he was ayr:
Be war tharwith, and kepe ȝou fra the snair,   175
Tyne nocht ȝour laubour and ȝour thank betweyn.

Exempill takis of this prynce Ene,
That, for hys fatale cuntre of behest,
Sa feill dangeris sustenyt on land and see,
Syk stryfe in stour sa oft with speir in rest,   180
Quhill he hys realm conquest bath west and est:
Sen all this dyd he for a temporall ryng,
Preß ws to wyn the kynryk ay lestyng,
Addreß ws fast fortill opteyn that fest.

He may be callyt, as says Sanct Augustyn,   185
Ane delicat, owr esy, Crystyn knycht,
Refusys to thoill traval, sturt or pyne,
And but debait wenys till optene the fycht.
To wyn the feild, and nevir preif thy mycht,
That war nyce thyng! Thy kyng Cryste in batell   190
Quhat sufferit he for the, O catyve wight?
Lyis thou at eyß, thy prynce in bargane fell?

Aschamys of our sleutht and cowardyce!   f. 242^r
Seand thir gentyles and the paganys ald
Ensew vertu, and eschew euery vyce,   195
And for sa schort renown warryn so bald
To susteyn weir and panys teyr ontald;
Than lat ws stryve that realm forto posseid,
The quhilk was hecht till Abraham and hys seyd;
Lord, at ws wrocht and bocht, grant ws that hald! etc.   200

Explicit prologus
Sequitur liber vndecimus

Eftir the feild Enee maid sacrifyce,
Offerand the spulȝe to Mars, as was the gyß.   C. i

Duryng this quhile, furth of the sey dyd spryng
  The fresch Aurora with the brycht dawyng.
Ene, albeyt hys hasty thochtfull curis
Constrenyt hym, as twychyng sepulturis
Of hys folkis now slane and berying,   5
Forto provide a tyme mast accordyng,
And gretly eik in mynd he trublyt was
For the slauchtyr and ded corps of Pallas;
Ȝit netheleß, as first the son vpsprent,
Scheddyng hys bemys in the orient,   10
As victor he onto the goddis als tyte
With sacryfyce can hys vowys acquyte.
Ane akyn tre, was huge gret and squar,
The branschis sned and kut abowt alquhar,
Apon a motys hycht vpset haß he,   15
And all with schynand armour cled the tre;
The coyt armour and spulȝe tharon hang
Of Meȝentius, the vailȝeand campion strang;
To the, gret god of stryfe, armypotent,
In syng of trophe tharon was vpstent   20
Hys cryst and hewmet all besprent with blude,
The brokyn trunschions of hys speris rude,
And hys fyne hawbryk, with speir, swerd and macis,
Assayt and persyt into twyß sax placis;
Hys stelyt scheild dyd on the left syde hyng;   25   f. 242^v
Abowt hys gorget, or hys nek armyng,
Was hung hys swerd with evor scawbart fyne.
And thus exortis Ene hys ferys syne,
The chiftanys all abowt hym lowkyt war,
Quhilk glaidsum warryn of this ioyus fair: 30
"O douchty men," quod he, "worthy in weris,
The grettast part of our warkis and afferis

142

Beyn endit now, sa that in tyme cummyng
All feir and dreid ar passyt of ony thyng:
Thir bene the spulȝe and first weirly weid　　　　　　　35
Reft from the prowd kyng be my handis in deid;
Lo, heir Meȝentius venquyst lyis doun bet.
Now to the wallys of Lawrent and the ȝet
The way is maid to Kyng Latyn to wend.
Tharfor addreß ȝour myndis, and attend　　　　　　　40
To armys and to weirfar euery ane,
Provydand in ȝour consatis for bargane;
So that ȝhe reddy be, and na delay
May stoppyn ȝou, nor stunnys ane other day,
Be ȝour awyn sleuth, for lak of gude forsycht,　　　　45
Gif ȝe onwarnyst beys callyt to the fycht.
Alssone as fyrst the goddis omnipotent
By sum sygnys or takyn lyst consent
The ensenȝeis and baneris be vphynt,
And all the ȝongkeris meyt for swerdis dynt,　　　　　50
Of thar tentis convoyt in array,
Se ȝhe all reddy be than, but delay.
And in the meyn quhile, lat ws to erd haue
The corpsys of our fallowys onbegrave,
Quhilk only honour is haldyn in daynte　　　　　　　55
At Acheron, the lawest hellys see.
Paß on," he said, "tha sawlys valȝeent,
Quhilk, with habundans of thar blud besprent,
Haß conquyst ws this realm apon sik wyß,
Do honour with thar funeral servys,　　　　　　　　60
And wirschip with thar finale last rewardis.
Bot first, befor all corpsis of tha lardis,
Ontill Evandrys dolorus cite
Of ȝong Pallas the body send mon we,
Quham, wantand na vertu nor prowes,　　　　　　　65
The wofull day heß ws byreft expreß,　　　　　　　　f. 243ʳ
And with a wofull slauchter caucht, allace!"
Thus said he, wepand salt terys our hys face;
Syne tuke hys vayage towart the ilk sted
Quhar Pallas lyfleß corps was lyggand ded;　　　　　70
Quham ancyent Acetes thar dyd kepe,
With flottyryt berd of terys all beweip;
The quhilk Acetes had tofor ybe
Squyer to Kyng Evander, from the cite
Of Parrha cummyn into Arcady,　　　　　　　　　　75
And at thys tyme was send in cumpany
With hys deir fostyr child he had in cur,
Bot not, as ayr, with happy aventur.
About the corps alhaill the multitud

143

Of servyturis and Troiane commonys stud,   80
And dolorus Phrigyane wemen, on thar gyß,
With hair down schaik, and petuus spraichis and cryis.
Bot, fra that enterit was Eneas bald
Within the portis of that large hald,
A huge clamour thai rasyt and womentyng,   85
Betand thar brestis quhill all the lyft dyd ryng;
So lowd thar wofull bewalyng habundis
That all the palyce dynnys and resoundis.
Thys prynce hym self, fra that he dyd behald
The snaw quhite vissage of this Pallas bald,   90
Hys hed vphald, mycht nocht the self sustene,
And eik the gapand dedly wond heß sene,
Maid by the sperys hed Rutilyane
Amyd hys sneith and fair slekyt breist bane,
With terys brystand from hys eyn, thus plenyt: 95
"O douchty child, maist worthy tobe menyt,
Haß fortoun me envyit sa far that, eft
Our weill is cummyn, thus thou art me bereft,
Sa that thou suld not se our ryng," said he,
"Nor 3it as victor with prosperyte   100
Onto thy faderis cite hame retour?
Syk promyß hecht I not the lattir hour
To thy fader Evandrus, quhen that he
At my departyng last embrasyt me,
And send me to conquyß a large empyre;   105   f. 243ᵛ
And, dredand eyk for the, that lordly syre
Vs monyst tobe war and avyse,
Becauß the men quhamwith to do had we
War bald and stern; said we had wer at hand
With bustuus folk that weill in stryfe durst stand.   110
Now, certis, he levand in hoip, invane,
For thy prosper returnyng haym agane
Perchans doith mak prayer and offerandis,
Chargand the altaris oft with hys awyn handis:
Bot we hys lyfleß child, quhilk aw na thyng   115
Onto the goddis of the hevynly ryng,
With womentyng heir menand tendyrly,
And vayn honour, accumpaneis by and by.
O fey onhappy kyng Archadian!
Now thy sonnys ded corps crewelly slane   120
Thou salbehald: allace, the panys strang!
This is our haymcom thou desyrit lang;
This salbe our triumphe thou lang abaid,
To se thy a son on hys beir tre laid!
Ha, quhat, is this my promyß and gret faith?   125
Bot, O Evander, beys not with me wraith;

Thou sall not se thy son was dryve abak
With schamefull wondis that he caucht in the bak;
Ne thou hys fader, war he alyve this day,
Suld nevir haue lak of hym, ne for hym pray   130
For hys desert he deit a schamefull deth;
And now with honour heß he ʒald the breth.
Bot, netheleß, quhat harm, ful ways me!
Quhou large support, hey, quhat beld or supple
In hym heß tynt Ausonya the ryng,   135
And quhou gret deill heß lost Ascanyus ʒyng!"

ʒong Pallas corps is till Evander sent, With all honour accordyng hys tyrment.

Quhen he bewalyt had on this maner,
This wofull corps he bad do lyft on beir,
And with hym send a thousand men in hy
Walyt of euery rowt and cumpany,
Forto convoy and do hym falloschip   5
At hys last honour and funeral wirschip,

And tobe present at the lamentyng
Of hys fader, to comfort hys murnyng;
Thocht smal solace was that to hys regrait,
Quhilk was sa huge, bot to hys estait   10
Accordit weill that sik thingis suld be,
Quhen all wightis mycht rew on hym to se.
Sum of Eneas ferys bissely
Flakis to plet thame presys by and by,
And of small wikkyris fortobeld a beir   15
Of sowpill wandis and of bronys seir,
Bund with the syonys or the twystis sle
Of small rammell or stobys of akyn tre.
Thyr beddis beldyt, or funeral lytteris,
Syk tumbys as for ded corpß efferis,   20
With greyn burgionys and branschys fair and weill
Thai gan ourheld, and stentys euery deill:
Amyd the quhilkis, of blumys apon a byng
Strowyt full hie, thai laid this Pallas ʒyng;
Lyggyn tharon als semly forto se   25
As is the fresch flowris schynand bewte,
Newly pullyt vp from hys stalkis smaill
With tendyr fyngeris of the damysaill,
Or the soft violet that doys freschly schyne,
Or than the purpour flour, hayt iacynthyne;   30
Quham all thocht the erth hys moder with sap
Hym nurys not, nor comfortis on hir lap,
ʒyt than hys schene cullour and figur glaid

Is not all went, nor hys bewte defaid.
Eneas syne twa robbys furth gart fold   35
Of rych purpour and styf burd of gold
Quhilk vmquhil Dydo, quheyn of Sydones,
Of sik laubour full byssy tho, I geß,
As at that tyme to pleß hym wonder glaid,
With hir awyn handis to hym wrocht and maid,   40
Wovyn full weill, and brusyt as rych wedis,
Of costly stuf and subtell goldyn thredis;
And with the tane of thir full dolorusly
Eneas cled the ȝyng Pallas body,
Tobe hys finall and hys last honour;   45   f. 244ᵛ
Hys lokkis and hys harys the self hour,
Quhilkis war forto be brynt in assys cald,
Into the tother habyt dyd he fald.
Abuf all thys, rewardis mony ane,
Yconquest in this batall Lawrentane,   50
In haill hepys with hym heß he send,
And bad thai suld tak gud kepe and attend
To leid the pray per ordour pompusly.
Feill horssys als he gaue thame by and by,
With wapynnys eik, and other precyus geir,   55
That he had reft hys fa men in the weir;
The presoneris alsso, quham he had tak,
He sent with handis bund behynd thar bak,
Quhilkis, at the obsequeis or entyrment,
To the infernal gostis suldbe sent,   60
And with thar bludis sched, as was the gyß,
The funerall flambe strynkyll in sacrifyß.
He bad the capitanys and the dukis all,
In syng of trophe or pomp triumphall,
Gret perkis bair or treyn saplyng that squair is,   65
Cled with the armour of thar aduersaris,
To wryte and hyng tharon baith all and sum
The namys of thar ennemyß ourcum.
Furth led was the onsilly Acetes,
Ourset with age, and sorow mycht nocht ceß;   70
Now bludyand hys awyn breist with hys fystis,
Now with hys nalys hys face rentis and brystis,
And oft down fallys spaldit on the erd,
With mony gowl, and a full petuus rerd.
And furth war led rych cartis for the nanys,   75
Besprent with blude of the Rutylianys.
And eftir com Aethon, hys werly steid,
Dispulȝeit of hys harnessyng and weid;
Wepand he went for wo, men mycht haue seyn
With gret terys floddyrrit hys face and eyn.   80

146

Ane bair hys helm, ane other bair hys speir;
For the remanys of hys harneß and geir,
Syk as hys rych gyrdill and cotarmour,
Turnus victor byreft hym in the stour.
Furth haldis syne the drery cumpany 85
Of Troianys, and Tyrrheyn dukis thame by;
And wofull Archadis, in syng of dolour, weris
Scheldis reversyt, and doun turnyt thar speris.
And efter that, per ordour, by and by,
Thai beyn furth passyt euery cumpany, 90
Eneas tho can styntyng and abaid,
And with a petuus regrait thus he said:
"The horribill batellys of thir sammyn weris
Tyll otheris funerall womentyng and terys
Callys ws from thens; we may nocht follow the, 95
Thyne entyrment forto behald and se.
Adew for ay, Pallas, beluffyt best,
Fair weill for evyr intill eternall rest!"
Na mair he said, bot went towart New Troy,
Entrand tharin with terys of ennoy. 100

Quhou Eneas onto the Latynys gave
Twelf days of respyt the ded corpsis to grave. C. iii

Be this war cum fra Kyng Latynys cyte
Ambassatouris, with branch of olyve tre,
Besekand favouris and benevolens;
That he wald suffir tobe careyt from thens
Tha corpsys ded, quhilkis on the feldis broun 5
Lay strowyt heir and thar, with swerd bet down,
And thame restor agane of hys gentre,
To suffyr thame begravyn fortobe;
Assuryng hym, thar mycht be led na weir
On venquyst folkis, that lyfleß mycht not steir, 10
And prayt spair thar pepill at syk myschans,
Quhylum clepyt hys frendis and acquentans.
Quhen that Eneas, heynd, curtaß and gud,
Thar peticioun sa ressonabill vndirstud,
As man that was fulfillyt of bonte, 15
Thar hail desyre full glaidly grantit he,
And forthir eik onto thame thus he said:
"O Latyn folkis, quhat mysfortoun onglaid
Haß ȝou involuyt in sa onhappy weir
That ȝhe chayß ws away, ȝour frendis deir? 20
Desyre ȝhe paix bot for thame that bene lost
By marcyall fayt, and slane into this ost?
And I, forsuyth, tyll all that levand be

147

Wald glaidly grant the sammyn, I say for me.
Neuer hyddyr had I cummyn, wer not, perfay,   25
Into this sted the fatys hecht for ay
Our restyng place providit and herbry;
Ne na weirfar with ȝour pepill led I.
Bot ȝour kyng haß our confiderans vpgeif,
And rather heß settyn all hys beleif   30
On Turnus vassalage and his hie prowes;
Thocht mor equale and ganand war, I geß,
To this Turnus, the brekar of our paix,
Till aventour hym self to de in preß.
Gif he pretendis in batale with a brand   35
To end the weir, or Troianys of this land
Forto expell, heir semyt hym vnder scheild
With wapynnys to recontre me in feild,
That nane bot ane of ws war left levand,
Quhais lyfe God lyst withhald, or hys rycht hand.   40
Now haldis on, and all the lyfleß banys
And corpsis of ȝour wofull citeȝanys
Do byrn and bery efter ȝour awyn gyß,"
Says Eneas, the Troiane war and wyß.
Than of hys speche so awondrit war thai,   45
Kepit thar silens, and wist nocht quhat to say;
And athir towartis otheris turnys, but mayr,
And can behald his fallow in a stair.
The eldast man amang thame, finaly,
Clepyt Drances, that had full gret envy   50
At ȝyng Turnus, all way to hym infest
For ald malyce or of cryme manyfest,
Begouth to speke and ansuer thus agane:
"O huge gret is thy fame, thou duke Troiane,
Bot far grettar all owt we may aspy   55
Thy dedis of armys and thy chevalry;
With quhat lovyngis equaill may I compair
The to the goddis in hevyn abuf the ayr?
Quhidder sall I fyrst extoll, and wonder in the,   f. 246ʳ
Thy gret gentryce and sa iust equyte,   60
Or thy gret fors and laubour bellicall?
Glaidly, forsuyth, now haymwart bair we sall
Ontill our natyve bundis and cite
Thir sa gret sygnys of humanyte:
And, gif that ony chanß can fynd the way,   65
We sall do fully all that evir we may
The to conione with Kyng Latyn in hy:
Lat Turnus quhar hym list go seik ally.
And forthir eik weil lykis ws at all
To help till rayß this fatale massy wall,   70

148

And fortober apon our schuldris war ioy
Thir stonys gret to this new wark of Troy."
Thus said Drances, and all the remanent
Tharto annerdis with haill voce and consent.
Twelf days of trewys thai band, to stanch debait,   75
Forto kepe paix, and werys sequestrat;
Than throu the woddis and thir holtis hie
Troianys and Latynys sammyn, he and he,
Quhar so thame list, wandris but danger.
The heich eschis soundis thar and heir   80
For dyntis rude of the scharp stelyt ax;
Down weltit ar with mony granand strakis
The fyrrys rekand to the sternys on hie;
The mekill syllis of the warryn tre
With weggis and with proppis beyn devyd;   85
The strang gustand cedyr is al to schyde;
Ne ceß thai not apon the iargand wanys
The gret akys to turß away atanys.

The kyng Evander complenyt sor and wareit,
Quhen his son Pallas ded was to hym careit.   C. iv

Than Fame with this, alsfast as scho mycht spryng,
As messynger of sa gret womentyng,
Flaw furth, and all with murnyng fillys sche
Evander kyng hys palyce and cyte,
Quhilk layt tofor had schawyn that Pallas   5
In Latyum landis sa victoryus was;
Now says sche, "Lo, is he brocht on heir!"   f. 246ᵛ
The Archadis ruschit to the portis in feir,
And euery wyght in handis hynt als tyte
Ane hait fyre broynd, efter the ald ryte,   10
In lang ordour and rabill, that all the stretis
Of schynand flambys lemys brycht and gletis,
Quhil all the large feildis of the light
Myght seueraly be raknyt at a sight.
The Troiane rowtis, on the tother hand,   15
With thame adionys thar folkis sair wepand,
Quham as the matronys beheld on sik wyß
So duylfully wend to the kyngis palys,
The dolorus town in euery streit and way
With petuus scrykis and gowlyng fyllit thai.   20
Than was na fors Evander mycht refreyn,
Bot in amyddis thame with gret disdene
He ruschis, plenand on wofull maner,
And fell on growf abuf ded Pallas beir,
Wepand and waland as his hart wald breke;   25

Embrasyt hym, bot no word mycht he spek
And scars at last with gret difficulte
The cundytis of his voce war lowsyt fre.
Quhen he mycht speke, than thir hys wordis was:
"This is nocht thy last cunnand, son Pallas,   30
Thou promyst not so vnto thy fader deir,
Bot at thou suld paß mair warly in weir,
And not in danger of the cruell Mart.
Owr weill I wist, with harmys at my hart,
Quhat aventour, and of quhou mekill mycht   35
Till ony ʒong man, the first feld in fight,
Was gret desire of new loif or glory,
And how sweit was renown of chevalry.
Allace, the first commancement and assays
To ʒyng men beyn in weir full fey always,   40
And rycht hard bene the first entechment
Of hasty batall to thame beyn not acquent.
My vowys nor my prayeris gret and small
War not accept to nane of goddis all.
O thou my blissyt spowß, decessit or now,   45   f. 247ʳ
Full happy of that ded in faith was thou,
That to thys sorow not preservyt was!
Bot be the contrar I, allace, allace,
Ourlevit haß my fatys profitabill,
And am alyve as fader miserabill;   50
Quham wald God in ʒon sammyn mortale weris
Rutilyanys had ourquhelmyt with thar speris,
That, followand to the feild my feris of Troy,
I mycht haue ʒald this sawle full of ennoy,
So that this funeral pomp, quhilk heir is wrocht,   55
My body, and nocht Pallas, hame had brocht!
Ne byd I nocht ʒou, Troianys, to argew
Of amyte and allyance bund of new,
Ne our rycht handis and promyß, quhilkis we
In frendschip knyt and hospitalyte: 60
This mysfortoun is myne of ald thirlage,
As tharto detbund in my wrachit age.
Bot had this hasty ded, sa ondigest,
Haue sufferit bot my son a stound to lest,
Quhill of Rutilianys he had slane thousandis,   65
And investit the Troianys in thar landis,
That is to say, in Latyum or Lavyn,
Weill lykyt me that he had endyt syne.
And forthir eik, Pallas, my son so deir,
Na mair rychly cowth I the lay on beir,   70
Nor with mair wirschip list me entyre the,
Than is providit be reuthfull Enee,

Be myghty Troianys and pryncis Tyrrheyn;
For all the Tuscane menȝe, as heir is seyn,
Gret trophe and rich spulȝe hydder bryngis,   75
On perkis rychly cled with thar armyngis
Quham thy richt hand in feild had put to ded.
Bot, O thou Turnus, in this sammyn sted
Amangis otheris heir suld thou haue be,
In form and maner of a stok of tre,   80
Gyf ȝhe of age had beyn equale and perys,
And baith elyke cummyn to ȝour strenthy ȝheris.
Bot now, allace, I, fey onhappy wight,   f. 247ᵛ
Quharto delay I Troianys from the fyght?
Paß haym in haist, and remember to say   85
Thir my desiris to ȝour prynce, I ȝou pray:
Evander says that thy ryght hand, Ene,
Is all the cawß that he delays to de,
Or that this haitsum lyfe sustene he wald,
Sen now is lost hys son Pallas the bald: 90
Sa till hym that he oblist is of det,
Baith to the son and the fader, to set
ȝon Turnus slauchter for owr recompens:
To the Eneas only, but offens,
And to fortoun, remanys this iournay ȝit,   95
Quharwith thou may thankfully be acquyt.
Tell hym, na lust to lyf langar seyk I;
Onlesum war syk plesour I set by;
Bot for a thraw desyre I to lest heir,
Turnus slauchter and deth with me to beir,   100
As glaid tithandis onto my child and barn,
Amang the gostis law in skowgis dern."

Heir athir party takis byssy cuyr
The ded bodeis to graif in sepultur.   C. v

The meyn sesson Aurora rasyt hir lycht,
Richt confortabill for euery mortall wight,
Rendryng agane the oportunyte
Of laubour and of wyrkyng, as we se.
The prynce Eneas, and the kyng Tarchon,   5
Gret byngis haß of treys mony one
Vpbeldyt, by the bowand costis bay.
Thydder euery ane dyd cary, but delay,
Efter thar eldris gyß, onto that sted
The corpsis of thar frendis that war ded,   10
As fortodo thar observans of det;
And thar vnder the smoky fyre haß set,
Quhill that the hevynnys hye dyd walxin dirk,

Involuyt with the reky stewys myrk.
And thryß on fut all sammyn euery man 15
In schynand armour abowt the fyris ran, f. 248ʳ
And thryß the wofull funerall inglys thai
Circulyt abowt on horsbak in array,
With gowlyng and with vocis myserabill;
Quhill that of trigland terys lamentabill 20
The feildis strowyt war in euery place,
Armouris all wet with wepyng, and thar face.
The clamour of the men and trumpys stevyn
Gan spryngyng vp on hight onto the hevyn.
Syne cumis sum, and in the fyre dyd slyng 25
The weirly wedis, spulʒe and armyng
Rent from the Latynys slane into the weir,
As helmys, scheildis, and rych swerdis seir,
Brydillys, and all thir stedis trappouris fair,
The hasty hurland charyot quhelys squair; 30
And other sum kest in the fyre syk geir
As weilbekend the corps was wont to weir,
Thar awyn wapynnys, and thar onsilly scheildis,
Quhilk mycht thame nocht defend into the feildis.
Full mony carcage of thir oxin gret 35
Abowt the fyris war brytnyt and downbet,
And bustuus bowkis of the byrsyt swyne,
Our feildis all byreft from euery hyne;
Thai steik the beistis, and swakkis in the fyre,
Endlang the costis all tho byrnand schyre; 40
And can behald quhou that thar feris brynt,
Observand weill the gledis half owt quent,
And eik the assys half brynt of the ded;
Ne may thai thens be harlyt of that sted,
Quhill at the hevyn ourquhelmyt the dirk nycht, 45
That ganand is for fyry sternys brycht.
And, netheleß, the Latynys lamentabill
In placis seir fyris innumerabill
Vpbeldit haß, and sum with wofull rerd
Feill corpsis deip bedelvys vnder erd; 50
And sum alsso in cartis haue thai sent
To townys in the feildis adiacent;
And sum alsso war send to the cite,
Tobe entyrit as thame accordyt be.
The remanent all sammyn assemlyt ourane, 55 f. 248ᵛ
But numbyr and but ordour, euery ane,
Of corpsys slane in huge heip byrn thai;
And thus on athir sydis, the hie way
And large feildis dyd oft of fyris schyne.
As that the thryd days lycht eftir syne 60

152

The dyrk nycht removyt from the sky,
The assys deip, murnand with mony a cry
Doun dyd thai cast, and scrapis owt atanys
The hait amyrris and the byrslyt banys;
And ȝit all warm, onculyt, sone thai haue   65
Bedelvyn thame, and in the erd begrave.
Bot, certis, than renewys the womentyng
Within the mychty burgh of Latyn kyng,
The rumour rayß and murmour principaly
Of bewalyng all owt the maist party.   70
The wofull moderis and matronys wepis heir,
The eldmoderis, and eyk the systeris deir
Thar mycht be hard with duylfull breistis greyt,
The ȝyng babbys walyng on the streyt,
That had thar faderis slane this hynder day,   75
Cryand, "Ichane, allace, and weill away!"
Thai curß and wary fast this vengeabill weir,
And Turnus wedlok bannys with mony a teir:
All in a voce thai cry, desirand hee
Suld ondertak the batall and melle,   80
And feght allane to mak end of this thyng,
As he the quhilk pretendis to weld the ryng
Of Italy with honour pryncipall,
Desyrand that he suldbe lord of all.
The brym Drances aggregis weill this thyng,   85
And buyr on hand baldly befor the kyng
Nane bot this Turnus challance wald Enee,
Turnus only to feght desyris he.
And, be the contrar, mony sensymentis
For Turnus schawys evident argumentis: 90
Of Queyn Amatha the gret authoryte
Dekkis and defendis hym with wordis sle;
And hys gret fame and actis triumphall
Hys querrell dyd susteyn agane thame all.   f. 249[r]

Befor Kyng Latyn and hys consale in deid
Venulus schawis responß of Diomeid.   C. vi

A buf all this, lo, the ilk stound onon
  Thyr messyngeris, all trist and wobegon,
Returnyt haymwart into thar maist neid
From the gret cite of Schir Dyomed,
Reportand answer, that alhaill was lost   5
Thar lang travale and maist sumptuus cost;
Schortly, thai had doyn thar na thyng at docht,
The rych gyftis nor gold avalyt nocht,
For all thar large requestis and prayeris;

To help the Latyn pepill in thar weris   10
Behuffyt thame to seik other supple,
Or to mak paix with Troiane prynce Ene.
Herand thir wordis, this ald Latyn kyng
Falys all curage, with gret lamentyng,
For patently the goddis wraik, hym thocht,   15
Schew that by fait Ene was thyddir brocht,
And manifest mycht of goddis hym dyd sustene,
That schew the new gravys befor thar eyn.
Quharfor, a gret consale assemlys he,
And callys the cheif ledaris of hys menȝe,   20
Chargeand thai suld in hys palyce conveyn.
Onto the riall chymmyß tho bedeyn
Thai flok so fast that euery way was hyd.
Thys ancyent kyng dyd set hym dovn amyd
The cepturyt men, as first and pryncipall,   25
Bot no thyng semyng glaid of cheir at all.
Than the ambassat, that was returnyt agane
From Dyomedis cite Etholiane,
He bad do schaw the credens that thai brocht,
Per ordour haill thar answer, faland nocht.   30
Silens was maid, ilk man hys tong held than,
And Venulus, of thame the gretast man,
Begouth fortill obey the kyngis charge,
And schew hys credens planly thus at large:
"O citeȝanys, we haue visseit Diomed,   35
And seyn thai strenthys by thame of Arge in deid
Vpbeldyt in the boundis of Italy;   f. 249ᵛ
The ways thiddir we haue met by and by,
And eschapyt all dangeris by the gait,
All thocht our iournay was nocht fortunait.   40
We haue twichit that sammyn douchty hand
By quham of Troy distroyt was town and land;
Quhilk now as victor, in the feildis plane
Besyde the skyrtis of the mont Gargane,
Within boundis of Iapigya sulȝe,   45
That now on days Apulȝe clepyng we,
Vprasyt heß the cite Argyripas,
Quham fra hys natyve pepill namyt he was.
Fra that we entryt war in hys presens,
And forto speke was geif ws audiens,   50
The gyftis and rewardys present we;
Our credens, our estait, and our cuntre,
Declaryt plane, and quha with wer ws socht,
And quhat occasioun had ws thidder brocht.
He hard ws weill, and on a frendly wyß   55
Thus answer maid with wordis war and wyß:

154

'O fortunat folk, quhar Saturn regnyt swa,
3he ancyent pepill of Ausonya,
Quhat mysaventour and onkyndly heyt
3ou steris from 3our lang rest and quyet, 60
Prouocand 3ou to movyng, rayß and steir
Sa peralus, onkowth and onthrifty wer?
For euery ane of ws that dyd offens
In Troys bundis with swerd and violens,
Or cruell handis set fortill invaid 65
Kyng Priamus, and of hys realm degraid
(I leif ontald all thai that in the feld
By Troys wallys heß swelt vnder scheld,
Or that the flude of Symois by the town
Drownyt in stremys warpis vp and dovn), 70
Our all the warld of ws hail the remanys
Beyn punyst sor with onrehersabill panys,
And sufferit heß all maner of turment.
Ful weill knawis my wordis, quhat I ment,
The sorofull constillatioun of Mynerve, 75
Quhilk causyt mony douchty man to sterve;
And on the costis of Euboica
The rokis beris witneß 3it alssua,
And the montane Caphareus, God woit, f. 250ʳ
That vengeans tuke and wraik apon our floyt. 80
From that weirfar and cursyt chevalry
We cachyt ar to syndry costis, far by
Our natyve bundis and ald heritage.
Lo, Menelay, ane of the cheif barnage
And Atrius son, yclepyt Atrydes, 85
To Protheus pillaris, hait Pyramydes,
Constrenyt is in exill forto wend;
Vlixes alsso, as full weill is kend,
Bewavyt is wyd quhar our all the see,
So that the Ciclopes of Ethna saw he. 90
Quhat suld I tell of Neoptolemus,
That other wyß to name is hait Pyrrus,
The hard myschans and tynsell of hys ryng?
Or quhou aganys Idomens the kyng
Hys kyndly goddis and cuntre dyd rebell, 95
And hym gan of hys natyve realm expell?
Or quhou the Locrys, Aiax Oelyus ost,
Now doys inhabyt the waist Lybyan cost?
Sen he hym self the gret Agamenon,
The kyng of Myce, and cheif ledar of on 100
Of all the Grekis ostis in batale,
Ha, schame to say, fowlely befell
That by the handis of hys awyn wife

155

The first nycht in hys palyce lost hys lyf.
And he that venquyst Asya lyis ded;   105
The sle adultrar occupiis hys sted.
The goddis eik sa far dyd me invy,
That in my natyve land neuer sall I spy
My chaist spousage, lyke as befor heß bene,
Ne Calydon my realm of crymys cleyn.   110
And now alsso, a grisly thyng to se,
Ane selcouth monstre, lo, betyd hes me:
My ferys lost with plumys in the ayr
As thame best lykis ar fleand our alquhar
(Allace of my folkis the vengeabill wraik!),   115
Transformyt in fowlys, wandris by the laik,
And of thar lamentabill and wofull sowndis
The large costis dynnys and redoundis.
Thir myschevys for my trespaß and cryme,   f. 250ᵛ
I may traist, heß betyd me sen that tyme   120
That I, witles and so rakleß, perfay,
The hevynly bodeis durst with swerd assay,
And with smert wond was our presumptuus
To violat the rycht hand of Venus.
Solist na mar,' quod he, 'persuaid me nocht   125
That to so dangerus batellis I be brocht.
Eftir the bettyng down of Troys wallys,
With the Tewcranys, quhat chance that euer befallis,
I will na mair debatis mak nor weris;
Nor of our ald stryfe thir hynder ȝheris,   130
That so myschews was and bad to se,
May I glaidly remember now,' said he.
'Tha gyftis rych and mony fair presandis
Quhilkis ȝe to me heß brocht furth of ȝour landis,
Return and beir onto the prynce Ene.   135
Contrar hys keyn dartis ellis stand haue we,
And hand for hand matchit hym in fycht:
Beleif me as expert, quhou stowt and wight
Is he owther in batale place or feld,
And how sternly he rasys vp hys scheild,   140
Or with quhou gret a thud in the melle
Ane lance towartis hys aduersar thrawys he.
Forthir,' he said, 'I certify ȝou alssua,
That, gif the forsaid grond of Phrygia
Twa othir sik men fosterit had or bred,   145
The citeis all of Arge mycht sor haue dred,
And the ofspryng of Dardan esely
Mycht in our realmys arryvit by and by,
So that Grece suld haue murnyt, euery tovn,
The fatis ald reuersit vp syd dovn.   150

156

Alhail the stop, resistans and delay
Mayd at Troy wallys, quhil the sege thar lay,
Was by the handis of Hector and Ene:
The Grekis conquyst lang tyme, trastis me,
By thame was styntit, apon sik maner   155
That it prolongit was quhil the tent 3er.
Athir of thame in bonte and curage
Excelland war, and full of vassalage;
Athir of thame maist souerane and douchty   f. 251ʳ
In dedis of armys, prowes and chevalry;   160
Bot this Ene was first all owt expreß
Of reuth, compassioun and of gentilnes.
Tharfor all sammyn adionys 3our rycht handis
In ferm allyance of concord, and sik bandis
Be ony wyß se 3he obtene,' quod he;   165
'For, gif thai start till armys in melle,
Be war with thame fortill debait, I red.'
Maist nobill kyng of kyngis, in this sted
Hys answer heß thou hard, as I haue tald,
And twichand this gret batale quhat he wald."   170

The kyng proponys with Enee to tak peß
Incontrar Turnus; tharto persuadis Drances.   C. vii

S cars had the messyngeris thir wordis said,
 Quhen all the Latynys, trublyt, full onglaid,
Fra hand to hand quhispyris fast and roundis,
On diuerß wyß demyng with murmour soundis –
Lyke as the swyft watir stremys cleir   5
Sum tyme rowtand men on far may heir,
Quhar it is stoppit with thir stanys round,
That of the ryveris brute and brokkyn sound,
Brystand on skelleis our thir demmyt lynnys,
The bankis endlang all the fludis dynnys.   10
Bot efter that thar mudis mesyt wer,
Thar waverand wordis stanchit and sik beir,
With reuerens first blyssand the goddis mycht,
The kyng thus carpys from hys trone on hycht:
"O Latyn pepill, forsuyth I wald al gait,   15
And so had beyn far better, weill I wait,
Full lang or now avisyt had we be
Twychand the common weill and materis hie;
And not at sik a poynt, apon this wyß,
Our consale to assembill and to avyß,   20
Quhen that our fays and aduersaris ar bown
Forto bysege the wallys of our town.
O cite3anys, we move and ledis at hand

157

Ane wer inoportune, quhilk is onganand,
Aganys folkis of goddis clan discend,   25   f. 251ᵛ
That beyn invincybill, and weill can defend
So that na bargane may thame irk nor tyre;
Nor thocht thai venquyst war, baith man and syre,
May thai desist, ne withdraw the melle.
Gif ony hope or confidens had we   30
In chevalry of the Etholianys,
Quhilkis in Napillis with Dyomed remanys,
And for thir men of armys thidder send,
Do all sik traste away, and ʒou defend:
Lat euery man in his awyn self haue hope.   35
Bot quhou febill sik traste is ʒe may grope,
And eik befor ʒour eyn cleir may ʒe se
In quhou gret perrell and proplexite
All other materis lyis now or standis;
All sic thyngis bene braid amang ʒour handis.   40
I will accuß nor argu now na wight.
All haill the forß or strenth mycht be in fycht
Exercyt was, I wait; sen all the flour
And pyssans of this realm dyd stryve in stour.
Now so it is that I will breifly end,   45
And in schort wordis mak onto ʒou kend
The dowtsum purpos in my mynd remanys;
Attendans geif, and harkis all at anys.
I haue, besyde Tyber the Tuscane flud,
Ane ald feld onprofitabill and rude,   50
Far strekand west to the bundis quhar remanys
The Scicyll pepill, quhilkis clepit ar Sycanys;
The folk Auruncane and of Rutuly
This grund sawys full onthriftely,
With scharp plewis and steill sokkis seir   55
Thai hard hillys hyrstis forto eyr,
And on thir wild holtis harsk alsso
In faynt pastur doith thar bestis go.
All that cuntre and band of hillis hie,
Sa full of rochis pynnakillis, as we se,   60
Lat it be geif for amyte and concord
To the Troianys, and Eneas thar lord;
Syne offer thame equale trety condyng,
And, as our perys, do call thame in this ryng;   f. 252ʳ
All sammyn lat thame dwell heir by and by;   65
Gif thai haue sik desyre to Italy,
Do lat thame beld thar cite wallys squar.
Bot gif so be that thai lyst ellis quhar
To othir costis or pepill forto wend,
Thar duellyng place for ay to apprehend,   70

158

And possibill be that of our boundis thai
May so depart, and from thens wend away;
Twyß ten schippis lat ws beld agane
Of strang tymmyr and treis Italyane,
And gif thai wald compleit ma in this land,   75
The stuf lyis all reddy by the strand;
Of thar schippis the numbir and maner
Lat thame command, and we sal furnyß heir
The irne graith, the wark men, and the wrychtis,
And all that to the schippis langis of rychtis.   80
And forthir eik it lykis me," quod he,
"To ber my wordis to this prynce Ene,
And to conferm our frendschip and our peß,
Ane hundreth gay ambassatouris, but leß,
Of gretast blude of the Latyn menȝe,   85
And in thar handis reke furth the paceabill tre;
And bair hym giftis and rewardis large,
Of gold and evoir mony sovm and charge,
The char or sete accordyng for the ryng,
Our rob ryall, ensenȝeys of a kyng.   90
Avyß heiron amangis ȝou for the best,
And help to bryng our febill weill to rest."
Ane Drances tho vpstud, and speke began,
The quhilk Drances was the self man
That, as we said haue laitly heir tofor,   95
Was rycht molest to Turnus euermor,
Quham the renovn of Turnus and glory
Prikkyt full sor with lurkand hyd envy;
Of moblis rych and plentuus was he,
And maste expert in speche and wordis sle,   100
Bot of his handis into batale sted
Full cald of curage, dolf as ony led,
And into consalys gevyng he was hald   f. 252ᵛ
A man nocht indegest, bot wyß and cald;
Bot ane seditioun or a brek to make   105
Sa masterfull, tharin was nane hys mayk;
The nobill kynrent of hys moderis syde
Maid hym full gret of blude, and full of pryde;
Hys fader was oncertane and onknaw.
And vp he startis in this ilk thraw,   110
With thir wordis Turnus to ourcharge,
Aggregyng on hym wrath and malyce large:
"O douchty kyng, thou axis consale," said he,
"Of that mater quhilk, as semys me,
Is nother dyrk nor dowtsum, bot full cleir,   115
That mysteris not our avicis beyn heir.
The pepill haill grantis that thai wait

159

Quhat forton schawys, and in quhat estait
Our materis standis; bot thai ar arch to schaw,
Quhispirand amangis thame, thai stand sik aw.　　　　120
Bot cauß hym geif thame liberte to speke,
Do way his bost, at thar breth may outbreke;
I meyn of hym, by quhais onhappy werd
And fraward thewys, now ded on the erd
Samony cheif chiftanys and dukis lyis:　　　　125
Forsuyth, I sall say furth all myne avyß,
All thocht with brag and bost, or wapynnys, he
Me doith await, and mannans forto de;
For by hys dedis may we se expreß
Thys cite haly plungit in distreß,　　　　130
Quhillys that he has maid hym to assay
The Troianys strenth, and stall sa sone away,
Havand assurans to withdraw and fle,
And into armys dois bost the hevynnys hie.
Bot, O thou all thar best and riall kyng,　　　　135
To all thir gyftis ekis bot a thyng;
Onto thir presandis and wyß wordis seir,
That to Troianys thou haß byd say and beir,
Ekis a gift, and lat neuer demyt be
The bustuusneß of ony may dant the.　　　　140
Bot that thi douchter, O thou fader gude,
Onto ȝon worthy prynce of gentill blude
Be gevyn, tobe thy son in law, I wyß,　　　　　　f. 253ʳ
As he that worthy sik a wedlok is;
And knyt vp paix, but mor disseuerans,　　　　145
With that eternall band of allyans.
And gif sa gret raddour or dreid haue we
Within our myndis or our breistis," quod he,
"That, for Turnus, we dar nocht do sik thyng,
Than lat ws for the weilfar of this ryng　　　　150
Beseik hym tharfor and with haill entent
Requir hym at he wald grant hys consent,
So that the kyng, at hys fre volunte,
Mycht oyß and do hys proper dewyte,
And, for the weill publik of this land,　　　　155
Desyre that he na wyß tharto ganestand.
O Turnus, hed and causar verraly
Of thir myschevis gret in Italy,
Quharto sa feill syß in playn perrellis now
Thir sylly wrachit citeȝanys warpis thou?　　　　160
Nane hoip of weilfar haue we in this wer:
For paix halely we all the requer,
Togiddyr with Lavinia the schene may,
Quhilk is the pand or plege, this dar I say,

Of paix tobe kepit inviolate. 165
And I, forsuyth, quhilk, as be thy consait,
Thou fenys thyne evill willar fortobe,
And for the common weill, sa mot I thee,
So fortocum I refuß nocht, gud broder,
Bot lo me heir, now formest of all other 170
Humylly the besekyng: I requer,
Haue mercy, lord, of thyne awyn frendis deir,
Lat be thy stowt mynd, go thy way but lak,
With ane mair strang rebute and dryve abak.
Ded corpsis bet down enew haue we seyn, 175
Our large feildis and boundis all betweyn
Left desolate and waist of induelleris.
Bot gif thy fame and gret renown the steris,
Gyf in thy breist sa hie curage and mycht
Thou haß consauyt, thynkand the sa wight, 180
And gif that on sik wyß this hald ryall
Suldbe thy dowry and rych gyfi dotall
Thou berys in hart, and is to the sa deir; f. 253^v
Do vndyrtake this thyng, and end the weir:
Addreß thy body baldly, and not spayr 185
Forto recontyr alone thyne aduersar,
To that entent, that Turnus all hys lyfe
May weld the kyngis douchter to hys wyfe;
So that we, dolf of curage as the led,
Be not doun strowit in the feildis ded, 190
In cumpaneis onberyit or bewalyt.
Bot thou, that haß in feild sa feil assalyt,
Gyf ony strenth thou haß or hardyment,
Or marciall prowes steryng thyne entent
For thy cuntre; aganyst the, for hys rycht, 195
Behald thy fa prouocand the to fyght,
3ondir all reddy to mak hys party gude;
Delay no mor, bot manfully go to it."

Turnus, at Drances speche commovit sair,
Rycht subtelly allegis the contrar.

C. viii

The fers mude of Turnus, this bald syre,
At sik sawys kyndillyt hait as fyre,
Sychand rycht sor deip in hys breist onon,
Thir wordis pronuncis with a petuus grone:
"Drances," said he, "forsuyth euer heß thou beyn 5
Large and to mekill of spech, as weil is seyn
Now, quhen the batale desyris wark at hand;
The consale syttand, first thou doys vpstand.
Bot not with wordis suld the cowrt be fillyt,

Set thou be gret tharin and ful evill willyt, 10
With haltand wordis fleand from the heir,
Quhen thou assouerit art of al danger,
Sa lang as that our strenthty wallys gude
Our ennemys debarrit doith exclude
Or quhil the fowceis of our fortereß 15
Rynnys not our of bludy spait, I geß.
Tharfor trump vp, blaw forth thyne eloquens,
As thou was wont to do, mak thy defens:
Bot than thou may, Drances, be myne avice,
Me to reproch of feir and cowardyce, 20
Quhen that thi rycht hand into batale sted
Samony hepis of Troianys hes laid ded,
And quhen thou takynnyt heß so worthely f. 254^r
With syng tropheall the feildis, as haue I.
Full eith it is fortill assay, and se 25
Quhat may our sprety fors in the melle;
And, as full weill is knawyn to ws eik,
Our fais beyn not far from hens to seik,
Bot plant about the wallis of our town:
Aganyst thame go mak ws reddy bown. 30
Quhy duellys thou and tareis thus al day?
Quhidder gif thy marcial dedis, as thai war ay,
Into thy wyndy clattrand tung salbe,
And in tha cowart feit, euer wont to fle?
Says thou I was repulsyt and dryve away? 35
O maist onworthy wight, quha can that say,
Or me iustly reprochyng of syk lak,
That I rebutyt was or dung abak,
By me quhen thou behald mycht Tyber flude
Boldyn and ryn on spait with Troian blude, 40
And all the famyll of Evander kyng
Brocht onto grond alhail and his ofspryng,
And the Archadis, confundyt and ourset,
With mony ma in armys I doun bet?
The grysly Bytias, and Pandarus his brother, 45
Thai ar expert gif I fled one or other,
And eik thai thousand sawlys on a day
As victor I to hell send hyne away,
Quhen that I was inclusyt at distreß
Amyd myne ennemyß wallis and fortereß. 50
Thou says, in weir na hoip is of weilfar:
O wytleß wyght, pronunce that, and declar
Sik chance betyd ȝon Dardan capitane,
And spa sik thyng onto thy dedis ilkane!
And forthir eik, sen thou art mad becum, 55
Ceß not forto perturbill all and sum,

162

And with thy felloun raddour thame to fley;
The febill myghtis of 30n pepill fey,
Into batale twyß venquyst schamefully,
Spar not fortill extoll and magnyfy;   60
And, by the contrar, the pissans of Latyn kyng
Do set at nocht, bot lychtly, and down thryng.   f. 254ᵛ
Now the nobill Myrmydon capitanys
Quakis in armys for feir of the Troianys,
And now Tedeus son Diomedes   65
Agast is, and Larissyane Achilles;
And Aufidus, the swyft flowand ryver,
Rynnys contyrmont frawart the sey for feir.
And quhill alsso this ilk schrewit wight,
That is controvar of mony wykkyt slycht,   70
Fen3eis hym fleyt or abasyt tobe,
That he dar not chide furth incontrar me,
Than with hys dreid and sle controvit feir
My cryme aggregis he on hys maner.
Desist, Drances, be not abasyt, I pray,   75
For thou sal neuer loß, schortly I the say,
Be my wapyn nor this rycht hand of myne,
Sik ane pevych and catyve saule as thyne:
Nay, lat it duell with the, as best may gane,
Within that wrachit corps, and thar remane.   80
Now, O thou gret fader and prynce souerane,
To the and thy consale I turn agane.
Gyf thou list no thyng trasting nor affy
Into our armys nor our chevalry,
Gyf that we be of help all desolate,   85
And haill at vnder into this last debait,
Distroyt for ay, and na help may mak,
For that our ost was anys drevyn abak,
And forton heß na return ne regreß;
Lat ws beseik for paix at sik distreß,   90
Mak hym request to rew apon our harmys,
And reke hym furth our ryght hand bair of armys.
Quhou beit, O, wald God in this extreme neid
That ony thyng of curage or manheid
Remanyt, as was wont with ws tobe!   95
Abufe the laif thame worthy thinkis me,
Maist fortunat in fatys marcyall,
And excellent in hie curage our all,
Quhilk wilfully, as that thame selvyn wald,
At thai ne suldyn sik myscheif behald,   100
Fell ded to grond by fatale happy werd,
And with thar mowth anys bait the erd.   f. 255ʳ
Bot gif we haue rycheß and moblys seir,

163

And nevir assayt ȝit fresch ȝong power,
And, in our helpyng, of Italianys   105
Citeis and pepillys habundis and remanys,
Or gif that also to the Troiane syde,
With effusioun of blude and wondis wyde,
This victory betyd is (trastis me,
Thai haue als feill ded corpsis as haue we,   110
Gyf this tempestuus trake of the batale
On baith the halfis is all owt equale),
Quhy failȝe we so schaymfully our mycht
Into the first entre of the fycht?
Quhy quakis thus our membris vp and dovn,   115
Befor the bludy blast and trumpis sovn?
For tyme, feill syß, and eik the variant chance
Of our onstabill lyfe hung in ballance,
Reducit heß full mony onlykly thyng
To bettir fyne than was thar begynnyng;   120
And fortoun interchangabill with blenkis quent
Full mony ane dissauyt heß and schent,
Syne efter in a thraw, this weill I wait,
Restoryt thame agane to thar ferm stait.
I put the cace, set the Etholianys,   125
With Dyomed and the pepill Arpanys,
Lyst not cum in our helpyng nor suple;
Ȝit than the bald Mesapus weill wylbe,
And the happy Tolumnyus alsso,
With all tha other dukis mony mo   130
That fra so feill pepillys beyn hydder sent:
And na litill renown, be myne entent,
Followys the chosyn folkis of Italy,
Nor thame that duellis in Lawrent feildis heirby.
Haue we not eik the stalwart Camylla,   135
Of the famyll and kynrent of Volsca,
Ledand thir armyt ostis and stern feildis,
In byrnyst plait arrayt and schynand scheldis?
Bot gyf the Troiane pepill, euery ane,
Desyris me to feght in feild allane,   140
Gif that be plesand onto the, schir kyng,
And I sa far, efter Drances menyng,
Gaynstandis the common weill; into that cace,   f. 255ᵛ
That schame sal nevir betyd me in na place,
For victory me hatis not, dar I say,   145
Nor lyst syk wyß withdraw thir handis twa,
That I refuß suld to assay ony thyng
Quhilk mycht sa gret beleif of weil inbryng.
With stowt curage agane hym wend I will,
Thocht he in prowes paß the gret Achill,   150

164

Or set in cace sik armour he weris as he,
Wrocht by the handis of God Vlcanus sle.
To ȝou, and Kyng Latyn my fader in law,
I Turnus heir, quham full weill ȝe knaw
No thyng behynd, nor tobe reput leß,   155
To nane of all our eldris in prowes,
This saul and life, the quhilk sa weil I lufe,
Doith promyß and awowis for ȝour behufe.
Thai say, allon me challancis Ene;
And I beseik gret God he challance me: 160
Ne byd I not that Drances deir aby
Ocht with hys deth, quhar that apposit am I;
Nor, quhidder this turn to goddis wrethfull wraik,
Or hardyment and honour, we ondertake,
Na thing at all tharof salbe his part –   165
The chans is myne, I will it not astart."

Duryng this disputatioun, as is said,
Enee hys ost abowt the town haß laid.   C. ix

Quhill thai thus at gret altricatioun wer
 Amangis thame self in dowtsum thingis seir,
Eneas all his ost and haill army
Heß rasyt, trumpyng to the town in hy.
A messynger com ruschand in with haist,   5
Amyd the rowtis ran as he war chaist,
That with huge rumour and a feirfull dyn
Fillit onon the kyngis riall in,
And with gret dreid the cite stuffit alquhar;
Schawand quhou that thar fays cummyn war   10
In plane batale arrayt, to conclud,
The Troiane barnage from Tibir the flude,
With ordinance of Tuscan, that dyd spreid
In forfront al the large feildis on breid.
Onon the pepillis hartis effrayt wer,   15 f. 256ʳ
And commonys breistis proplexit all for feir;
In sum, the greif and ire dyd fast habund,
Rasyt with brethfull stangis full onsond,
And with a felloun dreid all on steir
Thai hynt to harnes, and cryis eftir thar ger: 20
"Harneß, harnes," all the ȝong citeȝanys
With fellon brute and noys schowtis atanys;
The febill and agyt faderis wobegone
Can pleyn and weip with mony a petuus grone.
In euery part the gret clamour and cryis   25
In diuerß opinionys rayß vp to the skyis –
Nane other wyß than as sum tyme we knaw

The flycht of byrdis fordynnys the thik schaw,
Or than the rawk vocit swannys in a rabill,
Sondand and swouchand with noys lamentabill   30
Endlang the bemand stankis and stremys cleir
Of Padusa, sa full of fyschis seir.
Turnus, that fand hys tyme sa oportune,
Now baldly says he: "Cite3anys, haue doyn;
Do call 3our consale, takis avysment,   35
Sittand at ey3 ilkane say his entent,
Carpys of paix, and ruy3 it now, lat se,
Quhen that thai 3onder invadis 3our cuntre,
3our mortale fays enarmyt 3ou to assaill."
Na mar he said, bot startis vp sans faill,   40
And of the cheif palyce ischit furth in hy,
Thus carpand to the noblys stud hym by:
"Go tyte, Volusus, to the banereris
Of the Volscanys, and thame that standartis beris;
Charge thame thar ensen3eis forto ray3 on hycht,   45
And in thar armour adre3 thar men to fyght:
And 3he, Mesapus, Coras, and 3our broder,
The horsmen all enarmyt, ane and other,
Convoys furth onto the feildis braid.
A party of the cite3anys," he said,   50
"Do stuf the entreis, and the portis defend;
Sum to the towris and wall hedis ascend;
The remanent of all our hail men3e,
Quhen I command, lat thame set on with me."   f. 256ᵛ
Onon our all the cite by and by   55
Vp on the wallys ryn thai than in hy.
The kyng Latyn hys consale, full onglaid,
And gret materis quhilkis he begunnyn had,
Left and differrit quhil ane other day,
Trist in his mynd, and trublit of that delay;   60
And mony ways hym self he accusyt,
That he sa lang had slewthit and refusyt
To ressaue glaidly the Troiane Ene;
Repentyng sor, for weill of his cite,
That he had not requirit hym and draw,   65
Or than, tobe his mawch and son in law.
Sum tho, thar cite entre forto kepe,
Befor the portis delvis trynschis deip;
Sum to the 3ettis weltis weghty stonys,
And sum gret iestis and sillys for the nonys;   70
The ba3 trumpet with a bludy sovn
The syng of batell blew our all the tovn.
The wallis than thai stuffit rownd abowt
With diuer3 sortis of mony syndry rowt,

166

Baith wifis, barnys, childer, men and page   75
(Na kynd of stait was sparit tho, nor age);
The heyast poynt and lattir resistens
Callit euery wight to laubour and defens.
The queyn also, Amata, furth can hald
Onto the tempill and Pallas souerane hald,   80
Born in hir char, and walkyng hir abowt
Of matronys and nobil wemen a rowt;
Offerandis and gyftis brocht with hir scho had;
Nixt hand hir went Lavynia the maid,
The cauß of all this harm and wofull teyn,   85
That dovn for schame dyd cast hyr lusty eyn.
The matronys entris in the goddis presens,
And smokis the tempill with sweit vapour and sens,
And reuthful vocis warpis lovd on hie.
Alssone as thai attenyt the entre,   90
"O thou," said thai, "Pallas armipotent,
Tritonia clepit, maid, and president
Of batale and of weris eueryone,   f. 257ʳ
With thy virginal handis breke onon
3on Troiane revaris wapynnys and his speir;   95
Hym self als tyte dovn to the grund thou ber,
Vndre our portis and our wallis hie
Down warp hym ded, that we that sycht may se."

Heir Turnus and Camylla gan devyß
Practikis of weir, the Troianys to suppryß.   C. x

Turnus hym self, als fers as ony gleid,
  Ful bissely addressyt on his weid,
Desyrus of the batale and bargane.
Intil a cloß curaß Rutilyane
Be than his body weill embrasyt had he,   5
Hys burnyst armour, awfull for to se,
With lymmys claspit in platis gilt with gold
And hed all bair; 3it, as hym selvyn wold,
Hys dedly brand he beltis by his syde;
And, schynand all of brycht gold, fast can glide   10
Throw owt the palyce ryall heir and thar,
Reiosyt in his mynd, as thocht he war
In ferm beleif fortill ourset his fo;
And on sik wyß gan walkyng to and fro,
With hart hyngand on the ioly pyn.   15
As sum tyme dois the curser start and ryn,
That brokkyn hes his band, furth of his stall,
Now gois at large out our the feldis all,
And haldis towart the studis in a rage,

167

Quhar merys rakis in thar pasturage,   20
Or than onto the deip rynnand ryver,
Quhar he was wont to drynk the watir cleir;
He sprentis furth, and full provd walxis he,
Heich strekand vp his hed with mony a ne,
Out our his spaldis and nek lang by and by   25
His lokkyrrit mayn schakand wantonly –
Siklyke this Turnus semys, quhar he went.
And, as he bradis furth apon the bent,
The maid Camylla cumis hym agane,
Accumpaneit with hir ostis Volscane.   30
Befor the portis dovn lyghtis the queyn,   f. 257ᵛ
Quham all the rowt heß followyt bedeyn,
Discendand from thar horssis esely;
Syne on sic wyß this lady spak in hy:
"Turnus," says sche, "gif ony hardy wight   35
May traste or assur in thar awyn mycht,
I vndertak, and dar promyß, allane
To mach in feild the ostis Eneadane,
And baldly dar recuntir in melle
All the horsmen of the Tuscane menʒe.   40
I the requyr, suffir me to assay
With my retenew and thir handis tway
The first danger in batale, or I stent:
Byde thou behynd on fut in enbuschment,
And kepe the wallis of this tovn," scho said.   45
Turnus his eyn hes fixit on this maid,
That weirlike was and awfull onto se,
Syne on this maner to hir ansueris he:
"O thou virgyn, glory of Italy,
Quhat thankis ʒeld or rendir the may I,   50
Or quhat may I refer of thy renovn?
Bot, sen thou art to all thyng reddy bovn,
Surmontyng all in curage souerane,
Now at this tyme of sic laubour and payn
Grant me my part, so that on athir syde   55
Betwix ws twa the bargane be dyvyde.
Hark, I sall schaw ʒou myne avyß," quod he,
"ʒon detestabill and myschews Enee,
As that the rumour surly heß maid kend,
And als my spyis schawis was thidder send,   60
A certane horsmen, lycht armyt for the nanys,
Hes send befor forto forray the planys;
Hym self ascendis the hie band of the hyll
By wentis strait and passage scharp and wyll,
Schaip on our cite fortocum prevely.   65
Tharfor a prattik of weir devyß will I,

168

And ly at wait in quyet enbuschment
At athir pethis hed or secrete went;
In the how slak, be ȝonder woddis syde,
Full dern I sall my men of armys hyde.   70
Set thou apon the Tuscan horsyt rowt,
With pynsellis semlyt sammyn with a schowt.
The stalwart Mesapus with the sall go,
The Latyn barnage, and the brethir two,
That capitanys come fra Tyburtyn cite,   75
With all thar ordinance and hail menȝe:
Tak thou the cuyr with thame to rewle and steir
Alhaill that ryall army into weir."
Thus said he, and with sic wordis at schort
Mesapus to the fight he dyd exhort,   80
And all his feris, syne euery capitane;
And syne towart his aduersaris is gane.
Thar lay a valle in a crukyt glen,
Ganand for slycht till enbusch armyt men,
Quham, wonder narrow, apon athir syde   85
The bewys thik hampirrit and doith hyde
With skowgis darn and full obscur, perfay,
Quharthrow thar strekit a rod or a strait way,
Ane narrow peth, baith owtgang and entre,
Full scharp and schrowit passage wonder sle;   90
Abufe the quhilk, apon the hill on hycht,
Quhar men may spy about a weil far sycht,
Thar lyis a playn to the Troianys onknaw;
Bot, quha so list towart that sted to draw,
It is a stellyng place and sovir harbry,   95
Quhar ost in stail or enbuschment may ly,
Quhidder men list the bargane to abyde
Owder on the rycht hand or on the left syde,
Or on the hycht debait thame for the nanys,
And on thar fays welt dovn weghty stanys.   100
Thyddir ȝong Turnus held and dyd ascend,
As he that all the passage weil bekend;
The place he tuke, and ful prevy, onknaw,
Lyggis at wait vnder the darn wod schaw.

Quhou that Opis was doun from Dyane send,
And of quhat kyn Camylla was discend.   C. xi

The meyn sesson, Latoneis douchter Dyan,
Within hir set of hevynnys souerane,
The swyft Opys, a nymphe ane of hir feris,
Ane haly virgyne of hir sort mony ȝheris,
To hir callis, rycht dolorus and onglaid,   5

169

And, sychand sair, to hyr syk wordis said:
"O virgyn deyr, lo now, Camylla gays
To cruell batall aganyst hyr mortal fays,
And, al invayn, with hir into syk werys
Our wapynnys and our armour with hyr berys.   10
I the declar and certifeis," quod sche,
"Abuf all other full deyr is sche to me;
Ne this luf, suythly, is nocht cummyn of new,
Nor ȝit of lait in Dyanys brest vpgrew,
And with a hasty sweitneß movyt my spreit,   15
Bot of ald kyndnes lang tyme onforleit.
For quhen hir fader, Metabus the kyng,
Was throw invy expellit hys ancyent ryng
Of Pryvernum, and for the cruelte
Of his pepill fled from that cite,   20
With hym he bair this ȝong infant sa deir,
Tobe his fallow in exill, and play feir,
And efter hir moderis name, hait Casmylla,
Camylla hes clepit, a lettir tane awa.
Befor hym in hys bosum he hir bair   25
And socht onto the wilsum holtis hair.
Hys cruel fays with thar wapynnys keyn
Hym ombeset on all partis in teyn.
With armyt men and wageouris the Volscanys
So neir almost bylappyt hym at anys,   30
Thar was na passage quhar away to fle;
For lo, amyd the went quhar etlyt he,
Amasenus, that ryver and fresch flude,
Abuf the brays bulryt as it war wod;
From the clowdis was bryst sik spait of rayn   35
The ryver flowis our the large plane.
He, dressand hym to swym, at the bank syde
For luf of the ȝong bab most neid abyde,
And, for his deir byrdyng dredand soir,
Ilk chance in haist dyd roll in his memor;   40
And scars this sentens prent into hys mynd,   f. 259ʳ
Hys douchtir forto cloß within the rynd
And stalwart sapplyn or bark of cork tre
(For in hys hand the self tyme had he
A bustuus speir, per cace, baith styth and stuyr,   45
As he that was a worthy weriour;
The schaft was sad and sound, and weill ybaik);
Ywympillit in this bark tho dyd he take
Hys ȝong douchter, and with hys awyn hand
Amyddis of this lans full suyrly band;   50
Quhilk tasand with hys rycht hand, sone on hye
Onto the hevyn abuf thus carpys he:

170

'O blissyt maid Latonya, our alquhar
Of wild forestis the inhabitar,
I, fader, heir professys servand to the   55
Thys tendir ȝonglyng, bund onto this tre;
Fleand hys fays throw the skyis, llo,
Knyt to thy schaft, lawly besekis scho.
Ressaue hir, lady, and testify, God wait,
As thyne alhail, onto the dedicate,   60
Quhilk now thou seis standis in danger,
Commyttit to the wyndis and the ayr.'
Thus said he, and onon with a swak
Hys gardy vp haß bendit far abak,
And threw the speir with all hys fors and mycht;   65
The stremys soundyt of the schaftis flycht.
Owr this ferß ryver to the farthyr bra
This fey onsilly bab, ȝong Camylla,
Flaw knyt onto this quhirrand schaft of tre.
Bot this Metabus, quhen that he dyd se   70
The gret preß of hys fays cum sa neir,
Na langar duelt, bot swam throu the ryver;
And cummyn to hys purpoß blyth and glaid,
The speir onon, sa buklyt with the maid,
In presand onto the thrynfald Dyane,   75
Furth of the gresy sward he has vp tane.
Na rurall byggyngis, nor ȝit na strang cite,
Wald hym ressaue within thar wallys he,
Nor, thocht thai wald hym to harbry haue tane,   f. 259ᵛ
Hys fers mynd couth not subdew to nane;   80
So that, in maner of hyrdis in pasturage,
On wild montanys he wonnyt all his age;
Quhar that his dochtyr, amang buskis ronk,
In dern sladis and mony scroggy slonk,
With mylk he nurist of the beistis wild,   85
And with the pappys fosterit he his child
Of savage stude meris in that forest;
Oft tymys he thar pappys mylkit and prest
Within the tendir lippys of his get.
And, fra the child myght fut to erd set,   90
And with hir solis first dyd mark the grond,
With dartis keyn and hedis scharply grund
Hir fystis and hir handis chargyt he;
And at hir schuldir buklyt heß on hie
Ane propir bow and litil arow cace;   95
And for hir goldyn garland or hed lace
In sted eik of hir syde garmont or pall,
Our the schuldris fro hir nek down with all
The grisly tygrys skyn of rent dyd hyng.

The self tyme ȝit sche bot tendir ȝonglyng   100
Thir dartis and the takillis swyft leit glyde;
And oft abowt hir hed the ilk tyde
Wald warp the stryngis of the stowt staf slyng,
Quhar with feill syß to grund ded wald scho dyng
The cran of Trace, or than the quhite swan.   105
For nocht scho was desirit with mony a man,
And moderis feill throu the townys Tuscane
Desirit hir thar gud douchter, invane;
For scho only, full ferm in hir entent,
Of Diane, goddes of chastyte, stud content,   110
And list to hant evyr in woddis with me
The dartis schutyng, and love virginyte,
Remanand incorrupt and a cleyn maid.
I wald, forsuyth, at this tyme scho abaid,
And had not hastit to sic chevalry,   115
Forto molest the Troianys stowt army;
Bot that ane of my ferys scho suld be,
As scho that is at all tyme deir to me.   f. 260ʳ
Haue done onon, thou nymphe Opys," scho said,
"With wikkyt fatis sen bestad is ȝon maid,   120
Thou slyde down from the hevyn, and that inhy;
The Latyn feildis thou vissy and aspy,
Quhar, in the wofull batale and melle,
To ane onhappy chance betaucht is sche.
Tak thir dartis, and sone owt of my cayß   125
That ilke revengeabill arow thou owt rayß:
Quha evir with wond doys hurt or violat
Hyr haly body onto me dedicat,
Quhiddir he be Troiane or Italiane,
All is in like, that he onon be slane,   130
And with hys blude myn offens deir aby.
My self thar eftir the reuthfull corps in hy
Amyd a boyß clowd sall cary away,
Onspulȝeit of hir armour or array,
And hir bygrave, reducit to hir cuntre,   135
In sepultur full gloryus," said sche.
Than Opys lyghtly of the hevynnys glad,
Throw owt the skyis sowchand fast doun slaid,
Persand the ayr with body all ourschrowd
And dekkyt in a watry sabill clowd.   140

172

Quhou that Eneas with hys haill power
Towart the cyte wallys drawis neir.

Dvryng this quhile, the Troiane power all
Approchys fast towart the cite wall,
The Tuscane dukis and horsmen rowtis alhaill
Arrayt in batale, euery ward and staill,
Our all the planys brays the stampand stedis,
Full galȝart in thar bardis and weyrly wedis,
Apon thar strait born brydillis brankand fast,
Now thrympand heir, now thar, thar hedis can cast:
The large grond worth grysly onto se
Of steill wapynnys and scharp speir hedis hie;
And as the fyre all byrnand schayn the feildis
Of brycht armour, heich helmys, and braid scheildis.
Aganyst thame alsso onon apperys
The bald Mesapus, valȝeant in weryȝ;
The agill Latyn pepill with hym was,
And duke Catyllus, with his brother Coras,
And eik the weyng of Wolscane pepill in feild
With the stowt wench Camylla vnder scheild;
And furth thai streik thar lang speris weill far,
Drew in thar armys with schaftis chargit on far,
Tasyt vp dartis, taclys and fleand flanys;
The contyr or first tocome for the nanys
Full ardent wolx, and awfull forto se,
The men byrnand to ioyn in the melle,
And furour grew of stedis sterand on stray.
Now thai, approchyng sammyn in array
Within ane arow schot on athyr syde,
Syne maid a litill stop, and still dyd byde;
Rasyt vp a schowt, bad on thame with a cry,
Quhil bruyt and clamour fordynnyt the sky.
Thar fers stedis dyd for the bargane cheir;
On athir half thai mak a weirlike feir;
And tharwithall at anys on every sydis
The dartis thik and fleand takyllys glydis,
As doith the schour of snaw, and with thar flycht
Dyrknyt the hevynnys and the skyis lyght.
Tyrrhenus tho, ane of the Tuscane rowt,
And Acontevs, a Rutilyane full stowt,
Togidder semblyt with thar speris ran,
To preif the first fall sammyn, man for man.
Thai meit in melle with a felloun rak,
Quhil schaftis al to schuldris with a crak;
Togiddir duschis the stowt stedis atanys,
That athyris contyr fruschyt otheris banys.

5

10

15

20

25

30

35

40

And Aconteus, lyke to the thundris blast, 45
Smyte from hys sadill a far way was cast,
Or lyke a stayn warpyt from the engyne,
That altofruschit dovn he dyd declyne,
With sik rebund and rewyne wonder sair
That he his lyfe hes sparpellit in the ayr. 50
All suddanly the Latynys tuke affray
And gaue the bak bedeyn, and fled away, f. 261ʳ
Thar scheldis our thar schuldris kest behynd,
And to the tovn spurris als ferß as wynd.
The Troianys dyd persewyng on the chayß, 55
And fast invadis thame Prynce Asyllas.
Quhen thai approchyng to the portis neir,
The Latyn pepill returnys all infeir,
Thar weill dantit horß nekkis quhelit abowt,
Syne gaue a cry, and on thame with a schowt: 60
The tother party than heß tane the flight,
Leit ga the brydill, and fled in all thar mycht.
Lyke as the flowand sey with fludis rude
Now ruschis to the land, as it war woyd,
And on the skelleys at the costis bay 65
Vpswakkis fast the fomy wallys gray,
And with his iawpys coverys in and owt
The far sandis our the bay abowt;
Now with swyft fard gois ebband fast abak,
That with hys bulrand iaschis and owt swak 70
With hym he sowkis and drawys mony stayn,
And levis the strandis schald and sandis plane –
The Tuscane folk the Latynys on sik wyß
Onto the cite wallys chasyt twyß;
And twyß thar self dyd fle and gif the bak, 75
With scheldis at defens behynd thame swak.
Bot tharefter the thryd assay thai mak,
The ostis sammyn ionyt with a crak,
That euery man heß chosyn hym his feir.
And than, forsuyth, the granys men mycht heir 80
Of thame that stervyn and dovn bettyn beyn,
That armour, wapynnys, and ded corpß bedeyn,
And stedis throwand on the grond that weltis,
Mydlit with men quhilk ӡald the gaste and sweltis,
Bedowyn lay full deip in thar awyn blude. 85
The stowr encressis furyus and woyd.
Orsilochus, a Troiane, with all his forß
Dressis his lans at ane Remulus horß,
For hym to meit he stude a maner feir;
The hed remanyt vnder the horssis eyr, 90
The steid enragit for the cruell dynt, f. 261ᵛ

174

And lansys vp on hycht als fers as flynt,
As he that was inpacient of hys wond,
That Remulus down weltis on the grond.
Catillus, ane of the brethir Tyberyne,   95
Iollas down bet, and thareftir syne
The gret Hermynyus, wondir byg of corps,
Bot far byggar of curage and of fors;
Quhais hed and schuldris nakyt war and bar,
And on his crovn bot lokrand ʒallow hair;   100
And thocht he nakyt was, and voyd of geir,
Na wond nor wapyn mycht hym anys effer;
Forgane the speris sa bustuus blomyt he,
That this Catillus stalwart schaft of tre
Throw gyrdis baith hys stalwart schulder banys,   105
And with the dynt stud schakand all at anys,
Transfixit so, and persand euery part,
It dowblis and renewys the manis smart.
The blaknyt dedly blude on athir syde
Furth ruschis owt of warkand wondis wyde;   110
The swerdis baithit wolx in bargane red;
Feill corpsis kyllit in the feild fell ded,
And caucht a douchty end to swelt in fycht,
By hurtis feill forto manteym thar rycht.

Quhou Camylla hir fays doun can dyng,
And venquyst Awnus, for all his fair flechyng.   C. xiii

The awfull maid Camylla the ilk tyde,
With cace of arrowis tachit by hyr syde,
Amyd the slauchter and melle apon hyr foyn
Prowdly pransys lyke a wench Amaʒon,
That, forto hant the bargane or assay,   5
Hyr rycht pap had cut and brynt away.
And now the sowpill schaftis baldly sche
On ather sydis thik sparpellis and leit fle;
Now, not irkyt in batale stith to stand,
Ane stalwart ax scho hyntis in hir hand;   10
Apon hir schulder the giltyn bow Turcas,
With Dyanys arowys clatterand in hyr cayß.   f. 262ʳ
And gif that so betyd into that fight
Hyr ferys gave the bak and tuke the flycht,
Into the chaiß oft wald scho turn agane,   15
And, fleand, with hir bow schuyt mony a flane.
Abowt hir went hir walit stalwart feris,
The maid Laryna and Tulla ʒong of ʒheris,
And Tarpeia, that stowtly turnys and swax
With the weil stelit and braid billit ax;   20

175

Italyanys born; quham the nobil Camylla
Had to hir lovyng and honour deput swa,
Tobeyn hir servandis in ganand tyme of paix,
And in batale to stand by hir in preß.
Lyke as of Trace the wenchis Amaӡonys   25
Dyndillis the flude Thermodoon for the nonys,
As in thar payntit armour do thai fycht,
Owder abowt Hippolita the wight,
Or by the weirlyk maid Penthesile,
Rolland hir cart of weir to the melle;   30
The wemen rowtis baldly to the assay,
With felloun bruyt, gret revery and deray,
Furth haldis sammyn our the feldis sone,
With crukyt scheldis schapyn like the moyn.
O thou stern maid Camylla, quhat sal I say?   35
Quham first, quham last, thou smait to erth that day?
Or quhou feil corpsis in the batale sted
Thou laid to grond, ourthrew and put to ded?
With the formast, Ewmenyus, that was one
Son to Clysius; quhais braid breist bone   40
With a lang stalwart speir of the fyr tre
Throw smyttyn tyte and persyt sone hes sche;
He cavis owr, furthbokand stremys of blude,
And with his teith eik, schortly to conclude,
The bludy erd he bait; and, as he sweltis,   45
Apon hys wond oft writhis, tumlys and weltis.
Abuf this nixt scho ekis other two,
Lyris, and ane Pegasyus alsso,
Of quham the tane, that is to say, Lyris,
As that he fordward stowpand was, I wys,   50
To hynt hys horssis reyn that gan to fundir,   f. 262ᵛ
And the tother present, to kep hym vndir,
Furth straucht his febill arm to stynt his fall,
To grund togidder ruschit ane and all.
And to thir syne the son of Hyppotes,   55
Amastrus hait, ded scho adionyt in preß;
And lenand fordwart on hir lance of tre,
Terreas and Harpalicus chasys sche,
Persewand eik full bustuusly onon
The bold Chromys, and strang Demophon: 60
Quhou feill dartis with hir hand kest this maid,
Alsmony Troianys ded to grund scho laid.
Ane Ornytus, ane huntar, far on raw,
In armour and in cognycens onknaw,
Raid on a curser of Apulӡe throu the feild;   65
Hys braid schuldris weill cled war and ourheld
With a ӡong bullis hyde newly of hynt;

Hys hed coverit, to salf hym fro the dynt,
Was with ane hydduus wolfis gapand iowis,
With chaftis braid, quhyte teith and bustuus powis.   70
To mak debait, he held intill his hand
A rural club or culmas in sted of brand;
And, quhar he went, amyd the rowtis on hie
Abuf thame all his hail hed men mycht se.
Camylla hym at myscheif heß on set,   75
Scho bair hym throw, and to the grund dovn bet;
Nor na gret curage, forsuyth, was that, na mycht,
For all his rowt tofor had tane the flycht.
Bot forthir eik this forsaid Camylla,
With mynd onfrendly, can thir wordis sa: 80
"Thow Tyrrheyn fallow, quhat, wenyt thou tobe
In woddis chasand the wild deir?" quod sche.
"The day is cummyn that ȝour prowd wordis hait
A womanis wapyn sal resist and debait.
And, not the leß, na litill renowne   85
From thens thou sal do turß away with the,
And to our faderis gostis blythly schaw
That with Camyllais glave thou art ourthraw."
Incontinent this madyn eftir thys
Slew Orsilochus, and ane that hait Butys,   90   f. 263ʳ
Twa biggast men of body and of banys
Of all the ost and fallowschip Troianys.
Bot this ilk Butys, standand hir befor,
Outthrou the nek dyd scho perß and bor,
Betwix the hawbrig and the helm inhy,   95
Quhar that his halß scho dyd nakyt aspy;
For our his left schulder hang his scheld.
Bot this Orsilochus fled hir in the feild,
And gan to trump with mony a turnyng went;
In circulis wyde scho drave hym our the bent,   100
With mony a curß and iowk, abowt, abowt;
Quhar euer he fled scho followis in and owt;
And at the last scho haß ourtak the man,
And throw hys armour all, and his harn pan,
Hir braid poll ax, rasyt so on hie,   105
With all hir forß and mycht syne strykis sche;
As he besocht for grace with gret request,
Scho dowblit on hir dyntis, and so hym prest,
With feil wondis his hed haß tort and rent;
Hys harnys hait our all his vissage went.   110
Than Awnus son, quhilk also Awnus hait,
On cace betyd approche in the debait
Towart this maid, and, alsone he hir saw,
Abasyt huvis still for dreid and aw:

177

Into the mont Appennynus dwelt he,   115
Amang Liguriane pepill of his cuntre;
And not, forsuyth, the lakest weriour,
Bot forsy man, and rycht stalwart in stour,
So lang as fatis sufferit hym in fycht
To excerß prettykis, iuperty or slycht.   120
This Awnus, fra that weil persavit he
Na way to fle nor eschew the melle
Nor mycht eschaip the queyn stude him agane,
Than he begouth assay hir with a trayn,
And with a sle dissait thus first he said: 125
"Quhat honour is till a stowt wench or maid
Fortill assur and trast in a strang horß?   f. 263ᵛ
Leif thy swyft steid, and traste in thyne awyn forß;
At nane avantage, quhen thou lyst to fle,
Lyght on this plane, and hand for hand with me   130
Addreß ws to debait on fut allone:
Thar sall thou se, thar sall thou knaw onon,
Quhamto this wyndy glor, voust, or avantis,
The honor or, with payn, the lovyng grantis."
Thus said he, bot scho than als hait as fyre,   135
Aggrevit sor, inflambit in felloun ire,
Alycht, and to hir mait the horß betaucht;
At his desyre onon on fut vpstraucht,
With equale armour bodyn wondir lycht,
The drawyn suerd in hand that schane full brycht,   140
And onabasyt abaid hym in the feild,
Abylȝeit only bot with a quhite scheild.
The ȝong man, wenyng with his sle dissait
He had begilit hir be his consait,
Abowt his bridill turnyt but mar delay   145
And at the flycht sprent furth and brak away,
And feil syß leit the horß sydis feill
The scharp irne spurris prik apon his heill.
"O," quod the maid, "thou fals Liguriane,
Our wanton in thy prowd mynd, all invayn;   150
O variant man, for nocht perfay," quod sche,
"Heß thou assayt thy cuntre craftis sle!
Dissaitfull wight, forsuyth I to the say,
Thy slycht and wylis sal the nocht beir away,
Nor haylscarth hyne do turß the hame fra ws   155
Onto thy faderis howß, the fals Awnus."
Thus said the wench onto this other syre,
And furth scho sprent as spark of gleid or fyre;
With spedy fut so swyftly rynnys sche,
By passyt the horssis renk, and furth can fle   160
Befor hym in the feild with gret disdeyn,

178

And claucht onon the curser by the reyn;
Syne set apon hym baldly, quhar scho stude,
And hir revengit of hir fays blude –   f. 264^r
Als lychtly as the happy goishalk, we se,   165
From the hycht of a rokis pynnakill hie
With swyft weyngis persewis wonder sair
The silly dow heich vp into the ayr,
Quham finaly he clippis at the last,
And lowkyt in his punsys sarris fast,   170
Thristand his tallons sa throu hir entralis
Quhill at the blude abundandly furth ralys;
And, with hir beik deplumand, on al sydis
The lycht downys vp to the skyis glidis.

Tarchon, gret chiftane of the Tuscan ost, The fleand folkis to turn agane can bost.

C. xiv

The fader of goddis and men with diligent eyn
Haß all hir dedis vnderstand and seyn,
And, situat in his hevynly houß on hie,
Inducis and commovis to the melle
Tarchon, of Tuscanys pryncipall lord and syre,   5
In breithfull stoundis rasyt brym as fyre;
So that amyd the ful myschewoß fyght,
The gret slauchter and rowtis takand the flycht,
On horsbak in this Tarchon baldly draw,
Wilfull his pepill to support and saw;   10
The wardis all of euery natioun
With admonitions seir and exhortatioun
And diuerß wordis tystis to feght, for schame,
Clepand and calland ilk man be his name,
Quhill thai that drevyn war abak and chaste   15
Relevys agane to the bargane in haist.
"O Tuscane pepill, quhou happynnys this," said he,
"That 3he sal evir sa doillyt and bowbartis be
Onwrokyn sik iniurys to suffir heir?
O, quhat be this? Quhou gret a dreid and feir,   20
Quhou huge dolfnes and schaymful cowardice
Hes ombeset 3our myndis, apon sik wyß
That a woman allon, and thus belyve,
Apon sik wyß sal scattir 3ou and dryve,
And gar sa large rowtis tak the flycht?   25 f. 264^v
Quharto bair we this steill egis in fyght?
Or quhat avalys to hald in hand, lat se,
For nocht thir wapynnys, gyf we a wife sall fle?
3e war not wont tobe sa lyddyr ilkane
At nycht batellys and warkis venerian   30

179

Or quhar the bowand trumpet blew the spryng,
At Bachus dans to go in caralyng,
Syne go to fest at tabill, and syt at deß,
Se cowpys full, and mony danty meß:
Thar was ȝour lust, plesour, and appetite,   35
Thar was ȝour bissy cuyr and ȝour delyte;
Quhen that the happy spay man, on hyß gyß,
Pronuncit the festual haly sacryfyß,
And the fat offerandis dyd ȝou call on raw
To banket amyd the dern blissyt schaw."   40
And, with that word, amydwart the melle,
Reddy to sterf, his horß furth sterys he,
And awfully onon with all his mayn
Ruschit apon Venulus, stud hym agane;
And with hys rycht arm can hys fa enbraß,   45
Syk wyß he dyd hym from hys horß arraiß,
And with huge strenth syne dyd hym cowch and lay
Befor his breist, and bair hym quyte away.
The Tuscanys rasyt a clamour to the sky,
And Latynys all thar eyn abowt dyd wry.   50
This Tarchon, ardent as the fyry levyn,
Flaw furth swyft as a fowle vp towart hevyn,
Berand with hym the armour and the man;
And fra his speris poynt of brak he than
The stelit hed, and syne seyrsis all artis,   55
Euerilk entre, and all the oppyn partis,
Quhar he mycht fynd into sa litil stovnd
A place patent to geif hym dedis wond.
And, be the contrar, Venulus full wight
Maid all debait and obstakill at he mycht,   60
And can hys hand from hys throt oftsyß chop
With all hys strenth, hys violens to stop.
Lyke as, sum tyme, the ȝallo egill be sycht   f. 265^r
The eddir hyntis vp and careis on hyght,
Syne, fleand, in hir feit strenȝeis sa fast   65
That oft hyr punsys outthrow the skyn dois thrast;
Bot the serpent, wondyt and al toschent,
In lowpyt thrawys wrythis with mony a sprent,
Hyr sprutlyt skalys vpset grysly to se,
With quhisland mouth strekand hir hed on hie;   70
All thocht scho wreill and sprynkill, bend or skyp,
Evir the sarar this ern strenys hys gryp,
And with hys bowand beik rentis grewsly,
Sammyn with hys weyngis soursand in the sky –
Noyn othyr wyß, this Tarchon tursys hys pray   75
Throw owt the Tyburtyn rowtis glaid and gay.
The pepill Tuscane, quhilum cum fra Lyde,

Seand the exempill and prosper chans that tyd
Of thar stowt duke, followys hys hardyment,
And with a rusch sammyn in the bargane sprent. 80
Quhen as ane Aruns, by hys mortal fait
Onto myschewos ded predestinate,
Circulis at the wait, and aspyis abowt
The swyft madyn Camyll, of all the rowt
In honest fait of armys maist expert, 85
And best betaucht to schute or cast a dart;
He sekis by quhat ways or fortoun
To fynd the fassoun and tyme oportune
Maist esely this lady to assaill;
And all the wentis and renkis, sans faill, 90
This furyus maid held mydwart the melle,
The sammyn gait and passage haldis he,
And prevely hir futsteppys dyd espy;
And quhar scho dyd return with victory,
With ful bakwart frawart hir aducrsar, 95
This ilk Aruns was ful reddy thar,
And thyftuusly onon the sam way he
Withdrew hys payß, and held on hir hys e;
Lurkand at wayt, and spyand rownd about,
Now this tocome, now that onset, but dowt, 100
At euery part thys pevech man of weyr, f. 265ᵛ
And schuke in hand hys oneschewabill speir.

Aruns the preist slays Camylla be slycht,
Syne cowartly onon takis the flycht. C. xv

Per chans that tyde Choreus, of gret estait,
Ane spiritual man blissyt and consecrait,
That to Cybele sum tyme preist had be,
A weill lang space ȝond in the melle
Abilȝeit rychly and full gloryus schane 5
In pompus armour and array Phrygiane:
Furth dryvys he the fomy sterand steid,
With weirlyke bardis cled, and sovir wcid
Of coyrbulȝe or leddir with gilt nalys,
Cowchyt with plait of steill als thik as skalys; 10
And he hym self, in brovne sangwane weill dycht,
Abuf hys onkouth armour blomand brycht,
Schaftis he schot, and takillys wrocht in Creyt,
With Lycyane bow nokkyt with hornys meyt,
And clattryng by hys schuldyr for the weir 15
Hys ganȝe cays and goldyn awblaster;
The helm of gold schane on the prestis hed;
Of safron hew, betwix ȝallow and red,

181

Was hys rych mantill, of quham the forbreist lappys,
Ratlyng of brycht gold wyre, with gyltyn trappys 20
Or cordis fyne was buklyt with a knot;
Of nedill wark all brusyt was hys cote;
Hys hosyng schane of wark of barbary
In porturatour of subtell brusery.
Thys man only of all the mekyll rowt 25
The maid Camylla followis fast about;
Quhyddir so it was that Troiane armour sche
Lyst hyng in tempill for memor of trophe,
Or than desyryt this wantoun huntereß
In goldyn attyre hir selwyn to addreß, 30
Quhilk scho in feild byreft hyr aduersar;
Throw owt the ost onwarly went alquhar,
Blynd in desyre this Troiane to assay,
In womanly appetyt ardent of this pray,
This precyus spulȝe, and array sa prowd, 35
Quharwith, as said is, was this preist yschrowd. f. 266ʳ
Thys forsaid Aruns liggyng at the wait,
Seand this maid onflocht at sik estait,
Chosys hys tyme that was mast oportune,
And towart hir hys dart adressyt sone. 40
With voce expreß hys prayer thus maid he:
"O brycht Apollo, souerane god mast hie,
Of haly mont Soractis the wardane,
Quham pryncipaly we wirschip euery ane,
Quhamto the fyry smok of sens, we se, 45
Blesys in the kyndillit byngis of fyr tre;
As we that wirschippis the with obesans,
Be support of thy devoyt observans,
Oft with our futsteppys and our nakyt solys
Down thryngis feil hait syndris and fyry colys; 50
Grant me, fader almychty, now I pray,
With our wapynnys this schame to do away.
I ask na trophe, nor the pompoß weyd
Of this maid dovn bet or repulsyt in deid,
Nowder byd I tharof spulȝe nor renovn; 55
My other dedis syne mot mak me bovn
To report honour and lawd efter this;
Bot at this tyme I byd na mair, I wyß,
Salf that this wench, this vengeabill pest or trake,
Be bet dovn ded by my wond and smert strake, 60
And syne that I may to my kynd cite
But ony glor return alyve," quod he.
Phebus hym hard and grantit to fulfyll
Of hys axin a party, at hys wyll;
Bot for the tother part, suyth to say, 65

He leit do waif with the swyft wynd away;
Consentand that he suld doun bet and sla
By hasty ded the awfull Camylla;
Bot, at hys cuntre hailscarth haymwart brocht
Suld se hym eftir that, he grantit nocht;   70
And in the clowdy blastis of the sky
That voce and wordis flaw away in hy.
So that, als fast as from hys hand, that stond,
Thirland the ayr this takill gaue a sound,
The rowtis can aduert and takis tent,   75 f. 266ᵛ
Turnand thar syghtis, ilk wight, with a blent
Towart the queyn, thar lady, this Camyll;
Bot scho nane heyd nor tent heß tane thartill,
Nowder of the hasty motioun of the ayr,
Nor ȝit the byrrand sovnd this flycht maid thar,   80
No ȝit persauyt this awfull schaft of tre
Discendand swyftly fra the hevyn on hie;
Quhill that the lance hir smate and hurt, perſay,
Quhar that hir pap was schorn and cut away,
And weggyt deip within hir cost stude,   85
Furth sowkis largely of this madynnys blude.
Hyr complicis alsammyn in this neyd
Start to thar lady in affray and dreid;
And sone thai claucht and lappyt in thar armys
This queyn, that funderand was for hir smart harmys.   90
Bot fyrst of all, for feyr and fell affray,
Thys Aruns fled full fast and brak away,
With blythnes mydlyt havand paynfull dreid:
For he na langar durst into this neyd
Assur forto debait hym with hys speir,   95
Na ȝit abyd the virgynys wapyn, for feyr.
And lyke as that the wild wolf in hys rage
Knawand hys recent falt and gret owtrage,
Quhen that he haß sum gret ȝong oxin slane,
Or than weryit the nolt hyrd on the plane,   100
Tofor hys fays with wapynnys hym persew,
Onon is he to the heich mont adew,
And hyd hym self full far owt of the way;
Hys taill, that on hys ryg befor tymys lay,
Vnder hys waym lattis fall abasytly,   105
And to the wod can hast hym intill hy –
Nane other wyß Aruns, that fleyt wight,
Fled, and belyve withdrew hym owt of sycht;
Content only to gyf the bak and fle,
Amang the thikast preß hym hyd heß he.   110
And this Camylla, stervand the ilk stound,
The schaft haß pullyt of hir dedly wound

With hir awyn hand; bot ȝit amang the banys
The scharp steill hed fixt to the rybbys remanys
In a full deip wond and a grewos sayr.   115
All paill and bludles swarthis scho rycht thar,
And in the deth closys hir cald eyn;
The rudy cullour, vmquhile as purpour scheyn,
Blaknyt, and fadys quyte owt of hir face;
And, ȝaldand vp the gost in the ilk place,   120
Onto ane of hir damysellis and ferys,
Clepyt Acca, that had beyn mony ȝheris
Only maste trast, and hald in speciall
To Camylla abuf the otheris all,
That knew alhaill the secretis of hir hart,   125
With quham hir thochtful curys wald scho part,
That tyme scho spak, and said on this maner:
"Acca, Acca, my leif systyr deyr,
Onto this hour I haue done at I myght;
Bot now this dolorus wond so heß me dycht   130
That all thyng dymmys and myrknys me abowt.
Go fast thy way, and hy the of this rowt;
Schaw Turnus thir my last commandis," quod sche,
"Byd hym entyr in fecht in sted of me,
And fra the cite thir Troianys dryve away.   135
Adew for evir! I haue na mar to say."
Sammyn with that word the renȝeis slyp leyt sche,
And slayd to grond, nocht of fre volunte.
Than the cald deith and last stondis mortall
The spreit dissoluyt from the corps our all;   140
Hyr sowpil crag inclynand and nek bayn,
Bowyt dovn hyr hed that was with deth ourtane;
Furth sprent hyr armys in the ded thrawyng,
And fra hir kest hir wapynnys and armyng.
The spreit of lyfe fled murnand with a grone,   145
And with disdene dovn to the gostis is goyn.

Opis the nymphe with dartis of Dyane, Camylla to revenge, haß Aruns slane.

A ne huge clamour than dyd ryß on hycht,
That semyt smyte the goldyn starnys brycht.
The bargane walxis mair cruell and het
Quhar that the stowt Camylla was down bet,
For all the rowtis of the bald Troianys,   5
The Tyrrheyn dukis semlyt all at anys,
And eik Evandrus wardys of Arcadys,
Sammyn in the preß thar aduersaris invadis.
Bot Opis tho, the nymphe, that weill neirby

Be thrynfald Dyane send was to espy,   10
Sat a lang space apon ane hillys hight,
And onabasyt dyd behald the fyght.
Syn tharefter onfar scho can espy,
Amyd quhar as thir ȝongkeris rasyt this scry,
With schaymfull deth ourtane, Camyll the maid;   15
Scho wepyt soir, and plenand thus scho said,
Sobband full deip law from hir breist within:
"Allace, virgyne, to mekill, and that is syn,
To mekill all owt, sa cruell punysyng
Haß thou sufferit, certis, for sik a thyng,   20
Becauß thou hest inforsyt with all thy mycht
Fortill ennoy the Troianys in this fight!
Quhat proffitis the in buskis thyne allane
To haue servyt so lang the blissyt Diane?
Or by thy syde, or than on schuldir hie,   25
So lang our quavyrris to haue born?" quod sche.
"And, netheleß, but honour in this sted
Thy queyn heß not the left in poynt of ded;
Nor this thy slauchter but ramemberyng
Amang all pepill sall not be, nor menyng;   30
Ne salt thou not that schame suffir, trast me,
Forto betald thou suld onwrokyn be.
Quha evir with wond heß schent or violait
Thy fair body, to Dyane dedicate,
He sal repent the tyme that euer thou stervit,   35
And with his deth aby, as he hes servyt."
Vnder the montane law thar stude fute hoit
A byng of erth, vphepit like a moyt,
Contenyng the cald assis and brynt banys
Of ald Dercennus, kyng of Lawrentanys,   40
Ourheld with akyn treis and bewys rank: f. 268^r
Thyddir this goddeß, hastand dovn the bank,
Hyr self heß careyt, and thar huvys styll,
And from this knowys hycht, or lityll hyll,
Abydis this ilk Aruns till espy.   45
And fra scho hym persavys glydand by,
In rich armour schynand wonder brycht,
And all invayn, prowd, wantoun, gay and lycht:
"Quhy haldis thou awaywart so?" quod sche.
"Dreß hyddermar thy futsteppis towart me;   50
Now cummys hyddir to peryß and to sterve,
And caucht dewly, as that thou heß deserve,
Thy reward for Camyllys ded, perde.
On Dyanys dartis, ha, suld syk ane de?"
And with that word, lyke a stowt wench of Trace,   55
The swyft gilt arow schuke owt of hir cace,

And, rycht amovit, hir hornyt bow haß bent,
Quharin onon the takill vp is stent;
Syne halys vp in ire and felloun haist,
Quhil that the bowand nokkis met almaist; 60
And now hir handis raxit hyt euery sted,
Hard on the left neyf was the scharp steill hed,
The stryng, vp pullit with the rycht hand in feir,
Went by hir pap almaste ontil hir eyr.
Aruns onon the motioun of the ayr 65
Sammyn with the quhislyng of the takill squar
Persavit heß, and eik the dynt atanys;
The dedly hed throu gyrd his body and banys.
Hys ferys all heß hym forȝet allane,
Quhar as he swelt with mony a wofull grane, 70
And in ane onkouth feld heß left hym ded,
Bedoif in dust and puldyr, will of red:
Syne Opys with hir weyngis swyft can fle
Abufe the skyis heich in the hevynnys hie.

Acca to Turnus schawys Camyllais chance, Hir army fled, and left all ordinans.

C xvii

The swyft army and active rowt wyth this
Of Camilla fled first the feld, I wyß,
For thai had lost thar lady and capitane: f. 268ᵛ
The pissans haill and ostis Tyburtane
Affrayt all togydder gave the flycht; 5
The bak heß tane Atynas bald and wight;
The chiftanys brak array, and went thar gait,
The banneris left all blowt and desolait,
Socht to warrand on horsbak, he and he,
Frawart thar fays, and held to the cite. 10
Nor nane of thame, sa mayt and sa agast,
The ferß Troianys, quhilk thame assalȝeit fast,
Onto the ded and myscheif dyd invaid,
With wapynnys anys to styntyng maid a braid,
Nor thame sustene ne ȝit resist thai mycht, 15
Bot all atanys sammyn tuke the flycht,
And on thar wery schuldris with gret schame
Thar byg bowys onbent haß tursyt hame;
And the stowt stedis with thar huvys sovnd
With swyft renkis dyndlyt the dusty grond. 20
The blak stowr of puldir in a stew
Als dyrk as myst towart the wallys threw;
On the barmkyn abufe, and turettis hie,
The wemen bet thar breistis, was reuth to se,
Rasand atanys a wofull wyfly cry 25

186

Went to the starnys and thyrlyt throw the sky.
And quha mycht formest, with swyft curß heß thame set
To brek in at the oppyn patent ʒet;
The rowtis of thar ennemyß myxt ourane
Apon thame ruschis, and ourthrawys mony ane;   30
Nor thar eschape thai nocht the wrachit deth,
Bot in the portis ʒaldis vp the breth,
Stekit amyd thar native wallys hie,
And amang howsis quhar sovir semyt thame tobe.
A part closyt the entre and the portis,   35
Ne to thar ferys, nor ʒit nane other sortis,
The ʒettis listyng oppyn, nor mak way,
Nor, thocht thai oft besekyng thame and pray,
Durst thame ressaue within thar wallys squar.
A duylfull slauchter onon vprisys thar   40
Of thame in armys stude the portis to defend,   f. 269ʳ
And thame with glavys war kyllyt and maid end.
The son furthschet, that pety was to seyn,
Befor thar wepand wofull faderis eyn;
Sum in the holl fowcy war tumlyt dovn,   45
Sa thik thame cummyrris the preß thrang to the tovn;
Sum hasty and onwarly at the flycht
Sclakis thar brydillys, spurrand in all thar mycht,
Can with a ramrayß to the portis dusche,
Lyke with thar hedis the hard barris to frusch.   50
The moderis eik and wemen albedene,
Fra tyme Camylla kyllyt haue thai sene,
Knawand thar was extreme necessite,
With all debait stude on the wallys hee.
Sik thyng to do that tyme and tak on hand   55
The perfyte luf thame taucht of thar kynd land,
And all agast dartis and stanys doun threw:
The syllys squar and hedyt styngis enew,
And perkis gret with byrslyt endis and brunt,
Full hastely doun swakkis, dunt for dunt,   60
And, for defens of thar kynd wallys hie,
Offerit thame self with the formest to de.
In the meyn quhile, as Turnus at the wait
Lay in the wod, fast by the passage strait,
All the maist cruell tithingis fillys hys erys,   65
For Acca schawys to hym and all hys ferys
The huge affray, quhou the batale was gane,
The Volscane ostis distroyt, and Camyll slane,
Thar noysum fays encressyng furyus rage,
And by thar prosper Martis vassallage   70
Discumfyst all hys ostis, euery rowt,
That now the cite wallys stud in dowt.

He walxis brayn in furor bellicall,
So desyrus of dedis marciall,
For the hard fatys and strang mychtis he 75
Of the gret Ioue wald that so suldbe:
The hyllys heich he left quhar at he lay,
And from the dern woddis went away.
And scarsly was he passyt owt of syght, f. 269ᵛ
In the plane feild cummyn all at rycht, 80
Quhen that the prynce Ene with all his men
Heß entryt in and passyt throu the glen,
And our the swyre schawys vp at hys hand
Eschape the dern wod, and won the evyn land;
So that baith twa with thar haill rowtis at last 85
In all thar speid held to the cite fast.
And na lang space thar ostis war in sondir,
Bot that Ene the feildis reik lyke tundir
Of dusty stowr persauyt a far way,
And saw the Latyne rowtis ryde away; 90
And ferß Eneas, wyrkar of hys harmys,
Turnus persauyt also ryde in armys,
The dynnyng of thar horß feit eik hard he,
Thar stampyng sterage, and thar stedis ne.
Incontinent thai had to batale went, 95
And in the bargane previt thar hardyment,
Ne war, as than, the rosy Phebus red
Hys wery stedis had dowkyt our the hed
Vnder the stremys of the occeane see,
Reducyng the dyrk nycht, thai mycht not se; 100
Alhaill declynyt had the days lycht.
To tentis than befor the tovn ilk wight
Bownyng to rest, al thai that war with owt,
And delvys trynschis all the wallis abowt.

Explicit liber vndecimus Eneados
Incipit prologus in duodecimum eiusdem

The Proloug of the xii Buk of Eneados f. 270ʳ

Dyonea, nycht hyrd and wach of day,
The starnys chasyt of the hevyn away,
Dame Cynthia dovn rollyng in the see,
And Venus lost the bewte of hir e,
Fleand eschamyt within Cylenyus cave; 5
Mars onbydrew, for all his grundyn glave,
Nor frawart Saturn from hys mortall speir
Durst langar in the firmament appeir,

Bot stall abak ʒond in hys regioun far
Behynd the circulat warld of Iupiter;   10
Nycthemyne, affrayt of the lyght,
Went ondir covert, for gone was the nycht;
As fresch Aurora, to myghty Tytan spows,
Ischit of hir safron bed and evir hows,
In crammysyn cled and granyt violat,   15
With sangwyne cape, the selvage purpurat,
Onschet the wyndois of hir large hall,
Spred all with rosys, and full of balm ryall,
And eik the hevynly portis cristallyne
Vpwarpis braid, the warld till illumyn.   20
The twynklyng stremowris of the orient
Sched purpour sprangis with gold and asur ment,
Persand the sabill barmkyn nocturnall,
Bet doun the skyis clowdy mantill wall;
Eous the steid, with ruby hamys red,   25
Abuf the sey lyftis furth hys hed,
Of cullour soyr, and sumdeill brovn as berry,
Forto alichtyn and glaid our emyspery,
The flambe owtbrastyng at his noyß thyrlys;
Sa fast Pheton with the quhyp hym quhyrlys,   30
To roll Appollo hys faderis goldyn char,
That schrowdith all the hevynnys and the ayr;
Quhill schortly, with the blesand torch of day,
Abilʒeit in hys lemand fresch array,
Furth of hys palyce ryall ischit Phebus,   35
With goldyn crovn and vissage gloryus,
Crysp haris, brycht as chrisolyte or topace,
For quhais hew mycht nane behald hys face,
The fyry sparkis brastyng from hys eyn,   f. 270ᵛ
To purge the ayr, and gylt the tendyr greyn,   40
Defundand from hys sege etheryall
Glaid influent aspectis celicall;
Befor hys regale hie magnificens
Mysty vapour vpspryngand, sweit as sens,
In smoky soppys of donk dewis wak,   45
Moch hailsum stovys ourheldand the slak.
The aureat fanys of hys trone souerane
With glytrand glans ourspred the occiane,
The large fludis lemand all of lycht
Bot with a blenk of hys supernale sycht.   50
Fortobehald, it was a glor to se
The stablit wyndis and the cawmyt see,
The soft sesson, the firmament sereyn,
The lowne illumynat ayr, and fyrth ameyn;
The syluer scalyt fyschis on the greit   55

Ourthwort cleir stremys sprynkland for the heyt,
With fynnys schynand brovn as synopar,
And chyssell talys, stowrand heir and thar;
The new cullour alychtnyng all the landis,
Forgane thir stannyris schane the beriall strandis,   60
Quhil the reflex of the diurnall bemys
The beyn bonkis kest ful of variant glemys;
And lusty Flora dyd hyr blomys spreid
Vnder the feit of Phebus sulȝart steid;
The swardit soyll enbrovd with selcouth hewys,   65
Wod and forest obumbrat with thar bewys,
Quhois blisfull branschis, porturat on the grund,
With schaddoys schene schew rochis rubicund;
Towris, turettis, kyrnellis, pynnaclys hie
Of kyrkis, castellis and ilke fair cite,   70
Stude payntit, euery fyall, fayn and stage,
Apon the plane grund, by thar awyn vmbrage.
Of Eolus north blastis havand no dreid,
The sulȝe spred hir braid bosum on breid,
Ȝephyrus confortabill inspiratioun   75
Fortill ressaue law in hyr barm adoun;
The cornys croppis and the beris new brerd
With glaidsum garmont revestyng the erd;   f. 271ʳ
So thik the plantis sprang in euery peyce,
The feildis ferleis of thar fructuus fleyce;   80
Byssy Dame Ceres and provd Pryapus,
Reiosyng of the planys plentuus,
Plenyst sa plesand and mast propyrly,
By Natur nurysyt wondir nobilly,
On the fertill skyrt lappys of the grund   85
Strekyng on breid ondyr the cyrkyll rovnd;
The variand vestur of the venust vaill
Schrowdis the scherald fur, and euery faill
Ourfret with fulȝeis of figuris full diuerß,
The spray bysprent with spryngand sprowtis dispers,   90
For callour humour on the dewy nyght,
Rendryng sum place the gerß pilis thar hycht,
Als fer as catal, the lang symmyris day,
Had in thar pastur eyt and knyp away;
And blisfull blossummys in the blomyt ȝard   95
Submittis thar hedis in the ȝong sonnys salfgard:
Ive levys rank ourspred the barmkyn wall,
The blomyt hawthorn cled hys pykis all;
Furth of fresch burgionys the wyne grapis ȝyng
Endlang the treilȝeis dyd on twystis hyng;   100
The lowkyt buttonys on the gemmyt treis
Ourspredand leyvis of Naturis tapestreis,

190

Soft gresy verdour eftir balmy schowris
On curland stalkis smylyng to thar flowris;
Behaldand thame sa mony diuerß hew, 105
Sum perß, sum paill, sum burnet, and sum blew,
Sum greyce, sum gowlys, sum purpour, sum sangwane,
Blanchit or brovne, fawch ȝallow mony ane,
Sum hevynly culloryt in celestiall gre,
Sum watry hewit as the haw wally see, 110
And sum depart in freklys red and quhite,
Sum brycht as gold with aureat levys lyte.
The dasy dyd onbreid hir crownell smaill,
And euery flour onlappyt in the daill;
In battill gyrß burgionys the banwart wild, 115
The clavyr, catcluke, and the cammamyld; f. 271ᵛ
The flour delyß furthspred hys hevynly hew,
Flour dammes, and columby blank and blew;
Seir downys smaill on dent de lyon sprang
The ȝyng greyn blomyt straberry levys amang; 120
Gymp gerraflouris thar royn levys onschet,
Fresch prymroß, and the purpour violet;
The royß knoppys, tutand furth thar hed,
Gan chyp, and kyth thar vermel lippys red,
Crysp scarlet levis sum scheddand, baith atanys 125
Kest fragrant smell amyd from goldyn granys;
Hevynly lylleis, with lokrand toppys quhyte,
Oppynnyt and schew thar creistis redymyte,
The balmy vapour from thar silkyn croppys
Distilland hailsum sugurat hunny droppys, 130
And syluer schakaris gan fra levys hyng,
With crystal sprayngis on the verdour ȝyng;
The plane pulderit with semly settis sovnd,
Bedyit full of dewy peirlys rovnd,
So that ilk burgioun, syon, herb and flour 135
Wolx all enbalmyt of the fresch liquour,
And bathit hait dyd in dulce humouris fleyt,
Quharof the beys wrocht thar hunny sweit.
By myghty Phebus operations,
In sappy subtell exalations. 140
Forgane the cummyn of this prynce potent,
Redolent odour vp from rutis sprent,
Hailsum of smell as ony spicery,
Tryakill, droggis, or electuary,
Seroppys, sewane, sugur, and synamome, 145
Precyus invnctment, salve, or fragrant pome,
Aromatik gummys, or ony fyne potioun,
Must, myr, aloes, or confectioun –
Ane paradyce it semyt to draw neir

Thir gal3art gardyngis and ilke greyn herber.					150
Maist amyabill walxis the amerant medis;
Swannys swouchis throw owt the rysp and redis,
Our al thir lowys and the fludis gray
Seirsand by kynd a place quhar thai suld lay.
Phebus red fowle hys corall creist can steir,				155		f. 272ʳ
Oft strekyng furth hys hekkill, crawand cleir,
Amyd the wortis and the rutys gent
Pykland hys meyt in alleis quhar he went,
Hys wifis, Coppa and Partelot, hym by,
As byrd al tyme that hantis bigamy.					160
The pantyt povn, pasand with plomys gym,
Kest vp his taill, a provd plesand quheill rym,
Yschrowdyt in hys fedrame brycht and scheyn,
Schapand the prent of Argus hundreth eyn.
Amang the bronys of the olyve twestis				165
Seir smaill fowlys wirkand crafty nestis,
Endlang the heggeis thyk and on rank akis,
Ilk byrd reiosyng with thar myrthfull makis.
In corneris and cleir fenystaris of glaß
Full bissely Aragne wevand was,					170
To knyt hir nettis and hir wobbys sle,
Tharwith to caucht the myghe and litill fle.
So dusty pulder vpstowris in euery streit,
Quhil corby gaspyt for the fervent heit.
Vnder the bewys beyn in lusty valys,					175
Within fermans and parkis cloyß of palys,
The bustuus bukkis rakis furth on raw;
Heyrdis of hertis throw the thyk wod schaw,
Baith the brokkettis, and with braid burnyst tyndis,
The sprutlyt calvys sowkand the red hyndis,			180
The 3ong fownys followand the dun days,
Kyddis skippand throw ronnys efter rays;
In lyssouris and on leys litill lammys
Full tayt and tryg socht bletand to thar dammys,
Tydy ky lowys, veilys by thame rynnys;				185
All snog and slekit worth thir bestis skynnys.
On salt stremys wolx Doryda and Thetis,
By rynnand strandis Nymphes and Naedes,
Sik as we clepe wenschis and damysellis,
In gresy gravys wandrand by spryng wellis,				190
Of blomyt branchis and flowris quhite and red
Plettand thar lusty chaplettis for thar hed;
Sum sang ryng sangis, dansys ledys, and rovndis,				f. 272ᵛ
With vocis schill, quhill all the dail resovndis;
Quharso thai walk into thar caralyng,					195
For amorus lays doith the rochys ryng:

192

Ane sang, "The schyp salys our the salt faym,
Will bryng thir merchandis and my lemman haym;"
Sum other syngis, "I wilbe blyth and lycht,
Myne hart is lent apon sa gudly wight."   200
And thochtfull luffaris rowmys to and fro,
To lyß thar pane, and pleyn thar ioly wo,
Eftir thar gyß, now syngand, now in sorow,
With hartis pensyve, the lang symmyris morow:
Sum ballettis lyst endyte of hys lady,   205
Sum levis in hoip, and sum aluterly
Disparit is, and sa quyte owt of grace,
Hys purgatory he fyndis in euery place.
To pleyß his lufe sum thocht to flat and feyn,
Sum to hant bawdry and onlesum meyn;   210
Sum rownys to hys fallow, thame betwene,
Hys myrry stouth and pastans lait ȝisterevin:
Smyland says ane, "I couth in previte
Schaw the a bovrd." "Ha, quhat be that?" quod he,
"Quhat thyng?" "That most be secrete," said the tother.   215
"Gud Lord, mysbeleif ȝe ȝour verray broder?"
"Na, neuer a deill, bot harkis quhat I wald;
Thou mon be prevy." "Lo, my hand vphald."
"Than sal thou walk at evin." Quod he, "Quhidder?"
"In sik a place heir west, we baith togydder,   220
Quhar scho so freschly sang this hyndyr nycht;
Do choyß the ane, and I sall quynch the lycht."
"I salbe thar I hope," quod he and lewch,
"ȝa, now I knaw the mater weill eneuch."
Thus oft dywlgat is this schamefull play,   225
Na thyng accordyng to our hailsum May,
Bot rathar contagius and infectlve,
And repugnant that sesson nutrytyve,
Quhen new curage kytlys all gentill hartis,
Seand throu kynd ilk thyng spryngis and revertis.   230
Dame Naturis menstralis, on that other part,
Thar blysfull bay entonyng cuery art,   f. 273ʳ
To beyt thir amorus of thar nychtis baill,
The merl, the mavyß and the nychtyngale
With mery notis myrthfully furth brest,   235
Enforcyng thame quha mycht do clynk it best:
The cowschet crowdis and pyrkis on the ryß,
The styrlyng changis diuerß stevynnys nyß,
The sparrow chyrmys in the wallis clyft,
Goldspynk and lyntquhite fordynnand the lyft;   240
The gukgo galys, and so quytteris the quaill,
Quhill ryveris rerdit, schawis and euery vaill,
And tender twystis trymlyt on the treis

For byrdis sang and bemyng of the beys;
In wrablis dulce of hevynly armonyis   245
The larkis, lowd releschand in the skyis,
Lovys thar lege with tonys curyus,
Baith to Dame Natur and the fresch Venus,
Rendryng hie lawdis in thar obseruance;
Quhais suguryt throtis maid glaid hartis danß,   250
And al smail fowlys syngis on the spray:
"Welcum the lord of lycht and lamp of day,
Welcum fostyr of tendir herbys grene,
Welcum quyknar of floryst flowris scheyn,
Welcum support of euery rute and vayn,   255
Welcum confort of alkynd fruyt and grayn,
Welcum the byrdis beild apon the brer,
Welcum master and rewlar of the 3er,
Welcum weilfar of husbandis at the plewys,
Welcum reparar of woddis, treis and bewys,   260
Welcum depayntar of the blomyt medis,
Welcum the lyfe of euery thyng that spredis,
Welcum storour of alkynd bestiall,
Welcum be thy brycht bemys, gladyng all,
Welcum celestial myrrour and aspy,   265
Attechyng all that hantis sluggardy!"
And with this word, in chalmer quhar I lay,
The nynt morow of fresch temperit May,   f. 273ᵛ
On fut I sprent into my bair sark,
Wilfull fortill compleit my langsum wark   270
Twichand the lattyr buke of Dan Virgill,
Quhilk me had tareit al to lang a quhile;
And tobehald the cummyng of this kyng,
That was sa welcum tyll all warldly thyng,
With sic tryumphe and pompos curage glaid   275
Than of hys souerane chymmys, as is said,
Newly aryssyn in hys estait ryall,
That, by hys hew, but orleger or dyall,
I knew it was past four howris of day,
And thocht I wald na langar ly in May   280
Leß Phebus suld me losanger attaynt –
For Progne had or than sung hir complaynt,
And eik hir dreidfull systir Philomeyn
Hyr lays endyt, and in woddis greyn
Hyd hir selvyn, eschamyt of hir chance;   285
And Esacus completis hys pennance
In ryveris, fludis, and on euery laik;
And Peristera byddis luffaris awaik:
"Do serve my lady Venus heir with me,
Lern thus to mak 3our obseruance," quod sche,   290

"Into myne hartis ladeis sweit presens
Behaldis how I beynge, and do reuerens."
Hyr nek scho wrynklys, trasyng mony fold,
With plomys glitterand, asur apon gold,
Rendryng a cullour betwix greyn and blew,   295
In purpour glans of hevynly variant hew;
I meyn our awyn natyve byrd, gentill dow,
Syngand in hyr kynd, "I come hydder to wow,"
So pryklyng hyr greyn curage forto crowd
In amorus voce and wowar soundis lowd,   300
That, for the dynnyng of hir wanton cry,
I irkyt of my bed, and mycht not ly,
Bot gan me blyß, syne in my wedis dreß,
And, for it was ayr morow, or tyme of meß,
I hynt a scriptour and my pen furth tuke,   305
Syne thus begouth of Virgill the twelt buke. etc

Explicit scitus prologus,
Quharof the autour says thus:

The lusty crafty preambill, "perle of May"
I the entitil, crownyt quhil domysday,
And al with gold, in syng of stait ryall
Most beyn illumnyt thy letteris capital. etc   310

Turnus, persavand the Latyn pepill faill,   f. 274ʳ
Promittis Eneas allone hym tyll assaill.   C. i

Quhen Turnus knew the Latyn pepill haill
Irk of the weir, and saw thar curage faill,
By the frawart aduersiteis of Mart,
Quhilk war tofor onbrokyn and stowt of hart,
And thocht the tyme requiris hym, but abaid,   5
Forto compleit the promys he had maid,
Semyng as towartis hym tho euery wight
To that effect addressyt thar luke and sycht,
Than, onrequirit, by insaciabill desyre
Langang to feght, and byrnand hait as fyre,   10
Full hie rasand hys curage and hys cheir,
He gan amyd the audiens appeir.
Fers as a wild lyoun ȝond in Trace,
By the huntar wondyt in the chace,
Quhen the smert straik in hys breist all fast is,   15
For ire the lokkyrris of hys nek vpcastis,
Than first begynnyng to rayß hys stern muyd,
Reiosyt of the bataill, fers and wod,
Onabasytly raschand the schaft in sundir,

195

And on the man liggand at wait thar vndir,   20
Hym to revenge, with bludy mouth doys bray –
Nane other wyß ferd Turnus the ilk day,
Smytyn so brym in fervent violens,
That all commouyt in the kyngis presens
On this maner begouth to speke and say: 25
"Thar sall in Turnus be fund na delay;
And al for nocht ʒon cowart Eneadanys
Thar promyß and thar wordis cumis aganys,
Willyng retreit thar behestis and sawys;
Sa salt thai nocht; we wil nane sik lawys: 30
I sal thar falshed resist and ganestand,
And feght contrar thar chiftane hand for hand.
Thou ryall prynce and fader, Kyng Latyne,
Do sacryfy and conferm this convyne: f. 274ᵛ
For owdyr sall I with thir handis twa   35
ʒon ilk Troiane, banyst of Asya,
Do put to deth, send down to hell," quod he,
"Lat Latyn pepill syttyng by to se
Quhou, myne allane with swerd in thar presens
I sall revenge and end our allyris offens;   40
Or than, gyf so betyd he wyn the gre,
Lat ws all venquyst to hym subiect be,
ʒeld hym the crown enduryng term of lyve,
And lat hym ioys Lavinia to hys wyfe."
Kyng Latyn tho with sad and degest mynd   45
To hym answeris, and said apon this kynd:
"O douchty ʒyngkeir, excellent of curage,
Quhou far as by thy forcy vassallage
My febill age thou doith exceid," quod he,
"Als far mair diligently pertenys me,   50
And ganand is, to consell and provyde,
And exemyn euery chance may betyde,
As I that haß in part a maner feir,
Be lang experiens knawand the dowtis of weir.
Thow weldis Dawnus thy faderis realm and land,   55
And feil citeis conquest with thyne awyn hand;
Tharto thou haß alsso a gentill hart,
Liberall and fre, and in weir most expert,
And Kyng Latyn heß gold to geif the eik.
Perfay, enew otheris, not far to seik,   60
Of madynnys beyn onwed in Latyum wyde,
And in the Lawrent feildis heir besyde,
Of blude and frendschip na thyng myssemand,
Bot worthy to be queyn of ony land.
Thoill me, I pray the, al dissait done away,   65
Thir wordis quhoyn of weght to the till say,

196

And sammyn prent thir sawys in thy wyt.
Onlesum is I suld in wedlok knyt
My douchtir till ald wowaris of this land,
That hir tofor had axit in sik band: 70
All the spa men and goddis revelyng
Declarit plane that was onlesum thyng.
And netheleß, I, venquyst cleyn but weir,
For luf of the my spowsys cousyng deir, f. 275ʳ
Ourcummyn be hir wofull terys and syte, 75
All maner bandys now heß brokyn quyte;
And fra my son in law, full wrangwisly,
Hys spouß onto hym promyst reft haue I,
And forthir on hym movit a wikkyt weir.
Sen syne in quhate chance I stand and danger, 80
And quhou fers batellis now persewys me,
Full weill thou wait and seis, Turnus," quod he,
"And quhou huge travale thou has tholit and pane,
As principall maste douchty capitane.
Lo, twyß in batale venquyst haue we be, 85
And now scantly within our wallit cite
The hope and weill of Italy defendis;
Now of our recent blude, as noterly kend is,
The flude of Tibir walxis hait agane,
And of our huge banys quhite semys the plane. 90
Quhou am I sterit thus in purpoß seir?
And quhidder flow I thus oft thar and heir?
Quhat mad foly all tochangis my thocht?
Gyf that I reddy be and dowtit nocht
The Troianys for my frendis to ressaue, 95
Gif so war Turnus ded war and bygrave,
Quhat, aucht I nocht far rather end the weir
He beand in prosperyte haill and feir?
Quhat wald our cosyngis, the Rutilianys,
Or quhat wald say the other Italianys, 100
Gyf the I suld thus wyß sa wilfully,
Axyng our douchteris wedlok and ally,
Expone or offer to the ded?" quod he.
"Forton defend that chance at sa suld be!
Behald the chance of batale variabill, 105
Persave of weir the fykkill ward onstabill:
Haue reuth and mercy of thy fader ald,
Quham Ardea now, hys cuntre, doys withhald,
Diuidit far and disseuerit from the,
And for thy saik quhou wobegone is he." 110
Thus said the kyng, bot the violent curage
Of Turnus hie mynd bowit neuer a stage;
Quha wald with cuyr of medycyne hym meyß,

The moir encressys and growys hys mail eyß;   f. 275ᵛ
And, eftir that he first mycht speke agane,   115
Thus he began expreym with wordis plane:
"O thou maist souerane fader, I the pray,
To salue my honour, thou wald do away
Thir curis, thochtis and solicitude
For me thou takis; and, schortly to conclude,   120
Suffir me forto pleg my deth in wage,
For gloryus renovn of vassillage;
For we, fader, can swak dartis and brandis,
Nocht with febill bot stalwart rycht handis,
And of our wondis the red blude ruschis owt.   125
To 30nder provd Troiane, clepit sa stowt,
Hys moder at this tyme salbe far to seik,
Quhilk goddes with hir subtell slychtis eik
Hir son, accustumat to tak the flycht,
Was wont to dek, and to hyde owt of sycht   130
Within a wifly clowd, as for a trayn,
And heild hir self alsso in schaddois vayn."

The queyn perswadis Turnus fra stryfe desist,
Bot he for batal can agane resist.   C. ii

Be than the queyn Amata, all in feir
 Of this onkouth and new maner of weir,
Wepyng full soir, all dedlyke, full of harmys,
Hyr son in law Turnus hynt in hir armys,
That was sa fervent in his ardent desyre.   5
"Turnus," said scho, "thou best belovit syre,
Be thir ilk wofull terys I the pra,
And be the wirschip thou aw till Amata,
Gyf ony honour of hir or thy kyn
Twichys or movis into thy breist within,   10
I the beseik a thyng, myne awyn knycht;
Desist and ceß to mach Troianys in fight.
Thou only comfort of our febill eld,
Thou all our rest, our weilfar and our beld,
Haue reuth and piete of my wofull baill: 15
In thy power and mycht restis alhaill
The wirschip and empyre of Kyng Latyn;
Hys howß and famyll, now lyke to declyne,
In the remanys, and is by the vpbor.   f. 276ʳ
I the assuyr, and certifeis tharfor,   20
Quhat aventour in this fight sall happyn the,
The self chance, Turnus, sall betyd me:
Sammyn with the, gif thou endis in that stryfe,
I sal depart furth of this irksum lyfe,

Nor nevir thrall sall I remane to se   25
3on ilk Eneas son in law to me."
Lavinia the maid, with soir smert,
Hyr moderis wordis felt deip in hyr hart,
So that the rud dyd hyr vissage glow,
And full of terys gan hyr chekis strow;   30
The fervent fyre of schame rysys on hie,
Kyndland mar large the red culloryt bewte,
So that the natural heit the blude dyd chace
Our all the partis of hir quhitly face;
Quhill that this virgyn, in this wofull rage,   35
Syk cullouris rendris from hir fresch vissage,
As quha byspark wald the quhite evor Indane
With scarlet droppis or with brovn sangwane,
Or quhar the scheyn lylleis in ony sted
War pulderit with the vermel rosys red.   40
The hait luf trublys sor the knyght,
That on this maid he fixis all hys sycht,
And all the mair he byrnys in desyre
Of bargane into armys, hait as fyre;
Syne to the queyn Amata, but abaid,   45
In few wordis on this wyß he said:
"O my deir moder, of thy wepyng ho,
I 3ow beseik, do not, do not so,
Persew me not thus with 3our grete and teris,
Nor quhen I paß onto thir mortall werys,   50
In marciall bargane contrary my fo,
Do wa to present me sik takyn of wo:
In Turnus myghtis lyis nocht," quod he,
"The chance of deth to mak hym selvyn fre,
I say, gyf deth this way be to me schaip,   55
Now may I not astart, nor it eschape,
For at this tyme instant my messynger,
Idmon clepyt, my credens hecht tober
Now to 3one Troiane tyrrand, rehersyng   f. 276ᵛ
My wordis, quhilkis lykis hym na thyng,   60
That is to knaw, to morow, als ayrly
As brycht Aurora in the orient sky
With rosy chariot lyftis vp hir hed,
The firmament schrowdyng in cullour red,
That he move not aganys Rutilyanys,   65
Hys ostis, nor nane army of Troianys,
Bot athir half fra batale, for the best,
Baith sall Troianys and Rutilianys thame rest;
And lat ws twa, this bargane to conclude,
Betwix ws only dereyn with our blude,   70
And into 3onder feld, in stalwart stryfe,

Lat athir seik Lavinia to hys wyfe."
Fra this was said, fast to hys in he spedis,
And bad onon do lat hym se hys stedis:
Behaldand thame reiosys he in hart,   75
To se thame stand sa fers with curage smart;
Quhilk kynd of horß quhilum, as thai say,
Orythia, the lusty fresch may,
Of Athenis the kyngis douchter and ayr,
As ane maste ryall presand, wonder fair,   80
Send from hir cuntre to Kyng Pilumnus,
Was forgrandschir onto this ilk Turnus;
The quhilk stedis, schapyn at all delyte,
Excedit far the snaw in cullour quhite;
To speke of speid, thar swyftnes was ontald,   85
For thai the wyndis blast forryn wald.
The byssy knapys and verlettis of hys stabill
Abowt thame stud, full ʒaip and seruyabill,
And with thar holl luyffis gan thame cheir,
Dyd clap and straik thar leyndis to mak thame steir,   90
Thar lokrand manys and thar crestis hie
Dressys with trelʒeis and camys honestlye.
Fra thens onto hys chalmyr went he syne;
Abowt his schuldris assays hys halbryk fyne,
Of burnyst maill, and schynand rychely   95
Of fynast gold and quhitly alcomy.
Tharwith alsso hys swerd addressis he,
Quhat way he wald it oys in the melle;
Hys sovir scheld assays he alsso,
And eik hys tymbret helm with crestis two;   100   f. 277ʳ
Quhilk swerd was maid onto Dawnus hys syre
Be Wlcanus, the myghty god of fyre,
That forgyt this blaid and temperit with hys handis,
Hait glowand dyppyt in the Stigiane strandis.
Syne with gret fors, enarmyt in all hys geir,   105
Full lychtly vp he hynt hys stalwart speir,
Quhilk tho amyddis the hall lenand stud
Vp by a pillar huge squar and rude,
Quhilum the spulʒe he byreft from ane
Clepyt Actor, a capitane Auruncane;   110
The schaft he schuke and branglys lustely,
Tharto with lowd voce thus can he cry:
"O now thou speir, that nevir failʒeit thy deid
Quhen I the callyt to my desyre in neid,
Quhilum the weldit Actor, mast douchty knycht,   115
Now the in hand withaldis Turnus wight;
Now is the tyme that I maste myster the;
Forto dovn bet the corps thou grant to me

200

Of ȝondir Phrigiane, is skant half a man,
That with my stalwart handis I may than 120
Hys halbrik of hys body to arraß,
Hakkyt and rent and persyt in mony place,
And in the dusty puldyr heir and thar
Suddill and fyle hys crispand ȝallow hair,
That ayr maid creyß, and curlys now sa weill, 125
Yplet ilk nycht on the warm broch of steill,
Dekkyt and donk, on hys wifly maner,
Of fragrant myr and other envnctmentis seir."
With sykkyn fury rage catchyt is he,
That thus he carpys till a schaft of tre; 130
And from the vissage of this ardent syre
The sparkis glydis as the hait fyre,
For verray fervour of the feirfull teyn
Schynys and brystis furth of baith hys eyn –
Lyke as the bull, that bargane begyn wald, 135
Gevis terribill rowstis and lowis monyfald,
Or than aggrevit, bustuus and furthborn,
Presys hys ire to assay with hys horn,
Lenand hys spald to the stok of a tre,
And with hys dynt the wynd torentis he, 140
Or, forto mak debait apon the land,
With hys hard clufe vpwarpys fast the sand.
In the self tyme, na leß of curage, Enee,
Cled in hys moderis armour awfull to se,
Scharpys hym self in furour marciall, 145
Rasand hys greif for ardour bellicall,
And ioyus wolx of weir to mak ane end
By syk proffer and poyntment as was send.
Syne comfortis he hys feryo dolorus,
And mesyt the dreid of sad Ascanyus, 150
Declarand thame the fatale ordinans,
Thar destyne, and goddis purvians;
And to the kyng of Lawrenteis, Latyn,
Twychand this forsaid trety and convyne,
Bad the messyngeris bair hame but delay 155
Sovir answer, as thai desyrit alway,
And of the peyß and trewys, as thai spak,
Proclame articulis and lawys of contract.

f. 277^v

Iuno, knawand Turnus last day at end,
To stop the bargane haß Iuturna send.   C. iii

S carsly vpsprang the nixt day followyng,
  Scheddand the bemys of hys bryght mornyng
Apon the toppis of the montanys hie,
As Phebus stedis first of the deip se
Rasyt thar hedis and noyß thirlys on hight,   5
Our all the feildis blawand the cleir lyght;
Quhen that the Troianys and Rutilianys
The grund myssouris, evynnys, dichtis and planys,
Vndir the wallys of the cheif cite,
Thar as the feild and fechtyng place suldbe;   10
Amyddis quham the harthis vp thai set,
Quharon the fyris suldbe maid and bet,
And to the common goddis eik bedeyn
The altaris coverit with the scherald greyn.
Sum otheris brocht the fontane watir fair,   15
And sum the haly ingill with thame bair;
With lynnyng valis or lyke apronys lycht
Thai war arrayt, and thar hedis dicht
In wyppys of the haly herb vervane.   f. 278ʳ
The legionys tho furth haldis to the plane,   20
And all the rowtis of Awsonyanys,
That otherwyß ar hait Italyanys,
Furth thryngis at the portis full attonys,
With lancis lang and pykkis for the nonys.
Thydder all the Troianys wardis, by and by,   25
And Tyrrheyn ostis ruschis hastely,
Bodyn full weill in nobill armour seir;
Nane otherwyß with wapynnys and with geir
Arrayt for the batale all at rycht,
Than thocht the fury of Mars thame callit to fycht.   30
Amyd the thousandis swyftly throw the planys
Furth sprentis lustely thir capitanys,
In rich purpour arrayt and fyne gold brycht,
Assaricus sonnys and Mnestheus wight,
And on the tother part strang Asilas,   35
And bald Mesapus also with hym was,
Neptunus son, expert in horß dantyng.
And eftir that the trumpet blew a syng,
Than euery partyment bownys to thar stand,
And gan thar speris stik doun in the land,   40
Set by thar scheildis, to behald the fyne.
The wemen wedois and the matronys syne,
Desyrus forto se the bargane stowt,
Of childyr and of commonys mony a rowt

202

That couth na wapynnys weld, nor armour weir,   45
With the onweldy agit folk infeir,
Clam on the hight and hedis of the towris,
The wallys all and howsis ryggyngis flowris;
And sum abufe apon the portis hie
Ascendit ar to behald the melle.   50
Bot Iuno tho dovn from the hycht, I wyß,
Of the montane that Albane clepit is
Now in our days (set than this hyllys dovn
Had nowder name, honour nor renovne),
Scho dyd behald amyd the feildis plane   55
Athir batellis and the ostis twane,
Baith of the Troianys and the Laurenteis,
And Kyng Latynus cite eik scho seys.
Onon to Turnus systyr vp on hie,   f. 278ᵛ
That clepit was Iuturna, carpys sche,   60
Thys goddes to that haly nymphe, mastres
Of wellys, stankis and rowtand stremys expreß,
Quhilk honour Ioue, the kyng of hevynnys hie,
Hyr gave for the byreft virginite,
Said: "O thou nymphe, wirschip of fludis cleir,   65
That to my saul is hald maste leif and deir,
Thow knawys weill, I the preferrit ay
To all the otheris damysellys, perfay,
Of Latyn cuntre, quhat so evir thai wer
That wrangwisly ascendit or drew neir   70
The bed onprofitabill of Iupiter mast hie;
And glaidly eik haue I not stakyt the
Intill a party of the hevyn alssua?
Hark now thy sorow, thou Iuturna,
And wyte me not bot I the warnyt haue.   75
Turnus and thy cheif cite haue I save,
Sa lang as that the fatis sufferit me,
And quhill werd sisteris sa tholyt tobe;
Bot now I se that ȝong man haste, but faill,
To mach in feild with fatis inequaill;   80
The lattir day and term approchis ne
Of fatale fors and strangast destyne.
Nowder this bargane ȝonder on the greyn
Nor confideratioun may I se with eyn.
Paß thou on, for thy deir brothir germane   85
Gyf thou dar suffir ony mar dreidfull pane;
To the this semys and pertenys," quod sche,
"Gyf that, perchans, ony bettyr may be,
Or eft betyd onto ȝon catyvis kend."
Scars had Iuno thir wordis brocht to end,   90
Quhen that the nymphe Iuturna bedeyn

203

Plente of terys furth3et from hir eyn;
Hyr fair quhite breist, thar as scho dyd stand,
Thryß or four tymys smait with hir awyn hand.
Saturnus get, this Iuno, says: "Tha terys   95
Na wyß to this tyme pertenys nor efferys.
Hast the, gyf that thou can be ony way
Withdraw thy brother from the deth away;
Or than do mak the ostis baith on steir,
Provok the batale, and thame move to weir,   100   f. 279ʳ
And this convyn and trety, new consave,
Do brek, disturb and with the wynd bywave.
I sall the warrand and the wyrkar be
To mak the baldly vndertak," quod sche.
On this wyß Iuno can this nymphe exort,   105
And left hir hail in weir and dowt, at schort,
With mynd full tryst, wobegone and onsound,
Full deip smyttyn with the sorowfull wound.

Heir followis the sacrifyce and prayer
Fyrst of Eneas, syne Kyng Latyn infeir.   C. iv

In the meyn tyme, the kyngis of athir rowt
From thar citeis and strenthis ischis owt.
Amyd a four quhelit char Latyn that thraw
With huge pomp by stedis fowr was draw,
Quhais haris and hys tymplis war weil dycht   5
With ryall crown of fyne gold burnyst brycht,
Quharon stud turrettis twelf, lyke bemys scheyn,
As it ane rych enornament had beyn
Of cleir Phebus, that was hys grandschir hald:
Nixt quham furth rollyt was Prynce Turnus bald   10
Within a twa quhelyt chariot of delyte,
That drawyn was with stedis twa mylk quhyte;
In athir hand held he, in feir of weir,
The braid hed brangland on the ievillyng speir.
The fader Eneas alsso furth withall,   15
Of Romane lynnage the originall,
Apon the tother half com thame agane,
With byrnyst scheild that brycht as starris schane,
And hevynly armour lemand all of lycht:
Besyde hym raid Ascanyus the sweit wyght,   20
That semyt weil, till euery manis doym,
Ane other gude beleif and hope to gret Roym.
Furth come the preste, quhamto accordyt mak
The sacrifice of concord and contract,
In vestment cleyn, for syk religioun wrocht,   25
And a 3ong byrsyt swyne befor thame brocht,

204

With a rowch twyntyr scheip sammyn infeir,
Quhais woll or fleyce was neuer clyp with scheir;
The bestis furth heß tursyt this ilke syre   f. 279ᵛ
Onto the altar blesand of hait fyre.   30
The princis tho, quhilkis suld this payce makyng,
Turnys towartis the brycht sonnys vprysyng,
With the salt meldyr in thar handis raith;
The forrettis of thir bestis toppys baith
Thai clyp and myssour, as tho was the gyß,   35
And cowpys full of wyne in sacryfyß
Abowt the altaris ȝettis he and he.
With drawyn swerd syne the reuthfull Enee
Hys orison furth maid, and thus he said:
"O thou brycht son, with thy scheyn bemys glaid,   40
Be wytnes now till my behest, I pray;
And this ilk grund mot testyfy quhat I say,
For quham sa gret payn and aduersyte
I sufferit haue feill syth on land and see;
And thou almychty Ioue heir my prayer;   45
Saturnus douchtir, thou hys spowß sa deir,
Now mor benyng than thou was of befor,
Sweit goddeß, heir me now, I the implor;
And gentill Mars now takis tent heirtill,
That withhaldis and writhis at thy will   50
Every batale, stryfe, weirfar or debait
Vndyr thy hie power deificait;
All fludys I call, fontanys and stremys cleir,
And all maner of reuerend goddis seir
Abuf the hevyn ydred and starrit sky;   55
And ȝow eik, blissyt wightis, I testify,
That vnder erth or law in hell doun beyn,
Or in the fomy seis stremys greyn:
Gif so betyd, that fallys the victory
To Turnus on the Ausonyan party,   60
It is conuenient, and we grant to fle,
As venquyst folk, till Evandrus cite;
Ascanyus sall als tyte thir feildis withdraw,
Nor Eneadanys neuer, from the ilk thraw,
Aganyst ȝou sall rebell nor move weir,   65
Ne with na wapynnys eft thys cuntre deir.
Bot gif so beys, Mars our god glorius   f. 280ʳ
The victory and ouyrhand grantis ws
(As I beleif far rathar sal befall,
And that als tyte conferm mot goddis all   70
Throw the gret mychtis of thar deite!),
Gif that sa fair fortoun betydis me,
Ne will I not command Italianys

205

Tobe subiect, nor obey the Troianys,
Ne ȝit this realm desyre I not to me;   75
Bot athir of our pepill mot go fre,
Onthrall, onvenquyst, in lawys all evynly
Confiderat in perpetuall ally.
The wirschipyng of goddis in sacryfice
I sal thame lern and tech at my devyß: 80
My fader in law, the kyng Latinus heir,
Most rewle the pepill baith in peax and wer;
My fader in law, as souerane lord and syre,
Duryng hys lyfe most bruke solempnyt empyre.
Suffir my Troianys than, as we ar bovn,   85
For me to beild a strenth and wallyt tovn,
And to this cite, quhar we sall duell at hame,
Lat the madyn Lavinia gif the name."
Thus first Eneas said, and efter syne
Apon this wyß hym followys Kyng Latyn,   90
Behaldand towart hevyn quhar he dyd stand,
And to the starnys vphevyis hys rycht hand:
"By this ilk erth, seys and starnys hie,
I sweir inlike wyß onto ȝou, Enee,
And by Latoneis byrth, or twynnys twa,   95
The brycht Apollo, and chast Diana,
And by the dowbill frontit Ianus, and all
The pyssans of the goddis infernal,
And by the dyrk sanctuary, blak as sabill,
Of grevoß Pluto, that god revengeabill: 100
The hie fader abuf mot heir my cry,
That dois with thundir sik concord ratify.
I twich thyr altaris and ingill present," quod he,   f. 280ᵛ
"And testifyis ilk godly maieste;
Sall nevir tyme, sesson nor day betyd,   105
To breke this peax on the Italian syde,
Ne this confiderans anys part in two,
Quhat way that evir happynnys the mater go;
Ne na manner of violens, bost nor aw
Sall ony wyß me tharfra withdraw,   110
Bot ferm and stabill all sall haldyn be:
All thocht the erth wald myddill with the see,
And with diluge or invndatioun schent
Covir and confund athir eliment;
Or thocht the hevyn in hell resolue wald,   115
Our promyß sall inuiolat be hald.
Lyke as this ilk ceptour wand ȝhe see,"
(Perchans that tyme a ceptour in hand bair he)
"Sall nevyr burgioun, nor spred branchis lyte,
Nowder rank levys, nor blosum of delyte,   120

Sen it is anys in wod, thar as it grew,
Law from hys stok hard by the rutis hew,
And wantis now hys moder of nurysyng;
For all the syonys and twystis wont to spryng
Or grow thar fra, as ʒhe may se perfay,   125
With egge lumys bene sned full quyte away;
Vmquhile a growand tre, thar it dyd stand,
That now thus by the crafty wark manis hand
Inclusyt is and coverit lustely
In burnyst gold and fynast alcomy,   130
And gevyn our forfaderis of Latyn land,
As ceptour ryall, fortober in hand."
With wordis sik and ferm relatioun
This fynal suyr confideratioun
Athir pryncis haß confermyt and sworn,   135
Amyd thar nobillys standyng thame beforn:
Syne, eftyr thar auld cerymonys and gyß,
The bestis dewly adrest for sacryfyß
Thai brytnyt haue amyd the flawmys red,
And rentis out, or thai war fully ded,   140
The entralys of thir bestis ʒit alyve;
Syne furth of platys or ballancis belyve
With pasyt flesch plenyst the altaris large,   f. 281ʳ
Tharon bestowand in hepys mony a charge.
Bot tho begouth of new this ilk bargane   145
Semyng to the Rutilianys, euery man,
Tobe ane rycht onevynly interpryß,
And diuerß rumour can in thar brestis ryß,
With mony syndry demyng and consait;
He thynkis thus, and he ane other gait;   150
And ay the nerrar and mar diligently
At thai the mater consider and aspy,
Weill thai persaue and behaldis, sans faill,
Thir campionys war not of strenth equaill.
And onto this opinioun the ilk thraw   155
Helpit mekill, that with still payß so slaw
This Turnus musand towart the altar past,
And it lawly adournyt with face doun cast,
With chekis walxin leyn, to thar semyng,
Quharon the soft berd newly dyd furth spryng,   160
As all to ʒyng with sic ane till haue daill,
Thai thocht hys vissage all becummyn paill.

Quhou Iuturna be slycht and enchantment
Brekis the peax, and hasty batale sent.   C. v

A nd eftyr that this ilk commonyng
  Thus walxand mar and mar by mony a syng
Iuturna hys systyr dyd persaue,
And saw the common wlgar hartis wave
In diuerß sentencis and ententis seir;   5
Than in amyd the rowtis drew scho neir,
In form and lyknes of Camertis bald,
Of nobill blude cummyn and lynnage ald,
And of hys fader the bruyt and renowne
Was magnifeit in wirschip wonder hie,   10
Tharto hym self maste douchty cheveller
In dedis of armys and in fait of weir.
Amyd the ostis this wyß dyd scho thryng,
Not onexpert to convoy sik a thing,
And diuerß rumouris in the preß skalis sche,   15
Syne siclyke wordis carpis apon hie:
"O Rutilianys, aschame ʒhe not for feir
Into sa gret a perrell and danger   f. 281ᵛ
A sylly sawle to put in aventour,
That for ʒow all sall vndirly sik cuyr?   20
Quhiddir ar we not equale in our entent,
To the Troianys in numbyr or hardyment?
Lo, all the Troianys and Archadianys
Befor ws heir arrayt on the planys:
The fatall pissans is hail in this sted,   25
And the Tuscanys that Turnus heß at fed.
Sa few tha beyn, ʒhe may behald and se,
That gif we list mak onset, trastis me,
The half of all our menʒe gret and small
Sall not fynd ʒondyr a fa to mach withall.   30
ʒon Turnus, to the goddis abuf full straucht,
To quhais altaris hym vowyt and betaucht
He heß for ʒou, as that ʒhe se," said sche,
"With fame eternal sal vpheit be,
As euermar alyve and maist name couth,   35
Carpit and sung in euery mannis mowth;
Quhen we, as thrallys, leif sal our natyve land,
And onto prowd tyrrantis, heß the ovirhand,
Salbe compellit as lordis till obey,
That now, thus sleuthfully, sa fant and fey   40
Hufys still on thir feldis as we war ded,
And for our self list schape for na remed."
With siclike wordis the myndis and consait
Of the ʒongkeris was inflawmyt hait,

208

And mair and mar now, all the feld abowt,   45
The murmur crepys out throw euery rowt;
So thai quhilkis air desyrit peax and rest,
And for the common weill thocht it was best
To mak end of the bargane on this wyß,
Ar alterit haly in ane other avyß;   50
For now desyre thai batale, but abaid,
Prayand God this contract had neuer bene maid,
And haß compassioun caucht in hart, but faill,
Of Turnus chans, semyng so inequale.
Thys self tyme eik heß Iuturna, I wyß,   55
Ane other grettar wondir ekit to this,
And heich vp from the hevyn befor thame plane   f. 282^r
A takyn heß scho schawyn auguriane;
Syk a syng, that nane other to that entent
Was mar effectuus nor conuenient   60
To trubbill Italian myndis and mak thame raif,
And with fals demonstratioun to dissaue.
For Iovis fowle, the ern, com sorand by,
Fleand vp heich towart the brycht red sky,
Befor hym catchand ane gret flycht or ost   65
Of fowlys that dyd hant endlang the cost,
Quhilk on thar weyngis, sair dredand hys wraik,
Skrymmys heir and thar with mony sprauch and craik;
Quhil suddandly this egill with a surß,
As he towartis the fludis maid hys curß,   70
Dispittuusly intill hys punsys he
Hes claucht a swan excellent of bewte.
Than the Italianys apon athir syde
Rasyt thar myndis to se quhat suld betyd,
And oone the other fowlys heich in the sky   75
Turnyt agane with money screym and cry,
To chaiß and to assail thar aduersar,
A wondir thing to se, vp in the air:
The lyght thai dirkyn with thar pennys thik,
And throw the skyis with mony a strake and pik,   80
Sammyn in a sop, thik as a clowd, but baid,
Thar ta thai dyd assalȝe and invaid,
Sa lang, quhil that by forß he was ourset,
And of the hevy byrdyng sa mait and het
That hys mycht falȝeit, and of his clukis rude   85
The egill leit hys pray fall in the flude,
And vp amang the clowdis flaw away.
Than the Rutilianys all, full glaid and gay,
With huge brute and clamour lowd onan
Salust this syng or takyn augurian;   90
Syne sped thar hand, and maid thame for the fight.

209

And, first of othir, Tolumnyus the wight,
That was a spa man and diuinour sle:
"3a, this was it, 3a, this was it," quod he,
"Quhilk oft I visseit and desirit by and by: 95
This gud takyn I ressaue and ratify,   f. 282ᵛ
And knawys the goddis favour in our supple.
Rutilianys, hynt 3our wapynnys, and follow me,
Quham now 3on vauengeour, 3on ilk stranger,
Affrays so with hys onworthy weir,   100
Lyke tyll onweldy fowlys on the cost,
And our marchis with fors and mekill bost
Inuadis, rubbis and spul3eis, as 3e se:
He sall, for fer, sone gif the bak and fle,
Mak sail onon, and hald for euer away   105
Throu the deip sey outour the fludis gray.
Tharfor 3he sall all sammyn, with ane assent,
Assembil now 3our rowtis heir present,
And into feild defend, as men of mayn,
3our kyng Turnus he be nocht reft and slane."   110
Thus said he, with that word als sa fast
Towartis his fais forganys hym dyd cast
A weirly dart onon with all his byr:
The sovir schaft flaw quhisland with a quhir,
Thar as it slydis scherand throw the ayr,   115
Oneschewabill, bath certane, lang and squar.
Sammyn with this, vp rysis for the nanys
Ane huge noys and clamour all at anys;
With sik affray and hydduus dyn and beir
The wardis all and ostis war on steir,   120
That, for the rerd and deray, hait in ire
The hartis kyndillis of euery bald syre.
Furth flaw the takill rycht our forgane his face,
Thiddir as for the ilk tyme stude, percace,
Nyne brethir germane, fresch and 3yng of age, 125
Nane in thar ost mair semly personage,
Quham the trew faithfull wife Tyrrhene ilkane
Bair till hir spowß Gilip Archadiane;
Of quham this dart hyt ane, thar he dyd stand,
A gudly spryngald, a fair 3yng galland,   130
Richt schaply maid, in armour schynand brycht,
And at the myddill markyt hym full rycht,
Quhar as the wovyn gyrdill or tysche
Abufe his navill was beltit, as we se,
And smate hym evyn into the sammyn place 135 f. 283ʳ
Neyr quhar the bukkill hys sydis dyd enbrace,
Throw gyrd hys body with a grevoß wond,
And spaldyt hym stark ded apon the grond.

Bot than hys bald brethir in a rowt,
Wod wraith for wo, sum hyntis swerdis owt,   140
Sum claucht in hand the dart with the steil hed,
And in thar blynd fury, full of fed,
Ruschit on thar fays with a feirfull braid.
Aganys quham to resist and invaid,
The rowtis of the army Lawrentanys   145
Ran to recontyr thame; and tho atanys
Agane assemblit, as a spait of flud,
The Troianys and the Tuscanys wraith and woid,
With thame of Arcad in arrayt feildis,
With burnyst armour and thar payntit scheildis;   150
Apon sik wyß that all, with ane assent,
Caucht haill desyre to feght apon the bent,
And to dereyn in feild with bytand brand
The haill mater. Sum schot doun with thar hand
The altaris markyt for the sacryfyß.   155
Belyve our all the lyft vp semyt ryß
The fell tempest of dartis schote and flanys,
So thik as ony schour of scharp hailstanys,
As dyd increß this flycht of stelit hedis.
Full grewos grew the bargane in all stedis: 160
Sum ran to the wyn flacconys for gret ire,
And sum hynt vp the furnacc full of fyre.
The kyng hym self, Latinus, for the affray,
Fled to the cite, and tursyt with hym away
Hys goddis and hys mawmontis, drevyn abak   165
With a schamefull rebute and mekill lak,
Left the concord ondone, not brocht till end.
Sum brydillys stedis and cartis vp dyd bend,
And sum in haiot with a lowp or a swak
Thame self vpcastis on the horsys bak,   170
And war all reddy in the stowr at hand
With drawyn swerd and nakit burnyst brand.
Mesapus, full desyrus in the preß
Fortill confund the trety and the peß,
A kyng Tyrreyn, Aulestes, in that sted   175   f. 283ᵛ
With kyngis ensenȝeis and with crown on hed,
Affrays sor, at hym dryvand hys steid;
The tother drew away for feir and dreid,
And bakwartis fallys on hys schuldris and crovn,
Onhappely, apon ane altar dovn,   180
Quhilk stud percace behynd hym on the land.
Mesapus than, full ferß, with speir in hand
Apon hym drave, thocht he besocht hym fair,
And with this schaft, that was als rude and squar
As it had beyn a cabyr or a spar,   185

Dovn from hys stowt cursor, na thyng skar,
Smait hym a grewoß wond and dedly byt,
And syne thir wordis said: "Ha, art thou hyt?
Ha, that thou haß! This is, be myne avyß,
To our gret goddis mair ganand sacrifyß." 190
Italianys hurlys on hym in a floyt,
Spulзeit hys corps, hys membris зit all hoyt.
Chorineus tho, that was a stowt Troian,
To meit ane Ebusus, com hym agan,
That wald haue smyt hym with a bustuus dynt, 195
And on ane altar a byrnand schide haß hynt,
And gan it rycht amyd hys vissage stair,
That blesyt vp hys lang berd of hair,
Quhilk, scaldit thus, a strang fleur dyd cast.
And forthir this Chorineus alsso fast 200
Ruschit on hys fa, thus fyrefangit and onsaucht,
And with hys left hand by the hair hym claucht,
Syne with hys kne hym possit with sic a plat
That on the erd he spaldit hym all flat,
And with hys styf stok swerd in sik estait 205
Throu baith the sydis at the first dynt hym smait.
And Podalirius with drawyn swerd list not ceß
Alsus the hyrd to persew throu the preß,
Quhilk ruschis abak for feir, hys life to save,
In the vangart, throw mony a poyntit glave; 210
Bot quhen he saw his fa sa neir invaid
That he na wyß mycht eschew nor evaid,
Vphesit he hys braid ax rude and squair,
And akwartly strake at hys aduersar, f. 284^r
Quhilk from amyd hys forhed, neir hys crovn, 215
Onto hys chyn the egge dyd carvyn doun,
That far onbreid hys armour, quhar he stude,
Was all bysprent and blandit full of blude.
Tho Podalirius the hard rest dyd oppreß,
Or cald and irny sleip of dethis streß, 220
And vp the breith he зald into thar sycht,
With eyn closyt in euerlestand nycht.

Enee sair wondyt of the feild dyd paß,
In quhais absens Turnus mair cruell waß. C. vi

Than the reuthfull and pacient Eneas,
Behaldand quhou all wrang the gem dyd pas,
Hys rycht hand onenarmyt to stynt thar fed,
Furth strekis and oncoverit heß hys hed,
And cryis and clepis on his pepill tho: 5
"My frendis deir, quhidder now hurll зe so,

Ilkane aganys other? Quhou may this be?
Quhat haß movit this hasty discord?" quod he,
"O, stanch ӡour wraith for schame, or all is lorn!
The payce and concord now is twichit and sworn,					10
And the articulis and the lawys dyng
Appunctit vp, and promist euery thing.
Of det and ryght I aucht apon this land
Allane Turnus recontyr, hand for hand:
Suffir me perform my dereyn by and by,					15
And do away all dreid and villany.
I sall with my hand sone mak ferm and stabill
Our appoyntment, for evir onvariabill,
For this ilke sacrifice violate in this sted
Sall rendir onon Turnus to me ded."					20
Amyd sic sawys, as he thir wordis said
Forto asswage thar mynd, but mar abaid
A quhirrand arrow, lo, with fedderit flycht
At swift randon dyd in hys the bayn lycht,
Oncertane fra quhat hand that it was sent,					25
Quhat kynd of schote, nor of quhat instrument.
The hie glory of sa notabill a deid					f. 284ᵛ
Is hyd, that nane knew quha it dyd but dreid,
Nor wist quha wrocht had to the Rutilianys
Sa gret wirschip and lovyng for the nanys;					30
Quhidder it betyd on cace and aventur,
Or of sum god be dispositioun suyr;
Nor nevir person eftir, he nor he,
Dyd hym avant he wondit had Ene.
Quhen Turnus all the chiftanys trublit saw,					35
And Eneas sair wondit hym withdraw,
Than, for this hasty hope als hait as fyre,
To mell in feght he caucht ardent desyre;
He askis horß and harnes baith atanys,
And haltandly in hys cart for the nanys					40
He skippis vp and musturis wantonly,
Furth sprentand throu the feildis by and by,
And at his will, quharso hym list tobe,
With hys awyn hand the renӡeis rewlis he;
And dryvand furth thus into his ire					45
Laid feill corpsis ded and mony bald syre,
Down strowand eik vnder fut in the plane
Diuerß otheris ӡit throwand and half slane:
Owder with his cart the rowtis he drave away,
Or, as thai tuke the flycht for gret affray,					50
Castyng speris and dartis scharp hynt he,
And leit thame thik amang his fays fle.
Sik wyß as bludy armipotent god Mars,

213

Besyde hys frosty flude Hebrum in Traß,
Full hastely bownand to batale feild,   55
Makis gret bruyt and clatteryng with hys scheild,
Quhen he list movyng weir mast chevalrus;
Furth steris hys stedis, ferß and furyus,
Quhilk fleys furth sa swith with mony a stend
Owtour the planys at large quhar thai wend,   60
That thai forryn and goys befor alway
ȝephyrus and Nothus, swyftest wyndis tway;
And, with the dyn of thar feyt and hys cart,
All Trace gronys onto the ferthar part;
Abowt hym walkis, as hys godly feris,   65
Dreid with paill face, Debait, and mortale Weris,
The Wraith, and Ire, and eik fraudfull Dissait,   f. 285ʳ
Lyggyng vndir covert at enbuschment or await –
Turnus siclike, als chery, prowd and lycht
Amyd the batale catchys to the fycht   70
Hys stedys, rekand of swete quhar thai raid,
And sa baldly hys fays dyd invaid,
With sik slauchter, that piete was to se;
And sik deray haß maid in the melle,
That hys swift stedis hovys, quhar thai went,   75
Spangit vp the bludy sparkis our the bent,
Quhil blude and brane, in abundans furth sched,
Mydlit with sand vndir horß feit was tred.
For he, or now, heß doun bet Sthelenus,
And kyllit eik Thamyrys and Polus   80
(The formast twa he slew machit at hand,
And this Polus, as he far of dyd stand);
On far eik slew he of Imbrasyus
The sonnys twa, Glawcus and Iasus,
Quham this Imbrasyus fosterit had, baith twa,   85
Into the far cuntre of Lycia,
And thame instrukit had full equaly
In fait of armys, and to hant chevelry,
Owder till assaill befor, or ȝit behynd,
Or with swift horß fortill forryn the wynd.   90
ȝond, in ane other part, amyd the feild
The ferß Eumedes walkis vnder scheild,
Quhilk was the son and air, as that thai tell,
Of agit Dolon valȝeant in batell:
The name he bair of hys forgrandschir wight,   95
Bot the strang handis and stowt curage in fight
Of hys awyn fader, this Dolon, he bair;
Quhilk at Troy vmquhile, as the sege lay thar,
And was of sa stowt curage and hie will
That he durst ask the chariot of Achill   100

214

To his reward, for that he sa baldly
The Grekis tentis tuk on hand to aspy;
Bot the son of Tedeus, Diomed,
Ane other fasson heß hym quyt his meid
For sa stowt ondyrtakyn, and hym slewch;   105
And ȝit for all his renovn, provit eneuch,
Ne durst anys pretend, for all hys dedys,   f. 285ᵛ
That he was worthy to weld Achillys stedys.
Bot to our purpoß: this forsaid Eumedes
As Turnus dyd behald ȝond in thc preß,   110
On the plane feld thar as he dyd ryde,
First weill a far way at hym leyt he glyde
A fleand dart; and furth with that, rycht thar,
Gan stynt hys horssis and his quhirland char,
And ferely dyd lepyng from hys cart,   115
And sone apon hys aduersar astart,
Quhilk tho was fall to grond, and half deill ded;
Syne with hys fut doun thryst in thc ilk sted
Hys fair nek bayn, and owt of hys rycht hand
Richt austernly haß he thrawyn the brand,   120
Quhilk schynand brycht into hys throte he wet,
And tharto ekyt thir wordys wondyr het:
"O thow prowd Troian, lyggand thar at grond,
Now may thou myssour the feld at thou haß fund;
Lo heir the bundis, lo heir Hesperia,   125
Quhilk thou to seik in weirfar was sa thra!
Thys is the bontay tha sal bair away
That dar with wapynnys or armour me assay."
To hym in feir also haß he laid
With a scharp castyn hed, but mar abaid,   130
Ane Butys, and eftyr hym ane Chloreus,
Syne Sybar, Dares, and Thersilocus,
And Thymetes, a man of full gret fors,
Castyn from hys staffage, skeich and hedstrang horß.
And as the blastis with thar bustuus sovn   135
From mont Edoin in Trace cumis thuddand doun
On thc dcip sey Egean fast at hand,
Chasand the flud and wallys to athir land;
And quhar the wyndis assalys, the suyth to say,
The clowdis fleys fast our the hevyn away –   140
The sammyn wyß, quhat way at Turnus went,
The rowtis red hym plane rovm on the bent,
And all the ostis fast abak dyd fle,
For with sik forß and fard furth dryvys he,
Hys bissy movand tymbrell euery art   145
Catchis the wynd and ayr forgane hys cart.
Phegeus, a Troiane, seand Turnus all mad   f. 286ʳ

Sa instantly assaill with strakis sad,
Na langar mycht hym thoill, bot with bald hart
Hym self kest in the way to meit hys cart;   150
And he the renys in hys ryght hand hynt,
Syne writhit heß about, or euer he stynt,
The fomy mowthis of the hasty stedis.
And as this douchty man, sa gud at nedis,
Thus hang and harlyt was in euery art   155
By the lymmouris and hamys of the cart,
That he hys body mycht nocht kepe nor held,
To covyr with hys armour and his scheld,
The speir hym followis with scharp hed and braid,
And rent hys hawbrik of dowbill plyis maid,   160
Hurt his body sum deill, nocht fully sond,
Persand the hyde, and maid a litill wond.
He, nocht the leß, agane hys fa furthsprent,
With hys braid scheild or target evir vp stent,
And in hys hand held drawyn the burnyst blaid,   165
Cryand for help his aduersar till invaid;
Quham tho (allace, gret piete was to se!)
The quhirland quheill and spedy swyft extre
Smate doun to grond, and on the erd lay plat;
And, as he fell, Turnus followis with that,   170
And evyn betwix the helm can hym arraß
And vmast roll or hem of hys curaß,
Smait of his hed clenly with hys brand,
And left the corps lyke a stok in the sand.

Na mannys cuyr nor craft of surrurgyne
Mycht heill Eneas, bot Venus medycyn.   C. vii

A nd as Turnus thus in the batale sted
  With the ovirhand sa feil corpsis laid ded,
The meyn quhil Mnestheus and traste Achates
Heß led the bald Eneas of the preß,
Ascanyus ȝyng with thame in cumpany,   5
And to the tentis brocht hym all bludy,
With steppis slaw furth stalkand all in feir,
Lenand ilk payß on a lang poyntit speir.
Wod wroith he worthis, for dysdene and dispyte   f. 286ᵛ
That he ne mycht hys ferys succur als tyte.   10
He wrythis, and enforsys tyll owt draw
The schaft in brokkyn, and the hed withall:
He axis help at all thar standand by,
Quhat was the nerrest way and maist reddy,
And bad thai suld with a scharp knyf that tyde   15
Scheir doun the wond, and mak it large and wyde,

Rype to the boddum weill, and tak gude tent
To serß the hyrnys quhar that the hed was went,
That thai mycht hast thame self, but mair delay,
To the batale, forto stynt this effray.   20
Now was thar than present in the preß
Iapis, that was son of Iasides.
Abuf all otheris to the god Phebus he
Was best belovyt and haldyn in dante;
With quhais favour vmquhile strangly caucht,   25
This god Appollo gladly haß hym taucht
Hys craftis and hys officis, by and by,
Of diuinatioun or of augury,
The musik tonys to play on harp waill sle,
And forto schute and lat swyft arrowis fle.   30
Bot this Iapis, fortill prolong, perfay,
Hys faderis fatis, quhilk as bedrall lay
Befor hys ʒet, of hys lyfe in dispar,
Had levyr haue knawyn the sciens and the lair,
The myght and forß of strenthy herbys fyne,   35
And all the cunnyng of vse of medycyne,
And with sik secrete craftis prevely
To leid hys lyfe and tyme mair esely.
Eneas standis byttyrly chidand,
Lenand apon a bustuus speir in hand,   40
Amyd gret confluens of thir childer ʒyng,
And eik his son Ascanyus sair wepyng;
Bot he na thing hym movit at thar terys.
Than this Iapis, sage and ald of ʒheris,
With habyt schapyn on surrugyn mak,   45
Vprollit weill and wymplit far abak,
Richt bissely with hys nait handis tway
Begouth fortill exem, and till assay   f. 287ʳ
The wond with mony crafty medycyn,
And mychty herbys taucht be god Appollyn;   50
Bot all for nocht his travale and hys pane.
Oft with hys rycht hand sersis he, invane,
To rype the owtgait of the wond sa wyde,
And forto seik the schaft on euery syde,
With hys wynrys and grippand turcas sle   55
To thrist the hed, and draw furth, pressis he;
Bot, for na chance that evir betyd may,
Wald forton dreß hys hand the sovir way.
Na thing avalyt hys crafty medycyne,
Nor ocht hym helpys his master Appollyn.   60
And now the grisly dreid, ay mair and mair,
Our all the feildis walkis heir and thar,
Nerrar drawys the perrell and effray,

So that all dyrknyt wolx the cleir day
Of dusty puldir in the hevyn dyd stand;   65
The horsmen all approchis fast at hand,
That dartis thik amyd the tentis fell.
Wofull clamour with mony cry and ȝell
Went to the skyis of ȝong men faucht in feild,
And thame that swelt, sair wondit vnder scheild.   70
Venus hys moder tho, this pane to meyß,
Caucht rewth and piete of hir sonnys dyseyß,
And from the wod of mont Ida in Creit
Vp heß scho pullit dittam, the herb sweit,
Of levis rank, rypit and wondir fair,   75
With sprowtis, sprayngis and vanys our alquhar,
As that we se on sik verdour spryngand,
And on the top a purpour flour curland:
Sik gresis gude beyn nowyß onknaw
To the wild bestis, quhen that ony thraw   80
Thai with the fleand arrow beyn ourtake,
The hed stikand owther in syde or bak.
Thiddir brocht Venus this herb (and scho was schrowd,
Baith face and body, in a watry clowd),
And with the herb alsso mydlit heß sche   85
The hailsum thryfty watir wondir sle,   f. 287ᵛ
That from hir brycht lippys scho ȝet inhy;
And temperis and enbalmys prevely
The plastyr tharwith, strynkland all ourane
The hailsum ius of herb ambrosian,   90
And the weill smelland herb hait panaces.
This ancyent surrigian, Iapes,
With sik watir or ius, that he nocht knew,
The wond mesys, and softnyt hes of new;
And suddanly the payn vanyst als cleyn   95
Of hys body, as thocht it had beyn
Bot a dyrlyng or a litill stond;
All blud stanchit and stud in the deip wond.
Tharwith baith hed and schaft com owt droppand,
But ony pull followyng of manis hand,   100
That strenth and fors of new to mak debait
Restoryt war onto thar ald astait.
"Harnes, harnes, bryng hym hydder in hy!
Quhy stand ȝe sa?" Iapis gaue a cry,
And with this word aganyst thar fays he   105
Heß first thar spreit inflammyt to melle.
"O Eneas," quod he, "I mak ȝou suyr,
Throw manis mycht was neuer wrocht this cuyr,
Nor be na mastir craft of medycyne:
Thou art not helyt by this hand of myne,   110

Bot be sum grettar god, full weill I se,
The quhilk to grettar warkis preservis the."
Eneas tho, desyrus of bargane,
Hys lymmys in legharnes gold begane
Claspyt full cloß and dyd hym self array,   115
Bad speid in haist, for he hatit delay;
He schuke and branglit fast his speir that tyde.
And eftir hys active scheild was by his syde
Cowchit full meit, and on his bak full thik
Seysit his curace or his fyne hawbrik,   120
Ascanyus ȝyng tendirly the ilk place,
With all his harneß bilappit, dyd embrace,
And throw his helmys vental a litill we
Hym kyssyt haß; syne on this wyß said he: f. 288ʳ
"O thou my child, do lernyng, I the pray,   125
Vertu and verray laubour till assay
At me, quhilk am thy fader, as thou wait;
Desyre tobe chancy and fortunate
As othir pryncis, quhilkis mair happy beyn.
Now sall my rycht hand thy querrell susteyn,   130
And the defend in batale by and by,
To mak the partis man of gret senȝeory.
Do thou siclyke, I pray the, myne awyn page,
Als fast as thou cumis to perfyte age,
Ramembir heiron, and revolue in thy mynd   135
Thy lynage, thy forbearis, and thy kynd;
Exempill of prowes in the steris frendis befor,
Baith fader Eneas and thyne vncle Hector."

Iuturna gydys hir brotheris cart rycht sle
Frawart the batal, he suld nocht mache Enee.   C. viii

Quhen this was said, furth at the portis hee,
  Schakand in hand a gret speir, ischit he.
With hym also to the feild ruschis owt
Anteus, Mnestheus, and ane full thyk rowt:
Alhaill the barnage flokkis furth atanys,   5
Left voyd the tovn and strenth with wasty wanys.
Than was the playn ourset, quha com behynd,
With dusty stew of puldyr maid folk blynd,
And, for stampyng and fell dynnyng of feyt,
The erd movit and trymlyt euery streyt.   10
Turnus, apon the party our rycht forgane,
Persauyt thame thus sterand throw the plane,
Thame saw also the pepill Ausonyanys,
And the cald dreid for feir ran throw thar banys.
First of the Latynys all, this ilke maid   15

Iuturna thame knew, and was not glaid;
Scho hard the soundis and the fell deray,
And quakand fast for feir heß fled away.
Bot this Eneas, full bald vndyr scheld,
With all hys ost drave throw the plane feld,   20
And with hym swyftly bryngis our the bent
A rowt coill blak of the stew, quhar he went.   f. 288ᵛ
Lyke as the bub or plaig of fell tempest,
Quhen that the clowdis brekis est or west,
Dryvys by fors throw the sey to the land,   25
Doand the cayrfull husbandis vnderstand
The gret myscheif tocum and felloun wraik;
Quhilk, with sair hartis quakand, "Allake, allaik!"
Says, "Lo, ȝon bub sall stryke dovn growand treys,
Doun bet our cornys, and by the ruyt vpheis,   30
And far onbreid ourturn all doys vpstand:
Hark, heir the swouch cumis brayand to the land" –
On siclyke wyß this ilk chiftane Troian
The corsy pasand Osyris heß slane.
Mnestheus kyllyt Archet, and Achates   35
Byhedit haß the wight Epulones;
Gyas doun bet Vfens the gret captane;
Dovn fell also the gret augurian,
Tolumnyus him self, that the ilk day
Threw the first dart hys fays till assay.   40
Vprysis than the clamour, and a scry
Quhilk semyt wend onto the starnyt sky.
Thar curß abowt than the Rutilianys
Heß tane the flyght, and gave the bak atanys,
Skatterit throw owt the feildis heir and thar,   45
Quhil stovr of puldir vpstrikis in the air.
Bot the chiftane, this vailȝeant Ene,
Dedenȝeit nane doun bet as thai dyd fle,
Ne thame invaid that met hym face for face,
All thocht thai fawght with wapyn, swerd or mace;   50
Bot throw the thikast sop of dust in hy
Only Turnus went to seik and aspy,
And hym allane, accordyng the tretye,
He askis and requiris into melle.
With dreid heirof the mynd was smyttyn so   55
Of Iuturna, the verray virago
(Quhilk term to expone, be myne avyß,
Is a weman exersand a mannys offyß);
Amyd the lyamys and the thetis thar
Doun swakkis scho Metiscus the cartar   60
That Turnus char had forto rewle on hand,   f. 289ʳ
And left hym lygand far ȝond on the land,

Fra the cart lymmowris warpit a gret way;
And scho in sted hyß office dyd assay.
And with hir handis abowt writhis sche 65
The flexibill renys frawart the melle,
Berand the lyknes in all maner thing
Of Metiscus voce, person and armyng.
Als feill wrynklis and turnys can scho mak
As dois the swallow with hir plumys blak, 70
Fleand and seirsand swiftly thar and heir
Our the gret lugyngis of sum myghty heir,
Apon hir weyngis scummand euery syde
Thir heich hallys, bene full large and wyde,
Gadderand the small morcellis est and west 75
To bair hir byrdis chepand in thar nest;
Now into gowsty porchis doith scho fle,
Now by the donky stankis soundis sche:
In siclike wyß this Iuturna belyfe
Throw owt the ostis gan the horssis dryfe, 80
Circuland abowt with swift fard of the cart
The fcildis our allquhar in euery art,
And schew hir bruthir Turnus in his char,
Now brawland in this place, now voustand thar;
Na be na way wald scho suffir that he 85
Assembill hand for hand suld with Enee;
Bot fled hym far, and frawart hym held ay,
Writhand hir cartis curß ane other way.
In na leß haist Eneas on the bent
Hys quhelys turnys and writhis mony a went; 90
The man he seirsis throw the effrait rowtis,
And on hym callis with lowd cry and hie schowtis.
And als feill syß as he his eyn kest
Apon his fa, al tymys he hym adrest
To chaß hym with swyft curß throu the melle, 95
On horssis that semyt ryn as fowle dois fle;
Bot evir als oft Iuturna ane other art f. 289ᵛ
Awaywart turnys and writhis hyr broderis cart.
And thus Eneas remanys all on flocht
In syndry motioun of ire, bot all for nocht. 100
Allace, ne knawis he not now quhat to do:
Diuerß thochtis and seir consatis, lo,
Hys mynd in mony contrar purpoß sent.
And as he thus was trublit in entent,
Mesapus, that on cace was neirhand by, 105
And in hys left neif haldis all reddy
Twa sowpill castyng speris hedit with steill,
Of quham that ane full sovirly and weill
Towart Ene addressit leit he glyde.

221

Eneas hovit still the schote to abyde, 110
Hym schrowdand vndir his armour and his scheild,
Bowand hys howch, and stude a litill onheld;
And, netheleß, this speir, that scharply schar,
Of hys basnet the tymbrell quyte doun bair,
And smait away the creistit toppis hie. 115
Than mair in greif and ire vpgrowis he,
Seand hym catchit with dissait and slycht,
Quhen that he heß persauyt in his sycht
Turnus horssis furth drevyn ane other art,
Awaywart turnyng sa feill syß his cart: 120
Tho mony tymys lowd did he testify
Gret Iupiter, quhou that sa wrangwisly
He was iniurit, and constrenyt to fight;
To witneß drew he als with gret onrycht
The altaris of confiderans violate; 125
And now at last, full furyus and hait,
The mydwart of his ennemyß dyd invaid.
With prospir chance of batale, sa onglaid
And terribill to his fays walxis he,
That hail, but ony differans of degre, 130
All goith to wraik, for na man list he spair:
A cruell slauchter he heß rasit thar.
All kynd of wreth and breithfull ire now he
Leyt slyp at large, but brydill, with ren3eis fre.

Heir followys of the slauchter monyfald   f. 290^r
Maid by Turnus and be Eneas bald.   C. ix

Quhat god sall now me techyng to endite
Samony wondis and this cairfull syte,
Or quha me lern in metyr to declar
Sa feill and diuerß slauchteris as was thar,
And gret deceß of dukis in that sted, 5
Our all the feildis strowyn lyggis ded,
Quham euery ane sammyn hys curß abowt
Now down bet Turnus, now Eneas stowt?
O Iupiter, was it plesand to the,
With sa gret motioun of crudelyte 10
Athir pepill suld rusch on other in preß,
Quhilkis eftir suldbe ane in etern peß?
Eneas first, that tareit not to lang,
Smate ane Sucron, a Rutilian strang;
A grevouß wond he hyt hym in the syde, 15
Throw owt hys rybbys can the stif swerd glide,
Persyt hys cost and breistis cundyt inhy,
Thar as the fatale deth is maste hasty:

This bargane first fermyt Troianys to stand,
That langeir fled Turnus fra hand to hand.   20
Tho Turnus haß rencontyrit in the preß
Amycus, and hys brother Diores,
Quham, fra thar horssis on the grond doun bet,
On fut in feild strangly he ombeset;
And the formast with a lang stif speir   25
Smate ded, and with a swerd the tother in feir,
Syne baith thar hedis hakkit of in hy,
And at his cart thame hyngis by and by,
The blude tharfra dreipand, tursys away.
The self stound Eneas at ane assay,   30
Or ane onset, heß kyllit Tanaus,
Talon also, and the stowt Cethegus;
Syne, eftyr thame, he kyllyt in the preß
The sad and ay sorofull Onytes,
Renownyt of Thebes blude, and the ofspryng   35
Discendyng down from Echion the kyng,   f. 290ᵛ
And of hys moder born, Peridia.
This othir chiftane, Turnus, killit twa,
That brethir war, and owt of Lycia send,
Appollois cuntre, Troianys to defend;   40
And efter thame ane Meneit heß he slane,
A ȝong man that was born ane Archadane,
That all his days evir hatit the melle,
Bot all for nocht, for he most neid thus de –
About the laik of Lern and fludis gray   45
Hys craft was forto fysching euery day;
A puyr cote houß he held, and buyr hym law;
Rewardis of rich folkis war to hym onknaw;
Hys fader eyrit and sew ane peyß of feld
That he in hyregang held tobe his beild.   50
And lyke as that the fyre war new vpbet,
And in sum dry wydderit wod vpset,
Baith heir and thar, at diuerß partis seir,
Amyd the sovndand buskis of lawrer;
Or quhar the fomy ryveris, red on spait,   55
Hurlys doun from the month a large gait,
With hydduus bruyt and felloun fard atanys,
Thar as thai ryn ourflowand all the planys;
Ilkane distroys, wastis and dryvis away
All that thai fynd befor thame in the way –   60
Na slawar baith this Turnus and Ene
Hurlys and ruschis ferß throw the melle.
Now, now, the brethfull ire and felloun thocht
Within thar myndis boldynnys all on flocht,
And tha breistis, can na wyß venquyst be,   65

Now bristis full of greif and cruelte;
Now lasch thai at with bludy swerdis brycht,
Fortill mak wondis wyd in all thar mycht.
The tane of thame, that is to know, Enee,
Kyng Murranus, of anchestry mast hie, 70
Sovndand the name of his forfaderis ald,
Our all the clan of Latyn kyngis bald
Observit man by man onto his day, f. 291ʳ
Furth of hys cart heß smyttyn quyt away,
And bet hym doun onto the erd wyndflaucht, 75
With a gret roik or quhirrand stane ourraucht;
That this Murranus the renys and the thetis,
Quharwith hys stedis ʒokkit war in thretis,
Vndyr the quhelis heß do weltit doun,
Quhar, as he lyggis in hys mortall swoun, 80
Of hys awyn stedis abuf hym rap for rap
The sterand hufis, stampand with mony clap,
Ourtreddis and doun thryngis thar master law,
And gan thar lordis hie estait mysknaw.
And Turnus heß recontryt ane Hilo, 85
That ruschand hurlit throw the melle tho,
Full ferß of muyd and austern of curage;
Bot this Turnus, for all hys vassalage,
At hys gilt halffettis a grundyn dart dyd thraw,
That fixit throu hys helm the schaft flaw, 90
Persand hys brane, quhill owt bruschit the blude.
Nor thy rycht hand, Creteus, sa gude,
Thou forcyast Greik, cumyn from Archad land,
Mycht the deliuer from this ilk Turnus brand.
Nor all hys goddis Cupencus in the plane 95
Myght defend from Ene, com hym agane,
Bot at hys breist with the steill poynt is met,
That thirlyt hes throu all, and hym doun bet,
That nother scheild nor obstant plait of steill
This catyvis breist hes helpit neuer a deill. 100
O Eolyn, the feildis Lawrentan
Heß the behald tharon dovn bet and slane,
And with thy braid bak in thy rich weid
The grund thou heß byspred rycht far onbreid:
Thar lyis thou ded, quham Gregioun ostis in fycht 105
Nother venquyß nor to the erth smyte mycht,
Nor ferß Achilles to the grund couth bryng,
That was ourquhelmar of Kyng Pryamus ryng:
Heir war thy methis and thy term of ded:
The houß and famyll or the nobill sted 110
Of thy kynrent stant vndir mont Ida, f. 291ᵛ
In the gret cyte of Lyrnessia,

Bot in the feildis of Lawrentane sulȝe
Thy sepultur is maid for ay tobe.
Apon this wyß the ostis and wardis haill   115
On athir part returnyt in bataill,
Aganyst othir to feght sammyn attanys,
All the Latynys and alhaill the Troianys;
Duke Mnestheus, and the stern Serestus,
And, on the tother half, Prynce Mesapus,   120
That of gret horß the dantar clepit was,
And with hym eik the stalwart Asylas,
The Tyrreyn rowtis semblit all atanys,
And Kyng Evandrus army Archadianys:
Euery man for hym self, as he best mycht,   125
At the vtyrrans of all hys forß gan fyght.
No rest nor tary was, thai so contend,
Sum to confundyng all, sum to diffend.

Quhou Eneas segit the tovn agane,
And Queyn Amata hir self for wo haß slayn.   C. x

At this tyme, the bargane induryng thus,
Eneas moder, the farest dame Venus,
Into hys mynd scho haß put this entent,
To hald onto the wallys incontinent,
And steir hys ost the cyte till assay   5
With hasty onset and suddane affray,
At gret myscheif the Latynys to effeir,
Quhilk of hys cummyng tho onwarnyt wer.
And as at he held movyng to aspy
Turnus throu syndry rowtis by and by,   10
On euery syde he haß castyn hys e,
And at the last behaldis the cite,
Saiklcß of batalc, frc of all syk stryfc,
But payn or travale, at quyet man and wyfe.
Than of a grettar bargane in hys entent   15
All suddanly the figour dyd imprent:
He callys Mnestheus and eik Sergestus,   f. 292ʳ
Chiftanys of hys ost, and strang Serestus,
And on a lytill mote ascendit inhy,
Quhar sone forgadderit all the Troian army,   20
And thik abowt hym flokkyng can, but baid;
Bot nother scheld nor wapynnys doun thai laid.
And he amyddis on the knollis hight
Onto thame spak thus, herand euery wight:
"Heir I command no tary nor delay   25
Be maid of my preceptis, quhat I sal say,
Nor se that na man be sweir nor slaw to ryn;

225

Till our hasty onset we wil begyn,
Sen Iupiter assistis onto our syde.
Now harkis quhat I purpoß do this tyde: 30
This day I sal distroy and cleyn bet doun
Of Lawrent haill the cite and the tovn,
Quhilk is the cauß of all our werying,
And quyte confund the kyng Latinus ryng,
Leß than thai wil ressaue the bridill at hand,   35
Be at obeysans, and grant my command;
And ʒon hie turrettis, and tha toppis hie
Of rekand chymnais ʒondir, as we se,
I sal mak plane and equale with the grond.
Quhat suld I tary or delay a stond,   40
Abydand heir into sik plyte," quod he,
"Quhil Turnus lyst feght with ws in melle;
Or quhil that he, ane other tyme agane
Ourcum and venquyst into batale plane,
May haue refuge to this tovn to releif,   45
Syne efter in feild vs recontyr and greif?
O citeʒanys, the hed is this cite
Of our weilfair, and cheif of iniquyte:
Turß thiddir inhy the hait byrnand fyre brandis,
And with the blesand flawmys in ʒour handis   50
Renewys and requir agane," said he,
"The trety sworn and promyst ʒou and me."
Quhen this was said, thai put thame in array,
Togiddir all the cite tyll assay: f. 292ᵛ
Thai pyngill thraly quha mycht formest be   55
With dowr myndys onto the wallys hie:
Knyt in a sop, with gret pissans thai thrist
The leddyrris to the wallys, or ony wist,
And hasty fyre blesis dyd appeir.
Sum otheris of the Troianys ruschit infeir   60
Onto the portis, and the first thame met
Hes kyllyt at the entre and doun bet:
Sum otheris schotis dartis, takillis and flanys
At thame quhilkis on the barmkyn hed remanys,
That with the flycht of schaftis heir and thar   65
Thai dyrknyt all the skyis and the air.
Ene hym self with the formast can stand
Vndyr the wallys, puttand to hys hand
To the assalt, and with lowd voce on hie
The kyng Latinus fast accusys he,   70
Drawand the goddys to wytnes, quhou agane
He is constrenyt on forß to move bargane,
And quhou at the Italianys thus twyß
At syndry tymys schew thame hys ennemyß,

And how falsly that day thai brokyn had 75
The secund confideratioun sworn and maid.
Amang the cite3anys, into gret affray,
Vpraiß discord in mony syndry way:
Sum bad oncloß the cite, and als fast
Warp vp the portis, and wyde the 3ettis cast 80
To the Troianys, and thar gret prynce Ene
Ressaue as for thar kyng in the cite;
Otheris start to thar wapynnys and thar geir,
Forto defend thar tovn in feir of weir.
As we may geif a symylitude, wail lyke 85
Quhen that the hyrd heß fund the beys byke,
Closit vnder a dern cavern of stanys,
And fillit heß full sone that litill wanys
With smoik of sowr and byttir rekis stew;
The beys within, affrayt all of new, 90 f. 293ʳ
Ourthwort thar hyvis and walxy tentis rynnys,
With mekill dyn and bemyng in that innys,
Scharpand thar stangis for ire, as thai wald fycht –
Swa heir the laithly odor raiß on hycht
From the fyre blesis, dyrk as ony roik, 95
That to the ruffis toppys went the smoik;
The stanys warpit in fast dyd rebund,
Within the wallis rayß gret bruyt and sound,
And vp the reik all void went in the air,
Quhar as na tenementis stud nor howsis war. 100
Betyd alsso to thir wery Latynys,
Quhilk so irkit at sik myscheif and pyne is,
Ane chance of mysfortoun, that all the tovn
With womentyng straik to the boddum doun.
For as the queyn Amata saw syk wyß 105
The cyte ombeset with ennymyß,
The wallys kyndlyt be with flambys heit,
The fyre blesis abuf the ruffis gleyt,
Na Turnus army cumand thame aganys,
Nor 3it nan ostis of Rutilianys; 110
Scho, full onhappy, in the batell sted
Wenyt 3ong Turnus feghtand had bene ded;
And tho for verray sorow suddanly,
Hyr mynd trublit, gan to rame and cry,
Scho was the cauß and wyte of all this greif, 115
Baith crop and ruyte and hed of sik myscheif;
And in hir dolorus fury thus myndleß,
All enragit for duyll tho dyd expreß
Full mony a thyng, and reddy to de with all
Rent with hir handis hyr purpour weid ryall, 120
And at ane hie balk teyt vp scho haß

227

With a lowp knot a stark cord or a laß,
Quharwith hir self scho spilt by schamefull ded.
And fra the Latyn matronys, will of red,
Persavit heß this vile myschewoß wraik,   125
Thai rent thar hair, with, "Harrow," and, "Allaik!"
Hyr douchter first besyde the ded corps standis,   f. 293ᵛ
Ryvand hyr gyltyn tressys with hir handis,
Hyr rosy chekis to tor and scartis sche;
Than all the laif, that piete was to se,   130
Of ladeis that about the ded corps stud,
Rentis and ruggis thame self as thai war wod,
That of thar gowlyng, greting and deray
The large hald resundis a far way,
Quhill from the kyngis palyce inveroin   135
Dywlgat went and spred our all the tovne
The fey onhappy fame of sik a deid;
Than euery wight tynt hart for wo and dreid.
With habyt rent Kyng Latyn on the gait
Walkis wobegone, astonyst of the fait   140
Of hys deir spouß, and of the cite syne,
That semyt brocht onto fynall ruyne:
Hys cannos hair, sair movit in hys entent,
With onclene puldyr has he all bysprent,
And mony tymys hym selvyn heß accusyt,   145
That he sa lang had lachit and reffusyt
To ressaue glaidly the Troiane Ene;
Repentyng sair, for weill of the cyte,
That he had nocht requirit hym, and draw
Or than tobe his mawche and son in law.   150

The quenys deceß fra Turnus cleirly wist,
Went to the sege Eneas to resist.   C. xi

In the meyn tyme, as weriour vnder scheild,
Turnus ȝond at the far part of the feld
A few menȝe persewand our the plane,
Quhilk at the stragill fled in all thar mayn,
Sum deill or than walxis dolf this syre,   5
Seand his horssis begyn to sowpe and tyre;
That euer the leß and leß ioyus was he
Of thar renkis and gait throu the melle.
Tharwith the wynd and sowchquhyng of the air
This feirfull clamour brocht to hym rycht thar,   10
Mixt with oncertane terrour and affeir;
The confusioun of sovnd smait in his eyr,
Com from the cyte, of fellon murmuryng,   f. 294ʳ
Rycht onglaid bruyt of cayr and womentyng.

"Ha, ways me!" he said, "quhat may this be?   15
Quhou beyn the wallys trublit of this cite
With so gret duyll and sorrow as I heir?
Or quhou thus ruschis so fellon noyß and beir
And clamour from the tovn at euery part?"
Thus haß he said, and can do stynt his cart,   20
And all enragit tyt the renȝeis abak;
Quhamto his sistir tho Iuturna spak
(As scho that was turnyt, as I said air,
In semlant of Metiscus the cartar,
That horssis, renȝeis, sydrapis and cart dyd sche   25
Rewle and direct amydwart the melle),
With sic wordis scho ansueris hym fute hait:
"Turnus, lat ws persew Troianys this gait,
Quhar victory ws schawis the reddy way;
Thar beyn enew otheris, be my fay,   30
Forto defend and weill manteym the tovn.
Ȝon is Eneas makis the brute and sovn,
That can invaid Italianys, as ȝe heir,
Mydlit in batalc on sik feir of wcir.
Tharfor lat ws with cruell hand in this sted   35
Lay als feill corpsis of the Troianys ded;
For with na leß numbir slane vnder scheild,
Nor leß honour, sall thou wend of the feild."
Turnus answeris: "O thou my sistyr deir,
I knew full weill at it was thou, langer,   40
That be thi craft and quent wylis sa sle
Our confideratioun trublit and trete,
And entrit in this batell quhilk thou wrocht:
And now, goddes, thy wylis ar all for nocht.
Bot quha was that send the from hevyn so scheyn,   45
So huge sturt and travell to susteyn?
Quhidder gif thou com to that entent to se
The cruell deth of thy fey brother?" said he.
"Quhat sall I do, lat se, quhar sall I now?   f. 294ᵛ
Or quhat succurß promittis fortoun, and quhou?   50
I saw my self befor myn eyn langeir
Gret Murranus, quham nane mair leif and deir
Onto me was that levand is this day,
Swelt on the grund, and with lowd voce, perfay,
On me dyd call, quhar as he lay onsound   55
At erth discomfyt with ane grisly wond:
And lo, doun bet and slane in hys defens
Is not alsso the stowt capitane Vfens,
That he suld not our lak and schame behald?
Hys corps and armour doys Troianys baith withhald.   60
Sall I als suffir thame doun the cyte dyng?

Of our myscheif thar restis bot that a thing.
Nor sall I not with this rycht hand inhy
Confund Schir Drancis langage onworthy?
Sall evir this grund behald or se sik lak,   65
That I sall fle, or Turnus gif the bak?
Is it all owt sa wrachit thing to de,
That, or thai stervyn, men suld rathar fle?
ȝhe Manes, clepit goddis infernal,
Beis to me frendly now, sen that all   70
The goddis myndis abuf ar me contrar;
Be ȝhe benevolent quhen that I cum thar.
Ane haly saule to ȝou discend sall I,
Saikleß of all sic cryme or villany,
Na wyß onworthy namyt fortobe   75
With my eldris and forfaderis mast hie."
Scars heß he said, quhen, lo, throu the plane
Ruschand amyd hys fays, com hym agane
Ane Sages, montit on a fomy steid
(And he was wondit sair, and gan to bleid,   80
In the face with ane arrow vnder the e),
Cryand, "Help, Turnus, be his name, quhar is he?
Turnus," quod he, "in the and thy twa handis
The extreme help and lattir weilfar standis:
Haue reuth and piete of thyne awin menȝe.   85
Now, as the thundris blast, faris Enee
In bargane, so enragit he doith mannayß   f. 295ʳ
The cheif cyte of Italy doun to arrayß,
And into fynal ruyne to bet doun
The principall palyce and all the ryall tovn;   90
And now onto the thak and ruffis hie
The flambys and the fyre blesys doys fle.
In the thar wltys, in the thar eyn, but faill,
The Latyn pepill dressyt heß alhaill:
The kyng hym self Latinus, the gret heir,   95
Quhispyris and musys, and is in maner feir
Quham he sal cheiß or call, into this thraw,
Tobe hys douchteris spouß, and son in law,
Or to quhat frendschip or allyans fyne
Is best hym selwyn at this tyme inclyne.   100
And forthirmor, Amata the fair queyn,
Quhilk at all tymys thyne afald frend haß bene,
With hir awyn hand doith sterve, now liggand law,
And for affray hir self heß brocht of daw.
Only Mesapus and Atynas keyn   105
At the portis doys the stour susteyn:
Abowt thir twa on athir syde thik standis,
Arrayt rowtis, with drawyn swerdis in handis,

Full horribill and austern athir barnage,
Cled in steill weid with wapynnys, man and page;   110
And thou, thus rollyng furth thy cart bedene,
Walkis at avantage on the void grene."
Turnus astonyst stude dum in studeyng,
Smyt with the ymage of mony diuerß thyng:
Deip in hys hart boldynnys the felloun schame,   115
All mixt with dolour, angyr and defame;
Syne fervent luf hym catchit in fury rage,
And hys bykend hardyment and curage.
As first the schaddois of pertrublans
Was dryve away, and hys rememberans   120
The lycht of resson haß recoverit agane,
The byrnand sycht of baith his eyn twane,
Sor aggrevit, towart the wallis he kest,
And from hys cart blent to the cyte prest.   f. 295ᵛ
Bot lo, a sworll of fyre blesys vpthraw!   125
Lemand towart the lyft the flambe he saw,
Amang the plankis and the loftis schire
Stremand and kyndland fast the hoyt fyre,
That caucht was in a mekill towr of tre,
Quhilk towr of sillys and gestis gret belt he,   130
And thar vnder, to roll it, quhelis set,
With staris hie and batelling weirly bet.
"Now, now, systir," quod he, "lo, all and sum
The fatis haß vß venquyst and ourcum:
Desist tharfor to mak me langar tary;   135
Lat ws follow that way, and thiddir cary,
Quhar God and this hard fortoun callys me.
Now standis the poynt, I am determyt," quod he,
"Eneas hand for hand fortill assaill;
Now standis the poynt, to suffir in bataill   140
The bittir ded and all paynfull distreß.
No langar, sistir germane, as I geß,
Sall thou me se schamefull onworthy wight.
Bot, I beseik the, manly as a knycht
Into this fervent furour suffir me   145
To go enragit to batale, or I de."
Thus haß he said, and from the cart inhy
Apon the land he lap deliuerly,
And left his sistir trist and dissolate;
Thrist throu hys fays and wapynnys all, fute hait,   150
And with sa swift fard schot throu the melle
That the myd rowtis and wardis schuddris he.
And like as the gret roch crag with a sovn
From the top of sum montan tumlyt doun,
Quhen at it is our smyt with wyndis blast,   155

231

Or with the drumly schowris spait doun cast,
Or than be lang proceß of mony ȝheris
Lowsyng tharfra the erd, and away weris,
Is maid to fall and tumbill with all his swecht,
Lyke till a wikkit hill of huge weght,   160
Halding his fard the discens of the bra
With mony skyp and stend baith to and fra,   f. 296ʳ
Quhill that he schut far on the plane grund,
And all that he ourrekis doith confund;
Woddis, heyrdis, flokkis, catale and men   165
Our welterand with hym in the deip glen –
Towart the wallys Turnus ruschit als fast
Throw owt the rowtis, by hys fard doun cast,
Quhar tho the grund wet and bedyit stude
A weill far way with effusioun of blude,   170
And large on breid the skyis and the ayr
For schaftis schot dyd quhissilling heir and thar:
A bekyn with hys hand to thame maid he,
And sammyn eik with lowd voce cryis: "Lat be!
Stynt, ȝe Rutilianys, se ȝhe feght na mair,   175
And, ȝhe Latynys, ȝour dartys castyng spar;
Quhou evir the forton standis at this tyde,
The chance is myne, the fait I mon abyde.
It is mair iust and equale I allane
For ȝou sustene the payn was ondertane,   180
And purge the cryme, so happynnyt now of lait,
Of this confideratioun violate:
Lat me stand to my chans, I tak on hand
Forto derene the mater with this brand."
Than euery man amydward thame betwene   185
Can draw abak, and maid rovm on the greyn.

Eneas feghtis and Turnus, hand for hand,
And Turnus fled, for he had brokkyn his brand.   C. xii

Thys fader than, this gret prynce Ene,
     Herand the name of Turnus cryit on hie,
The wallys left, and fra the tovn went away
Richt hastely, secludand all delay;
Styntis all the wark that he begunnyn had,   5
And hoppit vp for ioy, he was so glaid;
The huslyng in his armour dyd rebund,
And kest a terribill or a feirfull sound.
Vpraxit hym he heß amyd the place,
Als byg as Athon, the hie mont in Trace,   10
Or heich as mont Erix in Scycily,   f. 296ᵛ
Or than the fader of hillys in Italy,

Clepyt mont Apennynus, quhen that he
Doith swouch or bray with roky quhynnys hie,
And ioys to streik hys snawy top on hycht   15
Vp in the ayr amang the skyis brycht –
That is to say, amang all other wightis
Eneas semyt to surmontyn in hyghtis
The remanent of all the mekill rowt,
As thir montanys excedis the knollys abowt.   20
And than, forsuyth, Rutilianys egyrly,
And all the Troian ostis or army,
Towart thar dukis dyd return thar eyn;
The Rutilianys, I say, and eik bedeyn
All the Latynys that on the wallys stud,   25
And all thai als tofor as thai war wold
The barmkyn law smait with the rammys fast,
Now of thar schuldris can thar armour cast.
The kyng hym self, Latyn, abasyt to se
Twa men sa byg of huge quantite,   30
Generit and bred in realmys far insundir
Of seir partis of the warld, that it was wondir
Twa of sik statur, onmysurly of hycht,
Fortill assembill sammyn into fyght,
Or forto se thame, matchit on the greyn,   35
Dereyn the bargane with thar wapynnys keyn.
And than athir thir campionys vndir scheild,
Quhen voydit weill and rowmyt was the feild
That patent was the plane a weil large space,
With hasty fard on far heß tane thar rayß,   40
And can thar speris cast, or thai cum neir,
Quhil scheildis soundit and all thar other geir;
Ane marcial batale thai begyn, but baid,
And athir sternly dyd hys fa invaid.
So dyd the strakis dyn on thar steill weid,   45
The erd granys and dyndlys far onbreid,
Syne raschit togidder with swerdis, or euer thai stynt,   f. 297ʳ
And rowtis thik thai doublit, dynt for dynt;
With fors of proweß and fatale aventur
Mydlit sammyn the bargane thai endur.   50
Lyke as twa bustuus bullys by and by,
On the hie month Taburn in Champany,
Or in the mekill forest of Syla,
Quhen thai assembill in austern bargane thra,
With front to front, and horn for horn, attanys   55
Ruschand togiddir with cronys and feirfull granys,
That fe masteris and hyrdmen, euery wight
Abasyt gevys thame place, so brym tha fight;
For feir the bestis dum all standis by,

233

And all in dowt squelys the ȝong ky, 60
Quha salbe master of the catal all,
Or quhilk of thame the bowys follow sall;
Thai twa bullys, thus stryvand in that stond,
By mekill forß wyrkis other mony a wond,
And duschand festynnys fast thar hornys stowt, 65
Quhill that abundans of blude stremys owt,
That can do wesch, bedy, or all to baith,
Thar grym nekkis and thar spaldis baith;
That of thar rowstyng all the large plane
And woddis rank rowtis and lowys agane – 70
Nane other wyß Ene, the Troian heir,
And Dawnus son, Turnus, sammyn infeir
Hurlys togiddir with thar scheildis strang,
That for gret raschis all the hevynnys rang.
Thus Iupiter hym self heß atheris chance 75
A weill lang space to hungyn in ballance
Be equale myssour, and pasyt heß alsso
The fatis diuerß of thame baith two;
Quham the stowt laubour suld deliuer fre,
And quham the pasand wecht ourwelt to de. 80
Turnus at this tyme walxis bald and blyth,
Wenyng to caucht a stound hys strenth to kyth
But ony danger or aduersyte;
He raxis hym, and hevis vp on hie f. 297ᵛ
Hys bludy sword, and smait in al hys mayn. 85
A gret clamour gave the pepill Troian,
And eik the Latynys quakyng gaue a schowt,
Full prest thame tobehald stud athir rowt.
Bot this ontraste fals blaid is brokyn in sundyr,
And ardent Turnus brocht heß in gret blundir; 90
For it amyddis of hys dynt hym falys,
And dissolet hym left, that nocht avalys
To hym hys strenth, hardyment and mycht,
Leß than he tak for hys defens the flycht:
Ȝa, swyftar than the wynd he fled, I geß, 95
Quhen that he saw hys rycht hand wapynleß,
And persauyt the plummet was onknaw.
For so the fame is, at the ilk thraw
Quhen he first ruschit in hys cart inhy,
And gart do ȝok hys stedis by and by 100
To go onto the batale the sam day,
That, for the suddand onset and effray,
The cartar Metiscus sword hynt in hand,
And all forȝet hys faderis nobill brand;
And this ilk swerd was sufficient a lang space, 105
Quhill that he followit the Troianys in the chaiß,

That gaue the bak, as we haue said or this;
Bot alsfast as it twichit and matchit is
By dyvyn armour maid by god Wlcan,
And tharon smyttyn in al Turnus mayn,   110
This ontrew temperit blaid and fykkill brand,
That forgit was bot with a mortal hand,
In flendris flaw, and at the first clap,
As brukkill ice, in litill pecis lap,
Quhill the small partis of the blaid brokin in twa   115
As glaß gletand apon the dun sand lay.
Quharfor this Turnus, half myndleß and brane,
Socht diuerß wentis to fle throu owt the plane;
With mony wyndis and turnys, all on flocht,
Now heir, syne thar, onsovirly he socht.   120
Troianys stude thik bylappit inveroun   f. 298ʳ
In maner of a conpaß or a crovn;
And on the ta half eik a laik braid
Hym so inclusyt that he mycht nocht evaid,
And on the tother syde fermyt als was he   125
With the hie wallys of the cheif cyte.
And thocht the wond tareis Ene sum deill,
Wrocht to hym by the takill with hed of steill,
To weild hys kne maid sum impediment,
That he mycht nocht braid swiftly our the bent,   130
With na leß preß and haist ȝit, nocht for thy,
He, fute for fut, persewys him fervently.
Lyke as, sum tyme, quhen that the huntar stowt
Betrappit haß and ombeset about
With hys ralys and with hys hundis gude,   135
The mekill hart swymmand amyd the flude,
Quhilk thar inclusit neidlingis mon abyd;
For he may not eschape on nother syd,
For feir of hundis, and that awfull bern
Baryng schaftis fedderit with plumys of the ern;   140
The rynnyng hund dois hym assail in threte
Baith with swift rayß and with hys questis grete;
Bot this hart, all abasyt of thar slycht,
And of the strait and stay bankis gret hycht,
Can fle and eik return a thousand ways;   145
Bot than the swypir Tuscan hund assays
And nerys fast, ay reddy hym to hynt,
Now, now, almaste lyke, or euer he stynt,
He suld hym hynt, and, as the beste war tak,
With hys wyd chaftis at hym makis a snak,   150
The byt oft falȝeis for ocht he do mycht,
And chakkis waist togiddir hys wapynnys wycht –
Right so, at this tyme, apon athir syde

The clamour rayß, that all the laik wyde
And brays abowt thame answerd, so thai ferd,   155
The hevyn our all eik rumlyt of ther rerd.
And Turnus, fleand, sammyn fast can call   f. 298ᵛ
Rutilianys, chidand baith ane and all,
Every man clepand by hys proper name,
To reke hym hys trast swerd for schame;   160
And by the contrar, awfully Ene
Can thame mannans, that nane sa bald suldbe,
And schew present the deth all reddy heir
To thar ondoyng, gif that ony drew neir,
And quakyng for affeir maid thame agast,   165
Schorand the cite to distroy and doun cast,
Gif ony help or supple to hym schew,
And, thocht he sair was, fersly dyd persew.
Thus fyve tymys round intill a rayß
About the feild can thai fle and chaiß,   170
And alß feill syß went turnyng heir and thar,
Lyke as befor the hund wiskis the hair.
And na wondir, for sa the mater lyis,
To na bowrdyng twichit thar interpryß,
Na for small wagis thai debait and stryfe,   175
Bot apon Turnus blude schedding and lyfe.
On cace, amyd this feild had grow of lait
Ane wild olyve to Fawnus consecrait,
Quharon grew bittyr levys, and mony ȝheris
Was hald in wirschip with all maryneris;   180
At the quhilk tre, quhen thai eschapit had
The stormys blast, and wallis maid thame rad,
Tharon thar offerandis wald affix and hyng
Onto this god vmquhile of Lawrent kyng,
And tharon eik the clathis bekend vpstent.   185
Bot tho the stok of this tre doun was rent
By the Troianys, mysknawand it hallowit was,
To that entent to plane the batale place.
Eneas byg lance or hys castyng speir
Percayß apon the poynt was stykand heir;   190
Thiddir this schaft the gret fors of his cast
Had thraw the ilk stund, and thar fixit fast,
Amang the grippill rutis fast haldand,   f. 299ʳ
Weggit full law the lance on end dyd stand.
The Troiane prynce it grippis in that sted,   195
Willyng in hand to pull owt the steill hed,
With cast tharof to follow hym at the bak,
Quham he throw speid of fut mycht nocht ourtak.
Bot than Turnus, half mangit in effray,
Cryis: "O thou Fawnus, help, help, I the pray!   200

And thou Tellus, mast nobill god of erd,
Hald fast the speris hed by ȝour werd;
As I that evir haß wirschipit on thir planys
ȝour honour, that be the contrar Eneadanys
Heß violet and prophanyt be stryfe," quod he,
"With blude scheddyng, and down hewyn ȝour tre."
Thus said he, and no thyng invane, I wyß,
The goddys help he axit, for, at hys wyß,
A full lang tyme wrelis and tareis Ene
Furth of the teuch rutis of this ilk tre
Hys speir to draw, and bytis on his lip;
Bot festynnyt sa is in the war the gryp,
That by na maner forß, thocht he was wight,
Furth of the stok the schaft vp pull he mycht.
And as he brymly thus inforcis fast
To draw the speir, this goddeß at the last,
I meyn Iuturna, douchter of Dawnus kyng,
Owt throu the feld com rynnand in a lyng,
Changit agane, as that befor scho was,
Into Metiscus semlant and lyknes,
And to hir brother heß hys swerd betauch;
Quhar at Dame Venus gret disdenȝe caucht,
Sik thyng suldbe tholit this bald nymphe to do;
Than suddanly to the speir rakis scho,
Baith schaft and hed onon, or evir scho stent,
At the first pull from the deip rute heß rent.
Than athir restit and refreschit weill
Baith in curage and scharp wapynnys of steill,
He trastand in hys swerd that weill wald scheir,
And he full prowd and stern of hys byg sper.
Incontrar otheris baldly lang thai stand
In marciall batale athir resistand,
Ilkane full wilfull otheris till ourthraw,
At sic debait that baith thai pant and blaw.

205
210
215
220
225
f. 299ᵛ
230

Quhou Iupiter and Iuno dyd contend
Eneas stryfe and Turnus fortill end.

C. xiii

The fader almychty of the hevyn abuf,
In the meyn tyme, onto Iuno his lufe,
Quhilk tho down from a watry ȝallow clowd
Beheld the bargane tharof na thing prowd,
Thus spak and said: "O my deir spouß, quhat now?
Quhat end salbe of this mater, or quhou?
Quhat restis finaly now at all lat se.
Thou wait thi self, and grantis thou wait, Enee
Is destinat onto the hevin to cum,

5

And fortobe clepit with all and sum 10
Amang the goddis a god indigites,
And by the fatis forto rest in peß,
Sesit abuf the sterry skyis hie.
Quhat purposis or etlys thou now lat se,
Or into quhat beleif, or quhat entent, 15
Hyngis thou swa in the cald firmament?
Was it honest a godly dyvyn wight
With ony mortal strake to wond in fight?
Or ȝit ganand, the swerd lost and adew,
To rendir Turnus, lo, hys brand of new, 20
And strenth encresß to thame at venquist be?
For quhat avalit Iuturna, but thy supple?
Desist heirof, now at last, be the lest,
And condiscend to bow at our request;
Ne suffir not thy hyd sorrow, I pray, 25
Na langar the consume and waist away,
That I na mar sik wofull thochtis se
Schyne nor appeir in thy sweit face," quod he,
"For now is cum the extreme lattir punct. f. 300ʳ
Thou mycht, quhil now, haue catchit at disiunct 30
The silly Troianys baith be sey and land;
And eik thou mycht alsso at thyne awin hand
A fell ontelabill batal rayß or weir,
Deform the howshald, and bryng all on steir
Be mony diuerß ways of fury rage, 35
And all with murnyng mixt thar mariage:
Bot I forbyd ȝou ony mar sic thing."
Thus spak and carpis Ioue, gret hevynnys kyng.
Saturnus dochtir, Iuno the goddeß,
Ansuerit on this wyß, castand doun hir face: 40
"O Iupiter, deir lord, certis," said sche,
"Becauß this thy gret will was knawyn to me,
On forß tharfor, and incontrar my mynd,
I left the erd and my frend Turnus kynd.
Ne, war not that, suld thou me se allon 45
Thus sittand in the ayr al wobegon,
Sustenand thus al maner of myscheif,
And euery streß, baith lesum and onleif;
Bot at I suld, gyrthit with flambis red,
Stowtly haue standyn in ȝon batale sted, 50
And suld haue drawyn ȝon Troianys, ane and all,
Into fell mortal bargane inimicall.
I grant, I dyd persuading owt of dreid
Iuturna to paß doun at sik neid
To hir brothir, and for his lyfe eik I 55
Approvis weill, and als dois ratify,

238

To vndertak mair than to hir pertenyt;
Bot I forsuith persuadit neuer, nor menyt,
That scho suld dartis cast, or takillis draw,
Nor with the bow mak debait ony thraw: 60
I swer tharto be the onplesand well
Of Stix, the flud and cheif fontan of hell,
Quhais only dreidfull superstitioun heir
The goddis kepis, that nane dar it forswer.
And now, forsuith, thy will obey sall I,   65
And giffis owr the cauß perpetualy,
And heir I leif sik werys and debait,   f. 300ᵛ
The quhilk, certis, I now detest and hait.
Bot for the land of Latium or Itaill,
And for maieste of thyne awin blude, sans faill, 70
A thing I the beseik, quhilk, weill I wait, is
Na wyß include in statutis of the fatis:
That is to knaw, quhen that, as weill mot be,
With happy wedlok and felicite
3on pepillis twane sall knyt vp peax for ay, 75
Bynd confiderans baith coniunct in a lay,
That thou ne wald the ald inhabitantis
Byd change thar Latyn name nor natyve landis,
Ne charge thame nother tobe callit Troianys,
Nor 3it be clepit Phrigianys nor Tewcranys, 80
Ne 3it the Latyn pepill thar leid to change,
Nor turn thar clething in other habyt strange.
Lat it remane Latium, as it was air,
And lat the kyngis be namyt euermar
Pryncis and faderis of the stile Albane;   85
The lynage eik and gret ofspring Romane
Mot discend tharfra potent and mychty,
Vndir the virtuus titill of Italy.
Troy is doun bet – doun bet lat it remane,
With name and all, and neuer vpryß agane." 90
Than gan to smyle Iupiter the gret kyng,
That is producear of men and euery thing:
"Syster german," quod he, "to Iove art thou,
And secund child to Saturn ald; ha, quhou
Sa gret a storm or spait of felloun ire   95
Vndir thy breist thou rollis hait as fyre?
Bot wirk as I the byd, and do away
That wreth consauyt but ony cauß, I pray.
I geif and grantis the thi desyre," quod he,
"Of fre will, venquyst, referris me to the. 100
Thir ilk pepill clepit Ausonyanys,
On other wyß callit Italianys,
The auld vsans and leyd of thar cuntre

239

Sall bruke and ioys, and eik thar name salbe
As it is now, and as thar stile remanys: 105
Alanerly thar personys the Troianys   f. 301ʳ
Sall entyr myddill and remane thame amang:
The fassonys and the ritis, that nocht ga wrang,
Of sacrifice to thame statute I sall,
And Latyn pepill of a tung mak thame all.   110
The kynd of men discend from thir Troianys,
Mydlit with kyn of the Italianys,
Thou sal behald in piete and gentilneß
To go abufe baith men and goddis expreß;
Nor neuer clan or other nation by   115
Lyke thame sall hallow, ne ʒit sanctify
Thy wirschip, eik and honour, as thai sal do."
Iuno annerdit, and gaue consent heirto,
Ful blith and ioyus of this grant, perfay,
Fra hir ald wraith heß writhit hir mynd away;   120
And in the meyn tyme onto the hevyn hir drew,
And left the clovd, and bad Turnus adew.
Thys beand done, as said is, on sik wyß,
This hie fader can with hym self devyß
Ane other craft, and providis the way   125
Quhou that he sal Iuturna dryfe away
From helpyng of hir brother intill armys.
Thar beyn twa vengeabill monstreis full of harmys,
Clepit to surname Dire, wikkit as fyre,
That is to say, the goddis wraik or ire,   130
Quhilk myschewoß and cruell sisteris twa,
Sammyn with the hellys fury Megera,
The Nycht thar moder, that barntyme miserabill,
Bair at a birth, for na thing profitabill;
And all elike wymplit and cled thir trakis   135
With eddris thrawin, and harys full of snakis,
And tharto ekit weyngis swift as wynd.
Thir wikkit schrewys reddy sal ʒe fynd
Befor the troyn of Ioue, and eik also
Within the wanys of cruell Kyng Pluto.   140
Thai scharp the dreid to mortale wrachit wightis,
Quhen euer the kyng of goddis by his mychtis
The deth, or the contagius seikneß seir,
Disponys hym to send in the erth heir,   f. 301ᵛ
Or quhen that hym list do smyte and affray   145
Citeis with weirfar, as deservit haue thai.
Ioue ane of thir, full swipper to discend,
Furth of the hevin abuf onon heß send,
And bad hir hald doun baldly to the erd,
Forto resist Iuturnais ire and werd.   150

240

And scho onon doun flaw, to pleß the lard,
And to the grund thuddis with hasty fard.
Nane other wyß than from the stryng doith fle
The swift arrow owt throw the ayr we se,
Or, into bittyr vennom wet, sum flane   155
Castyn or schot by sum archer Persayn,
By sum Persayn or man of Cydony
The schaft thrawyn, that quhyrris throu the sky,
And, quhar it hyttis, wyrkis a wond of pyne,
Oncurabill by the craft of medycyne,   160
And sa swiftly slydis throu the clowdis gray
That quhar it went nane may persave the way –
On sik maner the nyghtis douchtir onflocht
Throw the skyis doun to the erth sone socht;
And efter that scho saw the Troian ostis,   165
And Turnus rowtis arrayt on the costis,
Scho hir transformyt in lyknes of a fowle,
Quhilk we a litil howlet cleip, or owle,
That sum tyme into gravis, or stokkis of tre,
Or on the waist thak, or howß rufis hie,   170
Sittand by nycht syngis a sorowfull toyn
In the dyrk skowgis, with scrykis inoportoyn.
This vengeabill wraik, in sik form changit thus,
Evyn in the face and vissage of Turnus
Can fle and flaf, and maid hym forto grow,   175
Scho soundis so with mony hyß and how,
And in hys scheild can with hyr weyngis smyte.
A new dolfnes dissoluyt hys membris tyte;
For verray dreid and for gret horrour als
Vp stert hys hair, the voce stak in hys hals.   180
Bot as Iuturna soyn on far dyd heir
Of this fury the quhislyng and the beir,
The swouchyng of hir weyngis and hir flycht,
This woful sister hyr hair rent for that sycht,   f. 302ʳ
With nalys ryvand reuthfully hir face,   185
And smytand with hir nevis hir breist, allace!
"Turnus, my best belovit brother," quod sche,
"Quhat may thy sistir help now, wa is me!
Or quhat now restis to me, wrachit wight?
Thy life prolong quhou may I? Be quhat slycht   190
May I oppone me to resist or stryve
With sik a monstre? Na, nane wight alyve.
Now, now, I leif the feild, and goys away.
O ȝe myschewoß fowlis, I ȝou pray,
Do me na mair agryß trymland for feir;   195
The clappyng of ȝour weyngis I knaw and heir,
And eik the dedly sovndis weill onfar.

241

The provd command of myghty Iupiter,
That gydis al thing by hys maieste,
Dois me not now astart, for I it se. 200
Is this the ganȝeld that he rendris me
In recompens of my virginite?
Quharto eternal lyfe heß he me geif?
Quharto suld I on this wyß euer leif?
Quharto is me byreft the faculte 205
Of deth, and grantit immortalite?
For, gif I mortal war, now, now suythly,
Thir sa gret dolouris mycht I end inhy,
And with my reuthfull brother go withall
Amangis the dym schaddoys infernall. 210
O deir brother german, without the
Is na thing sweit nor plesand onto me.
O now quhat grund, land or erd tewch
Sal swelly me tharin half deip enewch,
And, thocht I beyn a goddeß, doun me draw, 215
And send ontil infernal wightis law?"
Thus mekil said scho, and tharwith bad adew,
Hir hed valit with a haw claith or blew,
And murnand gretly thar as that scho stud,
This goddes dowkit deip vnder the flud. 220

At Eneas Turnus a stane dyd cast, f. 302ᵛ
Bot Eneas haß slane hym at the last. C. xiv

Ene with this instantly list not ceß
Forto recontyr Turnus in the preß,
And hys big speir apon hym schakis he,
Quhilk semyt rude and squar as ony tre,
And with a bald and bustuus breist thus spak: 5
"Quhat menys this langsum delay ȝhe mak?
Quhy tary ȝe for schame, Turnus, all day?
Quharto withdrawis thou the so away?
We pyngill not for speid na curß to ryn,
Bot we debait suld, this barreß within, 10
With wapynnys keyn and with our burnyst brandis,
Togiddir met dereyn it with our handis.
Do change thy self, or turn at thy awyn eyß
In all maner of figuris as the pleiß;
Gaddir togiddir and assembill now, lat se, 15
All that thou haß of strenth or subtelte;
Wyß now to fle vp to the starnys on hycht
With fedderit weyngis forto tak thy flycht,
Or forto cloyß thy self this ilk thraw
Into sum cavern vnder the erd law." 20

Turnus, schakand hys hed, said: "Thou fers fo,
Thy fervent wordis compt I not a stro,
Thy sawis makis me not agast, perfay:
It is the goddis that doith me affray,
And Iupiter becummyn myne ennemy." 25
Ne mor he said, bot blent about inhy,
And dyd aspy quhar that a gret roke lay,
Ane ald crag stane huge gret and gray,
Quhilk on the plane, percace, was liggand neir,
A marche set in that grund mony ʒeir 30
Of twa feildis, forto decern tharby
The ald debait of pley or contrauersy;
Scarsly twyß sax stowt walit men and wight,
Quhilk now the erd producis, heß sik mycht
To charge it on thar schuldris or to beir; 35
Quham full lychtly Turnus, that nobill heir,
Hynt in hys hand, and swakkit at his fo, f. 303ʳ
And raxit hym on hicht thar vndir alsso,
And tharwith chargit a full swyft curß ran.
Bot sa confundit is this douchty man 40
That he ne knew hym selvyn in that sted,
Nowder quhar that he ran, nor quhar he ʒed,
Nor felt hym self liftand on the land
The mekill stane, nor steir it with his hand.
Hys kneis stummerit and hys lymmys slydis, 45
The blude congelit for feir within his sydis,
So at the stane he at his foman threw
Fayntly throwowt the voyd and waist air flew,
Ne went it all the space, as he dyd mynt,
Nor, as he etlyt, perfornyst not the dynt. 50
Lyk as, sum tyme, in our swevyn we tak keip,
Quhen langsum dravillyng or the onsond sleip
Our eyn oursettis in the nyghtis rest,
Than semys ws full bissy and full prest
That we ws streke, and doith adreß inhy 55
Lang renkis forto mak and ryn swiftly;
Bot all for nocht, for at the first assay,
Or in the myddis of the start, by the way,
All fante we faill, as forfeblit war we;
The tung avalis not, it will not be; 60
Ne ʒit the strenthis in our body knaw
Semys sufficient to ws at that thraw;
For, set we preß ws fast to spek owt braid,
Ne voce nor wordis followys, nocht is said –
Siklyke wyß heß this goddeß myschewß 65
Ombeset all the ways of Turnus.
Quhat evir to do by hys strenth etlyt he,

243

Scho maid obstakill; all that ganestandis sche.
Than in hys mynd becom his wittis strange
And begouth forto vary and to change;   70
And oft he dyd behald Rutilianys,
And oft the cite with all that ryall wanys.
He hovirris all abasyt for dreid and feir,
And gan do quaik, seand at hand the speir;
Ne can he fynd quhiddir away to wend,   75
Nor on quhat wyß hym self he may defend,
Nor with quhat strenth assaill hys aduersar,   f. 303ᵛ
Nor be na ways persaue hys cart or char,
Nor se hys sistir, that had hys cartar be.
And as he stud on hovyr thus, Ene   80
The fatale dedly speir in hand gan tayß,
And with hys eyn markit and walit haß
Ane place be fortoun to smyte oportune,
And with the hail fors of hys body soyn
Furth from hys hand weil far the lance gan thraw.   85
Neuer sa swyftly quhidderand the stane flaw
Swakkit from the engyne onto the wall,
Nor fulderis dynt, that causis towris fall,
With sik a rummyll com bratland on sa fast.
Lyke the blak thud of awfull thundris blast   90
Furth flaw the schaft to smyte the dedly straik,
And with it brocht cruell myschewos wraik;
Quhilk throu the hawbrik skyrtis persyt haß,
And the extreme bordour gan arraß
Of hys strang scheild, cowchit of sevyn ply,   95
And quhirrand smait hym throw the thee in hy,
That with the dynt huge Turnus, full onsound,
With faldyn howchis duschit to the grund.
Vpstart Rutilianys sammyn complenyng
With a ʒelloch and cairfull womentyng,   100
Quhill all the hillys rumysit thame abowt,
And far on breid thyk woddis gaue a schowt.
And Turnus, than, quhar he at erth dyd ly,
Addressis furth full humyll and lawly
Towart Ene hys syght and eyn tway,   105
And strekis eik hys rycht hand hym to pray,
And thus he said: "Forsuyth I haue deserve
The deth, I knaw, and of thy hand to sterve,
Ne wil I not beseik the me to spair.
Oyß furth thy chance: quhat nedis proceß mar?   110
Bot gif that ony cuyr or thocht," quod he,
"Of ony wofull parent may twich the,
Haue rewth and mercy of Kyng Dawnus the ald
(Thou had forsuyth, as I haue hard betald,

244

Anchises, sik a fader as is he), 115
And me, or than, gif bettir lykis the,
My body, spulȝeit and the life byreft,
Onto my folkis thou may rendir eft.
Thou heß me venquyst, I grant, and me ourcum.
Italian pepill present all and sum 120
Heß sene streke furth my handis humylly.
Lavinia is thy spowß, I not deny:
Extend na forthir thy wraith and matalent."
Eneas stern in armys tho present
Rolland hys eyn toward Turnus dyd stand, 125
And lyst nocht stryke, bot can withdraw hys hand,
And mor and mor thir wordis, by and by,
Begouth inclyne hym to reuth and mercy,
Abydand lang in hovir quhat he suld do,
Quhen, at the last, on Turnus schuldir, lo, 130
The fey gyrdill hie set dyd appeir,
With stuthis knaw and pendes schynand cleir,
The belt or tysche of the child Pallas,
Quhilk by this Turnus laitly venquyst was,
As we haue said, and with a grews wond 135
Slane in the feld, bet doun, and brocht to grund,
And Turnus, in remembrans of this thing,
Abowt his schuldris bair this onfrendly syng.
Bot eftir that Eneas with hys eyn
Sa cruell takynnys of dyseyß heß seyn, 140
And can sik weid byreft thar aspy,
All full of furour kyndlys he inhy,
Full brym of ire and terribill thus can say:
"Sall thou eschape me of this sted away,
Cled with the spulȝe of my frendis deir? 145
Pallas, Pallas, with this wond rycht heir
Of the ane offerand to the goddys makkis,
And of thy wikkit blude punytioun takkis."
And sayand thus, full ferß, with all hys mayn,
Law in hys breist or cost, lay hym forgayn, 150
Hys swerd heß hyd full hait; and tharwithall
The cald of deth dissoluyt hys membris all.
The spreit of lyfe fled murnand with a grone,
And with disdeyn vnder dyrk erth is goyn. etc.

Explicit liber duodecimus Virgilii in Eneados

Heir the translatour of this buk makis mensioun of   f. 304^v
thre of hys pryncipall warkis. etc.

L o thus, followand the flowr of poetry,
  The batellys and the man translait haue I;
Quhilk ʒoir ago in myne ondantit ʒouth,
Onfructuus idylneß fleand, as I couth,
Of Lundeys Lufe the Remeid dyd translait;   5
And syne off hie Honour the Palyce wrait:
"Quhen paill Aurora, with face lamentabill,
Hir russet mantill bordowrit all with sabill, &c."

To knaw the naym of the translatour. etc.

T he Gaw onbrokkyn mydlyt with the Wyne,
  The Dow ionyt with the GLAß rich in a lyne:
Quha knawys nocht the translatouris naym,
Seik na forthar, for lo, with litill pyne
Spy leill this verß: men clepys hym swa at haym.   5

Quod the compilar G D etc.

Heir begynnys the Proloug of the Threttene and last Buk of Eneados ekit to Virgill be Mapheus Vegius

T owart the evyn, amyd the symmyris heit,
  Quhen in the Crab Appollo held hys sete,
Duryng the ioyus moneth tyme of Iune,
As gone neir was the day and supper doyn,
I walkyt furth abowt the feildis tyte,   5
Quhilkis tho replenyst stud full of delyte,
With herbys, cornys, catal, and frute treis,
Plente of stoir, byrdis and byssy beys,
In amerant medis fleand est and west,
Eftir laubour to tak the nychtis rest.   10
And as I lukit on the lift me by,
All byrnand red gan walxin the evyn sky:
The son enfyrit haill, as to my sight,   f. 305^r
Quhirlit about hys ball with bemys brycht,
Declynand fast towart the north in deid,   15
And fyry Phegon, his dun nychtis steid,
Dowkit hys hed sa deip in fludis gray
That Phebus rollis doun vndir hell away;

And Esperus in the west with bemys brycht
Vpspryngis, as forrydar of the nycht. 20
Amyd the hawchis, and euery lusty vaill,
The recent dew begynnys doun to scaill,
To meyß the byrnyng quhar the son had schyne,
Quhilk tho was to the neddir warld declyne:
At euery pilis poynt and cornys croppis 25
The techrys stude, as lemand beryall droppis,
And on the hailsum herbis, cleyn but wedis,
Lyke cristal knoppis or smal siluer bedis.
The lyght begouth to quynchyng owt and faill,
The day to dyrkyn, declyne and devaill; 30
The gummys rysis, doun fallis the donk rym,
Baith heir and thar scuggis and schaddois dym.
Vpgois the bak with hir pelit ledderyn flycht,
The lark discendis from the skyis hycht,
Syngand hir complyng sang, efter hir gyß, 35
To tak hir rest, at matyn hour to ryß.
Owt our the swyre swymmys the soppis of myst,
The nycht furthspred hir cloke with sabill lyst,
That all the bewte of the fructuus feld
Was with the erthis vmbrage cleyn ourheld; 40
Baith man and beste, fyrth, flude and woddis wild
Involuyt in tha schaddois warryn syld.
Still war the fowlis fleis in the air,
All stoir and catall seysit in thar lair,
And all creatur, quharso thame lykis best, 45
Bownys to tak the hailsum nychtis rest
Eftir the days laubour and the heyt.
Cloß warryn all and at thar soft quyet,
But sterage or removing, he or sche,
Owder best, byrd, fysch, fowle, by land or sey. 50
And schortlie, euery thing that doith repar f. 305ᵛ
In firth or feild, flude, forest, erth or ayr,
Or in the scroggis, or the buskis ronk,
Lakis, marrasis, or thir pulys donk,
Astablllit lyggis still to slepe, and restis; 55
Be the smaill byrdis syttand on thar nestis,
The litill mygeis, and the vrusum fleys,
Laboryus emmotis, and the bissy beys;
Als weill the wild as the taym bestiall,
And euery othir thingis gret and small, 60
Owtak the mery nychtgaill, Philomeyn,
That on the thorn sat syngand fra the spleyn;
Quhais myrthfull notis langyng fortil heir,
Ontill a garth vndir a greyn lawrer
I walk onon, and in a sege down sat, 65

Now musyng apon this and now on that.
I se the Poill, and eik the Vrsis brycht,
And hornyt Lucyn castand bot dym lycht,
Becauß the symmyr skyis schayn sa cleir;
Goldyn Venus, the mastres of the ʒeir, 70
And gentill Ioue, with hir participate,
Thar bewtuus bemys sched in blyth estait:
That schortly, thar as I was lenyt doun,
For nychtis silens, and this byrdis sovn,
On sleip I slaid, quhar sone I saw appeir 75
Ane agit man, and said: "Quhat dois thou heir
Vndyr my tre, and willyst me na gude?"
Me thocht I lurkit vp vnder my hude
To spy this ald, that was als stern of spech
As he had beyn ane medicyner or lech; 80
And weill persavit that hys weid was strange,
Tharto so ald, that it had not beyn change,
Be my consait, fully that fourty ʒeir,
For it was threidbair into placis seir;
Syde was this habyt, round, and closyng meit, 85
That strekit to the grund doun our his feit;
And on his hed of lawrer tre a crown,
Lyke to sum poet of the ald fasson.
Me thocht I said to hym with reuerens:
"Fader, gif I haue done ʒou ony offens, 90
I sall amend, gif it lyis in my mycht: f. 306ʳ
Bot suythfastly, gyf I haue perfyte sycht,
Onto my doym, I, saw ʒou nevir ayr,
Fayn wald wyt quhen, on quhat wyß, or quhar,
Aganyst ʒou trespassit ocht haue I." 95
"Weill," quod the tother, "wald thou mercy cry
And mak amendis, I sal remyt this falt;
Bot, other ways, that sete salbe full salt.
Knawis thou not Mapheus Vegius, the poet,
That onto Virgillis lusty bukis sweit 100
The thretteyn buke ekit Eneadan?
I am the sammyn, and of the na thyng fayn,
That heß the tother twelf into thy tong
Translait of new, thai may be red and song
Our Albyon ile into ʒour wlgar leid; 105
Bot to my buke ʒit lyst the tak na heid."
"Mastir," I said, "I heir weill quhat ʒhe say,
And in this cace of perdon I ʒou pray,
Not that I haue ʒou ony thing offendit,
Bot rathar that I haue my tyme mysspendit, 110
So lang on Virgillis volume forto stair,
And laid on syde full mony grave mater,

That, wald I now write in that trety mor,
Quhat suld folk deym bot all my tyme forlor?
Als, syndry haldis, fader, trastis me,   115
ʒour buke ekit but ony necessite,
As to the text accordyng neuer a deill,
Mair than langis to the cart the fift quheill.
Thus, sen ʒhe beyn a Cristyn man, at large
Lay na sik thing, I pray ʒou, to my charge;   120
It may suffyß Virgill is at ane end.
I wait the story of Iherom is to ʒou kend,
Quhou he was dung and beft intill hys sleip,
For he to gentilis bukis gaif sik keip.
Full scharp repreif to sum is write, ʒe wist,   125
In this sentens of the haly Psalmyst:
'Thai ar corruppit and maid abhominabill
In thar studeyng thyngis onprofitabill':
Thus sair me dredis I sal thoill a heit,
For the grave study I haue so long forleit."   130   f. 306ᵛ
"ʒa, smy," quod he, "wald thou eschape me swa?
In faith we sall nocht thus part or we ga!
Quhou think we he essonʒeis hym to astart,
As all for consciens and devoit hart,
Fenʒeand hym Iherom forto contyrfeit,   135
Quhar as he lyggis bedovyn, lo, in sweit!
I lat the wyt I am nane hethyn wight,
And gif thou haß afortyme gayn onrycht,
Followand sa lang Virgill, a gentile clerk,
Quhy schrynkis thou with my schort Cristyn wark?   140
For thocht it be bot poetry we say,
My buke and Virgillis morall beyn, bath tway:
Len me a fourteyn nycht, how evir it be,
Or, be the faderis sawle me gat," quod he,
"Thou salt deir by that evir thou Virgill knew."   145
And, with that word, doun of the sete me drew,
Syne to me with hys club he maid a braid,
And twenty rowtis apon my riggyng laid,
Quhill, "Deo, Deo, mercy," dyd I cry,
And, be my rycht hand strekit vp inhy,   150
Hecht to translait his buke, in honour of God
And hys Apostolis twelf, in the numbir od.
He, glaid tharof, me by the hand vptuke,
Syne went away, and I for feir awoik
And blent abowt to the north est weill far,   155
Saw gentill Iubar schynand, the day star,
And Chiron, clepit the syng of Sagittary,
That walkis the symmyrris nycht, to bed gan cary.
ʒondyr dovn dwynys the evyn sky away,

And vpspryngis the brycht dawyng of day 160
Intill ane other place nocht far in sundir
That tobehald was plesans, and half wondir.
Furth quynchyng gan the starris, on be on,
That now is left bot Lucifer allon.
And forthirmor to blason this new day, 165
Quha mycht discryve the byrdis blisfull bay?
Belyve on weyng the bissy lark vpsprang,
To salus the blyth morrow with hir sang;
Sone our the feildis schynys the lycht cleir,
Welcum to pilgrym baith and lauborer; 170 f. 307ʳ
Tyte on hys hynys gaif the greif a cry,
"Awaik on fut, go till our husbandry."
And the hyrd callis furth apon hys page,
"Do dryve the catall to thar pasturage."
The hynys wife clepis vp Katheryn and Gill; 175
"3a, dame," said thai, "God wait, with a gude will."
The dewy greyn, pulderit with daseis gay,
Schew on the sward a cullour dapill gray;
The mysty vapouris spryngand vp full sweit,
Maist confortabill to glaid all manis spreit; 180
Tharto, thir byrdis syngis in the schawys,
As menstralis playng "The ioly day now dawys."
Than thocht I thus: I will my cunnand kepe,
I will not be a daw, I will not slepe,
I wil compleit my promyß schortly, thus 185
Maid to the poet master Mapheus,
And mak vpwark heirof, and cloyß our buke,
That I may syne bot on grave materis luke:
For, thocht hys stile be nocht to Virgill lyke,
Full weill I wait my text sall mony like, 190
Sen eftir ane my tung is and my pen,
Quhilk may suffyß as for our wlgar men.
Quha evir in Latyn heß the bruyt or glor,
I speke na wers than I haue doyn befor:
Lat clerkis ken the poetis different, 195
And men onletterit to my wark tak tent;
Quhilk, as twiching this thretteynt buke infeir,
Begynnys thus, as furthwith followis heir.

Explicit prologus in decimumtertium librum Eneados

Sequitur liber decimustertius de maphei vegii carmine
traductus per eundem qui supra interpretem etc.
G. D.

Rutilian pepill, eftir Turnus deceß,
Obeys Eneas, and takis thame to hys peß.

As Turnus, in the lattir bargan lost   f. 307ᵛ
  Venquyst in feild, 3ald furth the fleand gost,
This marciall prynce, this ryall lord Enee,
As victor full of magnanymyte,
Amyddis baith the rowtis baldly standis,   5
That tobehald hym apon athir handis
Astonyst and agast war all hym saw.
And tho the Latyn pepill haill on raw
A fellon murnyng maid and wofull beir,
And gan devoid and hostit owt full cleir   10
Deip from thar breistis the hard sorow smart,
With curage lost and doun smyttyn thar hart –
Lyke as the huge forest can bewaill
Hys granys doun bet and his branchis skaill,
Quhen thai beyn catchit and alltoschakyn fast   15
With the fell thud of the north wyndis blast.
For thai thar lancis fixit in the erd
And lenys on thar swerdis with a rerd,
Thar scheldis of thar schuldris slang away:
That bargan and that weir fast wary thai,   20
And gan abhor of Mars the wild luf,
Quhilk laitly thay desyrit and dyd appruf.
The brydyll now refuß thai nocht to dre,
Nor 3ok thar nekkys in captiuite,
And to implor forgyfnes of all greif,   25
Quyet, and end of harmyß and myscheif.
As quhen that twa gret bullys on the plane
Togiddir rynnys in byttir gret bargane,
Thar lang debait mydland quhar thai stand
With large blude scheddyng on athir hand,   30
Quhill athir of thame onto the batalis fyne
Hys awyn bestis and heyrdis doys inclyne,
Bot, gyf the pryß of victory betydis
Till ony of thir twa on athir cydis,
Onon the catall, quhilkis favorit langer   35
The best ourcummyn as thar cheif and heir,
Now thame subdewis vnder his ward inhy
Quhilk haß the ovirhand wonnyn and mastry,
And of fre will, all thocht thar myndis be thra,
Assentis hym till obey – and evin rycht swa   40
The Rutilianys, all thocht the gret syte   f. 308ʳ
Thar breistis had bedowit and to smyte,
With gret effray of slauchter of thar duke,
3it thocht thame levir, and haill to purpoß tuke,

To follow and obey, for all thar harmys,   45
The gentill chiftane and bettir man of armys,
And thame subdew to the Troian Enee,
And hym beseik of peax and amyte,
Of rest and quyet evirmar from the weir,
For thame, thar landis, moblis and other geir.   50
Eneas tho with plesand voce furth braid
And, standand abuf Turnus, thus he said:
"O Dawnus son, quhou com this hasty rage
Into thy breist with foly and dotage,
That thou mycht nocht suffir the Troianys,   55
Quhilkis at command of goddis onto thir planys
And by power of hie Iove ar hiddir cary,
Within the bundis of Italy to tary,
And, all invane, thame so expellyng wald
Of thar land of behest and promyst hald?   60
Lern forto dreid gret Iove, and nocht gaynstand,
And to fulfyll glaidly the goddis command;
And for thar greif weill aucht we tobe war:
Sum tyme in ire will grow gret Iupiter,
And oft remembrans of the wikkit wraik   65
Solistis the goddis tharof vengeans to take.
Lo, now of all sik furour and effeir
The lattir meith and term is present heir,
Quhar thou aganyst reson and equyte,
Aganyst lawte, and brokyn all vnyte   70
Of confideratioun sworn and bund or now,
The Troian pepill sair trublit heß thow.
Behald and se the extreme fynale day,
To geif all otheris gud exempill for ay
That it mot nevir lefull be agane   75
Tyll ony to contempne gret Iove invane,
As forto rayß with sik dreid and effeir
Sa onworthy motioun of wikkit weir.
Now beis glaid, bruke thyne armour but pled;
Allace, a nobill corps thou lyggis ded,   80   f. 308ᵛ
The gret Turnus, and, as to my demyng,
Lavynya haß the cost na litill thyng:
Nor thou na schame nedys thynk in na part,
That of Eneas hand thou kyllit art.
Now cumis heir, Rutilianys, but delay,   85
The body of ȝour duke turß hyne away.
I grant ȝou baith the armour and the man:
Hald on, and do tharto all that ȝe can,
As langis onto the honor of bereyng,
Or tobewaill the deth of sik a kyng.   90
Bot the gret pasand gyrdill and sik geir

That Pallas, my deir frend, was wont to weir,
To Evandar I will send, fortobe
Na litill solace to hym, quhen he sall se
Hys felloun fa is kyllit thus, and knaw,   95
Full glaid tharof, Turnus is brocht of daw.
And netheleß now, ʒe Italianys,
That otherwyß be clepe Ausonyanys,
Ramembir heirof, and lern in tyme cummyng
With bettir aspectis and happy begynnyng   100
To move and tak onhand debait or weir;
For, be the blyssit sternys brycht I sweir,
Neuer nane ostis nor ʒit armour glaidly
Aganyst ʒou in batal movit I,
Bot constrenyt by ʒour fury, as is kend,   105
With all my forß I set me to defend
The Troian party and our awyn ofspryng,
As, lo, forsuyth this was bot lesum thing."
No mor Eneas said, bot tharwithall
Addressys hym towart hys cite wall,   110
And throu the feildis socht full ioyusly
To hys new Troian reset and herbry.
Sammyn hym followis all the rowt atanys,
The pissans haill and ʒynkeris of Tewcranys,
And our the planys, glaid and wondir lycht,   115
Thar swyft stedis, as the fowle at flycht,
Throu speid of fut assays by and by,
And oft with bittir mouth dyd crying, "Fy!"
And can accuß the Latyn pepill all,
Oft fant folkis and sleuthfull dyd thame call;   120   f. 309ʳ
That with thar rerd and bemyng, quhar thai fair,
For the deray full heich dynnys the air.

Quhou Eneas, glaid of hys victory
Lovyt the goddis, and can tham sacryfy.   C. ii

And thocht Ene the bissy thochfull curis
Constrenyt haß as twychand sepulturis
Of hys folkis yslane, and bereyng,
With funeral fyre and flambis accordyng,
ʒit, netheleß, in hys breist rollys and sterys   5
Ane grettar mater and largyar, as efferis.
For first the soueran honour on thar gyß
On the altarys with detfull sacrifice
He ordand haß, and than, fra hand to hand,
Eftir the ryte and vsans of thar land,   10
The ʒyng oxin gan thai steik and sla:
Within thar tempill haue thai brocht alssua

253

The bustuus swyne, and the twynteris snaw quhite,
That with thar clovis can the erth smyte,
With mony palt scheddand thar purpour blude.   15
Furth haue thai rent thar entralis, full onrude,
And gan denude and strippyn of thar hydis,
Syne hakkyn thame in talȝeis, and besydis
The hait flambis brochit heß thame laid.
And furth thai ȝet the wyne in cowpis glaid,   20
God Bachus giftis fast thai multiply;
With platis full the altaris by and by
Thai can do charge, and wirschipis with fat lyre;
The smelland sens vpblesis in the fyre.
Than throu that hald thai fest and mak gud cheir,   /   25
Vprayß the mery rerd and ioyus beir:
Thai dyd extoll and lovyng with gret wondir
Gret Iupiter, the feirfull god of thundir;
And Dame Venus thai wirschippit alsso;
And the, Saturnus douchter, Queyn Iuno,   30
Now pacifyit and bettir than befor,
Ane huge lawd thai ȝald to the tharfor;
And eik hym self Mars, the gret god of armys,
Thai magnyfy as wrekar of thar harmys;   f. 309ᵛ
Syne haill the remanent of the cumpany   35
Of the goddys thai name furth by and by,
With hie vocis and with lowd cryis
Lovit and born vpheich abufe the skyis.
Befor thame all maste gracius Eneas
Hys handis twa, as tho the custum was,   40
Towart the hevyn gan vplift and arays,
And syne the child Ascanyus dyd embraß,
Sayand a few wordis, that all mycht heir:
"O thou my son and only child mast deir,
In quham only restis thy faderis beleve,   45
Quham throu samony laubouris of myscheve
I careit haue, catchit full mony gatis
Be the hard fortoun and the frawart fatis,
Lo, now our rest and quyet fund for ay!
Lo, now the last and maist desyrit day,   50
To mak end of our harmyß and distres!
Our paynfull laubour passit is expreß:
Lo, the acceptabill day for euermor,
Quhilk I full oft haue schawin the befor
Quhen ontill hard bargan callit was I,   55
This was tocum and betyd by and by
Be dispositioun of the goddys abufe.
And now, my derrest child, for thy behufe,
To morn, soyn as Aurora walxis red,

254

To the cite of Lawrent, that ryall sted,   60
I sall the send, as victor with ovirhand,
Tobe mastir and to maynteym this land."
And eftir this he turnyt hym agane
Onto hys folkis and the pepill Troian,
And from the boddum of hys breist weill law   65
With soft spech furth gan thir wordis draw:
"O ȝe my ferys and my frendis bald,
Throu mony hard perrellis and thikfald,
Throw sa feill stormys baith on land and se,
Hiddir now careit to this cost with me,   70
Throu sa gret fervour of batall into stowr
And dowbill fury of weirfar in armour,
Be sa feill wynteris blastis and tempestis,   f. 310ʳ
By all ways noysum and onrestis,
And all that horribill was, or ȝit hevy,   75
Wofull, hydduus, wikkyt, or onhappy,
Or ȝit cruell or myschews; now stad
In bettir hoip, return ȝour mynd, beys glaid:
Now is the end of all ennoy and wo,
The term is cumyn, heir sall thai stynt, and ho: 80
And, lyke as we desyrit for the best,
With Latyn pepill in ferm peax and rest
We sall conioyn, and leif in vnite;
And Lavinia, of that ilk blude," quod he,
"Quham I defendit haue in strang bargan,   85
Of Troiane kyn, with blude Italian
Sammyn mydlit, to me as spouß in hy
Sal ȝeld lynnage to ryng perpetualy.
A thing, my fallowis and my frendis deir,
I ȝou besekyng, and I ȝou requer: 90
Bair ȝour myndis equale, as all anys,
And common frendis to the Italianys,
And to my fader in law, the kyng Latyn,
Obeis all, and with reuerens inclyn –
Ane myghty ceptre and riall beris he –   95
This is my mynd, this is my will, perde.
Bot into batale and douchty dedis of armys,
Ȝou forto wreke and revenge of ȝour harmys,
Lern forto follow me and tobe meik,
Ȝhe contyrfyt my reuth and piete eik.   100
Quhat glor is ws betyd full weil is knaw,
Bot the heich hevyn and starris all I draw
To witnessyng, that I, the sammyn wight
Quhilk ȝou deliuerit heß into the fight
From sa huge harmys and myschevis seir,   105
I sall ȝou seyß and induce now, but weir,

In far largyar rewardis myghtyly
And ȝou rendir ȝour desert by and by."
With sik wordis gan he thame comfortyng
And in his mynd full mony syndry thyng   110
Of chancis bipast rollyng to and fro,   f. 310ᵛ
Thynkand quhou he is brocht to rest alsso
With na litill laubouris, sturt and panys;
And with excedand luf of the Troianys
Full ardently he flowis all of ioy,   115
Glaid at the last from danger and ennoy,
So huge and hevy perrellis mony fald,
Thai war eschapit, and brocht to sovir hald.
Lyke as quhen that the gredy gled on hycht
Scummand vp in the ayr oft turnys hys flycht,   120
With fellon fard wachand the chiknys lyte,
Thar deth mannasand, reddy forto smyte:
The cristit fowle, thar moder, tho full smert
For hyr pullettis, with harmys at hir hart
Affrait gretly of thar wofull chance,   125
Gan rax hir self and hir curage avans,
Forto resist hir fa scharpand hir byll,
And with haill fors and mycht and egir will
Apon hir aduersar baldly settis sche,
Quhill, at the last, to gif the bak and fle   130
With mekill payn and verray violens
Scho hym constrenys, and to pyk hym thens:
Hyr byrdis syne, clokkand, scho sekis on raw
And all affrait dois thame sammyn draw,
Ennoyt gretly for hir childir deir: 135
And quhen thai beyn assemlit all infeir,
Than glaid scho worthis and thar meyt gan scrape
For that thai haue sa gret perrell eschape –
Nane other wyß the son of Anchises
With frendly wordis thus amyd the preß   140
The Troian myndis gan meyß and asswage,
As man fulfillit of wit and vassalage,
Dryvand furth of thar hartis all on flocht
The ald dreid and byrnand hevy thocht,
That weill thame lykis now thar ioy and eyß   145
At last fundyn eftir sa lang diseyß;
And it that layt tofor was tedyus
To suffir or sustene, and ennoyus,
Now to ramember the sammyn or rehersyng   f. 311ʳ
Doys to thame solace, comfort and lykyng,   150
Bot maist of all onto the gret Ene,
Quhilk in excelland vertu and bonte
Excedit all the remanent a far way.

And for sa feill dangeris and mony affray
The goddis power and mychty maieste   155
With gyftis gret and offerand wirschippis he,
Eyk Iupiter, the fader of goddis and kyng,
Gan to extoll with maist souerane lovyng.

Quhou Turnus folkis for hym maid sair regrait, And Kyng Latyn contempnys his wrachit estait.   C. iii

In the meyn tyme the Rutilianys ichone
The gret ded corps reuthfull and wobegone
Of thar duke Turnus slayn, as said is air,
Within the cite of Lawrentum hair
With mekill murnyng in thar myndis enprent,   5
And from thar eyn a large schour furth sent
Of teris gret, as thocht the hevin dyd rayn,
And far on breid dyd fyll the erys twayn
Of Kyng Latyn with cry and womentyng,
That all to irkyt was the nobill kyng,   10
And in his breist the self tyme in ballance
Was rollyng mony diuerß selcouth chance.
Bot quhen he hard thar lowd womentyng
Incressyng mair and mair, and Turnus ȝyng
With sa grysly a wond throw gyrd heß seyn,   15
Than mycht he nocht fra terys hym conteyn;
And syne this rowt, sa tryst and wobegone,
Full curtesly chargis be still onon,
Baith with hys hand and wordis in his presens
Inionyt haß and commandit thame silens.   20
Lyke as quhen that the fomy bair heß bet
With his thunderand awfull tuskis gret
Throw owt the cost and eik the entralis all
Ane of the rowt, the hund maste principall;
Than the remanent of that questing sort,   25
For this onsilly chance effrait, at schort
Withdrawys, and abowt the master hunteir   f. 311ᵛ
With quhyngeand mouthis quakand standis for feir
And with gret ȝowlyng doith compleyn and meyn;
Bot quhen thar lord rasys hys hand bedeyn   30
And byddys ceß, thai hald thar mowthis still,
Thar quhyngyng and thar questyng at his will
Refrenys, and all cloß gan thame withhald –
The sammyn wyß thir Rutilianys, as he wald,
Gan at command debait thar voce and ceß,   35
To heir the kyngis mynd, and held thar peß.
Than thus, wepyng, from hys hart ruyt waill law
The kyng Latyn begouth thir wordis schaw:

"O quhou gret motioun, quhat alteryng onstabill,
Quhou oftsyß interchangit and variabill   40
Beyn the actis and dedis of man!" quod he,
"With quhou gret trubbill, but tranquylyte,
Is quhirlit abowt the lyfe of man, behald!
O dampnabill pryde and ambitioun, that wald
Bruke crovn or ceptre, prowd in thyne entent,   45
Quhilk beyn sa fragyll, and not permanent!
O fury, O lust, that beyn our gretumly
Bred in our brestis, to covat senȝeory!
Thou blynd desyre insaciabill, may not tary,
Our mortal myndis quhidder doith thou cary?   50
O glory and renoun of loyß, invayn
Conquest with sa feill perrellis and huge pane,
To quhat conditioun or to quhat estait
Thou sterys furth thir prowd myndis inflait!
Quhou mony slichtis and dissatis quent   55
With the thou tursis, quhou mony ways to schent,
Quhou feill maneris of deth and of distreß,
Quhou feill tormentis, gret harm and wikkytnes!
Quhou mony dartis, quhou feill swerdis keyn,
Gyf thou beheld, thou heß befor thyne eyn!   60
Allace, thou sweit vennom schawis, and ȝit
This warldly wirschip heß the dedly byt.
Allace, the sorofull reward in all thyng
Of realmys, and thame covatis forto ryng,
Quhilk costis oft na litill thing, but weir.   65
Allace, the hevy byrdyng of warldly geir,
That nevir hour may suffir nor permyt   f. 312ʳ
Thar possessour in rest nor peax to syt.
Allace, the miserabill chance and hard estait
Of kyngly honour sa mysfortunate: 70
The chance of kyngis standis onderlowt,
To mekill dreid ay subiect, and in dowt
From thar estait to dekey suddanly,
That all quyet and eyß is thame deny.
O Turnus, quhat avalit the to steir   75
In huge bargan so and feir of weir
All Italy with sik deray atanys,
And to perturbe the strangis Eneadanys,
Constrenyng thame hard batal to assay?
Or quhat avalis now, I pray the say,   80
Fortill haue brokkyn, violate or schent
The haly promyß and the bandis gent
Of peax and concord oblisit and sworn?
Quhou was thi mynd to rent and all to torn
With samekill impaciens on this wyß,   85

That the lyst move the weir, but myne avyß,
With tha pepill, sa strang, bald and sage,
That beyn discendit of the goddys lynnage,
And at command of Iove the god of thundir
Ar hyddir careit? and forto mak sic blundir,   90
That wilfully, but motyve, so belyve
Enforsyt the thame from our cost to dryve?
And forto brek the band that promyst we
Of our douchtir till our gude son Ene?
And with thy hand hard bargan rayß and steir,   95
Quhen I planely denyit to move weir?
Quhou was sa gret foly and dotage
Involuyt in thy mynd with fury rage?
Quhou oft, quhen thou to awfull batale wend
Amyd thy rowtis, and on thy steid ascend   100
In schynand armour arrayt all at rycht,
I assayt the to withdraw from fycht,
And feill tymys defendit the and forbad
To go the way that thou begunnyn had,
And all efferit, quhen thou wald depart,   105
Amyd the ȝet the stoppit with sair hart!
Bot all for nocht; no thyng mycht styntyng the.   f. 312ᵛ
Quhat I haue sufferit sen syne, quhou standis with me,
Our cyte wallys wytnessyng ful het,
With tenementis and biggyngis half doun bet,   110
And the large feldis strowit quhite of banys,
And haill the pissans of Italianys
All wastit and distroyit thus, allake!
The huge slauchtir and myschews wrake,
And all the fludis walxyn red or brovn   115
Of mannys quelling gret and occisioun,
The lang abasit quakyng feirfull dreid
And hard laubour, quhilk in extreme neid
I in myne age sa oft heß ondertane,
In sa feill dangeris quhar remed was nane.   120
Bot now, Turnus, heir thou lyggis ded:
Quhar is the nobill renovn of thy ȝouthed?
And quhar is thyne excellent hie curage?
Quhiddir is went thy strenth and vassallage?
Quhar is the staitly bewty of thy face?   125
Quhar is thy schynand figur now, allace?
Of thy fair vissage quhidder ar gone but weir
Thy plesand forret schaply and eyn cleir?
Ha, quhou feill terys and wofull dolouris smart
Sall thou, Turnus, rendir to Dawnus hart!   130
And with quhou large wepyng, duyll and wa
Ourfleit sal all the cite of Ardea!

Bot thai sal nocht behald the with sik lak
Througyrd with schamefull wond caucht in thi bak,
Ne noyt the of na cowardyß in thar mynd,   135
Nor that thou was degenerit owt of kynd,
And to thy wofull fader, will of red,
At lest this salbe solace of thy ded,
All thocht thy harmys doith hym soir smart,
That gret Eneas swerd heß persyt thy hart."   140
And sayand thus, with terys of piete
Hys chekis baith and face ourchargit he:
Syne, turnand hym towart the mekill rowt,
The reuthfull corps of this ilk Turnus stowt
Bad turß away and cary furth onon   145
Ontill hys faderis cite wobygon,
And commandit to do the body cald   f. 313^r
All funerall pomp, eftir the vsage ald.

Quhou Turnus corps till Ardea was sent,
Quhilk was by suddand fyre brynt doun and schent.   C. iv

The Rutilianys onon all in a rowt
�This ded corps, that slayn lay, start abowt;
The gentill body of this stowt ȝongkeir
Thai haue adressit and laid on a rich beir,
And with hym eik feill takynnys by the way,   5
Reft from Troianys in the bargan, bair thai,
Baith helmys, horß, swerdis and other geir,
Scheildis, gittarnys and mony stalwart speir.
Syne eftir this hys wery cart furth went,
Of Troian slauchter and hait blude all bysprent.   10
Furth haldis wepand Metiscus, the carter,
As he that in the craft was not to leir,
Ledand the steid bedowyn all of swete
And chekis wait of flotterand terys grete,
Quhilk steyd had careit Turnus oft tofor   15
As victor hame with gret triumphe and glor
Full pompusly, apon ane other wyß,
Efter fervent slauchter of his ennymyß.
Ȝondir otheris, about hym inveroun,
Baris thar armour and scheildis turnyt dovn;   20
The remanent syne of the haill barnage
Followys wepand, knycht, swane, man and page,
With habundans of mony trigland teyr
Wetand thar brestis, wedis and other geir;
And thus wery furth went thai euery wycht   25
Amyd the dirk silens of the nyght,
Betand thame self with wondir drery cheir.

260

And Kyng Latyn with all thame with hym wer
Towart hys palyce gan return onon
With mynd trublit, trist and wobygon   30
For sa excelland ded corps as was slane.
Terys all sammyn furth ȝettis eueryane –
Baith agit men, matronys and childer lyte
The cite fyllis with womentyng and syte.
Dawnus, hys fader (na wyß wittand tho   35   f. 313ᵛ
He suld remane to se sik duyll and wo,
Nor that his son hys stalwart spreit had ȝald
And maid end in the lattir bargan bald,
That thus was brocht to tovn ded by his feris
With sik plente of bittir wepand terys),   40
The sammyn tyme with other dyseyß was socht,
At mekill sad dolour and hevy thocht.
For as the Latyn pepill war ourset
Into batall by Troianys, and dovn bet,
And Turnus be his hait and recent ded   45
Had with hys blude littit the grund all red,
A suddan fyre within the wallys hie
Ombeset halyly Ardea cite;
The biggyng of this fader wobegon,
Brynt and doun bet, of reky flammys schone,   50
And all returnys intill assys red;
The fyry sparkis into every sted
Twynkland vpspryngis to the starnys on hie,
That now na hope of help may fundyn be,
Quhidder so it was onto the goddis lykyng,   55
Or that the fatis befor list schaw sum syng
Of Turnus deth, in horribill batal slane.
And quhen the pepill saw remed was nane,
Belyfe the wofull trublit citesanys
Thar drery brestis betand all atanys,   60
Gan fast bewaill with petuus wepand face
Of this onhappy chance the wrachit cace;
In lang rabill the wemen and matronys
With all thar forß fled reuthfully atonys
From the bald flammys and brym blesys stowt.   65
And lyke as that of emottis the blak rowt,
That ithandly laubouris and byssy be,
Had beldit, vnder the ruyt of a heich tre,
Intill a clift thar byke and duellyng sted,
To hyd thar langsum wark and wyntyr bred;   70
Gyf so betyde thai feill the ax smyte
Apon the treis schank, and tharon byte,
So that the crop doun weltis to the grund,
That with the felloun rusch and grysly sond

261

Thar small cavernys all tobrok and rent is; 75 f. 314^r
Than spedely this litill rowt furth sprentis
All will of red, fleand thai wait nocht quhar,
Tursand thar byrdyngis affraytly heir and thar –
Or lyke as that on the howß syde the snaill,
Schakand hir coppit schell or than hir taill, 80
Fleand the byrnand heit that scho doith feill,
A lang tyme gan do wrassill and to wreill,
Thristand fast with hir feit onto the wall,
And ȝit hir hed with forß and strenthis all
Frawart the fervent flammys fast withdrawys; 85
Scho scaldis, and with mony wrikis and thrawys
Presys forto eschew the feirfull heit –
Nane other wyß in sa feill perrellis gret
Thir woful citesanys gan thame self slyng,
Ruschand with trublit mynd intill a lyng 90
Baith heir and thar, and wist not quhar away.
Bot maist of all, allace and weil away!
With reuthfull vocis cryand to the hevyn,
The agit kyng Dawnus with wofull stevyn
Gan on the goddis abuf clepe and call. 95
And tho amyd the flambis furthwithall
Ardea the fowll, quham a heron clepe we,
Betand hir weyngis, thai behaldyn fle
Furth of the fyre heich vp in the air,
That baith the name and takyn our alquhar 100
Baris of this cite Ardea the ald,
Quhilum with wallis and towris hie ontald
Stud weirly wrocht, as strenth of gret defens,
That now is changit and full quyte goyn hens
With weyngis wyde fleand baith vp and doun, 105
Now bot a fowle, was ayr a ryall tovn.
Astonyst of this nyce and new cace
And of the wonderus mervellis in that place
(Quhilk semyt no thing litill fortobe)
As thocht thai send war by the goddis hie, 110
The pepill all confusyt still dyd stand,
Thir byrdyngis on thar schuldris caryand,
And movit nowther fut, tung nor mouth: f. 314^v
And Kyng Dawnus, for this affray onkouth
With ardent luf smyttin and hait desyre 115
Of hys cheif sete distroyt and brynt in fyre,
The hard dolour and the sorow smert
Haldis full cloß, deip gravyn in hys hart.

262

Fra that Dawnus his son Turnus saw ded,
Huge lamentatioun maid he in that sted. C. v

A myd all this deray and gret effeir,
  Fame, of dyseyß forrydar and messynger,
Com hurland with huge movyng fast to tovn
And with large clamour fyllys inveroun
Thar myndis all, quhou ane ded corps new than 5
Was cumand at hand with mony wofull man,
And Turnus lyfleß laid with mortal wond,
In feld discomfist, slane and brocht to grund.
Than euery wight, trublit and wobegon,
The blak blesand fyre brandis mony on, 10
As was the gyß, heß hynt into thar handis;
Of schynand flammys glitteris all the landis;
Thus thai recuntyrrit thame that cumand weir,
And sammyn ionyt cumpaneis in feir.
Quham alsfast as the matronys gan espy, 15
Thai smait thar handis and rasyt vp a cry,
That to the sternys went thar wofull beir.
Bot fra Dawnus the corps of hys son deir
Beheld, he gan stynt and arrest hys paiß,
And syne, half deill enragit, in a rayß, 20
With huge sorow smyte, in ruschis he
Amyd the rowt, that reuth was forto se,
And apon Turnus corps hym strekis doun,
Enbrasyng it ongrouf all in a swoun,
And, alsfast as he spek mycht, heß furth braid 25
With wordis lamentabill, and thus wyß he said:
"Son, the dyseyß of thy fader thus drest,
And of my febill eild the reuthfull rest
Now me byreft, quhy heß thou so, allace,
Into sa gret perrellys and in sik cace 30
Me catchit thus, and dryve quhidder?" quod he,
"And vndir cruell bargan, as I may se, f. 315ʳ
Now fynaly thus venquyst and ourcum,
Quhar is thy worthy valour now becum?
Quhar heß the douchty constans of thy spreit 35
Me careit thus from rest and all quyet?
Is this the notabill honour and lovyng
Of thy manhed, and glory of thy ryng?
Is this the gret wyrschip of thyne empyre?
O my deir son, quhilum thou bald syre, 40
Bryngis thou ws hame sikkyn triumphe as this?
Is this the rest and eyß thou dyd promyß
To thy fader, sa tryst and wobegone,
And oft ourset with ennemyß mony one?

263

Is this the meith and finale term or end   45
Of all laubouris, as we desyrit and wend?
O ways me, wrachit and wofull wyght!
Quhou hastely doun fallyn from the hight
Thir slyddir warldly chancis dryvis fast!
With quhou gret fard ourrollyt and down cast   50
So hastely beyn thir fatis, behald!
He that was laitly sa stowt, heich and bald,
Renownyt with gret honour of chevelry
And haldyn gret throu owt all Italy,
Quham the Troianys sa awfull felt in armys   55
And dred sa oft hys furour, wrocht thame harmys,
Myne awyn Turnus, lo now apon sik wyß
Ane lamentabill and wofull corps thou lyis:
Now dum and spechleß that hed liggis thar,
Quhilum in all Italy nane sa fair,   60
Nor nane mair gracius into eloquens,
Nor nane so byg but harnes, nor at defens!
Son, quhar is now thy schynand lustyhed,
Thy fresch figour, thy vissage quhite and red,
Thy plesand bewte, and thyne eyn twan   65
With thar sweit blenkand lukis mony ane,
Thy gracyus glitterand semly nek lang,
Thy vocis sovn, quhilk as a trumpet rang?
The glor of Mars in batale or in stowr
Is conquest with sik aventouris sowr: 70
Had thou sic wyll thy selvyn to submyt
To fervent bargan and to dedis byt,   f. 315ᵛ
Quhen thou departit of this sted fra me,
Forto return with sik pompe as we se?
O haitfull deth! that only, quhar thou lykis,   75
With thy revengeabill wapynnys sa sair strikis,
That thou thir prowd myndis brydill may;
To all pepill elyke and common ay
Thou haldis evyn and baris thi ceptre wand,
Eternaly obseruand thy cunnand,   80
Quhilk gret and small doun thryngis, and nane rakkis,
And stalwart folkis to febill equale makkis,
The common pepill with the capitanys,
And 30uth and age assemblys baith attanys.
Allace, detestabill deth, dyrk and obscur!   85
Quhat chance onworthy or mysaventur
Heß the constrenyt my child me to byreif,
And with a cruell wond thus ded to leif?
O systir Amata, happy queyn," quod he,
"Be glaid of sa thankfull chance hapnyt the,   90
And of thyne awyn slauchtir be blith in hart,

264

Quharby thou haß sa gret dolour astart,
And fled sa huge occasions of myscheif,
Sa hard and chargeand huge wo and greif!
O goddis abuf, quhat ettill ȝe mor to do   95
Onto me wrachit fader? sen ellys, lo,
My son ȝhe haue byreft, and Ardea
My cite, into flambis brynt, alssua
Consumyt is and turnyt in assys red,
With weyngis fleys a fowle in euery sted.   100
Bot ha, Turnus, mar trist and wo am I
For thy maste petuus slauchter sa bludy:
Wantit this last myschance ȝit or sik thing
To thyne onweldy fader, auld Dawnus kyng.
Bot sikkyrly, with sic condıtıoun aẏ   105
Thir warldly thyngis turnys and writhis away,
That quham the furyus Forton lyst infest
And eftir lang quyet bryng to onrest,
Brayand apon that catyve for the nanys,
With all hir forß assalȝeis scho attanys,   110
And, with all kynd of torment, in hir greif   f. 316ʳ
Constrenys hym with stundys of myscheif."
Thus said he, wepand sadly, as man schent,
With large flude of teris hys face bysprent,
Drawand the sobbys hard and sychis smart,   115
Throw rageand dolour, deip owt from hys hart;
Lyke so as quhar Iovis byg fowle, the ern,
With hir strang tallonys and hir punsys stern
Lychtyng, had claucht the litill hynd calf ȝyng,
Torryng the skyn, and maid the blude owt spryng; 120
The moder, this behaldand, is all ourset
With sorow for slauchter of hir tendir get.

Kyng Latyn till Eneas send message
For peax, and eyk hys douchteris mariage.   C. vi

The nixt day followyng with hys bemys brycht
Ihe warld on breid illumnyt heß of lycht:
The kyng Latinus tho seand, but let,
Italyanys discumfyst and ourset
By the fatale aventour of weir,   5
And weill persavit quhou and quhat maner
The forton haill turnyt to strang Enee;
And in hys mynd revoluyt eik heß he
The huge dowt of batall and deray,
Full mony feirfull chance and gret effray,   10
Hys confideratioun and hys sworn band,
The wedlok promyst and the ferm cunnand

265

And spousal of hys douchtir hecht withall:
Of all the rowt ontill hym gart he call
A thousand worthy men walit at rycht,   15
The quhilkis the Troian duke and dowchty knycht,
Quham he desyrit, suld convoy to town;
In robbys lang also, or traill syde govn,
With thame he ionyt oratouris infeir
And to thame gaif feill strait commandis seir,   20
And forthir eik, quhen thai depart can,
Of hys fre will thame chargit euery man
That, sen be favouris and admonysyngis
Of the goddis, by mony feirfull syngis,
Expedient it was the kyn Troian   25   f. 316ᵛ
Conioyn and myddill with blude Italian,
At tharfor glaidly to thame gang wald thai,
And with gud willis vissy, and assay
Forto convoy the said Eneadanys
With ioy within hys hie wallys attanys.   30
In the myd quhile, hym self full bissy went,
The cite, quhilk was disarayt and schent,
To put to poynt and ordinans agane,
And the onweldy common pepill ilkane
To cauß adreß eftir thar faculte –   35
Thar myndis mesys and estabillis he,
And gan thame promyß rest in tyme cummyng,
And quhou, within schort tyme, he suld thame bring
Intyll eternall peax for evirmar.
Syne chargit he the pepill our alquhar,   40
In ioy, blithneß, solace and deray,
Tryumphe to mak, with myrth, gam and play,
As was accordyng, and in lugyngis hie
Thar kyngly honour and sport ryall tobe;
And merely commandis man and page,   45
With ane assent, blith wlt and glaid vissage,
Hys gud son thai suld do welcum and meit
And with hail hart ressaue apon the streit
The Troian pepill, festand thame in hy
With glaid semlant, ryot and melody,   50
And to furthschaw seir takynnys of kyndnes,
And of new peax so lang desirit soleß.
Be this the rowt, as thai instrukkit wer,
In full gude rewle and ordinans infeir
Ar entrit in the Troianys new cite,   55
And on thar hed garlandis of olyve tre;
Peax thai besocht as cheif of thar message.
Quham gentill Eneas, euery man and page,
Within hys palyß ryall to presens

Chargit convoy, and gafe thame audiens,   60
And of thar cummyng the causys and maner
With vissage full debonar dyd inqueir.
Than the agit Drances with curage hoyt   f. 317^r
Begowth the first hys tong forto noyt,
As he that was baith glaid, ioyfull and gay   65
For Turnus slauchter, that tho was doyn away;
And thus he said: "O gentill duyk Troian,
Ferm hope and glory of the pepill Phrigian,
To quham of piete and dedis of armys fair
In all the warld thar may be na compair: 70
We venquyst folkis to witnessyng doith call,
And by the goddis sweris and goddessis all,
Contrar hys willis sair the kyng Latyn
Beheld the gret assemly and convyn
Of the Italyanys and folk of Latyn land;   75
Agane his stomok eyk, I bair on hand,
Owtragyusly the contract is ybrokkyn,
Ne nevir he in deid nor word heß spokkyn
That mycht the Troian honour trubbill ocht,
Bot far rathar, baith in deid and thocht   80
(Sen that the goddis responsis swa heß tald),
The weddyng of hys douchter grant ȝou wald,
And with full gret desyre, full weill I knaw,
Oft covat ȝou tobe hys son in law.
For all the brek and sterage that heß beyn   85
In feir of weir and burnyst armour keyn,
With sa gret rage of laubour and of payn,
The wild fury of Turnus, now lyis slayn,
Inflambit with the stang of wikkytnes,
And infekkit with hie haitrent expres,   90
Heß brocht on hand and movit sa to steir,
Agane thar will to rayß batale and weir
The Latyn pepill constrenyng by and by,
Quhilk thai playnly refusyt and gan deny:
Hym all the ost, turnand bakwart agane,   95
Besocht to ceß, and draw fra the bargan,
And suffir the gret Anchises son of Troy
Hys wedlok promyst enioys but ennoy.
Syne the maist nobill kyng Latyn, full fayn
Hym forto breke and to withdraw agane,   100
Hys auld onweldy handis twa dyd hald,   f. 317^v
Hym to requir hys purpoß stynt he wald
(For weill he saw, in our ardent desyre
Of the bargan he scaldit hait as fyre),
Bot all our prayeris and requestis kynd   105
Mycht nowder bow that dowr mannys mynd,

Nor ȝit the takynnys and the wondris seir
From goddis send with dyvyne ansuer,
Bot that evir mor and mor fersly he
Furth spowtit fyre, prouocand the melle.   110
And, for syk succudrus ondertakyng now,
Hys awin myscheif, weill worthy to allow,
He fundyn heß, quhilk finaly, on the land
Thou beand victour with the ovirhand,
Hym bet to grond heß maid do gnaw and byte   115
The blak erd intill hys mortall syte.
Now lat that ilk rahatour wend inhy
The blak hellys byggyngis to vissy
Vndir the drery deip flude Acheron –
Lat hym go serß, sen he is thiddir gone,   120
Other ostis or barganys in hys rage
And als ane other maner of mariage.
Thou, far bettir and gret deill worthiar
To bair the riall ceptyr and tobe ayr,
Succeid to realm and heritage sall   125
Of Lawrent cuntre with the moblys all:
In the alhaill the howß of Kyng Latyn
And hys onweldy age, lyke to declyne –
Hys hope and all beleif restis in the,
And the only Italianys all," said he,   130
"Abufe the schynand sternys, as gold brycht,
Full wylfull ar fortill vphie on hycht;
As maste excelland worthy weryour
Thai the extoll in batale and in stowr,
Thy hevynly armour eik with lowd stevin   135
And thy verray renoun syngis to the hevyn.
The grave faderis of consale venerabill
In thar digest decretis sage and stabill,
The ancyent pepill onweldy for age,
The glaid ȝong gallandis stalwart of curage,   140
The lusty matronys newfangill of sik thyng,
Wenschys onwed, and litill childryn ȝyng,   f. 318ʳ
All, with a voce and haill assent at accord,
Desyris the as for thar prynce and lord,
And ioyus ar that into feild fut het   145
Vndir thy wapynnys Turnus lyis doun bet:
The all Itaill, clepit Ausonya,
Besekis heirof, and forthirmor alssua
Doith the extoll maste worthy, wyß and wight;
In the only returnyt is thar syght: 150
The kyng hym self Latinus, now full ald,
Hys ancient onweldy lyfe to hald,
Heß only this beleif and traste," quod he,

"That he hys douchter may do wed with the,
Quhilk of kyn, successioun and lynnage, 155
Be that ilk souerane band of mariage,
Of Troian and Italian blude discend
Sall childryng furth bryng, quhill the warldis end
Perpetualy to ryng in hie impyre.
Tharfor haue doyn, cum on, thou gudly syre, 160
Thou gret ledar of the Troian rowt,
Cum entyr in our weirly wallys stowt,
Ressaue this worthy notabill fair proffyr
And saisyn tak of honouris quhilkis we offir."
Thus endit he, and all the remanent 165
Intill a voce sammyn gave thar consent,
Quham the reuthfull Eneas with glaid cheir
Ressauyt heß full tendyrly infeir,
And, in few wordis and a frendly mynd
Thame ansuerand, he carpys on this kynd: 170
"Not ȝou, nor ȝit the kyng Latyn, but leß,
That wont was forto ryng in plesand peß,
Will I argw of this maner offens:
For suyth I wait the wilfull violens
Of Turnus all that gret wark brocht abowt, 175
And I am sovir eik and owt of dowt
Sa gret danger of batale it was he
Provokit swa and movit to melle,
For ȝyng desyre of hie renown, perfay,
And loyß of prowes mair than I byd say. 180
And netheleß, quhou evir it be, I wyß, f. 318ᵛ
This spowsage Italian at me promyst is
Ne will I not refuyß on nakyn wyß,
Nor forto knyttyng vp as ȝhe devyß
This haly peax with frendly allyans, 185
With etern concord but disseuerans.
The sam Kyng Latyn, my gud fader ald,
Sall hys impyre and venerabill ceptour hald,
And I Troian for me vp in this feild
Ane new ressel and wight wallys sall beld, 190
Quhilk cite sall ressaue hys douchteris naym;
And my goddis domesticall, that fra haym
With me I brocht, I sall with ȝou conioyn;
In concord and in vnyte all common
In tyme tocum sammyn athir falloschip 195
Vndir a law sall leif in gret frendschip.
In the meyn tyme, go to and speid ws soyn
Onto our wark that restis ȝit ondoyn,
And lat ws byrn the bodeis, and bery eft,
Quham the hard wofull rage heß ws byreft, 200

And into batale kyllyt lyis ded;
Syne, tomorn ayrly, as the son worthis red,
And with hys cleir days lyght doyth schyne,
Blithly we seik to cyte Lawrentyne."
Thus said he, and the Latynys, quhill he spak, 205
With vissage still beheld hym stupifak,
Of hyß wyß gracius answeris wonderand all,
And of sik wordis debonar in speciall;
Mayr evidently gan mervell he and he
Of hys gret warkis of reuth and sik piete. 210
Belyve, with all thar forcis, euery wyght
Weltis doun treys grew full hie on hycht,
And hastely togiddir gadderit haß
In hepys gret, the funerall fyre to rayß,
And thar abuf thar citiȝanys heß laid, 215
Vndir quham syne thai set in blesys braid:
The flambe and reik vpglydis in the ayr,
That of the laithly smokis heir and thar
The hevyn dyrknyt and the firmament. f. 319ʳ
Thai hynt from all the feildis adiacent 220
Innumerabill rowch twyntir scheip syne,
And of thir akcorn swellyaris, the fat swyne;
And tydy ȝyng oxin steik thai fast
And in the funerall fyris dyd thame cast.
The large planys schynys all of lycht, 225
And, throw thir hait scaldand flambys brycht,
Stude blowt of bestis and of treys bair:
With huge clamour smyt, dyndillit the ayr.

Quhou Kyng Latinus metis with Eneas keyn,
And frendly talkyng was thir twa betweyn. C. vii

Be this the schynand secund days lyght
Vprasit Phebus with goldyn bemys brycht:
Than all the Troianys and Ausonyanys
Full blithly in a rowt assemblit attanys,
Montit on horß and held thar ways syne 5
Onto the mastir cite Lawrentyne,
With wallys hie and biggyngis weirly maid.
Befor thame all rewthfull Eneas raid;
And nixt per ordour Drances, that to the kyng
As agit man carpis of mony thyng; 10
Syne come hys only child Ascanyus,
That other wyß was clepyt Iulus;
Nixt hym Alethes, with mynd full digest,
Grave Ilyoneus, Mnestheus and stern Serest;
Syne followys thame the forcy Sergestus, 15

270

Gyas alsso, and stalwart Cloanthus,
Eftir quham, mydlit sammyn, went arayn
The other Troianys and folk Italian.
In the meyn quhile the Latyn citeȝanys
Withowt thar wallys ischit furth atanys,   20
That with gret lawd, in mych solempnyte
And triumphe ryall haß ressauyt Enee.
Be this thai cummyn war onto the town,
Quham with blith front, to meyt thame reddy bown,
The kyng Latyn with huge cumpany   25
Thame welcumis and festis by and by.   f. 319ᵛ
And fra that he beheld amyd the rowt
Eneas cumand, the Dardan capitan stowt,
Hys verray figur dyd hym nocht dissaue,
For, quhar he went, excellent all the lave   30
And hyear far a gret deill semys he,
That far on breid his ryall maieste
And pryncely schynand contenans dyd appeir.
And quhen that he cummyn was so neir
That athir gudly to othir speke mycht   35
And heir the wordis carpyt apon hycht
And, lyke as thai desyrit, on the land
To lap in armys and adion hand in hand,
The kyng Latinus, as a curtas man,
With glaid semblant thus first to speke began: 40
"Weill be ȝe cummyn finaly, Enee,
And the ferm hope heß not dissavit me
Of my desyrus mynd, now full of ioy;
O schynand gloryus light to folkis of Troy!
Quham the command of the gret goddis mycht,   45
Throu sa feill chancis catchit and evill dycht,
In Italy within our boundis plane
Heß destinat and ordanyt to remane,
All thocht that manis wanton willfull offens,
Be our malapert and ondantit licens,   50
In thar fury with brag and mekill onrest
Tha haly lawis trublit and infest,
Prouocand and commovand the goddis greif;
So that alsso, quhidder me war loith or leif,
Full oft resistand and denyand the weir,   55
Constrenyt I was and warpit thar and heir,
That, mawgre my hed, me behuffit susteyn
The hard dangeris of Mars and mekill teyn.
Now is it endit, bot, certis, na litill thyng
Haß it cost sum man sik vndertakyng –   60
The godly power, wilfull vengeans to tak,
Havand disdeyn at sik deray was mak,

Onto tha wikkyt sawlys for the nanys
Heß send condyng punytioun and iust panys.   f. 320ʳ
Haue doyn, gret Troian prynce, now I the pray,   65
Sen baith the crop and rutys ar away
Of all seditioun and discord, I wyß,
And wyrkaris of sa gret trespaß and myß;
Cum and ressaue thy spowß and mariage
To the promyst; succeid to heritage.   70
Realmys I haue, and citeys mony ane
Full strangly beldit with hie wallis of stane,
And sum alsso that I in weir conquest
And thar barmkynnys to grund bet and doun kest;
Bot only the beleif and beld," quod he,   75
"Of my wery age and antiquyte,
A douchtir haue I, quhilk suldbe myn ayr,
Quharfor in tyme cummyn for euermar
I the ressaue and haldis in dante
As son in law and successour to me."   80
To quham the gentill Eneas reuerently
This ansuer maid agane, and said in hy:
"Maist riall kyng, all tyme accustumate
To lyf in plesand peax, but all debait,
Of this weirfar and sa gret stryfe," quod he,   85
"I trastit evir thar was na wyte in the:
Tharfor, my derrest fader, I the pray,
Do all sik dowtis of suspicioun away,
Gyf ony sik thochtis restis in thy mynd,
And trastis weill Enee afald and kynd.   90
Now am I present, reddy as ȝe wald,
That ȝou ressavis and fra thens sall hald
As fader in law, and in all chancis, per de,
As verray fader that me bigat, but le:
The figour of the gret Anchises ded   95
I se heir present to me in this sted,
And I agane in fervent hayt desyre
ȝow forto pleß, my fader, lord and syre,
Sall byrn in lufe, as sum tyme wont was I
Towartis hym me engendrit of his body."   100

Heir Eneas, that worthy nobill knycht,   f. 320ᵛ
Was spowsyt with Lavinia the brycht.   C. viii

Wyth sikkyn sermond athir othir grat,
  And sammyn to the cheif palyß with that
Thai held infeir: than mycht thou se with this
The matronys and ȝong damysellis, I wyß,
That gret desyre heß sik thing tobehald,   5

272

Thryng to the stretis and hie wyndoys thik fald;
The agit faderis and the ȝyng gallandis
Per ordour eik assemlyt reddy standis
In gret rowtis, to vissy and to se
The gudly personys of the Troian menȝe.   10
Bot specialy and first of all the laif
The gret capitan Enee notyt thai haue,
Attentfully behaldand euery wight
Hys stowt curage, hys byg statur and hycht,
And in thar mynd comprasyt hys kyn maste hie,   15
Hys plesand vissage and knychtly large bonte;
And, glaid and ioyfull, extoll and loif thai can
The gret apperans of gud in sik a man,
And sa fair gyftis and beleif, but leß,
As thai desyrit, of finale rest and peß.   20
Lyke as quhen the gret ithand weit or rayn,
From the clowdis furth ȝet our all the playn,
Haldis the husbandis ydill aganys thar will
(Lang with hys crukyt beym the plewch lyis still);
Syne, gif brycht Tytan list do schaw hys face,   25
And with swyft curß far furth a large space
Doith cach hys stedis and hys giltyn char,
And kythis hys goldyn bemys in the ayr,
Makand the hevynnys fair, cleir and scheyn,
The weddir smowt, and firmament sereyn;   30
The landwart hynys than, baith man and boy,
For the soft sesson ourflowis full of ioy,
And athir otheris gan exhort inhy
To go to laubour of thar husbandry –
Nane other wyß the pepill Ausonyan   35
Of this glaid tyme in hart wolx wonder fayn.
Be this the kyng Latyn, lord of that land,   f. 321ʳ
With maste nobill Eneas hand in hand,
Within the cheif palyß, baith he and he,
Ar entryt in the saill ryall on hie;   40
Quham followys nixt the ȝyng Ascanyus fair,
That was hys faderis only child and ayr;
Syne folk of Itaill, mydlyt with Troianys,
Ar entrit in that riall hald attanys:
With pompoß fest and ioyus myrth our all   45
Resoundis tho baith palys, bowr and hall,
And all the chymmys riall rownd abowt
Was fyllyt with thar tryne and mekill rowt.
And tharwithall, of chalmyr by and by,
With sa gudly a sort and cumpany   50
Of ladeis fair and damysellys onwed,
Innumerabill almast, als furth was led

The fair fresch Lavinia the may,
Amyd thame schynand in hir ryall array;
The crystall bemys of hir eyn twane,   55
That as the brycht twynkland starnys schayn,
Sum deill eschamyt, towart the erth doith hald.
Quham as this Troian prynce first gan behald,
Of bewte, schap and all afferys, perfay,
Sa excelland that wondir war to say,   60
At the first blenk astonyst half wolx he,
And musyng hovirris styll on hir to se,
And in hys mynd gan rew the hard myschans
Of Turnus, quham na litill apperans
Sa baldly movit to dereyn bargan,   65
To rayß the weir and feght for sykkyn ane;
For weill, he thocht, the hope of syk a wight
To dedys of armys aucht constreyn ony knycht.
Syne, to abbryge our mater, hand in hand
Thai war coniunct intill eternall band   70
Of matrimonye, and tho at all devyß
Thar wedlok with honour, as was the gyß,
By menstralys and herraldis of gret fame
Was playd and sung and throw the cowrt proclame.
Than ioy and myrth, with dansyng and deray,   75
Full mery noyß and sovndis of gam and play
Abuf the bryght starnys hie vpwent,   f. 321ᵛ
That semyt forto perß the firmament,
And ioyus vocis ryngis furth alsso
Our all the palyß ryall to and fro.   80
And syk ryot indurand amyd the preß,
Ene thus carpys to traste Achates,
And bad hym go belyve, but mair delay,
Do fech the rych robbys and array,
The fresch attyre and all the precyus wedis,   85
Wrocht craftely and weif of goldyn thredis
Quhilum be fair Andromachais hand,
By quham thai war hym gevyn in presand;
And eyk the collar of the fyne gold brycht,
With precyus stanys and with rubeys pight,   90
Quham scho also abowt hir halß quhyte
Was wont to weir in maste pompe and delyte,
Quhill that the Troian weilfar stud abufe;
The gret cowpe eyk, the quhilk in syng of lufe
Quhilum Kyng Priam to hys fader gave,   95
Ald Anchises, of fyne gold and engrave.
Than, but delay, Achates at command
Brocht thir rych gyftis, a wonder fair presand;
Syne to hys fader in law, the kyng Latyn,

274

The precyus cowp gave he of brycht gold fyne,   100
And to hys spowß, Lavinia the may,
The wedis ryall and the collar gay.
Than athir dyd thar dewly obseruans
With breistis blyth and plesand dalyans,
To festyng, entertenyr and cheryß   105
Thar ferys abowt on the maist gudly wyß:
With diuerß sermond carpyng all the day
Thai schort the howris and dryvis the tyme away.

Gret myrth and solace was maid at the festis,
Rehersand mony historeis ald and gestis.   C. ix

Be this it walxis layt towart the nycht,
And fast declynyng gan the days lycht,
The tyme requiryng, eftir the ald maner,
To go to meytc and syt to the supper;
Onon the bankat and the mangeory   5   f. 322ʳ
For fest ryall accordyng, by and by,
With all habundans pertenyng to syk thyng,
As weill efferit in the howß of a kyng,
With alkyn maner ordinans was maid
Amyd the hallys heich, lang and braid,   10
Apparalyt at all devyß and array.
Onto the bankat haill assemlyt thai
And on the carpettis spred of purpour fyne
To tablis set, quhar thai war servit syne
With alkyn danteys and with metys seir   15
That all to rakkyn prolixit war to heir –
As quhou the crystall eweris to thar handis
The watir gave, and quhou feill servandis standis
To mak thame ministratioun in all curys,
And quhou thai trasyng on the large flurys   20
With blyth vissage intil euery sted,
And quhou that first on burdis thai set bred;
Sum with mesys gan the tabillys charge;
Ane other sort doith set in all at large
The cowpys gret and drynkyn tassis fyne,   25
And gan do skynk and byrll the nobill wyne,
That to behald thame walkyn to and fro
Throw the rowm hallys and sa byssy go,
And thame at tabillis makand sa glaid cheir,
A paradyß it was to se and heir.   30
Bot with hys eyn onmovit Latyn kyng
Gan fast behald the child Ascanyus ȝyng,
Wondrand on his afferis and vissage,
And of the speche and wordis grave and sage

Of sik a childis mowth syk wyß suld fall,   35
And of his digest and reddy wyt withall
Befor the 3heris of maturyte;
And of feill thingis hym demandis he,
Athir to other renderand mony a saw;
And syne wald he alsso, ane other thraw,   40
Full tenderly do kyß hys lusty face
And lap hym in hys armys and embrace;
And, wondirly reiosyt, declar wald he   f. 322ᵛ
Happy and to the goddis bedettit Ene,
Quhilk hym had gevin syk a child as that.   45
And quhillis thai thus at the supper sat,
Eftir that with samony danteis seir
Thar appetit of metis assuagit wer,
With commonyng and carpyng euery wyght
The lang declinand and ourslippand nyght   50
Gan schape full fast to mak schort and ourdryve:
Now the Troianys hard aventouris belyve
Rehersyng our, and all the Grekis slycht;
Now the ferß bargan and the awfull fight
Of Lawrent pepill callyng to thar mynd,   55
As quhou and quhar, quhamby and be quhat kynd
The ostis first discumfist war in feild,
And quhar that athir rowtis vndir scheld,
With dartis castyng, dynt of swerd and mayß,
Constrenyt was to fle in syk a place,   60
And leif the feild, and quha best dyd hys det,
Quha bald in stowr eyk maid the first onset,
And quha first, on ane startland cursour gude,
Hys burnyst brand bedyit with red blude.
Bot principaly Eneas Troian bald   65
And Latinus the kyng sage and ald
Of conquerouris and soueran pryncis dyng
The gestis can reherß fra kyng to kyng,
Twichand the stait, quhilum be days gone,
Of Latium that myghty region,   70
Quhou vmquhile Saturn, fleand hys sonnys brand,
Lurkyt and dwelt in Italy the land,
Be quhilk rayson he dyd it Latium call;
That kynd of pepill, dwelt skatterit our all
In montanys wild, togyddir maid conveyn   75
And gaif thame lawys and statutis, and full beyn
Tawcht thame to grub the wynys, and al the art
To eyr and saw the cornys and 3ok cart;
And quhou the gret Iupiter, god dyvyne,
To this hys faderis resset socht heß syne;   80
And quhou that he engendrit thar alssua

On Atlaß douchter, the fair wench Electra, f. 323r
Schir Dardanus, that efter, as thai sayn,
Hys awyn brother Iasyus heß slayn,
Syne from the cyte Choryte in Italy
To sey is went with a gret cumpany
And gan arryve eftir in Phrigia,
And belt the cyte on the mont Ida,
And quhou that he, in syng, for hys baner,
From Iupiter ressauyt, hys fader deir,
The fleand egill displayt fair and playn,
Ane knawyn takyn to pepill Hectorian,
As the first nobill armys and ensenȝe
Baith of the Troian ancistre and menȝe,
By hym erekkit and vprasyt stud,
Was first begun, and cheif stok of that blude.
Thus, with syk maner talkyn, euery wight
Gan dryvyn our and schortis the lang nycht.
Tharwith the bruyt and noyß rayß in tha wanys,
Quhill all the large hallys rang attanys
Of mannys voce and sound of instrumentis,
That to the ruyf on hie the dyn vp went is;
The blesand torchys schayn and sergis brycht,
That far on breid all lemys of thar lycht;
The harpys and the githornys plays attanys;
Vpstart Troianys and syne Italianys
And gan do dowbill brangillys and gambatis,
Dansys and rowndis traysyng mony gatis,
Athir throu other reland, on thar gyß;
Thai fut it so that lang war to devyß
Thar hasty fair, thar revellyng and deray,
Thar morysis and syk ryot, quhil neir day.
Bot forto tellyng quhou with torch lycht
Thai went to chalmer and syne to bed at nycht,
Myne author list na mensioun tharof draw –
Na mair will I, for sik thingis beyn knaw;
All ar expert, eftir new mariage,
On the first nycht quhat suldbe the subcharge.

Eneas foundis a wallit town and squair; Quhamto Venus can diuerß thingis declar. C. x

And thus thai festyng days nyne at all, f. 323v
With large pompe and kyngly apparall
Accordyng sych a spowsage as was this,
And quhen the tent morrow cummyn is,
Than this ilk souerane and maste douchty man,
Eneas, forto found hys town began;

Fyrst gan he mark and cirkill with a pleuch
Quhar the wallys suld stand, thar drew a sewch;
Syne Troianys fundis tenementis for thame self,
And gan the fowceis and the dichis delf.   10
Bot lo, onon, a wonder thing to tell,
Ane huge bleyß of flambys braid doun fell
Furth of the clowdis, at the left hand straucht,
In maner of a lichtynnyng or fyre flaucht,
And dyd alicht rycht in the sammyn sted   15
Apon the crown of fair Laviniais hed,
And fra thyne hie vp in the lyft agane
It glaid away, and tharin dyd remane.
The fader Eneas astonyst wolx sum deill,
Desyrus this syng suld betakyn seill;   20
Hys handis baith vphevis towartis hevin
And thus gan mak his boyn with myld stevin:
"O Iupiter, gif euer ony tyme," said he,
"The Troian pepill, baith by land and see,
Thyne admonitions, command and impyre   25
Obeyt haß, page, man or syre;
Of gif that I 3our power and godhed
Dred, and adornyt intyll ony sted
3our altaris, or ony wirschip dyd tharto;
And be that thyng 3it restis forto do,   30
Gif ony thyng behynd 3it doith remane –
With this 3our happy takyn augurian
3eld ws 3our plesand rest and ferm peß,
Mak end of all our harmys and cauß thame ceß."
As he sik wordis warpys owt that tyde   35
Hys goldyn moder apperis hym besyde,
Confessand hir tobe the fair Venus,
And with hir blissyt mowth scho carpis thus:
"Son, do syk thocht and dreid furth of thy mynd,
Ressaue thir godly syngis in bettir kynd,   40   f. 324ʳ
And ioyusly enioys, myn awyn Enee,
The gret weilfar fra thens sal betyd the.
Now is thy rest and quiet fund and kend,
Now of thy harmys is cummyn extreme end;
Now at the last, as thou desyris, perfay,   45
This warld with the sal knyt vp peax for ay.
Abhor thou nocht the fyre and flambis brycht,
From thy deir spowsys hed glaid to the hycht,
Bot constantly thy mynd thou now addreß;
It salbe scho, I the declar expreß,   50
That sall with blude ryall thy douchty name,
Thy successioun, renown and nobill fame,
And Troian pryncis, of thy seid discend,

Abufe the clowdis hie and sternys send.
Scho sall of thy lynnage, my son Enee,   55
Bair childryng full of magnanymyte,
Of quhais ofspryng sik men sal succeid
That all this large warld far onbreid
With thar excelland wirschip sall fulfill,
And by thar mychty power, at thar will,   60
As conquerouris, vnder thar sen3eory
Subdew and rewle this warldis monarchy;
Of quham the schynand souerane glor sall wend,
And far be3ond the occean see extend,
Makand thame equale with the hevynnys hie;   65
Quham, finaly, thar ardent gret bonte
And soueran vertu, spred sa far onbred is,
Eftir innumerabill sa feill douchty dedis,
Sall mak thame goddis and thame deify,
And thame vpheiß full hie abufe the sky.   70
This flambe of fyre the wirschip and renovn
Doith signyfy of thy successioun;
The god almychty from his starrit hevin
Haß schawin tharfor this syng of fyry levin:
Tharfor, in recompens of sykkyn thyng,   75
And samekill wirschip of hir sal spring,
This cite, quhilk thou closys with a wall,
Eftir thy spowsis name clepe thou sall.
And forthir eyk, the goddis quhom thou hynt   f. 324ᵛ
Of Troy, that tyme quhen it in flambys brynt,   80
Penates, or the goddis domesticall,
Thou set alsso within the sammyn wall:
Tharin thou gar thame soyn be brocht inhy
In hie honour, and tyme perpetualy
Thar to remane, eternaly to dwell.   85
I sall to the of thame a wonder tell:
Thai sall sa strangly luf this new cyte,
That, gyf thame happynnys careit fortobe
Tyll ony other sted or place tharby,
All be thame self agane full hastely   90
Thai sall return to this ilk town of thyne,
That thou beildis in boundis of Kyng Latyn;
3a, quhou oftsyß that thai away be tayn,
Thai sal return haymwart agane ilkane.
O happy cyte and weil fortunat wall,   95
With quham sa gret rellykis remane sall,
Quharin thou sall in tyme tocum, but leyß,
Govern the Troian folk in plesand peß!
Eftir this at last Latyn, thy fader in law,
Wery of hys lyfe and far in age draw,   100

Doun to gostis in the campe Elyse
Sall wend, and end his dolly days, and de:
Onto hys ceptre thou sall do succeid,
And vnder thy senȝeory, far onbreid,
Sall weld and led thir ilk Italianys,   105
And common lawis for thame and the Troianys
Statut thou sall; and syne thou sall ascend,
And vp to hevyn glaidly thy self send:
Thus standis the goddis sentens and decreit."
Na mair scho said, bot, as the gleym doith gleit,   110
From thens scho went away in the schyre ayr,
I wait nocht quhidder, for I com neuer thar.
Enee astonyst, havand hys mynd smyte
With syk promyß of renown and delyte,
Hys blissyt moderis command gan fulfill: 115
And now at plesand rest, at hys awyn will,
The Troian pepill rewlit he in peß.
With this the kyng Latynus can deceß   f. 325ʳ
And left the ceptre vacand to hys hand;
Than the reuthfull Ene our all the land   120
Of Italy succedis in hys sted
And gan full large bundis in lordschip led,
That halely obeyt to hys wand,
And at hys lykyng rewlit all the land.
Now equaly of fre will euery ane,   125
Baith pepill of Troy and folk Italian,
All of a ryte, manerys and vsans,
Becummyn ar frendly but discrepans;
Thar myndis and thar brestis in amyte,
In ferm concord and gret tranquylite,   130
Gan leif at eyß, confiderat in ally,
As vnder a law sammyn coniunct evynly.

Quhou Iupiter, for Venus cauß and lufe, Haß set Eneas as god in hevyn abufe.

C. xi

Venus with this, all glaid and full of ioy,
Amyd the hevynly hald, rycht myld and moy,
Befor Iupiter down hir self set
And baith hir armys abowt hys feyt plet,
Enbrasand thame and kyssand reuerently;   5
Syne thus with voce expreß scho said inhy:
"Fader almychty, that from thy hevynly ryng
At thy plesour rewlys and sterys al thyng,
That manis dedys, thochtis and aventuris
Reknys and knawys, and tharof heß the curis;   10
Weill I ramember, quhen that the pepill Troian

280

With hard onfrendly forton was ourtane,
Thou promyst of thar laubouris and distreß
Help and support, and efter dyseyß soleß.
Nowder thy promyß, fader, nor sentens   15
Heß me dissauyt, for lo, with reuerens
All the faderis of Italy heß se,
But discrepans, fully thir 3heris thre,
In blyssyt peax my son enioyß that land;
Bot certis, fader, as I vndirstand,   20
Onto the starnyt hevynly hald on hie
Thou promyst rayß the maste douchty Enee,   f. 325ᵛ
And, for hys meryt, abufe thy schynand sky
Hym forto place in hevyn and deify.
Quhat thochtis now doith rollyng in thy mynd,   25
Sen, ellys, doith the vertuus thewys kynd
Of this reuthfull Eneas the requyr
Abuf the polys brycht to rayß that syre?"
The fader tho of men and goddis all
Gan kyß Venus hys child, and tharwithall   30
Thir profund wordis from hys breist furth braid:
"My deir douchtir Citherea," he said,
"Thow knawys quhou strangly the mychty Ene
And the Eneadanys all of hys men3e
Ithandly and onyrkyt luffyt haue I,   35
On se and landis catchit by and by
In perrellis seir, and quhou that ofttyme eik,
Havand piete of the my douchtir meik,
For lufe of the, for thar dyseyß was wo;
And now I haue, lo, finaly alsso   40
All thar harmys and ennoy brocht till end,
And maid Iuno, as that full weill is kend,
Fortobecum frendly and favorabill:
Now lykis me, forsuyth, all ferm and stabill
My sentens promyst to compleit," quod he,   45
"Quhen that the riall Troian duke Ene
Amang the hevynnys institut I sall,
And hym to numbyr of the goddis call:
All this I grant with gud willis per fay,
Tharfor, se that thou clenge and do away,   50
Gif thar be in hym ony mortall thyng,
And syne abuf the starnys thou him bryng:
I sall alsso heich ony of hys kyn,
Quhilk of thar proper vertu lyst do wyn
Perpetuall lovyng by dedis honorabill,   55
And doith contemp the wrachit warld onstabill;
Thame in lyke wyß abufe the hevynnys hie
I sal do place and deify," quod he.

281

The goddis abuf alhaill gave thar consent,
Nor ryall Iuno, at that tyme present, 60
Lyst not contrary, bot gan perswaid full evyn f. 326ʳ
To bryng the gret Ene vp to the hevyn,
And frendly wordis of hym carpys thar.
Than Venus slaid discendand throw the ayr
And socht onto the feildis Lawrentan, 65
Neir by quhar that Numycus throu the playn,
That fresch ryver, flowys to the see,
Dekkyt abowt with redis growand hie;
Quharin the body of hir son sa deir
Scho maid do wesch, and vnder the stremys cleir 70
All that was mortale or corruptibill thyng
Gart do away; and syne, at hir lykyng,
The recent happy sawl with hyr hynt sche
And bair it vp abuf the ayr full hie
Onto the hevyn, quhar reuthfull Eneas 75
Amyd the starnys chosyn haß his place;
Quham the famyll and kynrent Iulian
Doith clepe and call amangis thame euery ane
Indigites, quhilk is alsmekill to say
As god induellar, at thar sudiornys ay; 80
And, in remembrans of this ilk turn,
Thai gan hys templis wirschip and adorn. etc. finis

Explicit liber decimus tertius Eneados

Conclusio

Now is my wark all fynyst and compleit,
Quham Iovis ire, nor fyris byrnand heit,
Nor trynschand swerd sal defaß ne doun thryng,
Nor lang proceß of age, consumys al thyng.
Quhen that onknawyn day sal hym addreß, 5
Quhilk not bot on this body power heß,
And endis the dait of myn oncertan eld,
The bettir part of me salbe vpheld
Abufe the starnys perpetualy to ryng,
And heir my naym remane, but enparyng; 10
Throw owt the ile yclepit Albyon
Red sall I be, and sung with mony one.
Thus vp my pen and instrumentis full 30r
On Virgillis post I fix for evirmor,
Nevir, from thens, syk materis to discryve: 15 f. 326ᵛ
My muse sal now be cleyn contemplatyve,
And solitar, as doith the byrd in cage,
Sen fer byworn is all my childis age,

And of my days neir passyt the half dait
That natur suld me grantyn, weil I wait.   20
Thus sen I feill down sweyand the ballans,
Heir I resyng vp ȝyngkeris observans:
Adew, gallandis, I geif ȝou all gud nycht,
And God salf euery gentill curtaß wight! Amen.

Heir endis the thretteyn and final buke of Eneados
quhilk is the first correk coppy nixt efter the translation
Wrytin be Master Matho Geddes scribe or writar to
the translatar

Heir the translatar direkkis hys buk
and excusis hym self etc.

My Lord, to ȝour nobilyte in effect,
To quham this wark I haue abufe direct,
Gawyn, ȝour cousyng, provest of Sanct Geill,
Gretyng in God ay lestyng, and gud heill.
Ressave gude will, quhar that my cunnyng falys,   5
And gyf within this volume ocht avalys,
Or is onto ȝour plesour aggreabill,
Than is my laubour sum thyng profytabill.
Quhar I offendit, or mysteris correctioun,
Vndir ȝour salfgard and protectioun   10
I me submyt; ȝhe be my scheld and defens
Aganys corruppit tungis violens,
Can nocht amend, and ȝit a falt wald spy:
Quhen thai bakbyte, quhen evir thai clepe and cry,
Gyf neyd beys, for ȝour kynysman and clerk   15 f. 327^r
Than I protest ȝe ansuer, and for ȝour wark.
Gyf thai speir quhy I dyd this buke translait,
ȝhe war the cauß tharof, full weill ȝe wait;
ȝhe cawsyt me this volume to endyte,
Quharthrow I haue wrocht myself syk dispyte,   20
Perpetualy be chydit with ilk knak,
Full weill I knaw, and mokkyt behynd my bak.
Say thai nocht, I myne honeste haue degraid,
And at my self to schute a but heß maid?
Nane othir thyng, thai threpe, heir wrocht haue I   25
Bot fenȝeit fabillys of idolatry,
With sik myscheif as aucht not namyt be,
Oppynnand the gravis of smert iniquyte,
And on the bak half wrytis wyddyr synnys
Plente of lesyngis, and ald perversyt synnys.   30
Quhar that I haue my tyme superexpendyt,
Mea culpa, God grant I may amend it,

283

With grace and space to vpset this tynsell;
Thocht not be far sa largely as thai tell,
As that me semys, ȝit offendit haue I;   35
For weill I wait, our wark to mony a wy
Sall baith be plesand and eyk profitabill,
For tharin beyn seir doctrynys full notabill;
It sal eik do sum folk solace, I geß,
To paß the tyme, and eschew idylnes.   40
Ane othir proffit of our buke I mark,
That it salbe reput a neidfull wark
To thame wald Virgill to childryn expone;
For quha lyst note my versys, one by one,
Sall fynd tharin hys sentens euery deill,   45
And al maste word by word, that wait I weill.
Thank me tharfor, masteris of grammar sculys,
Quhar ȝe syt techand on ȝour benkis and stulys.
Thus haue I not my tyme swa occupy
That all suld hald my laubour onthryfty;   50
For I haue not interpryt ne translate
Every bural ruyd poet dywlgait,
Na meyn endyte, nor empty wordis vayn,   f. 327ᵛ
Common engyn, nor stile barbarian;
Bot in that art of eloquens the flude   55
Maste cheif, profund and copyus plenitud,
Surß capitall in veyn poeticall,
Soverane fontane, and flum imperiall;
Quham gif I haue offendit, as thai meyn,
Deym as ȝe lyst, quhen the wark is ourseyn.   60
Be as be may, ȝour frendschip, weill I wait,
Wrocht mair at me than dyd myne awyn estait;
For kyndnes so myne eyn almaist maid blynd,
That, ȝow to pleyß, I set all schame behynd,
Offeryng me to my weriouris wilfully,   65
Quhilk in myne e fast staris a mote to spy.
Bot quha sa lawchis heirat, or hedis noddis,
Go reid Bochas in the Genolygy of Goddis;
Hys twa last bukis sall swage thar fantasy,
Leß than na resson may thame satyffy.   70
I rak nocht quhidder fulys hald me devill or sanct,
For ȝou maid I this buke, my Lord, I grant,
Nowder for pryce, det, reward nor supple,
Bot for ȝour tendir request and amyte,
Kyndneß of blude grundyt in natural law.   75
I am na cayk fydlar, full weill ȝe knaw;
No thing is myne quhilk sall not ȝowris be,
Gyf it afferis for ȝowr nobilyte;
And of ȝour moblys and all other geir

284

3he will me serve siklyke, I haue na weir.   80
Bot as twychyng this our wark now in hand,
Quhilk oft is said was maid at 3our command,
To quhat effect, gyf ony wald inqueir;
3e may ansuer, thocht I neid nocht 3ow leir,
That Virgill mycht intill our langage be   85
Red lowd and playn by 3our lordschip and me,
And other gentill compan3eonys quha sa lyst;
Nane ar compellit drynk not bot thai haue thryst:
And quha sa lykis may tastyng of the tun
Onforlatyt, new from the berry run,   90
Reid Virgill baldly, but mekill offens
Except our wlgar toungis differens,   f. 328ʳ
Kepand na facund rethoryk castis fair,
Bot haymly playn termys famyliar,
Na thing alterit in substans the sentens,   95
Thocht scant perfyte observyt beyn eloquens;
I will weill otheris can say mair curyusly,
Bot I haue said eftir my fantasy,
I covait nocht to prefer ony wight,
It may suffice I said na thing bot rycht;   100
And, set that empty be my brayn and dull,
I haue translait a volum wondirfull:
So profund was this wark at I haue said,
Me semyt oft throw the deip sey to waid;
And sa mysty vmquhile this poecy,   105
My spreit was reft half deill in extasy,
To pyke the sentens as I couth als playn,
And bryng it to my purpoß, was full fayn;
And thus, becauß the mater was onkowth,
Not as I suld, I wrait, bot as I couth.   110
Quha wenys I say thir wordis bot invane,
Lat thame assay als lang laubour agane,
And translait Ovid, as I haue Virgill;
Perchans that wark sall occupy thame a quhile:
3it haue I hard oft said be men na clerkis,   115
Tyll idyll folk full lycht beyn lukand warkis.
To 3ou, my Lord, quhat is thar mair to say?
Ressaue 3our wark desyrit mony a day;
Quharin also now am I fully quyt,
As twichand Venus, of myn ald promyt   120
Quhilk I hir maid weil twelf 3heris tofor,
As wytnessith my Palyce of Honour,
In the quhilk wark, 3he reid, on hand I tuke
Forto translait at hir instance a buke:
Sa haue I doyn abufe, as 3e may se,   125
Virgillis volum of hir son Enee,

Reducit, as I cowth, intill our tong.
Be glaid, Ene, thy bell is hiely rong,
Thy faym is blaw, thy prowes and renown
Dywlgat ar, and sung fra town to town,   130
So hardy from thens, that other man or boy   f. 328ᵛ
The ony mair reput traytour of Troy,
Bot as a worthy conquerour and kyng
The honour and extoll, as thou art dyng.
My Lord, all thocht I dyd this wark compyle,   135
At ȝour command, intill owr wlgar style,
Suffir me borrow this a word at the leist,
Thar with to quyte my promyß and beheste,
And lat Dame Venus have gud nycht adew,
Quhamto sum tyme ȝhe war a servand trew.   140
I haue alsso a schort comment compilyt
To expon strange histouris and termys wild;
And gif ocht lakis mar, quhen that is doyn,
At ȝour desyre it salbe writtyn soyn.
And forthir, so that I be nocht prolixt,   145
The etern Lord, that on the ruyd was fixt,
Grant ȝow and ws all in this lyfe weilfair,
With euerlestand blyß quhen we hyne fair! Amen

Quod Gawinus Dowglas etc.

Ane exclamatioun aganyst detractouris and oncurtaß redaris that beyn our studyus, but occasioun, to note and spy owt faltis or offencis in this volum, or ony other thryfty warkys etc.

Now throw the deip fast to the port I mark,
For heir is endyt the lang disparyt wark,
And Virgyll heß hys volum to me lent:
In sovir raid now ankyrrit is our bark;
We dowt na storm, our cabillys ar sa stark;   5
We have eschapyt full mony perrellus went:
Now God be lovyt haß syk grace tyl ws sent!
Sen Virgyll beys (wyd quhar in Latyn song)
Thus be my laubour red in owr wlgar tong.

Bot quhat danger is ocht to compyle, allace,   10   f. 329ʳ
Herand thir detractouris intil euery place,
Or evir thai reid the wark, byddis byrn the buke:
Sum beyn sa frawart in malyce and wangrace,
Quhat is weill said thai love not worth ane ace,
Bot castys thame euer to spy owt falt and cruyk;   15

286

All that thai fynd in hydlys, hyrn or nuyk,
Thai blaw owt, sayand in euery manis face,
"Lo, heir he failʒeis, se thar he leys, luyk!"

Bot, gyf I le, lat Virgyll be owr iuge,
Hys wark is patent, I may have na refuge;   20
Tharby go note my faltis on by on:
No wondir is, the volum was so huge,
Quha mycht perfytely all hys hie termys luge
In barbar langage, or thame dewly expon?
Bot weill I wait, of hys sentens wantis non.   25
Quha can do bettir, lat se quhar I forvayt;
Begyn of new; al thing is gud onassayt.

Far eithar is, quha lyst syt doun to moyt,
Ane otheris sayaris faltis to spy and noyt,
Than but offens or falt thame self to wryte: 30
Bot forto chyde sum beyn so brym and hoyt,
Hald thai thar peax, the word wald scald thar throte,
And haß sik custum to iangill and to bakbyte,
That, bot thai schent sum, thai suld bryst for syte.
I say na mair, quhen all thar rerd is rong,   35
That wight mon speke that can nocht hald hys tong.

Go, wlgar Virgill, to euery churlych wight
Say, I avow thou art translatit rycht,
Beseyk all nobillys the corect and amend,
Beys not afferyt tocum in prysaris sycht;   40
The nedis nocht to aschame of the lycht,
For I haue brocht thy purpoß to gud end:
Now salt thou with euery gentill Scot be kend,
And to onletterit folk be red on hight,
That erst was bot with clerkis comprehend. etc.   45

Quod Douglas etc.

Heir fullowys the tyme, space and dait of the translatioun   f 329ᵛ
of this buke

Completyt was thys wark Virgilian
 Apon the fest of Mary Magdelan,
Fra Crystis byrth, the dait quha lyst to heir,
A thousand fyve hundreth and thretteyn ʒeir;
Quhilk, for othir gret occupatioun, lay   5
Onsteryt cloß besyd me mony day;
And netheleß, quhidder I serve thank or wyte,
Fra tyme I tharto fyrst set pen to wryte,

287

Thocht God wait gyf thir bundis war full wyd
To me, that had syk byssynes besyde,   10
Apon this wyß, as God lyst len me grace,
It was compylit in auchteyn moneth space;
Set I feil syth syk twa monethis infeir
Wrait neuer a word, nor mycht the volum steir,
For grave materis and gret solicitud,   15
That all sik laubour far besyde me stud.
And thus gret scant of tyme and bissy cuyr
Haß maid my wark mair subtell and obscur,
And nocht sa plesand as it aucht tobe;
Quharof 3he curtaß redaris perdon me.   20
3he writaris all, and gentill redaris eyk,
Offendis nocht my volum, I beseik,
Bot redis leill, and tak gud tent in tyme,
3he nother maggill nor mysmetyr my ryme,
Nor alter not my wordis, I 30u pray.   25
Lo, this is all; now, bew schirris, haue gud day. etc.

Quod Gawinus Douglas etc.

Mantua me genuit, Calabri rapuere, tenet nunc   f. 330ʳ
Parthenope; cecini pascua, rura, duces.

Of Mantua am I beget and boir,
In Calabre decessit and forlor,
Now stant I grave in Naplys the cite,
That in my tyme wrait notabill warkis thre:
Of pasturage, and eik of husbandry,   5
And douchty chiftanys full of chevalry.

Quod G. Douglas etc.

288

Variant Readings

Note

C is the Cambridge manuscript ; E, the Elphinstoun ; R, the Ruthven ; L, the Lambeth ; B, the Bath ; Bt, the Bannatyne ; and 53, the 1553 print. The variants in E R L B 53 have been listed with only enough of the context to show their place in the line. ' . . ' between two words indicates that there are two variants in the same line, separated from each other by material identical with C. Square brackets indicate omissions.

BOOK VIII

Prologue, heading. E heyr begynnis the proloug of the aucht buik ; R L Prologus ; B *omits* ; 53 The Prolouge of the eyght buke of Eneados

1. E [Of] ; R 53 quhat doith to ; L dowit : 3. R slaid of [a] ; 53 swennyng : 5. R wald and ; 53 wald, mare woful ane wycht : 7. 53 ar : 9. E lurdanly ; R lurdanely is : 10. C E R L B 53 *lines 10–12 are bracketed on the right, and line 13 placed to the right of line 11. Later stanzas are arranged similarly* : 15. R Sturty : 16. E our . . . tway mycht : 22. C E R L B [wate] ; E [he] : 23. E bernis best ; R [nocht] : 29. E R Thair ; E refusis ; B loukis : 30. E [thame] : 31. E grum ; R 53 he grevis ; R B gammys ; 53 games : 33. R myschevis ; R 53 [is] : 35. R [land] : 40. E myllar mynschis : 41. E drouth of drinking : 42. R crakkit weill cant ; 53 wele : 48. R glasteris at the gangat ; R 53 [and] : 51. E efter a grene guß ; 53 greys : 54. E L B 53 mynd . . . ga na ; R mynde : 56. R 53 hant thay : 57. E [byngis] ; 53 bringis : 58. E byssely the bane ; R [and] bayne ; 53 leuer and ane byce : 59. 53 or [for] : 60. E To semble wyth thar schaftis the schur and settis to schoir ; 53 The sembyl : 61. E *omits* ; R 53 to the schor : 62. R cryis for the : 64. R The feist : 65. E [full] ; R for 3or : 66. E ramis ; L B ramys : 67. E ryt ; R L 53 ryot : 68. 53 skurriouris : 74. C it *interlined* : 77. C L B caym is ; 53 Cayn : 78. R [sik] : 79. R warldis ; L in warld is ; 53 wan, thryft : 80. E blag : 81. E plaikis ; 53 Practis ar repute to : 83. R and of : 84. E landis : 85. E Burges ; R in the ; 53 the bage . . . thar bawggis : 86. R Knichtis and ; R 53 plukkis : 87. R myscunnandnes : 92. E loud lyte ; 53 lawde : 93. R plane boddum : 95. E quent assens ; 53 quentassence : 97. 53 treitcheoure : 99. E garris [to iag] ; E 53 ged staff : 105. R [the] : 106. R papis and : 109. C wyrkis ; E wirkis : 116. R [wald] : 121. E R knappar ; R 53 grace ; 53 knappare : 123. E wordis ; B quod he freik : 125. L Quhat ; 53 brangillis : 126. E [churle] ; R go chak : 127. 53 Muse the not so hie than : 131. E vnto : 132. E leindis in : 133. E sleip syne : 136. E [a] : 137. R [and] : 138. R [thar] [thar] : 139. E liffyr . . . quhart ; R levir ; 53 leuir : 140. E R L 53 ar ; R [thar] : 145. E R the ane lessoun ; L B a ; 53 ane lessoan : 147. E riotest ; L B ryotast ; 53 royetest . . . ratt, rime : 148. R on : 152. R eldwand : 158. E lessoun and this I me lyk ; 53 [me] . . . I the like : 160. 53 drew one doun, derne in delf : 163. E [Bot] : 165. E grum ; R [as] ; L 53 at that : 166. R 53 grippit : 167. R modywert ; 53 And every modywart hil : 170.

53 sic ane truffuris : 171. E nocht werd ; R 53 and for ; L or for : 173. R With segeis ;
L but faill ; 53 but feal : 174. R L war we ; 53 war I : 176. E R L B 53 word in : 177. R 53
riotnes ; L and laving : 178. R This [I] : 181. 53 tre tre rute.

ending. E Heyr endis the prolug of the viii buik. Heir endis the prolug of the aucht
buik of Enedos and begynnis heyr the aucht buik. Heyr begynnis the viii buik of
aeneados ; R Here endis the prolug ; L B Heir endis the prolug of the aucht buke of
Eneados and begynnys here followand the aucht buke *etc.* ; 53 Finis. The aucht Buke.

VIII.i.

1. 53 *The book begins with the closing lines of Book VII* : 5. E in flocht : 6. R Avise . . .
[this] ; 53 Auising : 9. E How heyr ; R here and thare ; 53 sondry : 10. 53 Now seirsis :
12. E schaddowis : 15. R housß : 16. 53 seircheis : 19. C al *interlined* ; R [levand] : 21.
L land : 24. R with cure ; 53 soupis : 32. E R semyt : 35. E ruffly rudis dekis ; R reddy
dekkis ; L B leiffly : 38. R of the hie ; 53 of the goddis : 44. R and sale : 46. R the sikkir :
47. 53 And souir : 48. E fra hym ; L fra thyne : 52. E L B word : 54. E the bankis : 58.
E [hyr pappis] : 59. 53 the ciete : 60. R souerest sall ; 53 our : 64. E [fair] : 67. R [bot] :
68. E the kene in ; R lernyng in : 69. E [haue] : 72. R Cummys : 76. E L B montis :
77. E Eftir the ; B foirfaderis : 78. R pallentyne ; 53 [clepyt] : 80. E [the Latyn] : 81.
53 the hoist : 83. B the thy : 84. R thir fays apoun the : 87. 53 gdddes : 91. E all hyr
mannanis ; R malice : 95. E wallry hewit haw and haw : 97. R the brayis chawis the :
101. 53 huge and grete.

VIII.ii. heading. R as tyberiane

1. E The mycht flede : 3. 53 orient, and brycht : 5. 53 handis : 7. E R L 53 this wyse : 9. E
3e o ; R haly fludis : 10. R Quharefra ; R 53 the fresche : 11. R [as] ; 53 we do say clere :
12. E sourß ; 53 sowrssus : 13. E O thou o : 14. E R the blyssit : 17. C gif *interlined* ; 53
[rewth] : 20. E thai spring : 21. E the sall I the our : 24. 53 into the Italie ryng : 26. R
53 perrellis and dangeris : 27. E Conserne : 36. 53 bank, and his : 37. 53 With his : 39.
R Quhen ; R 53 this gise ; L vpoun this gyß ; 53 Qham : 40. 53 [the] : 41. R folk : 42. R
offerit apoun the ; 53 on the : 43. R 53 hir ; 53 fludis of that mycht : 47. C wyß *interlined* ;
E *runs 47–48 together* wyß mesand stank semyt for to be ; 53 Of sic : 50. R may ; 53
thy airis : 51. E L B Thair Eneas : 52. 53 on this : 54. E R barge : 57. R 53 accustumate :
58. R [at] ; 53 suld be : 59. E scheildis and fayr : 60. E L B mayr and mayr : 63. R routh
ilkman with lauboring ; L Can speyd ; 53 speid in rout : R of wellis : 65. E vpwart ; L
vpwarpis : 67. E R Endland ; 68. 53 out throw.

VIII.iii. heading. E B bandis and

2. 53 warld : 5. E heid : 9. 53 noblis : 14. E [gret] : 17. R 53 vnto : 21. R [the] : 23. R
essens : 27. E barge : 28. R [fast] : 30. R 53 of that : 33. 53 Quhen : 34. E was : 36. R to
returne : 37. R [3it] : 38. E 53 stand : 40. R strange ; 53 strang : 42. 53 or quhilk : 43. R
53 3e do ; R 3oure : 47. E as he ; R [furth] : 50. E peple ; R In : 51. E fra our ; R newe :
52. R That ilk : 54. E [to] suckyr ; R succoure : 55. E declayr . . . [hym] : 56. E Than :
57. E L B thiddir ; R cummyng : 58. R [vp] : 60. E wrocht : 61. E [evir] ; R [be] : 63.

53 lugeing : 64. R sall ressauit be : 68. 53 on the : 72. E biggit : 75. R [suld] reik furth : 76. L branchis : 77. E L B [that] ; R that I of thi supple and nede : 78. E of feir : 79. C thou *interlined* : 81. E of the ; R archadeis : 82. 53 meane [onto] : 85. R [our] : 86. R The flame ; L euer : 90. R of our : 91. R The belt ; R 53 and Ilion ; 53 ciete of troy : 92. R grant : 93. E electra gret atlas : 97. 53 Mercury is fader, to : 100. R hate is ; 53 archada : 101. L And thus : 103. R the same ; 53 the samyn : 104. R hevynnys ; 53 [speir] : 108. R [by] ; 53 ambassiat : 109. R the fryndschip : 110. R 53 [awin] : 111. R is my : 112. E [to] pray ; R And to the pray . . . in this : 113. R vnto dawnus : 115. R Quhilkis : 118. R [thame] : 120. R 53 thirldome ; L thrildoun : 121. E thi boundis : 124. L Quhilk : 126. 53 vs faith, and : 127. R begane haue : 129. E 53 expart in sic : 132. E to : 133. R His mouth his ene : 136. E O full glaidly ; 53 O thou, glaidly : 138. R may weill ; L Quhill blythlie ; 53 Full : 144. 53 pryame, son of kyng : 145. R *omits 145–152* : 146. E Salamya ; 53 salamonya : 149. 53 tyme and pylis : 151. E ioysit ; 53 tha troyane : 154. R we mervill : 159. R in hand : 160. E and band ; R or bynd forwart ; 53 Couenand . . . forwart our band : 161. 53 freinschip : 162. R the samyn : 164. R Or quhen ; 53 [quhen] : 165. 53 qwauir, and ful : 166. E R L 53 wantit : 172. E R 53 or ellis : 174. E Quhair to : 175. R 53 all lycht : 176. E. and supple ; R 53 succoure ; 53 and with supple : 177. 53 hyne one, to : 182. R onely full : 183. E Quhairfor ; 53 do alhallow : 184. E sembilland ; R gude semblant blith : 186. E L as our : 190. E scherardis : 198. R and baskettis : 199. R in : 202. R changeing mete.

VIII.iv. heading. E R L B 53 tellis ; E L B Ene [verray] ; R the sacrifice

1. R hungry ; 53 stanche it, was : 2. R to swage ; 53 of men, begouth : 3. R 53 supersti- ciouns : 4. E ancyent : 8. R And sa : 10. R persewit : 11. 53 this manere : 13. 53 henchis : 15. E bray : 16. E fousy ; R fowsyis : 20. R With grisly ; L entre quhair furth ; 53 furth in all : 24. R of his : 25. R hell : 26. R son bene neuer schyne ; 53 sonnys bene neuer nane : 28. R 53 of the : 31. E blude burn and bra ; R blude rvn : 32. E odour or fylth stynkand ; R 53 odoure ; R L 53 of filth : 36. R furth 3ett ; 53 3eskis : 41. 53 Becummyn : 42. 53 dantaris of the monstouris, or defence : 43. R dowtit : 45. R in the ; 53 strang melle : 46. E R L B [the] ; 53 hedis thre : 49. R 53 huge and gret ; 53 bullus : 51. E R B 53 Endlang ; L Endlange : 53. 53 furius : 54. 53 way for myscheif : 55. 53 thrawart : 56. E R 53 maner of : 58. C on assayt ; E on assait ; 53 from that land : 60. E tend : 61. E drive : 62. 53 that thay tred : 66. R [a] ; 53 quhine : 68. E hym to . 69. E meyne tym quhill all ; R thir beistis : 70. E Reparit : 71. E L B 53 *reverse 71–72* : 72. R Fra ; R 53 hens : 75. E dyndillit : 76. 53 Quhilk : 79. R in creif : 82. R to girne : 85. R 53 and his : 86. L held he a ; 53 [in] : 87. L his erd : 91. R [sped] : 94. C for *interlined* ; E [for] : 95. E leyit ; E L doun fall ; R [sic] : 98. R schet he the : 103. 53 Gnassing : 104. R [hill] : 105. E serß ; 53 He sesis : 106. 53 the craggy : 109. E the wall ; R vaill agane ; 53 him as he . . . vale is gone : 110. E quhyn a flynt ; 53 and flynt : 115. R this rent was worne ; 53 was : 116. R 53 and to schorne : 121. E [it] : 122. R braggis : 124. R wald went : 128. C a bak ; R L dynnyt quhill the : 129. E cave ; 53 caue : 132. R na quhen : 133. E a clak ; R 53 [a] : 134. E the terrable : 136. R inclosis the dirk : 138. 53 Or that : 145. R apoun the : 148. E R L B 53 kynd of : 150. E doun wappand ; L warpys : 151. E [that] : 152. E Fra his : 163. C habudit *in margin*, habundyt *blotted in line* : 165. E did gevin ; 53 So tha the : 166. E Thair as ; R cacus with wikkit ; L Thair was he : 169. 53 stren3eit : 170. E [blud] : 173. R 53 to [the] : 178. E R 53 satifyit : 182. 53 monstouris : 183. R ane

sloknyt : 186. E of this : 187. 53 kepis, euer solemnytlye [as 3e se] : 191. 53 cuchil : 192. 53 vnto was, in : 194. B That salbe : 195. R [done] ; 53 now 3oung gallandis in : 197. L hede and garlandis : 200. 53 [and] : 201. E L This : 204. E And haly ; 53 fallit in : 205. R scharply taistis ; 53 castis : 206. R greabill ; 53 [for].

VIII.v.

2. 53 [Throw] : 4. R 53 the ald : 8. E [thar] ; 53 All to : 9. 53 deliget : 18. E 3ongkeris 3onger in : 20. R 53 addressit thame : 21. E battellis : 23. E Quhen ; R step moderis : 24. C E B strangit ; R Liging abed in : 25. 53 to say : 26. R quhilkis : 28. R assegeit and brocht : 32. 53 thrawart : 33. E L B 53 sang ; R thus the said invincible ; 53 [thai] : 35. 53 The strang : 37. R eik that with ; L 53 handis : 39. R In crete . . . at will : 41. E L B the roik : 42. R 53 lyouns : 45. E half knaw : 48. R 53 Iouy : 51. R of the lerne : 54. R 53 Did the : 55. 53 Iouy : 61. L 53 sacrify ; 53 feist, and [thai] : 63. R principale ; 53 [last] : 65. R that flambis : 67. B for thar : 69. R And quhen : 70. R [To] : 72. E [by] : 74. E pasß : 80. E strang knycht culd plesance : 81. R inquere of euery : 84. L faderis.

VIII.vi. heading. E L B rehersit ; R reherß . . . Off elderis dedis . . . thar cuntre

6. R fawnus ; 53 faunis and apoun : 7. E L B elphis : 8. E R 53 samyn ; R 53 in the ; 53 [war] : 9. 53 And with : 10. E 53 rutis ; R ruttis : 14. R 53 conquest : 15. R movblis : 16. R ar thai dullit : 17. E R set : 18. R [of] : 19. E 53 [hie] : 20. C band *cancelled before* brand ; R fleand come : 21. 53 realme : 22. R Bot as thai ; R 53 vncouth : 23. R The : 27. 53 Was : 33. E eld than war : 34. R Begouth war that ; 53 the cullour : 35. E rage and weyr ; 53 And in [the] : 38. 53 Scany : 40. R Has loist : 42. R Strang : 43. R quham sen syne all the Italie : 44. 53 was clepit : 45. 53 his awin, trew : 48. R L Strange : 50. E thidder : 51. E B 53 mony singis ; R The remeid als : 56. E ther goddis tald : 57. R walkin furth thus bot : 60. E In to : 61. R 53 remembrance is ; 53 [the] : 62. R The : 63. E [was] . . . phatale ; 53 Quhilk has : 64. E [That] ; R in his ; 53 expores : 65. E prince : 67. 53 to him : 68. R did our reduce : 69. E franchis and of : 73. 53 Archady : 74. R To pay the ; 53 The pan : 76. E Quhat to . . . [thar] ; R men : 78. R of that dede : 79. R 53 manere plane : 80. R wyse he gest : 81. E tarpe tha he : 82. L [And] : 84. L wyld bestis ; 53 skrokky : 87. E The cry rurell : 89. R on the : 91. R doith : 95. E [oft] : 98. R cloude : 100. R [twa] toun steid is : 102. E fadris : 106. E was ay at vther ; R Saturnus : 111. R ar : 112. R [in] : 114. E L B houß ; 53 hous : 115. R And quhen cummyn to the place thai were : 118. 53 manys : 119. E on forß ; R 53 [the] : 120. 53 to do compteme : 123. 53 And thame : 127. R the bed ; 53 [him] : 130. L [a].

VIII.vii. heading. C quhilkis ; E R L B 53 quhilk

6. R and pepill : 7. E [gud] : 11. E Quhill sche quhill ; R of grete arge ; 53 Quhod : 12. E L B wallis deip and ; R 53 Bet doun ; 53 troianis : 17. R [spowß] : 19. 53 [the] : 20. R in : 22. E of : 28. R harnek : 36. E R wallis ; E in tym tene : 38. C to *interlined* ; E [ws] : 40. R belappit : 41. L [hait] : 42. R be kynde ; 53 bekynd : 43. E merich : 44. E L B in euery ; R Persand his banyst maid ; 53 his banes : 45. R [tyme] : 46. E L B sle ; R Thy : 50. 53 claucht : 52. R [in] ; 53 [the] : 53. R Welterand and : 54. 53 the mattere : 56. R 53 becummyn : 57. R [thou] : 58. L 53 nedis : 60. E sum tym ; R 53 samyn : 64.

R thy fader : 69. E [now] ; R [the] ; 53 thy grathis : 70. E be my mynd ; R [be] I the behecht : 71. R solist and diligence : 72. R 53 and science : 79. E R caiß ; 53 causis : 81. R 53 hate fyre : 83. E spouß : 84. E to be his : 86. R 53 swak : 88. E [and] : 91. R rise : 92. E or : 94. R to sustene hir entive ; 53 empty : 95. R incresß : 102. E spouß ; R spous : 104. E of hyr this : 105. E R 53 samyn ; B lawar : 106. B his bet ; 53 steris : 107. R him spedy : 108. E and nyle . . . and gledes ; R gledy : 109. E Out streking : 110. R 53 wyndy : 113. 53 on the : 114. E and brint ; L B and bront : 116. 53 studyes : 117. E dois ; R And ane huge [dyn and] ; 53 did : 118. R the cavis ; 53 in to the : 119. E bysß ; R bisß : 120. E Dois ; E L B and blesys ; R Did ; 53 bleisse : 124. 53 descendig euin : 128. E pan ; R The golward ; 53 and poync : 129. R ʒit nor formyt ; 53 fyreslaucht : 130. E of the goddis ; L Quhill : 136. E omits ; R Thareof . . . the schoure : 138. E thre blesis of ; 53 wyndis bricht : 140. R schulder : 144. R forgis of were ; L forgyt : 147. 53 polist : 150. 53 poudderis : 151. E luking loupit : 152. R [in] : 153. E wyndyr ; R and grete : 154. E bane hes in ; R negbane : 157. 53 I saw : 159. R [nedys] ; 53 [it] : 160. 53 and Pythus : 162. R 53 maisteris : 167. R irne and mettall throuch the ; 53 [thar] conduttis : 168. E [hait] : 169. 53 found it ran : 171. 53 tergane : 172. 53 into the feild : 177. R spargand ; 53 sperkland : 178. R Sum bissy watter ; 53 watteris, trinklis : 179. R coif of all : 181. E smyt his gret ; R 53 Amang ; R the grisly : 186. 53 [lump].

VIII.viii.

1. R that that fadeis flemnois Vlcanus ; 53 faderis : 2. E wynd : 6. R [the] : 7. R Ewalknyt ; 53 I walkynnyt : 10. E scois ; R fete put schois : 11. R buklit of the ; L vpoun ; 53 the wyse : 13. R Hang ; R 53 crafty : 15. 53 Ywomplit . . . spottis : 17. R [hie] : 18. E lordis paliß quhar that he : 19. E haldis : 20. R 53 quhare, that : 23. E sammyn : 27. L sone as as thai : 28. E [doun] ; R syne in the : 29. E thai com in ; R the fell : 34. E 53 cassin ; R nor takin doun : 36. E omits ; 53 pussance : 39. E closit one [the] tuscane : 40. C ar interlined ; 53 syde, as the : 44. E peple of landis : 46. L and fertill : 47. E L 53 schawis : 48. R And o thow maist : 49. L destany of fatis : 51. R fer thyne ; 53 [far] : 52. R 53 stude : 55. E the he tuscane hyllis ; R hegge : 56. C all interlined ; R of thare ; 53 This folkis ar in : 57. R valeʒement and ; 53 inhabitis : 58. 53 prude : 61. E that ; R intollerable ; 53 vntollerabil : 63. E tyrane : 66. E The quhilk bodeis : 69. 53 Quhilk quyk : 71. 53 on worsum : 72. E R 53 miserable : 74. E and way : 78. L [of] : 79. 53 halkit : 80. 53 in his . . . swalkit : 84. R in armeʒ ; 53 and his : 89. E Tho ther mony : 91. R thir schippis : 92. E R thar landis ; R endland ; L and thyr landis ; 53 on thir : 93. R [byd] : 94. E thaim that behaldis : 96. E walʒe and ; 53 galland : 99. E vertew of the ; 53 The verte I and : 102. R Bald agane : 103 R And [thocht] ; 53 his hie myscheif : 107. R grete of pepill and vnder : 108. R latynus landis ; 53 Latinis : 110. E 53 strang : 114. E Thayr throu hym ; E R delayit : 116. R [the] sceptour : 117. E essenʒeis ; 53 And al : 119. R and to be chiftane ; R 53 to thare : 122. E gane fayrly the : 123. E L B 53 of mony ; 53 reverses 123–124 : 124. R line added in later hand ; R L B 53 strang : 125. R and broik : 131. R quhem baith the . . . the blude : 132. R 53 so to conclude : 134. 53 and scharpe : 136. B and Rutilianys ; 53 To troianis : 137. R 53 the samyn : 138. 53 and our solace : 140. E And his : 142. R Had marciall dedis hantit : 144. L warkis and ʒyng ; 53 the werkis : 147. R 53 to thi : 150. R 53 was this ; 53 cassyn : 151. E R 53 Anchises ; L reverses 151–152, indicating order by B A in margin : 154. E [hard] : 160. E R B fyreflaucht : 166. 53 [dyd] : 167. R To rede ; R 53 apoun the ; L The rerd : 170. E fire in lewin : 177. 53

thusgate : 179. R 53 ȝit to spere : 183. R ane thing suld : 185. R 53 heich ; 53 doun from the : 189. E R 53 sall : 190. 53 Of tyber : 191. 53 helmes scheildis : 192. R 53 the fludis.

VIII.ix. heading. 53 son to ȝoung

1. R 53 the hie : 2. R he has : 11. E went into ; R to : 13. R 53 he has : 15. 53 sculd : 17. E R 53 flowand flude : 18. R And descendand : 22. E into ; R 53 tuskanys : 25. R [at] ; R 53 war : 26. R 53 lyoun ; 53 Ane dyn : 30. R coist of : 31. 53 wyffis : 33. E [the] narrar ; R More drewe the dreid nerrar drewe the danger ; 53 nerrare grew : 34. E walxis : 36. 53 with sad hart : 38. R wepand full tendirly : 39. R 53 son : 40. 53 Gyfe Iupiter : 41. R [sic] : 42. R and the : 46. R Heit hepis of the : 48. R L hillis : 49. R herilus with sent : 52. R [gevyn] : 53. E armis ; R be armoure : 55. 53 Fra quhan : 57. 53 of spulȝe clene : 60. C enbrasyng *cancelled before* maste : 62. E at his ; L at the : 65. B and devidit : 67. L of the : 74. R providit ; 53 presence : 76. R ȝe fatis : 82. R Bot of fals fortoun : 86. 53 is that all : 87. R is ane thing ; 53 of ony thyng : 89. 53 lustis presand : 90. R inbrace : 92. 53 smert enuoye : 97. E sicht ; L strange : 99. L Amang : 103. R So weill farrand and [so] : 104. 53 in tyl his : 105. E L B [dyd] : 106. L mair and gudly : 108. E occhiane : 109. 53 furie bemes : 110. E Closis : 115. E L B and follow : 116. R reik : 119. R 53 held away : 120. R buskis ; 53 scroggit : 123. L howy horß : 124. E Strampand.

VIII.x. heading. E eneas socht ; R The gudely

1. R schil ; 53 schaw, throw the : 7. L And sanctuar : 9. E And thik . . . and skuggy : 10. R L Belappit ; 53 cuchil : 15. R siluanus quhilk dedicate : 18. E [the] : 19. E strenthly : 20. E had all ; 53 Pallionus, al had stentit : 23. R 53 tentis tentit : 25. R barrounis : 27. 53 thocht thame best : 28. E horß ; 53 Thame selfe on hors : 33. R 53 gan behald : 35. R [cleuch] : 36. R to him scho tald ane tale : 37. R [And] : 38. R and [my] : 40. E sobyr : 43. L strange : 45. R chene : 46. R dere son : 48. E L B the bowand ; 53 bowan haik : 50. E wlx : 52. E 53 satifyit : 53. R thare armour : 56. L turnand : 61. R On : 62. E and variand : 65. 53 Scynand : 68. C gold *interlined* : 73. R [of] : 74. R 53 Of sundry : 76. R [the] : 77. E stok and nobill : 78. R battellis ar per ordoure : 79. R 53 thare importurate : 80. R grisly ; 53 gresly : 86. R 53 [and] ; 53 thaym souch, can : 91. R wall : 93. R War sevin : 98. 53 amang the : 99. E tityus ; R agit latyus : 100. R prince : 105. R With swyne.

VIII.xi.

1. 53 mycht draw : 3. C -te *added to* cruel- ; E cruell ; L crewell : 5. 53 obserue thy faith : 6. 53 furth draw : 9. R thare tharmes and thare : 12. R with schort : 15. B closyn : 19. R [ilk] persoun ; 53 persen : 20. R [he] ; 53 Lyke has he . . . boistyt men : 28. E 53 the hycht : 30. R lathlie ; 53 laithly : 35. 53 the gaulis, did : 36. R thai se : 37. R buß : 41. E 53 dois : 42. E rycht attyr ; R the riche : 45. 53 [or than] : 48. 53 ane feild : 53. 53 bullaris : 55. E The cheiff matronis ; R through : 58. C weill *interlined* ; 53 hens : 60. E dois remanis : 65. 53 sister fatis : 69. R man conformys cato : 71. E [the] ; 53 vtheris : 73. R for the ; 53 lopperand : 76. R In siluer swepand fast throw woddis grene : 77. R quhare na far.

VIII.xii.

1. L *note at foot of folio* Iesus maria : 3. 53 The ancient : 7. 53 thou, mycht thare : 9. 53 Mouand the battall : 10. 53 With sum sanctuaris : 11. R plenates : 12. R and mare : 14. 53 For his : 18. R The : 23. L than : 24. E and barbaryanis ; 53 supple, of Barbiaranis : 27. R 53 pepill : 31. R clpeit britanys : 32. R west parte ; 53 Quhilkis : 35. R all ruschand ; 53 ruschit : 38. R 53 fra the . . . souchis : 41. E landis ; R all vprent : 47. R vthir brynt bleisß : 49. R cassyn . . . lete fle ; 53 dartis casting . . . lete flete : 50. R Lang ; 53 irn, eand : 52. R blandit all of : 53. E L B the queyn ; R coistis : 57. E eldaris ; R [scho] ; 53 thir edderis : 59. R figoure ; 53 figure : 66. R L playt of ; R mailʒe ; 53 brym as ony fyre : 69. R In vane discorde ; 53 Inuent : 71. R Quhar . . . bellona goddes of : 73. R And vtheris goddis in thare cumpany : 74. R Actius appollo fleand in the sky : 79. 53 Sauye : 83. E Scaland : 84. R tentit barge : 85. R [god of] ; L hir wrath and : 88. C L B corpß ; E R 53 corps ; R 53 now of ; L new and slauchter ; 53 Amang : 91. R of thare : 92. R and braid spred : 96. E R L B 53 hid ; R 53 conduct : 97. 53 wallis sene : 99. E L B this gyß ; E L thair offerandis on ; R thar gyse : 100. R 53 in mortall : 102. E blythfull : 103. R [ryall] : 104. R reput and ; B [of] : 106. R In stretis : 109. R in corbell round : 111. R in sic riall : 114. 53 pepil : 115. R taking : 116. R [be] : 118. R [per ordoure] : 119. 53 langsum cryme : 121. E thai thrange ; R 53 war thai : 123. R 53 batellis ; R Munydanis ; L in beltles : 124. E quhilk in ; 53 [in] : 126. 53 [the] pepil of : 127. C E L B [of] ; 53 the pepil, of Cithea : 128. E [the] ; L *omits* : 130. 53 With stremyt now : 134. R danys thai did : 136. R ane barge : 142. R 53 schulderis ; R hynt and vp : 144. R gistis.

ending. E *as* C *except* Heyr endis the viii buik syne followis the proloug of the ix and syne the ix buik of the samyn proloug anno domini *etc. etc. etc. etc. etc.* ; R Here endis the aucht buke of eneados And begynnys the proloug of the nynte buke of the samyn ; L *as* C *adding* Finis, *followed by blank page* ; B *as* C ; 53 Finis.

BOOK IX

Prologue, heading. E The proloug of the ix buik of the aeneados ; R B *omit* ; L Prologus ; 53 The prologe of the .ix booke ; Bt The prollog of the nynt buk of virgell In commendatioun of vertew

1. 53 Bt lusty versis : 2. L and worthy ; 53 Bt of lusty : 3. R in thare merkis merkis ; 53 Bt thareon : 4. R Na vtilite ; 53 Bt no sic vnworthy werkis : 6. R Quham . 8. R blisß : 11. Bt [ʒa] : 12. Bt [syne] : 13. R to done ; 53 Bt as done to, thou : 16. R 53 Bt Clym nocht oure hie nor ʒit oure law to licht : 18. Bt *adds* Finis q gawyn dowglaß : 20. R to purpoiß said before : 23. E R 53 tenchis ; B thewchis : 24. 53 quhare euer thay : 25. E blythnes lattin : 27. R [eik] ; 53 sayand : 29. 53 we suld : 31. 53 knychtlie : 32. E of wassage ; R carpe on : 33. R woddis and treis : 36. E L B suld litill : 39. E Or mayr : 42. R ganys : 44. R knicht hant : 45. E byssit ; R bissert ; 53 or the : 47. 53 [the] gled, nor the : 49. R or the mastice behaldis : 50. E spalʒellis ; R spanʒartis ; 53 spanʒeartis : 54. R [hes] ; 53 bukis : 55. 53 enditit : 60. E he haill ; L distructioun : 61. R The nowmer : 64. R saying ; L the leid . 66. R 53 I laith : 70. 53 is bot gais : 73. R 53 full hardy : 77. R Bot be . . . fynd na proverb : 83. R amend : 84. L my sycht : 86. E dyd ; R valeʒe que

vale3e ; 53 vail3e quod vail3e . . . [deid] : 87. R [And] : 90. R and of hie : 94. 53 I ensew :
96. R my : 97. R oppone : 98. R begynnyth ; 53 begynneth, of.

ending. E *as* C *adding* Heyr endis the proloug of the ix buik and begynnis the ix buik
of the sam ; R *as* C *except* et incipit *and* in eneados ; L B *as* C ; 53 Finis. The nynth
buk of Eneados.

IX.i.

2. 53 ordinance, and materis : 6. E from the hewin ; R send : 9. C *reverses 9–10,
indicating correct order by* B A *in margin* ; E lawin ; R *reverses 9–10* : 13. R [ilk] : 15.
R 53 beheld : 17. E a vantage : 18. R 53 And sett ; 53 hef : 19. R [nevir] ; L [all] : 20. E
[durst haue] : 21. R 53 this : 23. 53 palentyne : 28. R To quhylom : 30. 53 3one cartis :
32. E Sone on : 34. R 53 to the : 41. E L the skyis ; R thir clowdis ; B of the skyis ; 53
the skies : 43. 53 becum : 44. R [cleir] : 47. 53 reuelacioun : 48. R 53 persaif : 50. R 53
I sall : 54. 53 sternis : 59. E in [the] ; L B [in] : 63. E did clatter : 65. L the gouernyng :
66. R 53 and childer : 72. E In lik : 73. E gandis : 74. R eftir the spate ; 53 space : 76. R
53 trowgh ; 53 now flowand : 77. 53 fatyl flude : 78. E band and ; R feild : 79. 53 waters :
80. R Swagit returnys ; 53 tyl thare.

IX.ii.

5. R Cacus : 7. E [ane] : 8. E 3our : 9. E wappyn ; R Swyithly ; 53 [hynt] : 10. E [the] ; 53
dartis fete, apoun : 12. R to thame cry : 16. C E departit ; R 53 thare : 17. E Command
geve thai : 18. R In : 20. R the place : 22. R with thare : 24. R 53 dykis : 27. R thir samyn
sett : 30. 53 on housis hie : 32. L schyftane : 36. R [hym] : 38. E *omits* : 41. R quhat that ;
53 [to] : 44. 53 gif the batal : 45. R 53 in the plane : 46. 53 byde, and drew : 52. R 53
rasit : 55. R grym : 56. 53 Saith here : 58. R 53 passage : 63. R 53 With : 65. E R Bayis ;
R 53 blatand : 66. R 53 the dammys ; 53 soueralie : 67. 53 in his : 69. R Rai3 in the are :
73. R Na ne : 75. R thare : 77. R and way : 79. E L B troiane : 82. E [was] ; 53 tharon :
85. R 53 dykis ; R drawin about : 86. R [the] : 88. R quhilk wilfully war glaid : 89. E
did he did cry : 90. R hynt : 91. L [the] : 96. R 53 bissis ; 53 crakkit : 97. R pikkit : 98.
53 ouerlotf hetschis : 99. 53 mext.

IX.iii. heading. E translatit . . . and goddes of the se ; R or goddis of the sey ; L *omits* ;
53 goddes

1. E reherß ; L reheris ; 53 rehers : 3. 53 Hed : 4. R Thus from : 5. E deidis auld : 11.
R 53 of the goddis : 13. E sicking : 16. R maist of : 18. R [the] : 20. R the cuchil ; 53
cuthil : 21. R [the] ; 53 maid ane : 22. R to wald : 24. R haboundand . . . gaistis : 29.
E doyß ; 53 dois canstrane : 32. 53 at the leist : 33. E na schippis ; L thair schippis :
35. E L Quhamby : 36. R 53 on : 37. 53 at hir : 41. 53 quham to : 43. 53 sele : 45. 53 that
euer in : 46. 53 dangeris sure : 47. E L B [heß] ; E grant : 49. R at the : 50. R [in] ; L
Arrayit : 51. R ourese : 53. R as that has : 54. E *omits* : 57. R mortale ; 53 [as] : 58. E
goddis : 60. E fomy bludis ; R mony woddis : 62. E L B [till] : 63. 53 brutheris : 66. R
53 swirlis : 67. E L [and] ; B [in] : 70. L and det : 72. 53 Turnis : 73. L Amonyst : 75. R
of the : 78. 53 of new plesand : 79. R Ane brand . . . thow did ; 53 cloud, then thay :

84. R 53 Doun from : 85. L fyllit at the : 88. E [my] ; R albeid : 89. 53 your : 90. E now
for as the : 91. 53 it befall : 94. E 53 ȝe list : 95. E 53 goddis ; B in the see ; 53 sowme :
100. E [dowkand] : 104. R barge and are : 108. E horß ; 53 hors : 109. R horß sound :
110. R B 53 bakwart : 111. E did stot ; R coursour did stour and lap abak ; 53 lepe :
114. E Bot : 115. E word : 116. R richt spretely : 117. R 53 ane fray : 118. R 53 The ; 53 at
the sey : 119. R quod : 122. E Quhayr thai . . . for to defens ; 53 for to fle for : 126. R 53
maner of hope : 128. E landis in : 129. R sall on na ; 53 sal in na : 130. 53 thousandis :
133. 53 that thay : 134. R at nocht ; 53 vane rufe : 135. 53 [be] : 136. E therof of felloun :
139. R euer this ; B in his cost : 143. R [my] : 146. E to the rewin : 147. E principalis ;
L [principal] : 150. R [of] . . . or weris : 151. R principall : 152. E L B I schaw ; R Giff I
had : 159. E [meyn] : 161. 53 their bene : 162. R That levis now ; L now in iuperte now
thai : 163. E R L B 53 men : 164. E geve : 165. E B handis ; 53 thare syre : 166. R [and]
all ; 53 thare toun : 167. R 53 valȝeant : 171. R nede ; 53 nedis wyth Uulcanus : 174. E All
that all ; R [hail] : 179. E R horß ; R 53 baly ; R and wyde ; 53 hors : 181. 53 determyt
haue we : 185. 53 vncertane : 187. 53 sa preteles men : 188. R that delayit : 192. R iorney
to tak : 193. R And eiß : 199. 53 War : 200. E ane thousand ; R And ilk ane hundreth ;
53 And eik ane : 204. F wordis ; R about the wardis : 205. 53 [dyd].

IX.iv.

1. R that fortreß : 5. R And five tymes : 6. E geve : 7. R the portis : 8. E [nocht] ; R
Ioyned ; 53 Ioned . . . be betrasit : 14. R For thare ; 53 For than : 15. R [son] ; 53 Had
put : 16. R capitane to ; 53 til his : 24. R has his : 28. R 53 And the ; R in all the ; B the
rowt : 30. 53 send, witly ful : 31. R na sa : 32. C schoyl *in margin* : 33. 53 his fader :
35. E L B harnyß : 36. R of his curage : 37. R ȝong ; 53 fluris : 38. R sprong : 39. R of
vnyte : 40. B and vniformyte : 41. 53 rest to, play : 50. R [lang] : 51. R [heir] : 53. R
quhite purpois ; 53 it is : 54. R or : 55. R sum surely : 56. E 53 haldis thaim : 57. R
begynnys now to schyne ; 53 ful syre : 58. R men : 60. E L B Queyne ; R Quhen ; 53
Quhene : 62. 53 thingis thou : 66. R wittering ; C wrytyng : 69. R [weill] ; R 53 nobill
famous ; 53 I knaw weil : 70. E na na thair ; R 53 na man : 71. B weill fund : 73. R the
fervent : 75. E L of his : 80. 53 [I] : 82. R [apon] : 83. R Instruct : 84. B no lernyt : 85.
R Amyddis ; 53 brag, the troyane : 86. 53 that all efferis : 87. R O my : 91. E R 53 dois ;
E this lyst dyspyß : 92. E L B Quhilkis ; R on sic ; 53 on this wyse : 93. E thus thou ; R
honour now pretendis ; 53 thus honour : 95. 53 ansuerit : 96. C E [I] : 100. 53 of the
sic consate : 103. 53 [my] : 107. R sall : 110. R B 53 or myscheif : 112. R or hard ; 53 was :
113. 53 the lifft : 115. R layd : 116. E [na] ; R wald nocht of na wyse ; 53 suffir than na :
119. R [to] do the corps : 120. R in ane memour vp in ane : 121. R it suld : 122. R that
dule : 125. 53 vtheris : 130. R 53 in vane ; 53 thou seis : 131. C ar ot ar of ; E cacis ay of :
133. R [thar] : 135. R [gat] on fute vnto : 136. R our intent.

IX.v. heading. L purcheß

1. 53 earth : 2. R Than ; 53 thochtis coissing : 3. E L B in : 6. 53 [stern] : 11. L feildis :
13. R B To ; R Nisus and to : 17. E Wyth harm : 18. R was with audience : 19. L haiste ;
53 seand first : 21. E [son] : 22. R and glaid : 24. R ȝow fur may : 25. 53 as we : 26. E
avysß ; 53 wisdome : 28. R drunkin ; 53 drounkyn : 30. 53 soithlie : 32. 53 strekit : 35.
L blake nycht dirknyß : 38. 53 grantit [sone] : 39. E and pallantyne : 40. 53 quhile,

hidder syne : 45. R 53 of the : 48. R thare wourdis : 50. R [vp-] ; 53 troy al tyme : 52. E
R L 53 3e nocht : 53. 53 deface : 54. B Sen na : 56. R thare . . . quod he : 57. R [of] : 58.
E Wyth steris ; R *added in later hand* : 60. E gevin ; 53 geuin : 64. R awne writing :
68. R his son from his life wappynnis pas : 69. R 53 as 3it quhilk is ; R bot ane page :
70. 53 forwart : 73. R 53 done ; 53 or : 77. R For ay my : 82. E L B [the] ; E kynrent all ;
R Quhare : 83. 53 secretis : 85. E [I] : 89. 53 In 3our wallis : 92. 53 noy : 93. 53 [rycht] :
94. L gravyt : 99. R [crafty] ; 53 anciant, crafty : 100. R L 53 Quhilk : 101. E be tyde ; 53
certis, that victouris [ws] : 102. R 53 conquest Italie : 103. 53 the toun : 105. R Behecht ;
L 53 Behald : 106. R How browdin : 108. E chyld : 109. R [the] ; L eik steid : 114. R
3our clawis : 115. L all thir : 116. 53 [rentis] : 119. R [O] ; R 53 3ong wourschipfull :
125. R in to oure worde : 126. R 53 gevin : 134. 53 ane thing grant : 136. E pammis
blude : 137. R [town] : 138. L compand ; B now comptand : 140. 53 [in] : 141. R Now
here : 148. R of wicht : 150. R Thy . . . to contort : 154. 53 I sal : 157. R hart : 163. E R 53
commandment : 164. E I ma the nyt I na : 166. R moder sal : 169. R this : 173. R The
quhilk ; 53 was wount : 174. R That all that I haue vnto the promyß ; 53 [the] : 176. 53
Iouy : 177. E and to : 182. 53 [it] : 183. 53 With ane : 184. L Than : 186. R rough . . . na
thing clene ; 53 With.

IX.vi. heading. R [thai]

1. 53 the way : 2. R Quhem ; 53 Quhen : 4. 53 Iouy : 7. R consatis : 8. R 53 men : 9. E
change : 11. R thare skatterit : 12. L amangis : 13. R ischit thame ; R 53 wentis : 14. R
53 amang : 17. 53 of ony : 20. E R fell . . . drunkin ; 53 Fordwart . . . drynkin : 24. R
helmys : 25. E R L B or the thetis : 26. R armouris : 28. R L this : 29. R Eurilianus :
53 thus now : 34. 53 gude tent thareto : 35. R wyde passage : 36. R throw the large
[streit] way ; B throu the : 37. R 53 thus : 38. E R 53 nor ; L behald : 46. R The straik :
52. E horß ; R amangis ; 53 hors : 54. R 53 was hakkit : 55. R [said] : 56. R [quhill] ; 53
[he] : 57. R wantit : 58. E be spred : 63. E and [in] play ; 53 ryet : 65. R 53 stekit : 66. C
of *interlined* : 68. R 53 sammyn : 77. E that he aufull : 78. 53 blate : 81. R that plane :
85. R to put to : 88. R [hard] : 93. 53 poent : 97. 53 mext : 98. R And at the last : 99. R
sic forß full : 101. R lichtly ; R 53 nixt that stude : 102. E did all : 103. R At the : 105. R
Stand at thare : 106. E bat seis ; R lat thame be : 107. R [his] : 108. 53 slaucter : 109. E
R 53 quhilk : 111. 53 day lyft : 113. E harme aneuch is doun of : 117. R [thai] : 118. 53 and
neft : 120. E tapystry ; R tapesey : 123. R Quhilk : 126. 53 The prudentis : 128. R and
the ; 53 ane of the : 131. 53 Romulus as he : 133. 53 franschip : 136. R [he] ; 53 [ded] :
137. E R 53 Romulus : 140. R syde it brasyn ; 53 brasit : 143. R tymbrell ; 53 creiftis.

IX.vii. heading. R Wolscenus ; L his fall

1. R [as] all this : 5. 53 and at the : 6. 53 schow : 7. R Wolscenus : 8. E 53 cumming : 9.
E the cite did : 10. 53 [held] . . . the new : 12. R Torned : 14. 53 Smytis Eurill : 16. E war
this ; R persavit ; 53 thus, war : 17. 53 this rout : 23. R [the] wodis : 24. R of dirknes : 26.
R knawin pethis turnys and wentis : 30. 53 schaddis : 31. C thyk *cancelled before* ful :
36. C also *interlined* ; R [new] : 38. E well gang ; L B will gang : 39. R Nysus he went :
42. 53 was clepit : 43. 53 Quhafore : 48. R the land : 56. R [the] : 57. 53 [at] persauit :
59. L harkand : 61. B Quhen : 62. R doutsum way : 64. R [hym] belowkit : 66. R 53
at nocht : 67. R that silly : 71. R ruschis : 76. E L B this wyß : 78. E beute and : 80. E

directeris ; R 53 directrice : 84. E R 53 maner of way : 85. L Or that thai : 86. E ruife of ; R and bawkis : 87. R 53 hang : 89. R this this grete : 90. E wolsum den ; R this wißdome then : 91. 53 mot go : 97. R scheild nerehand his : 98. R 53 in schunder : 102. E at his : 103. 53 derth : 106. L [se] : 109. 53 his chance, se : 110. R Ane nother : 111. R [with] : 112. E R L B part of : 113. R fixt : 114. B and bane : 115. 53 [capitane] . . . al wod : 116. 53 ane mendis : 117. R and syne his : 120. R 53 hart blude : 121. 53 with hat word : 122. R with ane : 125. E he hyd hym : 128. 53 [dede] : 130. L frendis : 136. 53 [and] : 138. R his self : 139. E remeyd ; 53 That thare : 140. R or thai war glaid : 143. L ruschis ; 53 duschit : 144. R 53 birstand : 148. R [the] : 149. E R 53 dois : 150. R chesboll : 151. R 53 in ; 53 Now doun : 152. R 53 ar : 153. R [Bot] in amyd ; L ruschis : 155. R he restis : 156. 53 preistis : 157. R Quhil her quhile thare on at : 158. R 53 wirkand : 159. R 53 he thame stoutly : 160. E [had] ; R as he na thing had : 161. 53 Bot : 163. E forganand [him] : 164. R 53 nocht he ; L was that he : 165. R he fra the life : 168. C to rest in *cancelled before* ded ; R lykit for to rest or ly : 175. R of romanys : 176. R sa hald : 184. R [gret] . . . slane he is ; 53 heros : 186. C R B corpß ; E L corps ; E [brytnyt] : 188. E hald deid ; R 3it flowand : 191. 53 blandit on the flude : 194. R hewmond ; 53 Mesaphus riche hewmond.

IX.viii. heading. 53 fast assaillis

4. E to fund : 8. L of maill ; 53 In place and : 10. R settis his folkis : 12 C of of this ; R The : 16. R followane ane : 23. R and the : 27. R The : 30. R messingeris : 33. E And paill : 34. R hir banyst reft : 35. 53 quhele said sche : 36. 53 spynnyl : 38. L mony scout : 41. E spedy spayß ; R 53 And wod . . . [a] : 44. E R 53 and rame ; R 53 amang . . . [and] roup : 49. R 53 wofull complantis : 50. R of the : 51. E L B Eurilly : 54. 53 this rage : 55. L B this ; 53 leif alase : 57. R [nor] tyme ; 53 grant : 58. E To thi thi : 59. R Quhil . . . into ; 53 When : 61. 53 As : 62. R The ; R 53 quenthing : 64. R the ; R 53 on the sand : 65. R So foullis ; 53 swage doggis : 69. R reduce agane thy : 71. R L 53 quhilk : 72. 53 boytht : 73. R werk with the : 76. R se the : 77. 53 lyis thou, manglit : 78. 53 tyrryt : 80. R thi confort : 81. 53 and sandis : 82. 53 3our handis : 84. 53 So swak : 87. R [me] wraich and : 90. 53 to smyte me therwith : 91. C life *cancelled before* cruel : 93. R madynnys all ; 53 troianis : 94. E enlang : 103. 53 handis : 104. R lugeing na hir : 107. R and clamour : 108. R Quhill that the : 110. 53 to stop : 111. R [of] : 113. R in buschement ; 53 surely : 117. 53 troyanis : 119. C the *interlined* ; R [the] : 120. E as thai ; R and sloppit : 121. C cace *cancelled before* place ; R thig : 122. R that oist in : 126. 53 with wappinnys : 127. R 53 weltering : 128. 53 thare be : 129. 53 That micht of force : 130. 53 thekis : 131. E fays and maner : 132. R 53 the volt : 133. C on syverit ; B on soverit ; 53 vnserit : 138. E [on thame] : 140. R brokin ; 53 [in] : 144. 53 now at thare : 146. R [for] to : 150. R bleisß ; 53 blesis : 151. E horß.

IX.ix. heading. R [3et]

1. R Caleope o thow god of musis all : 2. 53 [me] : 3. R or ; 53 octisioun : 4. C B corpß ; E R L corps ; 53 corpis, thare was : 6. R Quhare : 8. R dangere ; 53 daunger : 10. R 53 3e : 11. C weght *cancelled before* hycht ; R [tour of] : 12. E and wyth : 16. E athyr : 18. 53 discensis : 19. E schyllis ; L B schillis ; 53 and shotys : 26. R and in the ; 53 Vpblesis : 27. R 53 amang : 29. 53 schulderit : 34. B Quhare that : 35. R harlit : 36. R Than : 37. E towyr ; R 53 towris ; R that rusche : 38. 53 dynlit, with : 39. R welterit ; R 53 [the] ;

53 welteris : 40. L followys : 42. R spalis ; 53 with the : 46. L floryß ; 53 and lore :
47. R nernyus : 48. R 53 Latiuia : 52. E and onfarrand ; R Ane : 54. C *marginal note*
Turnus ; E L B 53 turnus rout ; R of turnus latyne rout : 57. R quhom to ; 53 ragent :
58. L ombesend : 61. gret *cancelled before* with : 62. R Apoun ane of the : 64. 53 eik :
67. C *marginal note 67–68* additio ; E alssone as has ; R Quhilk ; L B *lines bracketed
in MSS* : 74. E Quhair : 77. E rakles knaip : 79. 53 quhil he : 82. E had hym claucht ;
R 53 vpcaucht : 83. R 53 [a] : 84. 53 vp hie : 85. E L B [as] : 88. E bletingis softly the
gait ; L B his ; 53 feel : 89. E throu ioy : 91. 53 fowsyis : 92. E schyll ; 53 vthir : 95. R
craggis ; 53 [of] : 96. E crag bane ; R On ane ; 53 One Lucecius : 97. E towart ; 53 And
as he : 101. E *omits 101–105* : 104. R flambis : 105. R Na mare expert na this ; 53 Bane
mare : 106. E or tygius : 107. E L B [quhilk] : 110. R [eik] Dyrespus : 112. R [syne] : 117.
R 53 on the : 118. R full lichtly : 122. R thus he the liffe has : 127. E His : 133. E goddis
palice I hecht ; 53 Palacy did hecht : 134. E L B 53 byrnand : 136. R The styng . . . hed
he assayis : 138. R leding : 141. B ourtumlyt : 142. E 53 This.

IX.x. heading. E R L B 53 Quhilk

2. E [to] : 3. R 53 quhilk ; R [do] : 6. E wes the sornam : 7. E [3yngast] : 10. R 53 batellis :
16. R that thus takis : 17. R amyd the feild : 22. R cowart wrechis : 23. R [our] : 24.
E Quhat so wyld : 25. R vnthrift : 27. 53 ar 3e not : 28. 53 of the fare : 29. 53 bene of
naturu, derf : 30. 53 as bene men : 32. R we thame bar : 33. R [and] : 34. R L 53 schill :
36. R houndis harnes : 37. R 53 out throw : 38. E R horß : 41. R 53 laubour : 42. 53
mete : 46. R ar thai ; 53 we ar : 51. C *added in margin, beginning sheared* [Nor o-]-f
. . . ; E L B Or ; R [Nor] or to pair : 52. R hedis bare : 53. 53 tymes : 54. C on *interlined* ;
R And dry away : 55. R in purpur ; 53 3one : 56. C -dill lying (?) *cancelled before*
dyvyne : 63. R [to] hie ane stile ; 53 Be 3e : 67. 53 buschbome : 75. 53 about, of : 76. R
And like ; L blawyng : 77. 53 hors, Senonnus bendit : 80. R 53 Iovy : 83. R his hardy
commandment : 84. R the : 86. 53 altaris : 89. 53 tyde : 90. R equaill equale till : 91. R
horne3 crvne : 92. E and skattyr ; R and skattir with on soft sandis ; 53 schraip : 93.
E acceptit ; R accept ; L exceppis ; 53 acceppit : 94. E B he lyft ; R ane parte . . . mare
clere : 97. E Quhirland : 98. R he remulus : 101. R nor skornfully : 102. R 53 the by ;
53 The : 104. E Send ; R to the : 108. E curagis ; R curage ran : 110. 53 the riot : 114. L
Rutilianys : 115. L Troiane cite with cleir : 116. R 53 Iulius ; 53 thy victor : 117. 53 the :
118. R [is the way] . . . the hedis ; 53 that ledis : 121. 53 That al engendir . . . the sede :
122. R [of] : 123. R quhilk : 124. R to mak : 126. L Thy : 128. R [thus] : 130. R socht he
thar : 131. R that tyme changeit : 134. R 53 anchises : 135. E traistly ; R traist : 136. R 53
committit : 138. R to the : 142. R And with sic [3yng] : 147. R [thy] : 149. E eik renovne
he ; R The : 153. R and [of] : 158. R For ; R 53 of his ; L [in] : 159. E R 53 troianis ; L
[the] troianys : 162. R furth draw furth of the ; 53 this place : 166. E his hyinys : 168.
R perrellis during and ; 53 [all] : 169. E L B fra ; R Thir ; 53 [thar].

IX.xi. heading. R bitias baith twane Brethir kest

3. R 53 kyndely : 5. R 53 Quhilkis ; R lyn3ellis ; R 53 quhayngis : 7. R chaftis ; 53 takyllis
and schaftis : 9. C *or* On ? ; E One ; R L B 53 On ; R verray : 10. R rebound and : 11. E
increß : 13. E R 53 dois : 19. 53 tempestis : 20. R Quhilk ; 53 skatteris : 22. R the : 23. R 53
Quhen ; R fostaris : 24. B [vp] : 25. R Twa big : 27. E L B 53 and hyllis : 30. 53 to be : 32.

53 thay fais : 33. R thame durst : 34. R thare horß : 36. R thare richt : 39. R tymbrellis :
42. R flude ; 53 O : 46. R 53 ruschit : 49. R 53 With ; R menyt : 52. R to tak the flicht :
55. E R L myndis ; R L The : 56. L To that : 57. R 53 the place : 58. R that ne the : 59.
R Ischit : 62. R on that : 69. 53 the big : 71. R Syne to ; 53 Sone to : 72. L went : 74. R
it allane to : 78. E Furth buschyt : 79. R ground . . . [hed] : 80. C it *cancelled before*
festnyt : 83. R 53 mude ; L B muyd : 85. R For that : 86. R his lyfe : 87. E byrnand fyre ;
R byssy fyrand ; 53 fyre : 88. R phaltorica : 89. 53 thus : 92. E [traste] : 93. R 53 or : 94.
R 53 with the : 95. R 53 with the : 98. R eubrocone ; 53 Eubortone : 100. R 53 swelch :
101. R 53 [of] massy : 103. E he stude : 106. R slyde ; B Blak syk : 107. R in ylandis ; B
iland ; 53 Quhilk : 108. E R in aryme : 109. R in aryme : 110. E hard baid : 114. R 53 as
him self list : 116. C schamfull *in margin replacing cancelled* felloun : 118. L B portis.

IX.xii.

2. R this fortoun with him ; 53 thys : 3. R And quhen : 10. R Ruschand : 16. 53 beistis,
miserabil : 17. R 53 has him : 22. E fyre : 24. R [persauit] : 26. R He wounder : 28. R
turnus till ; 53 austerlie : 30. E L B onto ; E drowre ; R drowry : 32. E R L 53 dois ; R
[the] : 38. R allane with me : 39. R [at] : 41. 53 tothir two : 44. L [was] : 46. E Schoppit :
50. R [thus] enrollis : 51. R ane wound : 52. L ne na : 54. R Heving vp his : 57. 53 on
his : 59. R Ane felloun : 63. R vpspred : 67. R dredefull dreddour ; 53 dredour : 68. 53
They [Troianys] fled richt fast and syne did brak away : 71. R L 53 oppynnyt : 75. R
53 romanys : 78. R 53 vnsaciable ; 53 slauchter : 80. R 53 kelit : 85. R [hym] : 87. C B
corpß ; E R L corps ; R Synanthales vnto ; 53 corpis : 90. E L B in his ; R 53 and the :
92. C *added in margin* ; R 53 and the kene : 93. R *reverses* 93–94 Quhilk : 94. L his :
95. R dedely he : 97. 53 shynand : 100. R helpe he cryis : 103. E [thir] ; R efter thar :
104. C had *in margin* : 106. E inict ; R invnt ; 53 Inoynt : 107. E wemmon : 108. R 53
this ilk tyme doun dede is : 111. R poete was to : 113. R mvsing ; 53 musit, in harping :
114. E R his springis ; R [he] [a] : 115. 53 apoun.

IX.xiii. heading. 53 he fleis

2. R herand hale that : 3. R [doun] : 5. L within the : 7. 53 [to] : 13. R Oure vengit : 16.
R [sall] : 18. R awne silly : 19. E L B No : 20. R [Think ȝhe] na schame ; 53 [ȝhc] : 22.
53 obsence : 24. E all abyde : 25. B the rowt : 26. R 53 was stark : 28. R 53 ryver syde
on law : 32. R a schout : 33. C fast *interlined* : 40. R Nor : 44. E [a] ; 53 [wyß] : 45. R
abak ane : 49. R oure rebutit : 54. R 53 or : 58. E charge : 59. R 53 thare Turnus : 60.
R Nocht drewe : 61. R capitane : 64. 53 schakkit : 65. 53 as he : 66. E byß [helm] : 69.
R And brokin and birssin : 70. R was dyntis : 71. E bettit : 72. E Sa fayr ; R boiß : 73.
R 53 mycht na langer : 77. R [the] ; R 53 swete thik : 78. E R trymbland : 79. R ne gar
he : 84. C lap *interlined* : 86. R apon the wallis ; 53 thir wallis : 88. 53 slaucher.

ending. E *as* C *adding* Heyr endis the ix buik and begynnis the tent and the proloug
of the sam ; R Explicit liber nonus et incipit Prologus Libri decimi ; L B *as* C ; 53 Finis.

BOOK X

Prologue, heading. E R L *omit*; B Prologus decimi ; 53 The Prologe of the .x. Booke. Bt The prollog of the tent buik of Virgill compyld be the noble poet Mr gawyn dowglaß bischop of dumkeld : of godis workis to be incomprehensible be man wit or ressone / As for Example of the trinite

1. C Hhe ; E L B The : 5. E Quham . . . ganist : 6. R thir gracis : 7. R so that ilk : 9. R ordand : 10. E cauß . . . placis ; R thow schupe [seir] : 14. L Herbis : 15. R for to . . . frost and : 16. 53 Thocht that thou nedit not ; Bt Thocht *and* nocht *corrected to* Nocht *and* ocht : 17. E that kynd thou : 20. 53 Bt [thou] wrocht of nocht : 23. 53 [nane] accidence ; Bt nane *in margin* : 24. E [quhy] : 26. 53 Bt Sen : 27. 53 incommyt remanis ; Bt vncorrupt remanis : 33. R [baith] ; 53 thre disuinct ; Bt thre disunit : 34. R salbe ; 53 Bt As was and salbe : 38. E R 53 Bt dois : 39. C *or* All ane ? ; E R L B 53 Bt All ane : 40. R of life : 42. R He onely [Son] : 46. R [he] : 49. R 3it than : 50. 53 Bt [thai] : 52. R and euer : 53. C wysdome *cancelled before* word ; E R L B word his [and] : 57. R and bliß : 58. R is he bore ; Bt [hys] : 59. E Bt [tharof] ; R tharof has ; B Bot he : 60. E [Son] : 61. C he *cancelled before* that : 63. L B the thre : 65. R 53 Bt Thocht thir thre ; R seueraly : 71. R [knyt] : 75. R 53 Bt hete and licht : 76. R B 53 Bt hete and licht : 80. R Perpetuale ; Bt sowld heir hait haif : 84. 53 Bt [God] creature : 86. E nor cauß : 93. E [he] : 95. R 53 suffice ; 53 Bt the Crede ; Bt suffeiß : 96. 53 Bt excludit : 97. E [is of] ; L B [is] : 101. R thi wayis thy wayis : 102. R sa is : 105. B oxin : 109. R [kend] ; 53 scheiphardis : 110. R crip : 112. C Bt de- *erased before* -gre ; E L B degre : 113. 53 Bt maid : 114. R [hys] fulage : 116. R procedant : 117. B fowlis bestis and ; 53 in the see : 118. E hym in erd : 119. R to him : 124. R ofspringis : 127. E in thrall ; R bondis fle ; Bt bundin : 128. E clavis ; R schawis : 134. 53 will of mercy : 136. E this sone thine : 137. 53 Bt blude, luflye with wyne : 138. E [be] ; 53 Bt glory : 139. R The last ws gaif ; 53 Bt Thou last vs gaif . . . memory : 140. L dolouris : 142. E [synfull] ; 53 Bt synful, wrechit : 143. 53 Bt [peirles] : 148. R 53 Bt thy grace : 149. E [to] : 150. R 53 Bt This : 155. E wryt furth as : 158. 53 Bt thy help : 159. R of thare ; R 53 Bt futhir : 162. R Qwha that thi mandment ; 53 Bt mandmentis [ane] : 164. R clepit ; 53 fader clepis the ; Bt callis the : 165. R son : 166. E L our castell ; B castall : 168. R [thy] ; R 53 lovingis ; 53 Bt They but : 170. R maid of thi : 173. R 53 Bt thy hie realme.

ending. E *as* C *adding* Heyr endis the proloug of the x buik and syn followis the buik of the sam ; R *as* C *adding* et ; L *as* C *repeating* Amen. Explicit prologus *etc* ; B *as* C ; 53 FINIS. The .x. boke of Eneados ; Bt Finis q Mr gawyne dowglas.

X.i. heading. R Iupiter the grete goddis ; R L amang

2. 53 On heuinly : 5. R Amangis . . . abone the : 6. R 53 Within the : 10. L sagis : 11. L warpyt wyd : 12. E begouth him self ; R [hym self] ; B and first he said : 15. 53 decretis : 16. R 53 bakwart : 20. B contrar the : 22. R 53 inhabitatioun ; L inhabitioun : 23. 53 or thayrs has : 24. R raiß ; 53 rais were contriuit : 26. R The : 27. 53 preuoik : 29. 53 Herefor : 31. R quhelm ; L Ane gret myscheif ; 53 qualim send all : 32. R To thirl : 33. E *runs together 33–34* Than war iust tym to rug and reyf thus gait : 34. R 53 it tyme : 35. 53 Now all . . . decist said he : 36. E B mak ; 53 Glaidly and with one, mak : 37. R 53 on sic wyse : 40. 53 all, of : 42. R to beseik ; 53 I beseke : 43. E bene the glor : 44. R

[ws] : 46. 53 She : 48. R in stede wedis : 53 Trouch : 50. R 53 Amyd the : 55. E L B and blude ; E rynnis a ; 57. E euer mayr ; R suffice : 58. R skaill : 61. C enmemyiß : 64. 53 Aipois : 65. R To were on ; L 53 The : 68. R mot [eik] : 70. E R 53 repugnant : 74. R of help ; 53 [3it] : 76. C R L B responß ; E 53 respons : 77. R chargis : 79. B 53 and resson : 84. R war and lost : 86. E L B [the] : 88. R L throw the cloudis : 90. R the chance : 91. 53 I furth : 92. 53 vthir warld : 94. R all the cieties : 95. L vpoun : 96. E L B had of sic ; L thingis : 98. 53 list to avance : 99. 53 in to : 100. L romanys ; 53 Quham the : 102. 53 reik and : 104. E 53 of all ; R 53 perrellis : 105. R in to : 106. E thi new ; 53 the : 108. E L B hym on : 112. R Mot . . . omnipotend : 113. R [bot] : 114. R from the : 115. E almathus : 117. E clepit : 118. R eik : 124. R ciete of tyre of affrik : 126. R eschapit : 128. 53 seis : 131. R Troianis he socht till Italie ; 53 Italy : 133. 53 better, than : 134. C Haue *written over* Had ; E R assis ald : 139. E to the : 140. E 53 Panthus ; 53 quhilkis.

X.ii.

3. R to me said sche ; 53 to me, sais sche : 5. R [ayr] ; 53 aire, was troy : 6. R [hyd] : 7. L men : 11. L Itale : 13. R 53 Provokand : 16. C -is *added to* strenth- ; R To leuch his : 18. 53 wordis sere : 19. 53 [hym] : 22. R fallis : 23. 53 to : 24. R 53 Oure quiet : 28. E L B slychtis : 30. R 53 all hir ladyis ; 53 ding : 33. E thing only sum : 36. E L B as it ; 53 [it] : 39. 53 Pilumnus grantis : 40. 53 Nymphie : 41. R 53 leifsum : 42. R braidis ; R B and mortall : 46. 53 leifsum as : 48. R ald faderis : 49. L [breist] : 50. E [treuth] ; R spouß ; 53 spous : 52. 53 taking : 59. E L B [the] : 60. R goddes ; L in Itale : 61. C -is *cancelled in* ofspryng- ; R 53 contrare : 63. E mysknaw at this : 65. R quhare . . . [he] : 70. R Lat thare : 71. R the strange : 75. 53 the litill, Phrigiane gere : 78. E assal3eit ; R That wourthy ; R 53 exaltit ; 53 Quhat wourthy : 80. B werys : 82. R and sic : 84. R That : 87. R 53 in : 88. 53 [wapynnys] : 91. R Thay baid honest : 93. R And now to : 94. E riß ; 53 [ws] : 96. 53 Quhilkis : 99. L quhyspar : 100. C d *written over and cancelled before* full : 101. E Lik or ; R blastis ; 53 we persaue : 102. 53 souch : 108. R thing : 109. R [quhen] : 113. R bownyt sone : 114. R [playn] : 116. R [3our] : 117. R algatis this may : 118. R L consider ; 53 Latinus : 119. R 53 Nor 3it 3e : 121. R aduersite : 124. E in athyr ; L change ; B and werk : 125. R schewe : 126. R [of] : 127. R of Italianis : 129. R 53 thrawart ; R and monitions : 131. 53 nor Italianis : 134. R [haue] : 138. 53 [the flude].

X.iii. heading. L *note at top of folio* Ihus maria

11. E [in] : 13. E R L B son and ; 53 Icetrane : 18. E Followis : 19. B first : 20. L Presyt with all his ; B of his : 22. 53 semyt to he : 23. R 53 na his : 24. 53 or : 27. C to *cancelled before* into ; 53 preis ; 31. R And amyd : 35. E cruell ; R and riche : 36. R and the ; B [the] hed : 37. 53 euoure bene to : 40. R 53 gate : 41. E weill full dek : R 53 hang : 43. E cerkyle ; L B cirkill ; 53 so blyth : 46. 53 men mycht : 47. R Invictand ; 53 Unwyttand : 48. R Addresß ; R 53 wirkis : 50. 53 thou borne : 52. R on the grond ; R 53 goldin : 55. R dykis ; 53 dikis : 58. E [in] : 62. L out *cancelled before and after* throw ; 53 Sclidis : 63. E [Kyng] ; R evander hie : 66. L king of : 67. E L B [hym] : 70. R 53 he with him : 74. L thar till : 75. E warldly : 76. 53 All manues : 78. 53 glaidly : 81. R noblis : 82. C cunmand ; R 53 fordwartis ; 53 command : 85. E R At the : 87. R 53 strang : 92. L quhilk : 94. C *marginal note* wod ; E R L B wod ; 53 belouit freynd, wod and : 96. R

within him : 97. C cawsys *cancelled before* chancis ; R changis : 99. E B at hym at did :
101. 53 Quhil : 103. C seye *cancelled before* see.

X.iv. heading. R [of] Quhilk

1. E goddeß ; R 53 goddis : 3. 53 [lyand] and in : 7. E [the] : 10. R statelie snowte ; 53
Tyrgris : 11. E Swouchand ; R 53 out throw . . . he went : 12. R [hys] ; 53 [3ong] : 13. R
Vnder his leding ; 53 Vndder him ledin : 14. E Clusum ; 53 Clusyn : 16. R flambis ; 53
flamys : 21. R schippis : 22. R state : 26. 53 was send : 28. R 53 mycht : 32. R he knewe :
35. C curß ; E R L B courß ; R That richt : 36. R Off : 37. 53 betaikinnis : 38. E fyre : 42.
R the flude : 44. R 53 followis eftir the : 47. R vale3eant : 50. R 53 crete : 51. L in the :
52. R bank ; L 53 Endland : 53. 53 Or til : 55. 53 of pest : 57. R Signus and : 59. R And
the ; 53 Ane of the : 60. R [I] be : 61. 53 Cupanus with the : 62. R 53 tymbrell : 63. R
fetherame ; 53 fetherem : 65. 53 [or] : 66. R 53 fedderis : 67. E tell full dolorusly ; R 53 As
that thai tell ; R dolorus ; 53 dolours : 68. R amangis ; 53 skoggy : 69. 53 branchis, rising
lang : 71. 53 gan bew Phaetoun : 72. R Quhat . . . as playt : 74. R [to] : 75. R invyous ;
53 thochtis, and ennoyus : 77. R 53 ouerhede : 78. R his life : 80. R 53 souchand : 82. 53
equale : 83. L Amangis : 84. E 53 rowis ; R this : 86. E [throu] : 88. L and huge : 95. 53
[famus] : 98. R [name] : 100. R Off : 103. E R B clan and : 104. 53 owthir souir : 108. E
of noble ; R of the nobill : 109. L Men3encyus ; B Men3entius : 110. E 53 his cite : 111.
R 53 men in : 113. 53 [of] : 116. E Wyth thar : 118. E rowis ; 53 rollaris : 119. E of thar ;
R thare coistis ; 53 choftis : 120. B harys : 121. R Quhill all the : 122. E Vp wellis ; 53
Upwaltis : 124. 53 in his : 129. 53 [to] : 130. 53 bally : 133. 53 byismyng : 134. R 53 wallis
bokkand : 136. E [thryß] : 138. E bulge.

X.v. heading. E L B translatit ; R of the sey ; 53 Tald Eneas ; C *omits* the ; E R L B 53
the cite

2. R 53 in till ane . . . of licht : 5. R thocht : 8. E To steill ; R his ruddir : 10. R [thar] :
12. 53 [of schippys] : 14. E goddeß ; R goddes ; 53 goddis : 16. 53 [dyd] : 17. E numer :
18. R And laitly with the : 21. R [all] : 25. R his richt hand on the ; 53 est castell : 30.
53 Syne of : 31. E a thing : 34. R and the : 36. R of the fir of the busche tre : 38. E L B
is present : 43. 53 Thy cauillis : 44. R To se ; R 53 [the] throw : 46. 53 Hauing on : 49.
R goddes : 50. R [the] ; R 53 and rest ; 53 Amang : 52. B and clepit : 53. R fowsseis . . .
on ather : 54. R dartis and : 56. R all thing : 58. 53 with he thurianis : 59. R 53 Quhen :
60. E R Thy ; L gan command : 61. R all bydand ; 53 as biding the : 64. R Bot : 68. R
invisible ; 53 inuisibil : 71. C an *cancelled before* and : L Has brocht : 73. R 53 ocht my :
76. 53 [fell] occasioun : 77. R L departit : 79. L [sche] : 83. 53 pyngil for the : 86. R 53
suld be : 87. R neuertheles : 90. R and mak ; L [hys] : 91. E wodis : 92. R 53 mont : 94.
R 53 the towris and : 95. R lokkit in ane schare ; L in to : 96. L hardy : 97. E 53 Be 3ou :
98. E protecteris ; 53 protectour : 99. R 53 As ; R in oure : 100. 53 fute of it seile : 101. R
53 assist ; 53 awayne : 103. R vpsprang and the : 104. L Casand : 106. R 53 display : 107.
53 and turate : 108. R graith for the battaill thame : 109. B or than : 112. R 53 amyddis :
116. R The : 117. R The hate of : 119. R Tharewith : 120. R [of] : 121. 53 trumpettis : 123. E
crouping ; R 53 crowping : 126. E of we : 128. 53 sownes, flowand thaym : 129. R 53 thare
affere : 131. R rutilianis ; 53 Rutulianis in that : 132. R Italianis : 133. R 53 Quhil that ;
R towartis ; 53 endlang the : 135. 53 of scheppis : 136. R 53 tymber : 138. R 53 lemand

flambis : 140. E fir stremis ; R L fyre : 141. R ane comete : 145. R [with] : 149. R mycht :
151. 53 stalwart, hardy : 156. 53 folkis : 164. E be sawin [in] 3our stalwart : 165. L vpoun
his : 167. R 53 into 3oure myndis : 172. E 53 Quhilk ; R Quhilkis . . . settis : 173. R half
deid ; L tocum : 175. E Hop helpis hardyment ; L Hap helys hardment ; B hardyment.

X.vi. heading. E L B landis ; E [thame]

1. R mene tyme : 5. E L B swaffard ; R Quhilk [the swarf] : 6. E thai kep : 7. R in the
coggis ; 53 into the : 8. 53 Entillit : 10. L na schaldis schald : 20. 53 to hys and : 21. R
like as stok ; 53 chere and cheif : 23. R 53 by his : 28. R latyne round : 32. R the ; 53
dyd : 34. R 53 [a] dry channell ; L On ; 53 or ane bed : 35. E tyme onto schaikin : 36.
R quhil scho : 38. L the flude : 42. R 53 from the wallis ; 53 sliddry gar : 43. B 53 war ;
53 That of · 44. 53 drounkit : 46. R [na] . . . or bost : 54. 53 commouns, all hale : 57. E
[set] : 58. R 53 sydis : 62. R dyntis : 63. R 53 to lorne : 64. R his hid moderis [furth] ;
53 furth was : 65. R [god] ; 53 And to : 67. R 53 [he] : 68. E deid ; 53 dedis gap : 70. E
stawart ; 53 Kelit : 72. R And with ; 53 burdoun, al the routis : 76. 53 Melanpus : 81. R
at him ane darte : 86. 53 3owng berd : 87. E lustand desyr ; R the newe : 90. R 53 lyne :
91. R thy clan : 94. E fire ; 53 and fyrie : 95. 53 harme of : 96. E Schot ; R hewmont ; 53
the scheild his hewmond : 100. R me thy dartis ; 53 sayd : 102. R bedewit : 106. E in
the contrair ; R aduersare : 107. 53 towart : 109. 53 the Coislottis : 110. 53 Out throw :
111. 53 bruthir : 112. 53 when : 115. 53 Furht : 119. C *marginal note to improve legibility*
Numytor ; 53 Nymptoure : 120. 53 runseoun : 121. E swakyt ; R to Enee : 123. R achates
thre : 127. R The troianis ; B into : 128. R [And] : 131. R Baith voce sprete and life ; 53
spreith : 132. R 53 was : 134. E in ; R 53 ruschit : 137. R [ilk] : 140. E R 53 of the cite :
143. R barnarge that come : 144. R The ; 53 That cald : 147. E horsman trust ; 53 hors
men : 148. R Now persis his : 149. R 53 roll : 153. R And 3outh sum : 156. R all [sa]
wichtis ; 53 vtheris : 157. R Nor : 158. R rageand seand ; R 53 quhilk : 162. R Contrare ;
R 53 in thare : 164. R lokkit : 166. R The futer.

X.vii. heading. R 53 Quhilk

2. R archady : 4. E R L 53 round ; R barne : 5. R 53 bussis : 8. L [And] : 13. R quhilis
with power : 14. C r *cancelled before* enflambis ; 53 in the : 15. 53 hauyng : 16. R [a] ;
53 vther poyntit : 17. R fle henß : 18. R grete reuerence : 21. R oistis of : 24. E R L B
53 confidence quhilk restis : 26. 53 afore : 30. 53 myddis : 31. R L thikkest ; L [a] ; 53
thikest : 36. E ganestand : 37. R Nor vthir : 41. 53 abstekile : 43. R has left : 46. R fais he
ruschit ; 53 feris he ruschit : 47. E the 3outis ; 53 was : 50. 53 Qham : 51. R 53 his oist :
55. C it *interlined* : 56. 53 Hibane : 58. E or war : 59. R Wod wod for . . . myscheif : 60.
53 in this : 61. R sic was on : 62. R 53 blude : 65. R Than [Pallas] sett he apoun : 69.
E Defoulis : 70. R 53 forlyne : 71. C -ne *cancelled in* twa- : 75. R sic like : 76. 53 Na :
77. R errour on sic : 80. E [Pallas as] : 81. R [sic] ; 53 [rud] : 82. R 53 knawin : 84. R
smytit ; 53 smyttin : 88. 53 thy brand : 89. R ourtane : 90. R archady ; R 53 euerilkane ;
53 Archane : 91. E the barganist thar : 93. E L B for that behald : 94. 53 dochty : 96. R
As he becaus glaidly on thare fleing : 97. R [of] ; L or : 98. R 53 that ilk : 99. 53 [as] :
100. R [had] : 101. R [in] : 103. E tewras ; R For the handis of the ; 53 the handis :
104. C the *interlined* : 106. E R rutilianis : 108. C with *cancelled before* with : 110. 53
in the : 112. R Amangis : 115. R [he] that set thai : 116. L [that] : 118. E [the] ; R wyse

thre hundreth archanys in hye ; 53 Nor vthir : 121. R 53 Bot the Elesus ; R the kene ; L
Bot lo ; 53 in : 122. R 53 to assaill : 124. R And manfully : 125. R of fereß ; 53 and feris :
128. R of he : 130. C myxt *in margin replacing blotted* myxyt ; R quhill of myxt blude :
131. R 53 out of the ; 53 harne . . . harne pan : 132. R The . . . ane witty : 135. R Illesus ;
53 Elesus : 138. R Illesus ; 53 Elesus : 140. R in dedis : 145. E his ; R traist apoun this
cassyn : 146. R That I may throw Illesus body bere : 149. R 53 the bray : 151. R Illesus :
152. E wyth a : 156. R his hede : 158. C sik *in margin* ; E 53 nor bost : 160. R [At] ; R 53
compan3eouns : 162. R [gret] : 163. 53 [sop] : 165. E also ; R invalis : 166. L was : 172.
R And hyndmest : 173. B in steid : 179. 53 age : 180. 53 thay went : 182. R weill away ;
53 weleaway : 186. 53 omipotent : 187. 53 eftar.

X.viii. heading. R and pane

3. R 53 His : 4. E R 53 folkis : 9. R ceiß ; 53 ceis : 10. 53 enterly : 11. R Vnto me : 12. R
to sic : 13. R Glade : 14. E to decerne ; 53 to derne and to espie : 19. R bigging ; 53 of
the : 24. R to spy : 27. C L B belovyt ; 53 Owthir thou . . . belouit : 28. R O riche : 29.
C aduesar ; R for myne : 31. R end and maist : 32. R the boist : 33. R quhilk : 38. L
B towart : 39. E [as] : 41. R broud : 44. R In sic wyse ; 53 In sic like wise, Turnus to
cunnyng : 47. R to ane : 50. 53 help him or support : 53. E B of hewin ; R of the hevin :
54. 53 his maner : 55. R the mychty : 56. R that ilk : 62. R 3ald : 64. R In his tryumphe
with honour : 65. R [hard] : 66. R 53 did grone : 68. R haue wald : 69. E [for] : 70.
R 53 3ettis : 71. R To : 73. C *marginal note* nota ; R wofull mortall ; 53 [wofull] : 75.
R oncoverabill : 82. 53 amang : 83. R blude my kyn and gett : 87. R Off . . . iovy ; 53
Iouie : 89. 53 rutulianis : 91. R Turnus with ane : 94. E L B towartis : 95. 53 Apoun his :
96. E amaist : 98. R Quhen . . . sum parte ; 53 it reuersit : 102. E laying quhill : 107. C
poynt *in margin* : 108. L hys scheild : 113. 53 styntis : 114. 53 thirllis : 115. L at the ; 53
no schrynkand : 116. 53 [heß] : 118. C gidder *cancelled before* passys ; L passyt : 121. C
marginal note inimycall ; R [that] : 122. E [not] : 124. R vpoun him ; L [on] ; 53 apoun
him stand and : 125. R 53 Archady : 130. R [And] . . . quhil he be ; 53 3e be : 132. 53 With
sic solace : 134. R thare ; 53 perfray : 137. E B 53 ouer weltit ; L ourweltyt : 143. 53 Was :
144. R thir : 145. E was ; R 53 bespred : 146. R heuritius : 147. C *marginal note* payntit ;
R 53 payntit : 148. 53 In the wichty : 150. 53 [he] : 151. C L B *marginal note* nota : 152.
E [quhilkis] may be fall ; R 53 changis quhilk : 155. 53 perfray : 156. E the spul3e ; R
his spule3e ; B spul3e of this : 157. R by sa mekle : 159. E to his : 160. R playnt : 163. R
Thow pallas [dolour] and hir wourschip : 169. R 53 in [the] : 170. R L [the].

X.ix. heading. R 53 na ressoun ; 53 Enes

1. 53 Tho name : 3. E of his : 5. R 53 bot ane litill : 6. R That ; 53 to seke : 7. 53 Ane . . .
quhilk : 8. R [the] : 9. R nere : 11. L blait : 14. R the coist : 16. R pretand : 17. E [was] :
22. E L B band [of] : 24. C b *cancelled before* promyß ; R Remembring on ; 53 promyses
and commandis : 25. R L B 53 in his : 26. R quhilk he : 27. E [hecht] ; R 53 fulmon ;
R in the ; 53 war : 29. E R B 53 Vsens : 30. E Quhat : 31. 53 like to walkis : 32. E R L B
and byrnand : 33. E [was] ; R As we the gide with blude and : 38. R 53 as he : 39. R 53
about his : 46. E L B [silly] ; 53 [and] : 47. R To saif ; 53 awne son : 48. R mobill sere :
52. R fyne : 56. C s *cancelled before* na : 58. R L or : 61. E R 53 Thy : 62. R L Quhilk : 66.
R Into this : 67. 53 slaand : 70. 53 thing, perfay has : 71. E hym by the helm ; R helme

thus grippis : 72. R hand als fast : 73. R Bowit downe : 74. E hillis : 75. R far forme
thens : 76. 53 [the] : 78. E to the : 83. 53 to the ground : 85. R brand doun brettynnys :
88. R [preist] : 90. R schulder : 91. R hing his trophe and.

X.x. heading. R [the] ; R 53 kelit

1. L [blude] : 2. R chiftane gude ; L schyftane : 3. R cummyn : 4. L *note at foot of folio*
Ihus Ihus Maria ; 53 reueland : 7. E onto the heich ; R And to ane : 9. L avante : 11. E
[gret] : 12. R And thocht : 13. R hevynnys : 15. R 53 haris : 16. 53 Now now : 17. L Syne
blythlie : 18. 53 tarquyntus : 21. R 53 wynnyng : 23. E bot to the ; R tothir in fere : 25.
R paviß : 26. R Than ; 53 And to : 27. R 53 [full] him humbly : 30. R bathyn : 32. E
trublyst ; R inmortall : 34. R [was] : 40. R *added in later hand* ; spate of wattir of : 41.
E R [the] in the : 42. R Sall with emptive throttis ; 53 emptiue : 44. R the blude : 46. 53
Quhhilkis : 47. R 53 Neuma : 48. R [all of] : 49. E Wolscanis : 50. C fertill *in margin*,
rich *cancelled* : 54. R [armys and] ; 53 [say] : 56. E battale of gigantyne : 57. L 53 fyre
slaucht : 58. 53 [scharp] : 60. R enragit ; 53 enrageing : 61. R [with] : 65. R nympheus
. . . breistis : 66. R cariot : 67. B the ost : 68. 53 stukand : 70. R duke nyheus ; 53 wyde
apon his : 72. E [and] mony : 73. C hoit *cancelled before* hoyt : 74. C charyot *cancelled
before* hys ; 53 into : 75. R The : 80. 53 in that : 82. C *marginal note* sycht ; E 53 sicht ;
R 53 Forganis : 83. R [to] : 84. C nocht *interlined* : 85. R achilles thare persavis : 86. R
athir vmquhile in the feild : 87. R Nocht : 88. R of thi bergane : 89. R thare landis : 91.
R the lyger full lichtlie : 93. 53 pres : 94. L flayng ; 53 flame : 97. R and thare all : 98. R
he thame hit addressit in to : 99. R 53 in to his : 102. E groundyt : 103. R or list ; 104.
E schariot : 107. 53 schyde : 109. E R horß ; 53 hors : 110. R The ; L as : 111. 53 wrinchis
nor : 113. 53 the fais : 114. C Bo lo : 119. 53 and lurkand : 122. C vert *cancelled before*
awyn ; E 53 [thy] thewis ; E mak : 123. E haist of : 124. R [sik] : 125. 53 sylly, wofull :
128. R Euer at : 129. 53 langayr out of : 130. B Serve : 132. R 53 samyn : 133. *R omits
133–139* ; *marginal note in later hand* seven lines are here wanting : 136. 53 and haldis :
137. 53 thys in : 138. C B corpß ; E L corps ; 53 corpis has brocht : 139. 53 ryddand :
140. R *adds extra line* That rynnys ruschand euer in ane state : 144. R of the : 145. R
53 Quhilkis ; R segeit in to vane : 146. 53 has lesit.

X.xi. heading. E persawand ; R persauit has he

8. 53 Thy . . . pussance : 9. 53 I mene : 10. R 53 perrell : 18. E hes ; R had : 22. L
almychely : 24. E Bot as I ; R [at] I : 29. E his patient blude : 31. R 53 neuertheles :
33. R 3our ; 53 Discend : 34. R [to] rekynnand : 39 C *marginal note* etherial ; E R L
B 53 etheriall : 40. E [thus] : 41. 53 askis me, respit : 42. 53 B or ellis a : 45. R richt
ressoun we : 48. 53 thy gate : 50. R I may grant : 55. R alterate all agane : 60. R 53
[thy] ; R wourdis and fataill : 62. R that thow : 64. E Bot turnus : 68. R ane rathare :
71. 53 promyssis : 76. L behyd : 78. L So furth the ayr bownyß furth ; 53 Sche throw :
82. 53 schape ane : 87. E godly heyd ; L godlie heid ; B 53 godly hede : 91. C and*is* ;
E contynens ; 53 hir counterfete and : 92. E R [that] : 93. E of goddis that ; R and
gaistis ; 53 wrachis : 96. R [in] ; 53 driuylling : 103. R evaid and thare that he : 104. R
53 quhirland : 106. R [about] : 107. R [tane] : 108. R woundreth : 109. E corfort : 110.
R L [now] : 115. R [owt] ; 53 safer : 116. R saving ; 53 sauyn, gif : 117. R schoutand he :
118. R and drewe ; 53 brand, with schuke : 129. R vnder the hechis : 132. E and in the

schip can : 135. 53 That sone : 137. R 53 this samyn : 138. R 53 serchis : 141. R the lift and : 143. E hernis heyr to ; L heir to abyde : 144. E L that sammyn : 145. E R L 53 in : 148. E And dyd : 151. R 53 ioyned vp towartis the hevyn ; L *reverses 151–132, indicating correct order by* B A *in margin* : 152. R furth drivis : 154. R As me thow ; 53 As thou : 157. E drevin ; R 53 drive, or : 158. R *added in later hand* : 160. 53 neuir : 161. E L B eftyr : 163. R Quhilk is : 164. R 53 now allace now fechtand : 165. C E L B *parentheses in MSS* ; E [sa] ; R 3onder is schame : 166. E left ; R mynescheus : 168. R in granyng [of] : 169. R 53 to the ground : 171. C L B *parentheses in MSS* ; E [tymys] : 174. R On routtis : 176. R on : 177. 53 Quhil . . . on : 179. R 53 schald ; 53 in the : 180. R and the ; 53 in Cirtis : 181. R [fynd] : 182. R na rumour : 184. R in his mynde did [he] ; 53 he did : 186. 53 or wo : 187. R his fury : 188. R Or with ane swerde stifly in his hand : 189. R [and] : 191. E [the] ; R coistis lay : 193. L presis : 197. R saland out : 199. R 53 souerlie.

X.xii.

1. E L B this tyme quhill ; 53 in the fatis ; R the fatis : 2. 53 wyth furoure : 4. E in to his ; R [the] : 5. R [And] : 8. R 53 Semblit the ; R haill oist [of] : 10. R 53 thare routis : 12. R [schour] ; R 53 schaftis at him schutis : 13. E [a] ; R [to] rout : 14. L Strekis : 17. R the violence : 20. E our movyt ; R [hys] ; L from [in] his : 22. E R 53 [the] ; 53 fyllit : 25. 53 Palynus : 26. R brittynnys ; 53 Licagus : 28. R With quhilk [hym] : 29. R hoch ; 53 Palynus : 32. 53 sulderis : 33. 53 The : 36. 53 [and] ane euin : 37. L the nycht : 41. C E R L B 53 [samyn] : 44. R 53 thare ; 53 vnkend : 48. E venquest ; R [quest] mony cry and : 49. E L drivin : 51. R ald : 53. R 53 fed weill : 54. L Amangis : 55. L Besydis ; 53 laurent : 56. R betrappit as efferis : 58. R Standis all the ; R 53 vp the ; L Standand ; B in the bay : 59. R with his sterne ; 53 Graissand : 60. 53 [and] tene : 61. 53 hunt mene : 62. R 53 aggreue : 63. E approche : 67. 53 [all] : 69. R [iust] : 72. E L or : 74. E [durst] ; 53 durst nane cum : 76. E Hym : 79. R [the] : 80. R cummyn ; 53 cumming . . . Arto : 81. E one to : 83. R Quha : 89. 53 empty, rageand : 94. R 53 vprisis : 96. E trymbilis ; R trymlis ; 53 trouch : 98. L [the] : 103. 53 [in] : 107. E R L B 53 quhilk : 108. R wise and as : 109. 53 hys bake : 110. R 53 Vnwarnyst : 113. R 53 was of prattik mare all : 116. R with ane : 118. 53 beis, baith blyith : 126. R 53 sall neuer : 129. R 53 [lang] : 132. R 53 The : 133. L Men3entyus : 135. R 53 almychty : 137. E sayand this ; R thus wound and body did he drawe : 138. R *substitutes 137* : 139. E R 53 To . . . dois : 141. 53 anone ful richt : 142. C lycht *cancelled before* nycht ; 53 and euirlesting : 148. C Ly *cancelled before* Erycates : 149. E erd be our : 150. C *marginal note to improve legibility* had ; R [had] : 152. R in fute : 153. R him that went : 156. R expert : 158. 53 in the : 160. E or a ; 53 casting dar.

X.xiii.

1. R 53 equale : 2. C rasyt *cancelled before* apon ; 53 He : 4. E [ar] : 5. E in feyr ; R 53 in fere : 7. R wist nor he ; B wyß : 8. R thai fie ; 53 or quhare : 11. R of the : 14. C E R L B 53 [of] : 17. E L B [the] : 19. R And ; 53 principale : 29. E Quhilkis : 32. R [speir] ; B helm speir : 41. C fleand *in margin* : 43. 53 you : 45. R trophe and : 49. R [the] : 50. E byrnand : 52. C *in margin* ; E 3onder : 53. R achates ; 53 Achores : 55. R of the gret : 57. R archadence : 58. R [maid] : 60. R [thus] : 61. 53 dynt within the : 63. R behald can the ; 53 He deand he : 64. R 53 can behald his : 65. R [the] : 66. E [Quhilk] [all] ;

L Menȝentius ; 53 dyd all : 67. 53 his arge : 68. E [And] : 69. R [the] ; 53 playis : 70. E
[law] : 72. R [tho] : 73. E Ioyfull men and Meȝentius ; L Menȝentius : 80. E saltis teris ;
R teris out our : 86. C to *interlined* : 90. R the scheild ; 53 lance fast, fixit : 101. C with
cancelled before hys : 102. R thai lorde : 104. 53 feirs aduersare : 106. R he haldis him :
108. L furgh ȝettand : 111. E ȝong vnder ; L ȝonder ; B ȝon : 115. E in the ; 53 on [the] :
116. R quhen he schynes : 118. 53 Siclike Ene : 119. 53 vnbeset : 123. R 53 mannysand ;
C L B *parentheses enclosing line* : 125. R vndertakin to : 127. R art now now wyse : 128.
E allout : 129. 53 Lausus then al hale : 130. R [ceß] : 132. E schyr : 134. R [lattyr] : 136.
53 the ȝoungkere : 139. R This : 142. R rede blude ; 53 has fillit : 144. R law that sad :
145. R syne did : 149. E R L B in ; R Becummyng : 151. 53 draif abak : 154. E Empretit :
156. R walit : 161. R thow sum tyme : 166. R in to ; 53 or ellis into : 168. 53 counfort :
174. 53 handis : 177. E Besparkyt ; R 53 Besparkit : 178. R 53 was.

X.xiv. heading. E [the]

2. 53 flude : 3. R Stancheand : 4. 53 swete, and blude : 5. E R L B [hang] ; R His held : 6.
R grane ane branche : 8. C in *interlined* ; E L B [in] ; R on the : 9. 53 His crafty : 11. E L B
[wery] : 12. R oure the . . . sore grones ; 53 sary : 18. E [hym] : 19. R betid na : 20. R 53 for
him quhat sorow ; R has tane : 22. E cheyld : 24. L with a gryslie woynd ; 53 discumfest :
26. L quhilk ; 53 war tho betyde : 34. R [get] : 36. E L B [sa] : 37. 53 ony stede : 38. E thi
fais ; R 53 handis : 39. 53 sa I : 42. R thy sa : 45. R 53 vnsufferable ; L onsufferabill : 48. R
with ane : 49. R 53 the caus was : 51. R my name : 54. E [thar] : 55. 53 Expellit has, my :
59. R silly saul : 61. 53 offence : 65. R Bot sovirly : 67. C vp *cancelled before* hym : 69. R
[hys] : 71. R vndekkit : 75. 53 his hors : 77. 53 but ony mare : 78. R [sad] : 80. R [to] : 81.
E O my tyme ; 53 lang of (quod he) : 82. 53 reuengit : 84. L B with me bringyn : 86. 53
strenth, nor force : 87. E Mycht ; L that I be : 89. C myst forcy *cancelled*, moist *in margin* ;
R 53 o thow moist : 91. R vthir : 92. 53 dedenete : 93. R my maister : 94. E 53 cowartly ;
R cowardly : 95. R [bekend] : 96. E he at he a eyß : 97. C *marginal note* handis ; E R
L B 53 handis : 99. R Apoun . . . tymbrell : 101. C swyft *in margin* ; R [swyft] coursis :
105. R [of] his : 106. R fury ; 53 to : 108. R 53 His hors : 112. R gan eftir him ; 53 towart :
113. E L B says he fader : 114. R grantit me : 115. 53 begyn the bargane : 116. R [to] : 117.
E This ; L 53 carpis : 119. 53 se, and : 123. R has bereft me : 126. E [that] ; R wardly ; 53
warldly : 127. R 53 abhor I ; R [to] stoure in : 128. B of my goddis : 129. E me and ; 53
or ceis : 130. R 53 cummyn : 132. C at his fa a dart leyt *in margin*, leyt a dart at his fa
cancelled : 136. R thare dartis ; R 53 sufierit the : 137. R half thryiß as : 139. R [hys] : 143.
R of his · 149. R 53 at ane avantage : 150. 53 thyngis : 152. R horß : 154. 53 Upstendit : 156.
R syne with : 158. R [can] ; 53 hys teyld vnfald : 160. E R 53 dynlit · 162. E fordwart ; 53
Hynt furt : 163. R [he] ; L Menȝentius : 164. 53 stout feirs : 165. R that ilk : 166. R mycht
haue liftit : 167. B Tho se : 169. 53 dispitefull : 170. R thow me chydis reprevand : 171. 53
And Mannassis me the to ded : 173. 53 on feild : 176. L or ; 53 comnandis : 178. E [the] :
182. R In sepulture : 190. E And throu ; R gorgett ; 53 gorge it went : 192. 53 bruschis
. . . stremes grete : 193. C L *bracket around 193–198, marginal note* Additio ; R *heading*
Additio : 194. 53 Rutilianis : 195. 53 [the] : 196. E [bald] : 197. L 53 With draw.

ending. E *as* C *adding* Heyr endis the tent buik with al that belangis it and syn cumyis
the lewynt buik and his proloug anno domini *etc.* ; R *as* C *except adding* in, *and*
librum *for* eiusdem ; L B *as* C ; 53 Finis.

BOOK XI

Prologue, heading. E The proloug of the lewynt buik of the aneneados ; R B *omit* ; L
Prologus ; 53 The prolog of the xi buk of Eneados

1. R The ; 53 How hie : 2. E [gentill] : 3. E R 53 defy : 8. R dicist : 9. R previt mekill
thing : 10. R The haly : 11. E Iove : 13. R of the : 14. 53 mind : 15. 53 None vyle strokis :
16. R budge staff polax swer knyfe ; 53 budgeis, staf polax swerd nor mace : 17. E
repeats stanza, variants recorded as E and E2 ; E2 or in ; R takin that the ; 53 takin . . .
and fecht : 18. R Off myndis : 19. E *omits 19–20* ; E2 fundin ; 53 groundit : 20. R 30w :
22. E 53 the querrell : 23. E E2 addreß : 25. 53 mortall : 29. C says *in margin* : 30. E or
cors : 31. 53 thame not traisting, in ther fors : 32. R [mercy] : 35. R 53 heich : 36. 53
boet set : 37. R Off quhilk . . . that ane : 38. E a vice : 41. E out my mesur : 43. E R L
B thingis ; R 53 Nor : 48. E R 53 dois ; R 53 and manhede samyn smure : 50. R 53 he
avysit be ; L be avysyt : 52. 53 cowarines : 53. E comt : 54. E R 53 dois : 55. R [now] :
56. R 53 Quhareof of : 57. R Giff of crystis faith . . . we be ; 53 [faithfull] : 59. R may :
60. R Nor : 62. E witnessit ; R 53 witnessis : 63. R [hym reddy] : 68. R [gospell] : 72. E
fyr : 73. R and our : 74. 53 teachis : 80. 53 reuel : 85. R The secund fra the ; B The : 88.
53 The : 89. E maister in thi ; R is maister : 90. E this ward is ; R is : 91. R to feyndis ;
R 53 with slicht and all ; 53 to freyndis : 92. 53 the ancient : 94. R 53 the flesche : 95. 53
causit : 99. L [he] : 100. 53 contrary : 101. 53 in the land : 102. R hope of hope : 105. 53
at the defence : 106. R ar rent : 108. 53 the lord : 109. 53 thou art : 110. C E L B payn is
nochtis ; R pane as nocht is : 53 pane nocht is : 111. R 53 how with : 112. 53 And aye vnto
his wourd thy mynd be bent : 114. E bene : 116. R debait than ; B sic fycht ; 53 Thay
mayd . . . lithlie : 118. E R 53 will : 122. E venquest : 123. R [nevir] : 127. E venquest ;
R By dissate ; 53 vincust : 130. E R in all : 132. 53 any : 133. B and gret ; 53 greter : 137.
R bergane or strung ; 53 walis : 139. 53 and fele : 140. E his victory ; 53 [thar] : 142.
53 sa quha : 143. E [euer] ; R or campioun ; 53 conquerour, ane campioun : 146. R 53
techis ws so ; L [so] : 147. R 53 And to : 148. E dekit : 150. R malivolus : 151. L grace of
his : 154. E [may] : 155. R [thou fallys] : 156. L gettis heir ; 53 Of the . . . gettis it : 158.
R [thar] : 159. R 53 eternal : 160. L Restoryte ; 53 with the grace : 161. 53 the fall : 162.
R This : 164. E *reverses 164–165* ; R ar : 167. R [That] Thow gettis nocht : 168. E stand
in stable ; R stand : 170. 53 seruandis : 174. E *first hand resumes until 184* : 178. E That
of ; R cuntre I behest : 179. E be land : 181. R Quhill his realm he : 183. E Presß : 184.
53 attene : 191. R [for the] : 192. R 53 at bargane : 194. R 53 thir paganis : 199. R The
quhilk hecht hevyn throw the to succeid ; 53 echt : 200. E bocht and wrocht.

ending. E *as* C *adding* Heyr endis the proloug one the lewynt buik and eftyr cummys
syne the buik of samyng vytht the fyrst cheptour anno domini *etc.* ; R L B *as* C ; 53
Finis The .xi. booke of Eneados.

XI.i. heading. L *omits*

4. R Constrenyng : 9. R [eik] in mynde als he : 8. E deip corps ; R Off : 9. R nevertheless
as 3it the : 14. R sched and : 15. E L B montis : 17. R [armour] thareon gart hang ; 53
coist armour : 18. B a vail3eand : 21. E L hewmont ; R 53 hewmond : 24. 53 in : 25.
R 53 on his : 27. E stalwart fyne ; R scawart : 29. E L B lowkyt syne war : 30. R war ;
53 Quhilkis glaidsum werren : 32. R grete ; 53 party : 36. R hand : 38. 53 wallis, and

laurent : 41. R weilfare : 44. L other way : 45. R 53 Bot 3our : 46. R 53 [the] : 47. 53 god : 48. R 53 takynnys : 52. E 3e than [all] reddy be but ; R [than] : 53. E meyn tym ; 53 [in] : 54. R corps ; 53 and vnbegraue : 55. L Quhilk ony honour : 56. R lawis : 57. R [tha] ; B the ; C val3eent : 58. R Quhilkis : 59. R this wyse : 61. E *first hand resumes* ; 53 with the : 62. C E L B corpß ; R corps : 63. 53 Euandrus : 70. R lyand : 72. R flokkerend : 73. R befor ; 53 be : 75. 53 cum in to : 76. 53 that tyme : 77. R [in] : 78. R And : 79. R with multitude : 80. R commonis troianis stout ; 53 commouns troianis : 82. E L B [and] cryis ; R [schaik] : 85. B raiß : 86. C lyft *in margin*, lyft *blotted in line* : 87. R thir : 88. R place : 91. R nocht mycht ; 53 [mycht] : 95. E this plenyt ; R [thus] ; 53 brist, and : 96. R Ane : 98. 53 art thou : 100. 53 3it, ane victor : 101. R 53 ciete, haue retoure : 105. R [me] : 107. R avise be : 109. R Wald were and sterf sa we had were at hand : 113. R 53 dois : 116. R for the : 120. R [corps] : 124. R this bere be laid ; 53 awin son, on this bere : 127. R nocht murn thi : 129. R Now thow . . . war thow ; 53 Not thou : 131. L [he] : 132. R the spreith ; 53 he has : 133. R neuertheles : 136. R grete dule.

XI.ii. heading. R 53 Now Pallas ; 53 to hys

1. L in : 8. R 53 the murnyng : 11. 53 According : 14. R preisß thame ; 53 Flokis : 15. R [for] ; 53 beild vp ane : 17. L B or [the] twistis : 18. R and stobbis : 19. 53 beildit, on funerall : 20. R and as ; L *omits* : 23. R quhilk ; L on : 25. R Bigging : 26. R schynand bounte : 29. E doith : 30. R floure that hate : 32. R confort at hir ; 53 nurissis : 33. 53 schyne : 37. R [vmquhile] : 38. R [sik] ; B bissy so I ; 53 besely : 40. R handis it [to hym] wrocht ; B to hir : 46. E hair : 47. R Quhilk ; R 53 [for] : 52. 53 [and] : 54. R horß ; 53 as he : 55. 53 vtheris : 56. E [the] : 57. E he hed did tak ; R quhen he : 58. R 53 sendis : 59. E attyrment : 62. E 53 strinklit : 64. E R and pomp : 65. C of *cancelled before* or ; E R L B 53 of trene ; R 53 pykis : 66. 53 [the] : 69. 53 silly Achates : 70. R 53 age of sorow : 71. E R L B 53 bludy and ; 53 with his awin breist : 79. E L wend ; R wo 3e mycht : 86. R and of the thirrene : 87. R [of] dolour and weris : 88. E *second hand resumes* : 91. E abyd : 93. E ther ; 53 thire : 95. R Tellis : 100. E L and ennoy ; R 53 Enterit.

XI.iii. heading. C B corpß ; E corpiß : R eneas to . . . corps

1. R 53 cummyn : 2. R 53 Embassiatouris : 3. B of benevolens : 5. R corps . . . the bentis broun ; L 53 quhilk ; 53 corpis : 6. R Law : 7. E all thame ; R gentricee ; 53 gentrice : 9. 53 Assuring thame : 10. R Vnvyncust folkis : 13. E L B [that] ; L heyn : 16. R hate desire : 18. E quham ; R vnfortoun : 22. L this cost : 25. R cummyn I say perfay : 27. 53 promoult : 28. R Ne mare . . . lede we : 30. R [heß] · 31 R [his] ; 32. E equaly : 33. C our *interlined* : 36. R Or for to were oure troianis : 38. 53 in the feild : 40. R [with] hald our ; 53 ouer his : 42. C *marginal note* or wrachit ; E L B wrachit ; R 53 corps . . . wrechit : 45. E wondrit ; 53 this speich, so wounderit : 46. 53 [quhat] : 47. R towartis vthir ; 53 towart [vtheris] Turnus : 51. L at him : 52. E [or] ; R of the ; 53 Or auld : 55. E [far] : 56. L and the : 57. R loving ; 53 louyng equale, I may : 58. R [the] goddis : 61. E [gret] ; E L B fors or ; R For thi ; L thi for fors ; 53 Or the : 62. R hamewart fare we : 64. R Thir ar sa : 65. E L B [that] ; R change : 66. L fully at that : 67. 53 To the conoine : 68. 53 That Turnus : 70. R massy fataill : 74. R anherdis ; 53 Thare to cryis, wyth : 77. R of thir : 80. E B heschis : 81. E L B [the] : 82. R 53 strax : 83. R L [on] : 84. B [the] : 85. R [with] ; 53 propppis : 86. R chyde : 87. 53 girgirand.

XI.iv. heading. L was dede onto him

2. 53 of the grete : 3. R Flewe : 6. R latyne ; R 53 land : 12. R In : 14. 53 soueraly : 16. L
[folkis] : 17. 53 matronus : 18. R L B 53 went : 20. R 53 pietuous ; 53 glouling : 21. R 53
mycht nocht refrene : 22. R [in] : 23. R plene3eand ; 53 Plen3eand : 24. R aboue dane
pallas ; L B in growfe : 27. R at the last : 28. E was : 30. R 53 the last : 32. E mayr warldly :
36. 53 into : 37. R L 53 and glory : 38. L renown and of chevalry : 39. R commendment :
40. R bene werefull fey : 42. E nocht bene : 44. R nane goddis of all : 47. E persauit :
48. E L B [the] ; 53 Bot to the : 49. E fattale : 51. C mortal *cancelled before* sammyn ;
R [sammyn] : 55. E [that] : 57. R 3one troianis : 59. 53 hand and promyssis : 61. R
infortoun : 62. R And thareto ; 53 detborne : 63. R Bot [had] thy haisty : 64. R Had
sufferit ; 53 Sufferit haue : 67. 53 Latinum : 69. R [eik] : 70. R 53 lay the : 75. R Sa grete ;
53 Sa riche trophee, and riche : 76. R And parkis : 77. R 53 has : 78. R 53 the samyn ; 53
Durnus : 79. R 53 [thou] : 81. 53 equale, of peris : 89. R 53 his hatesum : 90. R [the] :
92. R and to the fader : 97. R lust of life lang : 98. R Welesum war : 100. R deith to
me : 101. E as to : 102. 53 and skuggis.

XI.v. heading. R dede folkis

2. R to every : 7. R coistis bowand : 9. E eldris dayis ; E L B into that ; R one that ; 53
eldaris, gif that vnto that : 10. C B corpß ; R L corps : 13. E walx in dyrk ; R [that] :
14. R reky skyes : 15. E triß : 16. 53 sceynand . . . feris ran : 18. 53 horsis bak : 19. 53
gowing : 20. C terys *cancelled before* trigland ; E teris miserable : 23. E L B trumphis ;
53 an trumpis : 24. 53 on hecht : 25. 53 dois : 26. R spule3eing ; L spul3eit : 27. R B Reft ;
53 in the : 28. E suerdis and riche scheyldis : 29. R 53 thare stedis : 30. L charyotis :
31. E R 53 And athir : 34. R 53 nocht thame : 35. R mony of thare cartage oxin : 37.
53 bustuous bonkis, of thr : 40. R Endland ; R 53 all the : 41. R [that] : 46. E fyr : 47.
R nevertheles : 50. C B corpß ; R L 53 corps ; 53 bedeluit : 51. E thai stent : 52. E To
turnus : 53. 53 was : 56. E *first hand resumes* ; R or but : 57. R 53 corps : 59. 53 [of] : 60.
E And that : 62. R 53 [a] : 63. R and trumpis out : 64. R amouris : 65. R vnclosit : 66.
R erde thame graif ; L thame all in ; 53 and to the erd thame graue : 70. R Ar bewalit
all : 73. L behald : 76. R Cryand ilkane allace ; 53 ych ane : 79. R All with ane : 82.
E to weir the ; R *omits 82–85* ; L [the] quhilk ; 53 pretendit : 85. 53 aggregris : 92. E
defendis he with : 94. R sustene amangis thame.

XI.vi. heading. L fra diomeid

3. E L B haymwartis ; R thare made nede ; L in : 9. E L B request : 10. 53 people : 11.
53 Behuffis : 12. R with the : 15. R 53 patientlie . . . he thocht : 17. E R 53 did hym : 24.
R [hym] : 25. R man : 26. E cheir athall : 30. R all haill ; L all thare ; 53 alhale : 34. E L
B planly furth at : 35. L 3e haue : 41. R the sammyn : 42. L quham at troy : 43. E now
in victor ; R L B is victor ; R in his : 44. E gardane : 45. E Iapidia ; R 53 the boundis ;
53 of Iaripia : 46. E L B in dayis ; R clepit : 47. R agrapas ; 53 Uprasing : 48. R 53 he
namyt was : 53. R were was socht : 54. L hydder : 55. C on *in margin* : 56. R 53 ansuerd
he with : 57. R 3e fortunate folk quhen ; 53 quham : 58. R 53 The : 61. E mofing ; R
moving rest and : 63. E evirane ; L B euer ane : 66. E R [of] : 67. R 53 all thame : 71.
E L B hail [the] ; R Off all : 72. E with our hersabil ; R oure hersable : 75. 53 of god

mynerue : 79. R And in the menetyme caphereus : 82. R We castin ar : 83. E and all
heritage : 85. 53 clepit : 86. R Pryamydes ; 53 Priamedes : 87. E *second hand resumes* ;
Constrenyt ws in : 91. R neptoloneus ; 53 I say of Neoptoloneus : 94. 53 Idomeus : 95.
R did to bell : 96. 53 hym agayne, of : 97. E the acris : 99. R 53 Syne ; R in grete : 101.
R And all . . . ost : 103. R [awyn] ; L B Than by : 108. C *marginal note* Honeste taxat
coniugis adulterum ; R native cuntre ; 53 [in] : 109. R sa as : 112. L selcough : 113. E
runs together 113–114 My feris lost lykis ar fleand our alquhair : 117. R of the : 118. R
coist ; 53 resoundis : 119. R Thare : 120. R 53 me betid : 121. R [I] : 125. E he ne persaude
ne nocht : 126. R [That] : 129. B debait : 130. R hundreth 3eris ; B hidder 3eris ; L 53
hunder 3eris : 131. 53 bald to : 133. R The : 134. E R L B 53 Quhilk ; E L B 53 out of :
135. 53 [the] : 140. R how sturely : 141. R how with grete ; R 53 [a] : 142. L towart ; 53
aduersaris : 143. 53 I said : 146. R had dred : 147. 53 And of the : 148. 53 realme : 149.
E L B gret suld ; R 53 grete suld : 153. R [by] the handis : 156. R prolongit ws : 158. L
B vassillage : 161. 53 That this . . . out al : 162. 53 conmpassioun : 163. R Thare [for] :
165. E R 3e se : 166. R in arme3 ; 53 we stert : 169. R haue 3e herd.

XI.vii. heading. R 53 and tharto

7. R with the ; 53 [is] : 9. R skellyis vnder dynnyt lynnys : 10. 53 dymmys : 11. R [that]
the mudis : 19. E nocht as sic : 20. 53 for to : 21. R Quhat that ; 53 Quhat our : 23. R
marginal note nota : 24. 53 inportune : 25. R goddis clene discend : 28. E Nor nocht
thai : 29. 53 resist : 30. E L B haue : 32. C L B *marginal note* additio : 33. R 53 for thare
men : 35. R self him hope : 36. C but *cancelled before* traste ; R traist as 3e : 37. R ene
eik 3e may ; 53 3e may : 38. E quhat gret : 39. R L vtheris : 40. R being braid amangis :
45. R [so] ; L [that] ; 53 is it so : 47. B of my mynd : 48. R harkyn ; 53 harknes : 51.
R *omits, leaving space* : 52. E R L quhilk : 53. 53 armitane : 55. B 53 stokkis : 56. E B
hirskis ; 53 Thare hard : 57. R hillis harß ; 53 hars : 58. E L 53 dois : 60. C as *interlined* :
69. 53 The othir : 70. R [ay] : 71. R [be] : 72. R May se departe : 76. C all reddy *cancelled
before* by ; R reddy all ; 53 ther lyis now all : 77. 53 and the maner : 80. R [the] : 82. R
L the prince : 83. R to constrene : 85. R blude and of : 90. R 53 for a : 91. 53 amang :
92. R oure pepill ; 53 febil, wile : 93. R and to speke ; L spake agane : 95. E sayd to
laytly : 102. R For cauld : 104. E and wyß : 107. R nobill lanrent : 110. R that ilk : 111. R
turnus and ourecharge : 112. E [on hym] ; L B in him : 117. R grantit : 118. R Quhilk :
121. R causis : 123. R mene by him : 126. R [all] : 127. R 53 braik : 128. E R dois ; R 53
mannace : 131. E L B 53 Quhilkis ; R Quhilk that he had : 133. 53 for to : 134. B doith :
140. 53 ony man dant : 142. 53 of whurthy blude : 146. R 53 With all eternall : 147. R
53 grete dredour or : 148. R mynde in oure : 149. R we wald do sic · 152. K [hym] :
159. E *first hand resumes* ; E L B Quhairfor : 161. R werefare : 162. E L B 53 [the] ; 53
halile : 164. R [the] : 165. E to [be] : 166. E my consait ; 53 quhilk is, by : 168. R [weill] :
169. E So fortune I : 170. E L B [now] : 174. E strange bute and : 175. C L B corpß ; E
anew ; R 53 corps ; R ynewe bett doun : 176. C bedeyn *cancelled before* betweyn ; R
[all] : 182. E R L 53 drowry ; R [thy] : 186. 53 recounter agane, thy : 187. R that effect :
192. E [thou] ; 53 assayit : 194. E Of mercyall ; L B O marciall : 196. R Behaldand thy
fa provocand to the ficht : 197. C L B *marginal note* additio propter emisticio : 198. E
second hand resumes ; 53 go tude.

XI.viii.

1. 53 mind : 2. R sic wourdis ; L hait has fyre : 3. R Sichand so depe richt in : 4. E L B petuus mon : 5. R 53 Drances forsuth quod he : 14. E 53 dois : 15. R forteresß : 16. E L B blude ; R gesß : 19. R [than] ; L beyne myne : 20. R oft fere ; 53 or cowardise : 22. R troianis he laid : 23. 53 vnwourthely : 24. E in feyldis ; R feild ; 53 fild : 27. 53 And als : 28. R 53 thens : 29. E plantit : 30. E thame to mak : 34. E in that [wont] ; R 53 in thi : 38. 53 and doung : 40. 53 troyanis : 41. 53 the femel, of : 42. E Brocht all to : 45. R lityus ; L bysyas ; 53 bytais : 48. E to heill ; R send haue away ; B send him away ; 53 Is vyctor : 52. R that I declare : 54. E And spy ; R 53 thingis ; R on thi : 56. R perturb : 57. 53 fellound : 58. 53 3our pepill : 63. R War 3e nobill : 64. R Quhilk in : 67. R assidus ; 53 Ansidus : 68. R contare mont : 69. R The quhilk also the : 70. C controvar *written more legibly in margin* : 72. R contrar : 77. R or : 78. 53 Sic and peuis : 80. R thy wretchit : 89. E return to regreß : 92. 53 richt arme : 93. E [beit] ; R beit I wald : 94. E curage of manheid ; R or of manhede : 96. R think : 99. R as thare selvyn ; L Quhill ; 53 Quhilkis [that] : 100. R ne schulden : 101. R 53 Feld : 103. E thou haue : 104. E freß ; R 53 And evir : 109. R 53 betid as traistis ; 53 victor : 110. C L B corpß ; E corpiß ; R 53 corps : 111. R Giff that tempestuous : 114. R of our ficht : 116. R blast of : 118. R hang ; 53 hing : 119. R ane likly : 122. L [ane] : 124. R 53 estate : 125. E *first hand resumes* : 127. E R L B and supple ; R 53 to cum ; 53 help : 128. R weill wylle : 130. E R L B 53 the othir : 134. R laurens : 135. E [we] : 136. R famyllis [and] : 137. E R 53 thair armyt : 139. E R B euer ane : 140. 53 to feill, fecht in : 141. C the *interlined and in margin* : 146. R Now list : 147. E [suld] : 148. R Micht mycht sa : 149. C will *cancelled before* I : 150. R in prowes he past : 153. B and my fader king latyne in law : 156. E owir elderiß ; 53 To name of : 157. R [the] : 158. E Doyß . . . 3owir : 159. E schallancis ; R challance ; L challangis : 160. E schallance : 161. E *second hand resumes* ; R [deir] : 162. 53 [that] : 163. E R 53 wraikfull wraik : 164. R or honour : 166. E [it] ; R [not].

XI.ix. heading. C ost *interlined* ; E as I said ; 53 his stoi, about

1. C gret *in margin* : 2. R of doutsum : 5. R ruschand with grete haist : 6. 53 rautis : 7. R huge armour and effererull ; 53 [a] : 10. R [that] : 15. R pepill : 19. R [a] : 22. R felloun cryis and noyis : 23. 53 [and] : 24. R [a] : 26. R vp in the ; 53 opinionus : 28. R birdis fedderis the : 29. R vocis of swannys : 30. E wyth sangis ; R 53 souchand ; R with noyus : 31. R 53 lemand stankis : 35. E tak : 36. R sais : 37. R it nocht lat : 38. R 3oure ciete : 39. R 53 [to] : 42. R L nobillis that stude : 44. 53 stanrdatis : 47. R thoras : 50. 53 part : 53. R the hale ; 53 3our hale : 56. E thai can in ; 53 thay vp in : 58. R quhilk : 60. E Thrist : 62. R sleuth ; 53 sleuchit : 64. B for weir of : 66. E maigh : 67. L Sum to thair : 72. E In sing : 74. R diuerß and mony : 77. L tho for age : 80. C and *in margin, replacing* of *cancelled* ; E L B of pallas ; R 53 And to : 82. L matronys ane nobill : 84. 53 Lauinna : 87. R *omits, leaving space* : 89. 53 warpis vp on : 90. R Also as : 94. C virginal *in margin replacing* virginyal *cancelled* : 98. 53 mych se.

XI.x. heading. E to suppreß

3. R [the] : 4. R cloiß turett : 6. E wofull : 7. C With *interlined*, Hys *cancelled* ; R with platis : 9. 53 The : 16. R [the] courseris : 18. 53 [out] : 19. E haldis our the ; R towartis

the studis fast in ; 53 stedis : 20. R 53 meris walkis : 21. R And than : 23. R proude walloppis he ; 53 waloppis hie : 25. E L B [lang] ; R 53 lang nek : 26. R 53 lokkerand : 28. R brandis : 33. L hir horssis : 34. R on this wise : 35. R 53 said : 36. 53 or 3it assure : 44. R 53 in the buschement : 47. R werely ; R 53 for to se ; 53 verely : 48. R on this wyse : 51. 53 to thy : 52. R [art] : 54. R tyme in sic : 55. E L B in athir : 56. R [the] bargane we divide : 59. R And that : 63. R His self : 64. R strate derne passage and will : 65. R Schapis in oure : 67. R ane buschment : 68. R and secrete : 71. 53 horssit tuskane : 75. R Thay : 77. E [thou] ; R thame and reule : 78. R that army in to ryall were : 82. R 53 towartis : 86. E R 53 dois ; R 53 hamperith : 88. R or [a] : 91. 53 thy hill : 92. R 53 mycht spy ; 53 fare sycht : 94. R the stede : 95. 53 sobir : 96. 53 enbushment : 104. R [wod].

XI.xi. heading. L *omits*

4. R sort may 3eris : 16. R vnfor3ett : 17. R 53 Mechabus : 20. R the ciete : 21. R bare now 30ng ; 53 the 30ung : 23. R his moderis : 27. C thar *in margin* : 28. E partyis ; R in all : 29. B wageouris of Volscanys : 32. R enterit he : 33. E Amasonus ; R Amastynis : 34. E brais bukit as ; R bokkit : 37. R to sovme at : 38. R And for the lufe [bab] : 39. 53 dreading : 40. 53 Ilk change . . . did row : 41. 53 prentis in his ; 53 his sentence [prent] : 45. E R 53 styf : 47. R chaft [sad and] : 48. R 53 his bark : 50. R the lance : 54. R O wylde : 55. R O fader : 57. R his fais : 58. R 53 the schaft : 59. R Ressaue this lady : 61. R stand in the : 66. 53 of he schaftis : 68. R 53 The : 69. R 53 quhirlland : 70. R 53 mechabus : 71. R 53 [cum] ; 53 fais him sa nere : 74. R ane maid ; 53 buklith : 75. R Ane present : 76. 53 had : 78. R Wald he ; 53 thyr wallys : 79. 53 [thocht] : 81. E R that the maner : 83. 53 buskis rouk : 84. R sloggy ; L scroggis ; 53 sloggy ouk : 87. R Off sa greyne rage stude : 88. C *marginal note* or breistis ; E L B 53 breistis ; R tyme he thare preistis : 89. C child *cancelled before* get ; E of his breystis get ; R his grete gett ; L B his breistis get : 90. R on erde : 91. R B his solis ; 93. 53 fist : 94. E R 53 buklyt on hes he ; 53 sulder : 95. R 53 and ane litill : 96. E L B and hed : 97. R 53 garmont of pall : 98. E R Oure hyr schulderis ; 53 hir suldderis : 101. E R L B did glyde ; R and thir : 102. R the hede : 103. R of [the] stout stiff staf slyng : 105. R or 3it the : 106. R desirit of : 109. C -ly *cancelled after* ferm- : 111. E to hand : 113. C Remand : 117. R 53 [scho] : 118. R [at] ; 53 is oft, al : 119. E [Opys] ; 53 anone now nymphe : 122. L and assy : 124. 53 has sche : 125. R Tak my dartis . . . this case : 128. R onto men : 129. 53 Quhithir · 130. 53 is elike : 131. R 53 dere by : 133. R Amyd the leß clowdis : 134. R and array : 138. E R swouchand ; 53 doun glade : 140. R Indekkit ; 53 Addekkit.

XI.xii.

6. R in his gardis and were wedis : 8. C E L B his hedis ; R 53 his hede ; R [can] ; 53 trypand . . . did cast : 9. R ground richt grisle : 10. R With : 13. R 53 anone also : 17. 53 or wolscane : 19. R speris on fer ; 53 stroke : 20. E L Drewin thair ; R chargit wele fer : 21. R [taclys] and felloun flanys : 22. R To counter the first ; B and first : 24. 53 to Ioue in : 25. R on stedis : 30. R and armour : 31. R The ferß ; 53 bargane there : 34. R fleand takis ; 53 [thik] : 35. E R 53 dois ; R 53 that flicht : 37. R [tho] : 39. R semblit and with : 41. R 53 met : 42. R all in schunderis with ; 53 schudderis : 45. R 53 [to] : 51. 53 ane fray : 52. E L B bedene all fled : 53. R All scheildis oure ; 53 sulderis : 55. E persaving : 57. 53 approche in, to : 66. R 53 the samyn wallis : 67. 53 coweris : 69. C

fard swyft *correct order indicated by* b a *interlined* ; 53 farde swift : 70. E bukand ; R bukkand iassis and oure swak ; 53 Iawis and ouerswak : 72. R 53 and schaldis plane : 73. C tuscane *interlined above cancelled* latyn ; latynnys *interlined and repeated in margin*, Tuscanys *cancelled* ; R on this wyse : 75. R 53 gaif : 79. E schosin : 85. E L B Bet doun lay : 86. E encreß ; 53 encrestis : 90. E R horß ; 53 hors : 92. E as fylt ; R 53 And lavsus apoun : 93. E onpacient : 94. R to the : 97. R 53 armynyus ; 53 cors : 103. R 53 Forganis ; R bownys he ; 53 bustuously : 105. C *marginal note* or braid ; E R L B 53 braid ; R 53 schulderis : 106. R stude stakkerand : 107. 53 persit : 108. R It doublit : 110. R of werkis woundis : 111. E batht ; R bathis : 112. C E L B corpß ; E in the feill fell ; R 53 corps ; R lay dede : 114. R 53 the richt.

XI.xiii.

1. E may ; R that ilk : 2. R caucht : 6. L brynt and cut *corrected by* b a *interlined* : 8. R Apoun [and] ; R 53 syde : 9. R nocht ilkit in ; 53 not I irkit : 11. R 53 schulderis ; R bow to raiß : 12. E his cace : 13. E L B [that] ; R that scho betid ; 53 that flicht : 14. 53 the ficht : 15. 53 the cais : 17. E Abowit : 18. R tella : 19. E R 53 swakis : 21. R quhen : 23. R [tyme] ; 53 seruand : 26. R 53 Dynnys . . . thamodane : 27. R patent ; 53 [payntit] : 31. R [the] ; 53 baldly, with the : 33. 53 on the : 34. R as the : 36. E [last] ; 53 thou strake : 37. C E B corpß ; E R L B into the ; R L 53 corps ; 53 how faill : 39. R 53 And with : 40. E L B breist and bone ; R And to ; 53 brode breist : 42. R smyting : 43. 53 furth bokkis : 44. R his beith eik : 46. R 53 writhit : 47. E scho nixt ekis wderis : 48. E [ane] ; 53 Loris : 49. 53 On quhom : 50. 53 stoupan : 51. E R horß ; 53 hors : 55. R And the tothir syne ; 53 to hir sine : 56. R Ane maistry hate ; 53 Amastous : 57. E in hir : 60. R bald troiane : 61. R 53 handis : 62. E R 53 to ground ded : 64. C and and ; 53 armur : 65. C L B *marginal note* Apulʒe is now callit Naplis : 66. R 53 [war] : 69. R 53 wolfis hidduous : 70. R [With] ; R 53 bustuous browis : 73. R [on] : 74. R [all] : 80. E on wreyndly : 85. R in ane litill : 92. R That all : 93. R [ilk] : 96. R 53 In at his hals quhare sche : 97. 53 ane scheild : 99. 53 to triumphe : 100. E L B him throu the ; R scho drewe him ; R 53 on the : 101. E L B [a] : 105. C rasyt *cancelled before* so : 106. E mycht and forß : 107. R of grace ; 53 hir grace : 110. C hait *in margin*, hayt all *cancelled before* our ; E His armis ; R hait out throw his : 111. 53 And Awnus : 112. R Approche betid on cace : 113. R and also he : 115. R mont aspynyus ; 53 opennyus : 118. E men : 119. L has fatis : 120. 53 Ieoperdy and : 122. R to fle to eschewe : 124. L to assay : 128. R Leif the : 129. E As nane : 133. 53 vost and : 137. E hyr horß ; B hir *cancelled before* the : 140. 53 that schameful brycht : 144. 53 with his : 147. R his horß ; 53 feil sydis let, his : 151. 53 bariant : 156. R and fals : 158. R or glede of fyre ; 53 and fyre : 159. R so spedy rynnys : 160. E R horß ; 53 hors : 163. R he stude ; 53 [hym] : 166. 53 rokit : 168. R vp heich ; R 53 in the : 169. 53 he chepis : 170. L punsys at the last : 172. E haboundanly ; R 53 Quhil all the ; 53 aboundly : 174. R licht dowis vnto.

XI.xiv. heading. R the grete . . . to retorne ; L [folkis]

3. 53 setuate : 4. E and convoys : 5. R Tarchone the tuskanes : 6. E soundis : 12. E admotiouns : 15. C thai *interlined* ; E L B Quhilk : 18. E sall on sa ; R bombartis : 20. E adreid : 26. E L B this steyll : 31. R L Or quhat : 34. E The cowpis full of mony dantis meß ; R 53 of mony : 35. R [ʒour] : 37. R [the] : 39. E ʒow can on ; R the first offerandis ;

53 And se fat : 40. 53 The banket : 42. E to start : 46. E B [from] ; R And twyiß he ; L him and his horß ; 53 Sic wise as he : 47. 53 With his huge : 50. 53 about thare, ene : 51. E fyre : 52. E R [vp] : 53. R of the : 54. R oft brak ; L brake the heid [than] : 57. R 53 mycht he fynd in to sic : 61. E oft tymes ; R 53 oft syis from his throt ; 53 schop : 63. 53 be slicht : 64. R 53 hynt : 65. R strene3eis hir sa : 66. R That of hir punsis throw oute ; R 53 hir skyn ; L 53 of : 68. R 53 Ylowpit thrawis and ; R writhit [with] : 71. E L B 53 and skyp ; R [and] : 74. L with hir : 78. L proper : 81. R ane armes ; 53 [ane] arnus : 82. R Or myschevous : 84. R camylla : 90. R and reikis : 92. R passage and gate held : 95. R 53 thrawart : 96. R armes full reddy was ; 53 Arnus : 97. R 53 samyn wise : 100. R Now his ; 53 Nowis to cum : 101. R And euery . . . peveß : 102. E R L B vnschewabill.

XI.xv. heading. R Arrus ; 53 Arnus

1. C that *cancelled before* of : 2. 53 spritual : 3. R Sybilla : 7. 53 drawis : 8. R werelike wardis : 10. 53 Conchit : 11. E [he] : 14. E L lycient ; 53 latiane : 19. C gold *cancelled before* quham : 22. L bruschit : 26. E followit : 28. R in memour : 30. R for to dreß ; L gold : 36. R L the prcist : 37. R arme3 *and so always* ; 53 Arnus *and so always* : 39. C hys *in margin* ; R Chosin : 40. R he dressit : 43. R O haly : 45. R 53 Quhen to ; 53 furie, smoik : 46. R Bleiß ; 53 Bleis : 48. R the devote ; 53 [thy] : 49. L And with 3our fut steppis : 50. R syndry feill hate and ; 53 hait, sundry and : 58. R As this : 59. R Sa that : 60. R or scharp straik : 66. 53 ane swift : 69. R Bot to his . . . hame war brocht ; 53 hame has brocht : 70. R 53 Suld he him : 73. R 53 hand [that] : 74. R 53 his takill ; R gan ane : 75. L haduert : 77. 53 thus Camyl : 79. 53 [the] haisty : 80. E L byrnand ; R this birrand . . . flicht mar thar ; 53 berrand : 83. R [that] hurte and smate ; 53 Qhuhil : 85. R wedgit ; 53 wedgeit : 88. R Tert to this ; 53 and dede : 89. C hir *cancelled before* in : 90. R scharp harmes : 94. R [he] : 95. C with *cancelled before* hys : 96. R Nor 3it amyd the virginis wappynnys for were ; L wapynnis : 99. R 53 3ong grete : 100. R in the ; 53 nolehird : 105. 53 [fall] : 116. R and blynd swarffis scho richt sone thare ; 53 swarffis : 117. R [in] : 118. E as sapour schene ; 53 rede cullour : 123. E haldyn speciall ; R Ony maist ; 53 and wald in : 129. 53 I hef done at my mycht : 131. B dynnys : 132. E R L B 53 fast away : 133. R command ; 53 this my : 137. R [that].

XI.xvi. heading. R Ops . . . has armes tane

1. R 53 clamour that did : 3. C hayt *cancelled before* het : 4. R 53 doun was : 5. B of [the] ; 6. R Thir : 8. C the *interlined* : 9. R ops ; R 53 weill thareby ; L opus : 11. R [ane] : 14. R 53 the 3oungkeris rasis ; R thare cry ; 53 this cry : 15. E R L B 53 Camilla : 18. E L B [to] : 19. R out and that is punyssing ; 53 all ouer : 20. E soverit ; R As thow has : 21. C *marginal note* in ; E R L 53 has ; R [with] : 22. R thare ficht : 23. R [the] : 24. R 53 this blissit : 25. R the syde : 26. R [quod] : 27. L his stade : 28. R The quene : 30. E murnyng : 31. E R L B 53 sall ; 53 thy schame : 32. L B onwrokyn de : 33. R euer that wound : 35. R he stervit : 36. R [his] : 38. 53 vpheit : 42. R Togiddir this : 48. C ha *cancelled before* wantoun : 50. 53 thiddir mare : 51. L B thydder : 52. R [that] ; 53 as thot thou : 54. E [syk] : 58. R has stent : 60. R [that] [and] : 61. 53 [hir] : 72. R Bedovyn in ; 53 Bedouin with : 73. R ops : 74. E the hillis he.

XI.xvii. heading. R Active to ; L left and ordinance ; 53 His army

3. R 53 had left : 5. R togidder and gaif : 8. E R L B [all] ; R blunt : 11. R 53 For nane ;
R nor sa agast : 13. R evaid : 15. L thi mycht : 16. E [all] : 19. 53 stedis stout : 20. R The
swyft : 22. C drew *cancelled before* threw ; E L B as nycht ; 53 Als thik as : 23. R abone
the ; 53 and the : 29. R nixt ouretane : 31. B to wrachit : 33. R 53 Stekand : 34. C L B
howß ; E L 53 [to] be ; R thai : 36. 53 And to . . . vther resortis : 37. 53 mak away : 38.
R thai ocht beseking : 40. E wpriß : 45. 53 how fousye : 54. L on 3one wallis : 55. 53
Sic tyme . . . tuk in hand : 56. R 53 caucht : 58. 53 hedis slingis ynew : 59. R brissillis
endis and brynt : 60. R dynt for dynt : 64. R first by : 65. E L B [cruell] ; E tydannis :
66. R And acca : 68. R L 53 camylla : 71. R Discomfit : 72. R stout in ; L stude about :
74. E marschall : 76. R that it suld : 77. 53 hillis hicht : 81. E L B [that] : 84. R 53 wyn :
85. R with all thare routis : 87. R thir hoistis : 93. E dymming : 94. R stering : 96. R
53 And in battaill preuit : 97. E L or than ; R 53 war on thame the : 98. R His weris :
100. R myrk nycht [nocht].

ending. E Heyr endis the lewyt bulk of aeneados and the proloug of the samyng forsaid
anno domini &c &c. Explicit liber vndecimus Incipit prologus in duodecimum ; R
Explicit liber vndecimus in eneados Et incipit prologus libri duodecimi &c ; L *as* C
except [eiusdem] ; *followed by a blank page* ; B *as* C *except* [in] duodecimi libri ; 53
Finis.

BOOK XII

Prologue, heading. E Heyr begynnys the prolong of the twelf buik And syne followis
the buik of the samyng anno domini etc. ; R B *omit* ; L The Proloug ; 53 *as* C

1. E L B and the : 7. E L B for his : 8. 53 farmament : 9. R regioun fare : 11. R of the flicht :
12. R went was : 14. R in euery *cancelled*, and evyr *in margin* ; 53 and euery hous : 15.
R 53 cremmesy : 16. R The : 17. 53 the wynd, of his : 21. E *marginal note* or stremis ; B
stremys, *marginal note* stremowris : 26. R liftis vp ; 53 seyis : 28. 53 emysperery : 29.
R 53 at the ; 53 Tha : 30. 53 him quhillis : 32. E schrowdyt ; R schroweth : 35. R [ryall] :
38. R hir face : 42. R influence : 44. E sapour ; R bricht as : 46. R With halesum : 47.
E L B troiane souerane ; R 53 phanis : 51. E L B [a] : 53. R and firmament : 54. 53 and
furth : 56. 53 grete stremes : 58. R B stowand : 59. R alichtnyt : 60. R 53 Forgane the ;
53 and beriall : 61. R The bene bonkis and the diurnale ; 53 dinruale bemes : 62. E
L B kest all of : 64. B ful3art : 65. E enbrouth ; R enbrowdit ; 53 embrede : 66. R the
bewis : 69. E [kynnellis] : 71. R phioll thayne and ; 53 fane phioll and : 76. R in his
barne ; 53 hir barin : 77. R bere is now on brerde ; B beir ; 53 bere : 78. 53 gardmond :
79. R on euery : 81. R and pomp priapus : 85. E lappis on the : 87. E In variant ; R
vyncust vaill : 88. E scherald full and ; R scherand : 89. R 53 and fyguris : 90. R 53
The pray : 91. E dewly : 92. R 53 thare licht : 93. R Als fell as : 94. R 53 gnyp : 95. R
blunt 3arde : 96. R sons half garde : 97. R The levis rang vpspred : 98. R The blunt :
99. R of the fresche : 100. R Endland the tale3eis : 102. R Ourespredand bewis on :
104. E L B culrand : 108. R Blancht : 109. L B cestiall : 110. L the hawit wally : 112. E
gold sum aureat : 115. R banward : 116. R [the] ; 53 camuomelde : 117. R furth spredis
hevinly : 118. E L B Furth dammes ; E R blak : 119. R dentilioun ; 53 in denthilion :
120. R [levys] : 121. R thareon levis : 123. E L B 53 tetand : 124. E vernall ; R vernaill ;
53 vernale : 128. R thare tressis : 129. R sikkin croppis : 130. R succurand hony : 131. R

[syluer] : 132. E in the ; R stringis on : 133. R [settis] ; 53 ponderit : 135. R 53 or floure :
137. R in the dulce : 139. 53 mycht : 142. R from the rutis ; 53 rutis rent : 144. B Tryukill :
145. E L B or synamom ; R succoure ; 53 succure : 147. R [or] : 150. R Thir garȝeard :
152. R rispy redis ; 53 souchis : 153. E R L B all the : 157. R B of the : 158. E R Pykand :
159. E pertelok ; R epartelop : 162. R plesand proude : 163. R Ischrowdin : 165. E L B
bromis : 169. E of cleyr ; R glasß : 170. R araying wafand : 171. 53 hys . . . his : 172. E
myght of litill ; R the nymphe ; L B or litill ; 53 the litil mige or fle : 173. B euer : 174. 53
gorby : 175. E L B bene the ; R and lufely valis : 179. E with brokettis ; R to brokettis :
180. 53 The sprutal : 186. R All snod . . . and beistis ; 53 And snod : 187. 53 wolk : 191.
R branschis of flouris : 192. B to thair : 193. C E L B 53 [sang] ; E Sum ȝing sangis ;
R [sangis] : 196. 53 dois : 199. E sangis : 200. E apounc gudly a wycht : 201. E R 53
rownys : 207. 53 quyte ouer of : 208. R in ilk place : 209. R 53 flatter : 210. E lawdry ;
R 53 vnleifsum : 212. E R ȝistrene ; 53 pastyme : 214. R [a] : 216. E awin brother ; R
[verray] : 218. R ȝone man be : 219. R wend : 221. E [so] ; 53 fresche : 223. 53 quod he,
I hope : 227. R [rathar] : 228. R impugnand : 229. 53 ettillis al : 230. R all thingis : 233.
R thare amouris ; 53 thare armouris : 235. R outbrist : 236. R In fortyfying [do] : 237.
C E L B 53 [and] ; R pykkis : 238. E sterling chyrmis diuerß stewnis ; R strimling :
239. R on : 240. R The : 241. R [so] : 242. E schewis at euery ; R in euery ; 53 euery
dale : 245. R L B and hevinlie : 247. R with notis : 250. R maid hartis to dance : 251. E
L B [al] : 253. R 53 fosterare : 256. E rut and ; L B rute and : 260. R reperrellare : 263.
E L kynd of : 264. R be the : 268. E L B temperat : 271. B last : 272. E Quhilk ane had
tareyt : 277. E stayt ; R 53 arising ; B stait : 278. E his held but : 280. R ly I may : 281.
R me to fangare : 282. E prong ; R Or . . . his : 283. E [hir] : 286. 53 completit : 287. 53
[on] : 292. C bynge cancelled, beynge in margin ; R 53 dois : 297. R [natyve] bird the :
298. R 53 on hir : 299. C greyn in margin ; R prikking : 302. R bed I mycht : 303. 53
dressis : 304. 53 messis : 306. L adds Amen ; 53 began : heading. R scotus prologus ;
53 omits : 307. C 307–310 added at bottom of folio ; the capital beginning Book XII is
not in fact gold : 308. R intitulit ; 53 intitillit : 309. L in gold.

ending. E Heyr endis the proloug of the xii buik of aeneados And eftyr cummys syne
the buik of the samyng etc. I. E. ; R B omit ; L Writtin be me Iohanne mudy anno xlv
ȝeris ; 53 Finis. The .xii. Booke of Eneados.

XII.i.

3. R 53 thrawart : 4. E R 53 was ; 53 vnwrokin : 5. L baid : 6. R that he : 7. E [tho] : 8.
53 And to : 9. 53 vnquirit : 10. L as hait as : 13. R [lyoun] of trace : 15. R breist as fast :
17. C muyd u written over o : 19. R omits 19–20 : 22. C the cancelled before ferd : 27. R
nocht ychone coward : 28. R worde ; 53 promyssis : 30. E R 53 sall ; 53 not, for we : 36. C
marginal note or forhowar ; E forhowar banist ; R 53 forhoware of ; L B marginal note
forhowar : 38. R by the se ; B the cancelled, to interlined : 41. 53 [gyf] : 43. 53 the terme :
45. 53 Latyne, so with : 46. E To his : 48. E fury vassalage ; R forcely : 49. E R 53 dois :
51. R is counsale to provide : 52. R tyde : 54. C L B Belang : 64. C to interlined ; R of
my land : 66. L to the say I : 67. E one thi : 69. R 53 [ald] ; 53 dochteris : 72. 53 Declarit
thaym that : 74. E R spouß : 76. 53 bandis, thou has : 77. 53 wranguslie : 80. B stude :
86. 53 As now : 88. R 53 notourly : 89. R wayis hate : 92. R [oft] : 93. E to chance ; R
maid feble and change my : 96. R turnus dede and war begrave : 98. E and heyr : 101.

C the *in margin* ; E L B this wyß ; R Giff we suld . . . fulefully : 102. R wedding : 104.
E chance it sa : 108. 53 doith : 114. E increß ; 53 incres : 115. E mycht first : 119. R *omits
to XII.ii.49* : 126. 53 The . . . thàt clepit is to stout : 127. C salbe *cancelled after* salbe ;
E [to] ; L B salbe forto : 129. 53 accustumate, ay to : 131. 53 wyfeler.

XII.ii. heading. E [stryfe] ; L fra fecht resist ; B fra stryfe resist

7. B To thir : 10. 53 in thi breistis : 14. E Thou art our : 16. E L B resistis alhaill ; 53 In
the . . . michtis rest alhale : 18. 53 famyl, thou lyke : 21. B of this : 24. 53 out of : 27. 53
sore teris smert : 30. E sall hyr : 35. E in [this] ; 53 from the : 49. E R 53 gretand ; L
this with : 50. R Bot that I may recounter my aduersaris : 55. R I sall gif : 56. E [it] ; 53
nor 3it eschape : 60. R lykis me : 63. R his hede : 67. E to battall : 69. R battaill ; 53 the
bargane : 71. E feyld the ; B feild and stalwart : 73. R his stable in he : 74. 53 lat do : 77.
E quhylis : 78. E fraß : 82. R ferde grant schir to ; 53 ferd grantseir : 86. R forrynnyng ;
53 blastys : 89. 53 how luffis : 90. R [Dyd] : 103. R temperit it with : 105. R [all] : 107.
E R 53 lemand : 108. 53 and gude : 110. R the capitane ; 53 Armicane : 111. E blanglis :
113. E the deyd ; 53 in dede : 115. 53 the maist : 116. E vphaldis : 119. E O 3onder ; R Off
3one : 120. 53 [handis] : 124. E Subdill ; R 53 crisp and ; 53 fule : 127. R 53 in his : 128.
53 [and] : 129. R sic ; R 53 caucht : 133. E The verray : 135. R bull ane bergane : 136. E
R 53 routis : 137. R aggrevous : 139. E R to ane stok ; E of tre : 140. R wyndis : 143. E
in curage ; R tyme the self of curage : 148. E sic prosper : 150. R 53 drede and said :
151. L batale ordinans : 152. E destyn : 154. E his ; 53 the forsaid : 155. E L B And the ;
E messinger : 157. E and weris as ; R [the] : 158. R efter contrak.

XII.iii. heading. E day and end ; R last delay at hand ; 53 delay and end

13. R goddis and eik : 15. R 53 fontanys : 17. E Vp lynnyng : 20. 53 tho behaldis : 23. R
portis out attonys : 30. R 53 callit thame : 32. R 53 thare : 38. C a *interlined,* and maid
cancelled : 43. R [for] : 45. R [weld] : 46. R age : 47. R hie hedis : 48. C L B howß ; R
rangeingis : 50. R Discendit ; 53 or to : 53. C L B *parentheses in MSS* ; R his hillis : 57.
53 of [the] : 60. R Iuturnus catakus sche : 68. 53 vthir : 69. E L B thame wer : 70. 53
draw : 71. R The beist maist proffittable : 79. 53 And now : 81. R 53 terme and day : 82.
E ane strangast : 83. R in the : 84. 53 [I] : 85. R 53 [thou] : 88. R 53 percase : 89. R Of oist
betid ; 53 Or ocht betyde : 90. E the wordis : 91. R Quhat that : 95. R [this] Iuno seis
the teres : 101. E L B now consave : 103. 53 and thy : 106. R [hir] : 107. E traist ; R [full].

XII.iv. heading. E praeyr ; R syne in king ; 53 syne of kyng

1. B king : 7. 53 [stud] sturettis : 8. E L B enorment ; R 53 adornament : 10. R 53 was
rollit ; 53 Nixt came furth : 11. R 53 cart : 13. E in feyld of : 14. R of the ; 53 [on the] :
16. 53 The romane : 19. R on licht : 20. 53 swete knycht : 21. C sycht *cancelled before*
doym : 23. E [the preste] : 28. R war neuer clippit ; 53 [was] : 29. E Be beistis : 31. E
R 53 quhilk : 32. E 53 Turnus ; R 53 towart : 33. C the *in margin* : 34. 53 beastis : 37. C
wyne *cancelled before* altaris : 40. 53 with the : 42. E most : 43. R 53 For quhen sa : 44.
E [and] ; 53 feilsyis : 45. R 53 Iovy ; 53 And now : 49. R [now] ; 53 Mars thou takis :
51. E R L B 53 and debayt : 54. 53 goddis reuerent : 55. R skarit sky ; 53 ydrad : 56. R
wicht : 58. R in my fomy : 60. 53 ansomane : 65. B and move ; 53 or : 66. R Nor 3it

with wappynnys ; 53 [na] eftir : 67. R be [Mars] : 68. 53 victorie in our hand : 69. 53
afer rathir : 70. 53 sal goddis : 74. R or : 77. E lawis onewinly ; R vincust : 80. R 53 And
I sal : 81. 53 latyne : 82. E rewill : 83. E is souerane : 84. B mot : 90. R 53 [hym] : 91. E
Behald and : 94. R in liknes vnto : 95. E L B and twynnis ; R [by] : 96. R or chaist : 97.
R frontis : 106. R Italianis ; 53 the peace : 108. R mater to go : 112. R erth with myddill ;
53 All thougt : 113. E R L B diluge and ; E L invadatioun ; B inadatioun : 116. C R L B
behald ; E sall neuer lat behald : 117. 53 we se : 118. C L B *parentheses in MSS* : 121. E
[is] ; R thare is it : 122. R the stok : 123. L moder and : 125. R 53 grew : 126. R edgit ; 53
edgeit : 127. 53 quhare it : 128. E Thus now thus : 131. B in latyne : 132. R 53 on hand :
133. R 53 relationis : 134. R 53 confederationis : 135. 53 had confirmid : 137. E [eftyr] ; 53
thir : 141. R 53 thar beistis ; 53 on lyue : 143. R tho altaris : 148. E breist ; L rumouris :
150. R [other] : 152. R Than the mater : 153. E behaldis sawis faill : 156. R 53 so law :
157. E Thus turnus ; R towartis ; 53 altaris : 159. R schekis waxin thyn : 160. R [furth].

XII.v. heading. E haestily

3. 53 hir sister : 5. E sentence : 7. E L B camert ; R of ane Camer : 12. R dede ; 53 *adds
extra line* Hardy and stout, liberal syncere : 13. E did scho did thring : 18. R [to] :
20. R vndely : 24. E in the : 28. 53 mak, vnset : 32. R and him betaucht : 33. R [that] :
40. C thus *in margin*, and *cancelled in line* ; R 53 That thus now : 42. R [for] : 47. R
ar desirit ; 53 are desyrit : 50. E L B vther wyß ; R wyse : 54. R vnequale ; 53 senyng :
55. R self ilk tyme has ; 53 The self : 57. R [the] ; 53 vp in : 59. E ane thing as nane ;
R in that entent : 60. B and conuenient : 63. R foul and cron come ; L soursand ;
53 forand : 65. R [hym] : 66. E on lang : 67. R Quhill on [thar] ; 53 Quhilkis : 68. B
Skymmys : 69. E Quhilk : 77. R and [to] : 79. R dirkynnyt : 80. 53 scraik : 81. E [as] ; R
as ane club : 82. E did assay : 83. R that quhile : 85. E crukis rude : 89. R huge rout and
clamoure huge : 90. R and takin : 92. 53 vtheris : 96. R [I] : 99. E L B 3ong ilk : 100.
R with this ; L Affrays ws so : 107. R [all] ; L [3he sall] : 108. E rowtis now present ; R
Assembill here 3oure : 110. E 3ong king ; R nor slane : 111. R [word] also fast : 112. R
53 Towart : 116. R Vnscheveabill : 123. R aganis : 125. 53 Myne brethir : 128. R spous
clepit archaden : 131. 53 scharplie : 135. R [evyn] : 140. R hynt thare ; L hyndis ; 53 hynt :
142. R bludy fury : 143. R felloun braid : 147. R Agane than semblit : 148. 53 wroith as
wode : 149. R archady : 153. R [in] : 155. L thair sacrifice : 158. B [scharp] : 161. R [the]
wyn flacernys of gret : 170. E R horß ; R Him self : 175. E L B The king ; E [tyrreyn] :
179. R 53 bakwart : 180. E R B Onhappy : 184. E R L B 53 his schaft ; 53 also rude : 186.
R swyft couresere : 187. R dedely wound and grevouß ; 53 dedelik bit : 188. E wordis
sa ha ; R thou quyte : 190. R [mair] gevand sacrifice : 194. R Eubuses [hym] : 196. E L
B the altar ; R [ane altar] ; 53 And on altare : 198. E R L and hair : 199. R flewour ; 53
fleoure : 200. R als fast : 201. R Richt on . . . thus fury and : 202. E by the fyr : 205. R
53 sic ane state : 209. 53 fere of his : 210. 53 vandgarde throw mony and : 216. E Into :
218. R blandlit : 220. E R 53 or irny ; E of the dethis.

XII.vi. heading. L B Eneas ; L out of the feild couth paß . . . mair cruell wa

2. B the gen ; 53 all wrang how : 3. C E L on enarmyt ; R 53 vnarmyt : 4. R vncovir :
5. R clepis of ; 53 [and] : 6. E L B hurt 3e : 7. R Aganis vthir ilkane : 11. R 53 [And] ; L
And tha ; 53 and eik the : 14. 53 hand to hand : 16. R fellony : 20. R to the dede : 22.

E wyth mair : 23. R 53 quhirland . . . with ane : 24. R in this : 25. R 53 [that] : 27. 53
glore : 28. 53 quhat : 30. R of the : 31. R betid becaiß : 34. E That present war persauit
in the melle ; L *omits, leaving space* ; B Did vant him self of wounding of Enee : 37. E
for his : 39. R with harnes : 43. R quhareso it list him be ; 53 hym list hym be : 45. L
hir ire : 46. C corpß ; E R L B 53 corps : 47. R strowit : 49. C dr *cancelled before* he ; R
cartis : 54. E frosty blude : 57. C he *interlined and in margin* : 59. E [sa] ; R 53 [swith] :
62. E swyftaust : 63. R And wyn the : 67. R [eik] : 68. R 53 ane buschement or wate :
76. R Spangand : 77. 53 Quhilk : 79. R [or] : 82. E L B [he] : 85. R Quhare this : 89. L
behyd : 92. 53 Wmedes the feris walkis : 99. 53 and her wyl : 101. R 53 quhare that ; R
he saw baldly : 107. R 53 durst he anys : 109. R the purpois : 111. R 53 as thar : 112. R
53 him did he ; 53 wele at him ane fer way at him : 114. E R B horß ; E and this : 115.
53 frelie, did lepand : 120. R [he] : 125. 53 hsperia : 126. E [to] ; R weilfar : 127. R 53
bounteth : 130. R [a] . . . habaid : 132. R 53 thersibotus : 133. E 53 [full] : 134. R Cassin :
135. E R wyth a : 139. R quhare he assalis ; 53 [the] soith : 140. R hevynnys : 142. E
[plane] : 145. L euer : 147. R *omits 147–150* : 154. R neid is : 156. R and hamouris : 157.
C nocht *in margin* ; E [mycht] ; 53 hys mody, micht : 162. R Persand his syde ; 53 the
syde : 168. R and the : 169. 53 donn : 170. B followit : 172. C the *cancelled before* vmast ;
53 At vmaist : 173. R hede cruelly.

XII.vii. heading. R [of]

2. C corpß ; E R L B 53 corps : 5. E *reverses 5–6* : 6. 53 all brudy : 11. R 53 withdrawe :
12. L hed withdraw : 14. R [way] : 16. E Sceir doun the wynd : 18. E that he had ; R
To seik . . . was wount : 19. 53 thay maist haist : 20. R [To] . . . stynt and this : 21. R
And was thar ; R 53 than new present : 22. R son to : 25. R stranthly : 26. R 53 has
him glaidly : 27. R 53 office : 29. E L B rycht sle : 32. R quhilk that : 33. R and of : 34.
R had knawin : 35. R and strenth of mychty herbis : 36. R and vse ; 53 [of] vse : 43.
53 at thys teris : 44. R Thus this : 45. C wyß *cancelled before* mak ; R schapin of ; 53
schapin of the : 50. R be the god : 52. E Off wyth : 53. E the wynd : 54. R [And] in
euery : 55. R twynris : 57. R That for : 58. R dresß his handis : 59. E avalis [hys] : 61. E
R grysly deid ; R [the] : 69. R [of] : 71. 53 thus pane : 72. R of his : 74. R dittane : 76.
E springis : 77. C se *interlined* : 79. R na way : 80. 53 Tho the : 81. R Tharewith : 82.
L stikand ewyne in ; 53 stikand out, in : 86. E L B thristy ; R hailsum spatil thrifty
wounder : 89. R springland : 90. 53 helsum : 91. R 53 penates : 96. R had nocht bene :
99. R And tharewith hed and schaft baith ; R 53 come furth : 100. R [pull] : 102. E
into : 103. R bring thame : 105. E agast thair : 115. R Claspis : 118. 53 by his his syde :
120. R and his ; L on his : 121. E L B in the : 124. R kissit his son and on : 125. R lerne :
126. R and wirk ay laubour : 129. R quhilk : 130. 53 the querrell : 133. E thin awin ; 53
Do 30u : 137. E in proves : 138. 53 Saith fader.

XII.viii. heading. L battale and suld

2. L ischis : 3. R To him : 4. R Eneas menestheus : 6. R with mony waisty : 9. R for the :
11. C agane *cancelled before* forgane ; E L B rycht our forgane : 12. R 53 Persauand :
13. 53 Than : 14. R come throw : 15. R that ilk : 17. E L B and [the] : 20. 53 draw : 21. R
drivis oure : 22. 53 Ane rouch : 23. E the bull or ; R ane bub . . . fyne tempest : 26. R
Wald the : 32. E sowch ; R such ; 53 swoich : 34. R 53 he has : 25. E L B achet and : 37.

E R L B Vsens : 40. R With the first ay his fais : 41. EL the scry ; R 53 ane clamour : 42. E R L B 53 went : 45. L out throw : 46. E and pulder ; R Quhilk : 47. R Bot this : 50. E L B and mace ; R 53 wappynnys : 52. R spy : 54. E in the melle ; R vnto the melle ; 53 vnto melle : 56. 53 virgo : 58. R 53 [a] : 59. R of the : 60. E L B the contrar : 61. B at hand : 69. R 53 wrinkis : 70. L B plumys bake : 72. R lugeing : 73. 53 skimmand : 74. E R L B heich hillis : 75. E mortallis : 77. E R 53 dois ; R 53 portis ; 53 [scho] : 78. R [the] sound pasß sche : 80. E R L B [owt] ; R horß : 84. E his place : 85. 53 [Na] : 88. B his cartis : 90. R [a] : 92. 53 [hie] : 93. R 53 [And] : 94. R tyme : 96. E R horß ; E that semyng . . . doith ; L B that semyne ; 53 hors : 104. E this was : 109. R 53 did he glyde : 110. R byde : 114. R and tymbrell : 115. E R L B 53 crestis : 117. R 53 caucht : 119. E R horß ; 53 hors : 120. 53 turnis : 131. R 53 [goith] : 132. R And cruell : 134. R bridill but reneȝeis ; 53 renȝe.

XII.ix. heading. E R L and [be]

1. 53 teaching : 3. R L 53 in mater : 4. R slauchter ; 53 war : 6. R 53 feild ; R strowit : 7. R Quhen : 10. R and crudelite ; 53 oh crudelite : 12. E L B [ane] ; R Quhilk : 13. E so lang : 14. R [strang] : 18. R breist endit ; 53 condict : 20. R The langer : 21. R To : 23. E R horß ; 53 hors : 25. E L B [the] : 28. R 53 hyngis thame : 29. E R L B 53 droppand ; E L B turß : 30. 53 self stede : 31. R At ane ; 53 Or at ane . . . Ianaus : 35. E [the] ; L B and hie ofspring : 38. 53 vther chif Captane : 39. R The : 42. R 53 in archadane : 43. R dais eftir : 44. R that he ; 53 nedis : 51. 53 war now : 52. E L B [in] : 55. E L B Or quhat : 56. 53 mouth, of ane large : 60. 53 omits : 65. R And thare : 66. E R L B 53 Now breistis : 67. R [at] : 69. R 53 [to] : 73. L this day : 76. E quhirrand our stane ourraucht ; R rouk of quhirlland ; 53 and quhirland : 80. R 53 soun : 82. R mony ane clap : 83. E Ourthreddis : 85. R turnus he recounterit ; 53 Ane Turnus : 86. E L B ruschit : 87. E R L B 53 mynd : 89. R In his : 96. 53 [defend] : 97. E [with] ; R 53 Bot as . . . has mett ; L it met : 98. E [hes] [hym] ; 53 doun him : 100. E Off cativis ; R has clepit : 103. 53 the riche : 105. R lyis now dede quhare : 106. E L B venquest ; E [the] erd : 107. 53 the erde : 109. R the methis and the : 110. R housß of famell ; 53 houssis : 111. R 53 Off the : 114. R The : 117. R 53 vtheris : 118. R And the latynis and all the haill troianis : 120. C E L B 53 [on] : 121. R horsß ; 53 horssis : 127. R Nor . . . war : 128. E confunding and sum.

XII.x. heading. E Quhen Eneas ; is ; L for wo hir self

1. R this thyme : 3. C scho interlined : 9. 53 [held] : 11. E R 53 cassin : 14. R men : 15. R of grete bergane : 17. E calllt : 19. C a interlined ; R ascending : 20. E [all] : 23. R 53 amyd : 24. R spak his erand : 25. E [I] : 28. R vnsett quha will : 29. C on interlined ; R 53 to : 31. R 53 and sone bet : 33. E R 53 wering ; L B weringe : 34. R 53 latynis : 36. L grand : 37. R thare toppis : 38. 53 chynais : 39. B equale is the : 41. 53 in sic place : 44. R vincuß in the : 45. R of releif ; 53 to beleif : 46. E efter the feild : 48. R L B 53 weilfare ; R [of] : 49. R and hate : 50. L fawmys : 54. R Togiddill : 57. 53 pussance : 58. 53 or thay wyst : 59. R 53 haistely : 62. R Thai kelit : 64. R L 53 quhilk ; 53 berinkin : 66. C heir cancelled before and ; R in the : 67. R Eneas [with] : 68. R puttis : 69. R and hie : 70. E accuß ; 53 Latinis : 72. E L B to forß and move ; 53 on hors : 73. 53 that he Italianis : 74. R And syndry : 78. R in to sindry : 80. R wyde to the ; R 53 wallis cast : 81. E the gret : 82. R [for] : 84. 53 of fere of : 89. R reik ; 53 better : 91. E Ouer

throwart ; R Ourthort ; 53 Ourthowrt : 92. R thare innys : 94. R laith : 98. R 53 the grete ; 53 [rayß] : 99. R went all wod : 100. C E L B howß ; 53 hossis : 101. R so to : 102. 53 at his myscheif and pynys : 104. R [With] : 105. E L B Fra [as] ; E this wyß : 107. E kinlit ; R kindillit he with : 110. 53 the oistis : 111. 53 Sche fell vnhappy : 115. R of wyte and all the : 120. 53 his handis : 123. R 53 spilt with : 125. C wraik *i corrected from y* ; R the vile : 126. B Thai renk : 127. R His : 140. R 53 Waxis ; R that fate : 141. 53 [and] : 145. R Off mony : 146. R 53 has : 149. R [nocht] : 150. E maigh ; R 53 or son ; 53 maich.

XII.xi.

1. R 53 In to the : 2. R in the : 5. R dolf as fyre ; B that syre : 6. E R horß ; 53 hors : 9. E swouching ; R 53 souching : 10. R 53 The ; 53 clamours : 11. R Next with : 13. R 53 ciete ane felloun ; R murnyng : 14. L B and cayr of : 15. R 53 wa is : 16. R the ciete : 18. E And quhow ; E L B [noyß] : 21. C ren3eis *rewritten in margin* ; R hynt the : 22. R Iuturna his sister thus spak ; 53 the Iuturna : 23. E B [I] ; R [was] : 24. R [of] : 25. E R horß ; 53 hors ren3eis syde, ren3eis : 28. R 53 thus gate : 31. R and to menteme : 34. 53 Mydlit the batall, in sic feare : 35. E Thairwyth . . . the steyd : 36. C corpß ; E R L B 53 corps ; R [the] : 38. R thai wend : 40. R this was ; L lang 3eir ; 53 lang gere : 41. 53 the craft : 42. R and tretit : 43. L his batale : 45. R For : 47. R [gif] . . . in that : 48. B thi deir brother ; 53 [fey] : 51. 53 I sal my self . . . lang gere : 52. R 53 nor dere : 53. E me that was ; 53 [me] : 54. R with ane loude ; 53 Swete : 55. E On the : 57. R [lo] . . . at his : 58. E capidane ; E L B Vsens ; R 53 vsence : 62. R Oure our myscheif that restis bot [that] : 63. R Now sall : 64. 53 drantes, lynnage : 68. E stervit : 72. R 3e be ; 53 He 3e : 74. R 53 and velany : 76. E forbearis : 77. E had : 78. E myd : 80. C gan *in margin* : 81. 53 the Eee : 82. R Cryis : 84. R weill standis : 85. E thin town men3e : 86. E thundir : 87. E R dois : 88. R 53 Itaile : 89. R 53 And to : 90. L and als ; 53 [palyce] : 91. E R L B 53 into : 92. E bleiß ; R 53 of the : 96. R of fere : 97. E R 53 his thraw ; 53 vnto : 100. E his selvyn : 102. C Quhilk *in margin* ; E L B [at] : 103. R dois ; R 53 [now] : 106. E doith ; 53 he dois : 107. R 53 athir hand ; R sic standis : 111. E this rolling ; 53 the cart : 112. R at ane vantage : 113. R astonate ; R 53 stude doun ; 53 astonaid : 116. E All mycht with ; 53 aagir and : 117. R cachis : 118. R 53 And has by kynd : 119. E R of the : 123. R 53 So aggrevit : 125. R a furoll : 129. R caucht within ane : 131. R to rollit ; 53 to rollyt : 132. R battaill : 133. E R [quod he] : 135. R and mak na : 136. R 53 hiddir : 143. 53 se, sa schamful : 150. 53 wappin : 151. E L B a swift ; R [sa] : 152. R [That] : 155. E [it] . . . thunderis blast : 158. R 53 Lowsing away the ; B [tharfra] : 159. E B swelcht : 162. R and stound : 163. E apone the ; R [that] ; 53 that the schout fer, in : 164. E 53 dois : 166. R depe den : 169. 53 Quhare to the : 170. 53 wele for way : 172. E Off schaftis ; 53 and quhissilling : 174. E cryis that be ; R All samyn ; L cryis he lat : 179. E equaly.

XII.xii. heading. R 53 Eneas and turnus fechtis ; R [fled] his band

6. 53 hoppis : 7. R of his : 10. C thus he montyt was *cancelled after* Athon, the hie mont in Trace *in margin* ; 53 he had : 12. R Or ellis hie : 14. E 53 Dois swoich : R Doith souk : 15. E L B And ioyus ; E snawy to on ; R his swan on hicht : 18. R surmonting the hichtis : 20. R As thare : 22. L 53 and army : 23. R thir dukis : 26. R [tofor] ; L befor : 28. 53 Now on : 32. E In ; R [it] : 33. R 53 vnmesurable : 36. R and bergane : 39. R and plane ; 53 the plame : 41. R 53 [thar] : 45. R And did : 47. R 53 raschis : 49. R and

proveß of : 52. E Campany : 53. R in Syla : 54. R 53 batall thra : 55. E horn to horn :
56. R ferefull bonys : 57. R The ; 53 That the : 58. E to brym to fycht : 59. E doun all :
60. E [the] : 62. 53 Of quhilk : 63. E [thus] ; R in this ; B the stownd : 64. R 53 [a] :
66. R [that] : 67. C t *cancelled before* all ; R 53 Than can do wesche body ; R and all :
68. C spaldis *in margin*, spaldyß *cancelled* ; R spaldis laith : 70. R rankis routis : 75.
R This ; 53 self, as has : 80. R Or quhen the ; R 53 oure weltit : 81. R waxis blith and
bald and blyth : 84. R raxit . . . huffit : 87. R gan ane ; 53 gan and schout : 88. 53 athir
out : 89. L 53 Bot his : 95. R That swifter na the : 96. E [that] : 98. R and the ilk : 100.
E the stedis ; L B he stedis : 101. E R 53 samyn : 103. 53 cartur : 106. R the cace : 108. R
or machit : 109. E L B 53 With : 111. 53 and fals brand : 116. E [gletand] ; R dum sand :
117. E myndles in brane : 118. R out throw : 125. R thothir : 129. R weild has Enee
made : 130. R [nocht] : 131. E [3it] : 133. E [that] : 135. E his rathis : 136. R amyddis : 137.
R Quhill thame · 138. R Quhen he : 140. R [the] : 141. B doith : 142. R swyft rest : 143.
E R L B 53 flycht ; L [all] : 146. R the swippis ; R 53 tuskand hound : 148. R or euery
he : 150. 53 ane suak : 156. R 53 all and eik . . . that rerde : 157. R 53 [fleand] ; 53 fast
agane can : 161. R 53 awfull : 162. 53 mannace : 164. R 53 [that] ; L gyf ony of thaim
drew : 165. R 53 for the fere ; 53 [thame] : 166. E [to] : 170. R can thame : 171. R with
tornyng : 172. C L B *marginal note* comparatio non Virgiliana ; R as the before : 173.
C the *interlined* : 174. R 53 twiching : 177. E grow alait ; 53 haid grow : 178. R wylde
olife olywe to : 182. 53 stomres : 183. R 53 wald thai : 186. R Bot than ; 53 the tre : 196.
C in *overwritten*, with *erased* ; R 53 to put out : 204. R honoure to be contrare : 208.
53 for that hys : 214. R vp put : 215. R [he] : 217. R 53 to dawnus : 221. R hir swerde ;
L B In to hir : 227. R And athir.

XII.xiii. heading. E did contend all haill ; E L B Promittis Eneas allone him till assaill ;
L contend in haill

3. 53 3allow wattry : 4. R and thareof : 5. R and sperit o my dere soun : 6. E [this] : 11.
53 Ane god amang, the goddis Indigites : 13. C *marginal note* saisit or vpheit ; E L B
Saisit or vpheit abuf ; R and vpheit ; 53 Vpheyit abone : 14. 53 or ellis thou : 15. R [Or] :
18. E L B Wyth mony : 20. R And render ; 53 Turnus, to his : 21. E increß : 22. E Fo
quhat : 23. R Decist quod he and at the last ; 53 and at last : 24. C d *cancelled before*
condiscend · 25. E the hyd : 26. 53 langare to consume : 28. 53 [face] : 29. R Full is ;
R 53 cummyn : 33. R 53 on were : 34. R bring sall al : 35. R and fury : 38. 53 spekand
carpis : 42. R was schewin : 43. E in contrary : 45. R 53 nocht thai thow suld : 48. 53
leifsum : 49. R girth it : 55. E [I] : 59. E [suld] ; R takill : 61. R vpblesand well : 62. R
the chefe : 63. R ony diede . 69. R latyne ; 53 Latin : 70. B awyn kyn, *marginal note*
blude : 71. E [weill] : 72. R includit : 75. 53 pepil : 76. R confederatioun ; B in ally ; 53
conione : 77. 53 That now ne : 78. E name now natiue ; L B or ; 53 nor Itale landis :
80. 53 Phrigiane : 81. 53 thare lord : 83. R atium ; 53 latine : 85. R stile allane : 86. R
remane : 87. L discent : 92. R perducer : 93. C thou *cancelled before* art : 95. R of spate
and felloun ; 53 or space : 96. R [thy] : 101. R This . . . Asiosanis : 102. R 53 And vthir :
104. 53 and vse : 105. 53 [As] : 106. R thir personis : 107. R intermyddill : 108. R 53
gang : 109. R [statute] : 113. C E L salbehald : 114. E [baith] ; R goddis and men : 115.
L 53 nor : 116. E L B 53 sacrify : 118. R thareto : 123. R this wise : 124. E This hir fader :
125. R cast : 130. 53 and Ire : 133. C *reverses 133–134, correct order indicated by* b a *in
margin* ; R 53 *reverse 133–134* : 135. R 53 thare trakis ; L cled thair thir trakis : 138. 53

reddys sall : 145. E L B [do] ; R L or effray : 149. E L B hald on baldlie ; 53 And hald
hir hald : 150. E Iuturna as ire : 151. 53 duun : 152. 53 hasty swarde : 153. E L B dois :
154. E A suyft : 156. R Cassyn : 157. B persane of man ; 53 sum persone : 158. E chaft ; R
53 quhirllis : 160. R 53 [the] : 164. E sum socht : 169. R in gravis ; 53 in granis : 170. R
53 [the] ; R or ruffis of housß ; 53 Or ane . . . or ruffis of houssis : 171. L by the nycht :
172. R with cryis : 176. 53 Sho : 177. B hir scheild : 179. R 53 grete honour : 180. E his
voce : 181. 53 couth here : 182. R the fury and quhissilling : 183. R 53 souching ; R the
flicht ; 53 hir flycht : 184. 53 Hys : 189. 53 to me restis : 190. R or how may ; 53 I se
quhat slicht : 191. E L B and stryve ; L oppyne ; 53 oppin : 195. 53 mare grife ; 198. 53
The power command : 200. E a start ; R [not now] : 206. R the immortalite : 208. 53
dolorus : 210. R 53 Amang : 213. E [land] : 216. R 53 send me : 217. C with *in margin* ;
R [sche] : 218. E L B clayth of blew : 227. E 53 [that] : 228. E L B The ; 53 depe, doukit.

XII.xiv.

1. 53 did not : 4. 53 rade : 6. 53 menis that : 7. E 3e tary 3e : 9. R Na pyngill : 12. 53 deryue :
14. R thou pleiß ; L 3e pleiß : 15. 53 Sadder : 16. 53 and subtillite : 18. R the flicht : 21.
R said thus ferß ; L saikand : 24. E R 53 dois : 27. B quhat that : 30. R 53 mony ane
3ere : 32. R pley and : 33. L [and] : 34. E producit : 39. R [full] : 41. E R him self ; R he
mysknewe : 42. E Nouder that quhair ; L or : 44. E *combines with 47, omitting 45–46*
The mekill stane he at his foman threw ; R sterit with : 48. E waist our flew ; R wod
and : 51. 53 our slewing : 55. E dois ; 53 [we] : 57. R [at] : 58. R [Or] . . . the strete and
by : 59. R fall : 62. E [to ws] ; R Semyt : 65. R Sic wise hes the ; 53 the goddis : 66. R
53 way : 69. C strang*is* : 70. E for [to] : 72. R B all the : 75. R Ne fend he fyndis : 76.
E quhat wayis ; R he mycht : 85. R Furth of ; 53 [weil far] : 86. R swidderand : 87. E
eengine : 88. E fulderis *corrected to* thunderis ; cauß ; 53 sulderis : 90. R Like to the
blak and awfull : 92. R menestheus wraik ; 53 brocht, meikil mischeuus : 95. E [of] :
98. R 53 faldand : 100. E and ane cairfull : 102. R gan ane : 103. C than *interlined* : 104.
E L B [full] : 106. R 53 strekis furth his ; L hand vp to : 112. R Of my . . . twichit : 113.
C the *interlined* : 114. R [had] : 115. R [a] : 120. R 53 Italianis : 123. R Extent : 128. E
Begoutht declyn ; R to inclyne : 129. 53 [in] : 130. R 53 Quhill : 133. E of tysche : 140.
E L B and dyseiß : 141. E [weid] ; R He can sic wede thare bereft : 142. R And fall :
145. R L freynd : 146. R this wourde : 147. 53 offerand, of the : 148. C *marginal note* or
slauchter ; E R L B 53 slauchter ; 53 the wikkit : 149. B And says ; 53 in all : 150. R Laith
in the breist ; B agayn : 151. 53 has hit : 153. 53 fred murnand : 154. R 53 vnder the dirk.

ending. E Heyr endis the xii buik of aeneados and his proloug and sua endis the
xii buikis of Aeneados maid be virgil and eftir cumis the xiii buik maid be ane
ane famoiß auchtor maupheus anno domini &c. &c. &c. &c. &c. Quod sit est finis
duodecimi libri Eneados Amen &c. ; R *as* C ; L *omits* ; B 53 Finis.

Mensioun, heading. R *omits* ; 53 *omits to beginning of Prologue XIII*

1. E Lo this : 5. B lundeis lyfe.

ending. L Writtin be me Iohnne mudy with maister thomas bellenden Iustus clerk
in the 3eir of god 1545 2* february &c. &c. &c. &c.

Naym, heading E R L B *as* C ; 53 *these lines occur at the end of Exclamatioun after Book XIII*

1. C *key words underlined* ; R [the] : 2. R the ionyt dow : 5. E Spy weill.

ending. E L B *add* Explicit duodecimos Liber et quicquid Vergilius in Eneados Scripserat. Sequitur prologus in XIII et ultimum Librum per matheum veggum superadditum ; E *adds initials* I.E. ; R G. D. The compilare G. D. ; L G. Dowglaß *followed by blank page* ; B G. Douglas ; 53 Finis.

BOOK XIII

Prologue, heading. E The proloug of the xiii buik of aeneados ; R *as* C *except* in the xiii buke and the last ; L Prologus ; B *omits* ; 53 The Prologue of the .xiii. Booke

2. E his feyt ; R [in] ; 53 fete : 4. E gone new was ; R was nere . . . suppertyme done : 6. R Quhilk : 11. E I blynkyt : 16. R phege on ; R 53 his dym ; 53 phigie, on : 17. R [hys hed] ; 53 sa depe his hede : 23. E L B did schyne : 25. R And euery : 26. 53 buriall : 27. 53 helsum : 29. E to quynkill ; L out of fayll : 31. E ryß : 36. E matyne honour : 40. L otheris vmbraig : 41. R [flude] ; B man [and] : 42. R [tha] . . . war insylde ; 53 in the : 43. 53 was : 45. C And euery thing *underscored* ; C E L B *marginal note* or all creatur ; R 53 all creature : 48. E [all] : 49. R L stering ; 53 mouyng : 50. C or *cancelled before* byrd ; R [by] : 51. E L dois : 52. E florest erd ; R [flude] : 54. R 53 thare pulis : 55. R [still] : 56. E L B [Be] ; 53 Bot the : 60. E L B *marginal note* or beistis ; L or small : 65. R on : 67. R the vocis bricht : 70. R [the] maistres : 71. E [gentill] : 74. R 53 thir birdis ; 53 nycht : 78. E lukit : 80. R he that bene : 82. 53 [that] : 83. R [that] : 85. R L 53 closit ; L 53 his habit : 90. E done to 3ou : 94. R 53 I witt quhen or quhat ; L I wyt . . . and quhair, *marginal note* or : 100. 53 lusty werk : 102. R [of] ; 53 same : 103. 53 thuelf : 104. B and sond : 105. R into oure : 107. R said [I] . . . quhat I say : 108. 53 3ou I : 112. R [full] : 118. R thrid quhele : 120. R Latt sic thing : 121. R as at : 125. E sum as writt ; B sum it write : 128. 53 thing : 129. E [thoill] : 131. R 53 3a son quod : 133. B think 3e : 135. R [hym] : 136. R bedovyn now in : 141. E potry : 142. 53 bene bot tway : 145. E R L B 53 sall : 146. E [that] : 149. 53 deo meo, mercy : 152. 53 [the] : 153. L be the hand me : 157. R [of] : 159. E 3one : 160. R 53 of the day ; 53 dawning : 162. B plesand : 163. R sternys in ane : 164. 53 is best, bot : 165. R to blasing : 168. R 53 bricht morowe ; 53 salute : 172. R Walk ; 53 Awalk : 173. 53 [furth] : 175. R clepit : 177. R powderit powderit : 181. R 53 thare schawis : 182. E plais ; 53 playis : 187. E R L B 53 mak vp wark ; R ane buke ; B tharof : 189. E this still : 191. R eftir eftir ane : 193. R 53 and glore : 194. 53 na vers : 195. R 53 poet : 197. 53 is twiching : 198. R furth wait.

ending. E *adds* Gawinus douglace Heyr endis the proloug of the xiii buik of eneados and eftyr followis the buik of the samyng anno domini &c. &c. &c. ; R *as* C *except* Explicit prologus et incipit liber in ; L B *as* C *except* G dowglas ; 53 Finis. The .xiii. Booke of Eneados.

XIII.i. heading. 53 Rutulianis

2. R [ʒald furth] ; B ʒald vp : 3. R and ryall : 4. 53 mangnanymyte : 8. 53 And to the : 9.
53 murnyng and ane : 11. R sorowis ; B Doun from : 13. R as he huge : 16. R fere thud :
18. 53 the swerdis : 20. R Thare bergane and thare : 21. R gan hawer of : 22. R Quhat :
24. R Nor ʒit thare : 25. 53 in all : 26. R Amyte and ; 53 harmys, in : 27. R [that] : 31. R
53 syne : 34. E in athyr : 35. R 53 quhilk : 38. E R 53 wynnyng ; B in mastry ; 53 Quhilk
as the . . . [and] : 39. R of thare fre : 42. R bedowit in to : 43. R of the slauchter : 44. R
53 hale thare purpois : 45. R For follow : 48. R of gudelie amyte : 49. 53 [the] : 50. R
thare boundis : 51. R 53 voce full braid : 54. L my breist ; 53 An to : 56. R Quhilk . . .
god ; L thair planys ; 53 in to thare : 57. R [of hie Ioue] : 59. 53 [thame] so excellyng :
60. R land and behest and promyß ; 53 [land of] : 61. C Ioue *cancelled before* gret : 64.
53 grete mupyter : 65. L [the] ; B And of ; 53 of that : 66. 53 [vengeans] : 69. R Quhare
now aganis ; 53 [thou] : 70. C and *interlined* : 71. R 53 and band ; 53 ar now : 72. 53
sare, and trublyt : 75. R be lefull : 80. R 53 corps now ; R lyis : 81. 53 demnyng : 83. L
And thou : 84. 53 handis : 86. E turß him away ; 53 tursis : 95. 53 this vnknaw : 97. R
[now] : 98. R L 53 clepit ; 53 Ausomanis : 100. R bitter : 103. R ʒit nane armoure : 105.
E by by ʒour ; 53 I kend : 107. 53 and of our : 108. R 53 leifsum ; 53 As al forsoith : 110.
R 53 Addressit ; 53 the ciete : 111. R thocht ful : 114. L haill of ʒyngkeris : 116. R That
swift ; 53 The : 118. 53 and crying : 120. L Of : 121. L [rerd].

XIII.ii.

3. E 53 bering ; 53 slane : 5. 53 neuertheles : 6. R and langer ; 53 grete : 7. 53 Bot : 8.
C altarys *in margin*, honouris *cancelled* : 12. R the tempill : 14. 53 the clufis : 15. R 53
plat : 18. R 53 be tailʒeis and be sydis : 19. R In the hate ; R 53 flambis bricht has : 23.
C wirschipip ; E R L B 53 wirschep ; 53 And gan : 24. E vpbleiß : 25. R makis : 28. R
and ferefull : 31. R 53 pecefyit in bettir : 32. R to the thai hald tharefore ; 53 to the thay
ʒald tharfore : 34. 53 workar : 35. C haill *in margin*, all *cancelled* ; R 53 of thare : 37. E
L B and eik wyth : 38. R 53 amang the : 39. E thame thame all : 40. R hand ; 53 [tho] :
44. E O ʒow : 45. R the faderis : 46. E 53 and mischeif : 47. E careit hame ; R haue and
catchit ; E taryit : 48. E *omits* ; 53 thrawart : 49. L *combines 49 and 50* rest and maist
desyrit day : 50. 53 the rest and : 54. R 53 has schawin : 58. C bafe *cancelled before*
behufe : 63. R turnyt hame agane : 64. 53 [the] : 67. R and [my] : 68. E my hard : 71. R
With . . . and battaill : 72. R and armoure : 74. R all the wayes : 75. R horribill wayis
or ; L and ʒit : 76. R B 53 and : 77. R and : 78. R 53 myndis : 80. E 53 cuming : 85. 53
Qham : 91. L mynd . . . atanis : 92. E to me Italianis ; R 53 As : 95. R [and] ; 53 weris :
97. R Bot in the : 99. E and be : 101. R 53 [ws] : 102. R Bot be the . . . all ydrawe ; 53
Bot he the . . . and sternes law : 104. R 53 thou : 105. R [sa] : 115. R 53 in ioy : 118. B
Thai was : 119. R [that] : 120. E Scummand ws in ; R and turnis hir ; B Cummand ; 53
of Turnus his : 125. R 53 of that : 128. R 53 mycht of : 129. E schowtis sche : 130. R hir
bak : 131. E verra : 132. 53 hence : 140. R freyndis : 141. R [and] : 144. L hevy byrnand ;
53 The bald drede : 146. 53 sa grete discis : 147. R 53 at late ; 53 [it] : 148. R and sustene
and invyous : 149. L and rehersing : 150. E conforting : 151. 53 in the : 152. E and beute :
154. R ane fray : 156. R L B 53 offerandis ; L wirschippit.

XIII.iii. heading. R [estait] ; L king latynnys

2. E deip corps : 3. R was : 4. R laurentyne : 6. E ther Enee : 12. 53 selcouth, diuers : 13. B that loud : 15. R With ane grisly wound : 17. R And than : 18. 53 Fail : 19. E word : 21. R [that] : 22. E awfull thunderand ; R thudderand : 25. R 53 remanyng of the : 26. L For his : 28. 53 quhyncheand : 29. E dois ; R 53 did : 30. R thare hand ; 53 [quhen] : 32. R This : 34. E L B the rutilianis ; 53 Thir same : 35. E Gan all command : 37. R That thus : 38. R this wourdis : 39. C B *marginal note* nota : 42. L gret rowbill : 45. L and ceptre : 46. E Quhill : 48. 53 3our breistis : 50. E L B dois ; R 53 do ; R we cary : 52. 53 [sa] : 54. E the proud ; R Do steris : 55. B Quhou may : 56. R [thou] turß : 57. 53 *substitutes 58* : 58. 53 Quhat labour curis falsched, and craftynes : 60. 53 afore : 62. E R B wardly : 64. R and of thame : 53 realme : 65. E R Quhilkis ; R [costis] : 66. R and wardly : 67. E suffyr may : 68. B and peax : 70. R 53 infortunate : 72. R subiect vnder dout : 73. R decaue : 74. R 53 is to thame : 76. R and ferefull were : 78. E B 53 strang ; R strange ; L e *cancelled in* strang- : 81. R violent : 82. 53 promyssis : 84. 53 Quhat was : 85. E onpaciens ; R pacience : 86. 53 That thay : 87. R the pepill ; R B 53 bald strang ; 53 thy pepill : 90. R 53 [and] : 92. 53 [from] : 93. E L B that band ; R thare band ; 53 forth brek : 96. E [move] : 99. L to till awfull : 100. R 53 the rowtis : 102. B to withdraw the : 103. E In feill ; R [the] : 107. R schuting the : 108. E haue I ; R syne thow standis ; 53 [sen] : 109. C hait *cancelled before* het : 111. E R 53 wyth banis : 112. R the possessioun : 113. C all *in margin* : 115. R 53 and broun : 116. C gret *in margin* ; E L B and gret ; R quellis : 119. 53 [I] : 123. R Or : 124. 53 is it went : 126. 53 the schinand : 129. R 53 dolour : 134. R 53 the bak : 135. R Ne nocht the ; R 53 thy mynde : 137. 53 the woful : 138. R L 53 At last ; B to thy : 139. E dois : 140. R The : 142. C baith and *cancelled before* chekis : 143. R torned.

XIII.iv. heading. E [by] ; R brynt and doun schent

2. R stent : 7. R horsß ; R 53 scheildis and : 8. R 53 Swerdis : 12. E [to] : 15. R has : 22. 53 [man] : 24. 53 *omits* 24–27 : 27. R with woundis : 28. R thame that with : 29. E Thowart : 31. R [sa] . . . wer : 32. R euery man : 33. 53 matronus : 35. E no thing witand ; 53 wyttand so : 39. E That this . . . [ded] : 46. R Has . . . littand : 47. 53 And suddane : 49. E L 53 of his ; R of hir ; R 53 biggingis : 50. R rekis : 52. E fyre : 54. R helpe of hope : 55. E was in the : 56. R suld schaw ; B fatis tharfor : 58. 53 remedy : 60. 53 batand : 62. R and wrechit : 63. R In ane lang : 65. E bleß ; R the braid flambis : 71. R to fell : 75. R 53 rentis : 77. R As will ; 53 Is wyll : 79. R [Or] [Syde] : 80. R 53 toppit : 81. E R 53 dois ; L hir byrnand : 83. E [the] ; 53 thare feit : 90. L Ruschit : 91. R Bare here : 92. 53 [all] : 94. C E L B 53 Dawnus and wofull ; E [kyng] : 95. E cled and ; 53 *omits* : 97. 53 the heroun : 98. R behaldand ; 53 behald and : 100. R and the takin : 102. R Quhom with : 108. 53 And oft the : 111. R pipill : 112. R 53 Thare : 115. R smytyn in harde desire ; 53 [hait] : 116. E cheif cite ; R ciete ; 53 this cheif cyite : 118. B deid gravyn.

XIII.v.

1. R the deray : 3. 53 huge murmure : 4. E L B fulfillis : 5. E myndis than how : 6. R [with] : 8. R discomfit : 15. R 53 the materis ; L [as] : 19. L his space : 24. L [a] : 26. R On this wise with wourdis lamentable he said ; 53 [and] on thus : 29. R [me] : 30. R In so : 34. R the wourthy : 35. E [heß] ; R my sprete ; 53 Quhare is thy douchty : 36. L *omits* : 38. R [thy] : 39. C and eyß *cancelled before* wyrschip : 42. 53 So this : 44. R

And of : 45. R the mentis the fynale terme and : 46. R desiris : 47. R 53 wa is : 49. R 53 sliddry ; R wardly ; L dryvist ; 53 drawis : 51. E this fatis ; R 53 thare fatis : 53. R and chevelrye : 55. R Quhen : 56. L sa fast : 57. R 53 this wise : 58. 53 now lyis : 62. R big but but harme3 ; L bur harnes ; 53 armes : 63. E B 53 lusty heid : 64. 53 in visage : 67. R The : 68. R The ; L the trumpet : 69. L of armys in : 70. L B venquyst : 71. 53 in to : 72. R To frawart : 73. E the steid ; R with me : 75. E hait full deid : 79. R Thy ; 53 the scepture : 80. E command ; 53 abseruand : 81. E and doun rakkis ; R thringand and ; L thrangis : 82. R 53 folk : 87. E L [to] ; 53 child thus to be reif : 88. R With sic ane : 90. C hes *cancelled before* hapnyt ; R 53 happy chance ; R 53 has ; 53 as : 91. R O thyne ; L begaid in : 92. 53 grete dishonour : 93. R and myscheif : 94. R changeand ; B changeabill : 95. R Off : 97. R bereft in ardea : 100. 53 Syth : 101. E [I] ; R And ha turnus moist : 102. 53 the maist : 103. R or skathing : 107. E Than quhen ; R That quhen : 110. R aschail3eis : 112. E of my scheif ; R 53 soundis : 113. 53 wepand sore : 115. R Drawis : 118 R and his : 120. R the kyn.

XIII.vi.

1. L with hir : 2. R has illummynit on licht : 3. E L B seand tho : 7. R [turnyt] : 10. R 53 change : 16. R 53 quhilk ; R wourthy knycht : 19. R To : 20. R full strate ; 53 command-mentis : 22. R Off hir : 23. R admonyssing : 24. R syng : 25. E L B to kyn ; R 53 king ; 26. E Adione : 27. E R 53 And thairfor : 30. E [hie] ; R his hie palice of stanys ; 53 the, hie : 31. R meyne quhile : 34. B And to onweildy : 40. E L B pepill attour : 43. R according in thare lugeingis ; 53 and al thare lugeingis : 50. 53 semblant ryall, and : 51. R And for to furthschaw sic : 52. E desyrit in solace ; R neve pece : 56. E R L B 53 heidis : 58. R L 53 Quhen : 59. R the palice : 60. R 53 gif : 61. E R cauß ; 53 caus : 64. R [the] : 65. E [he] : 68. 53 glore : 71. E L dois : 73. R will : 74. 53 assembil : 77. E L B brokyne : 79. E trublit : 81. C L B *parentheses in MSS* ; E R responß ; 53 respons : 93. R constrenyt : 97. E oft troy : 98. R in ioyes : 100. R 53 and [to] : 109. E Bot thar : 110. R 53 Furthspowtand : 111. R for to seke sucquedry ; 53 sucquedry vndertake : 113. 53 finale : 114. C the *in margin* : 115. E bet the ground : 117. E L B this ilk : 119. 53 flude, of : 121. E L B Othir gostis ; R and barganis : 124. L [to] : 126. E R 53 nobillis : 128. E And this : 129. R all his : 131. R sterne ; B and gold : 136. R [And] : 138. E secretis sege ; R In the : 142. R childe : 143. R consent : 144. R als for : 146. 53 Vnder the : 147. R 53 The auld Italy : 150. 53 returnite : 155. R of king : 157. E Itail blude : 158. L quhilk the : 160. R Haue done herefore : 161. R 53 The : 164. R And seisingis ; L 53 quhilk : 167. R Quhen : 168. C f *cancelled before* hes ; R in effere : 170. R ansuerand has carpit ; 53 carpit : 171. R 30w bot king ; L Not thou : 173. R 53 I will ; R argewe on ; R 53 and offence ; L of fens : 175. E L B brocht out : 177. R as was : 178. E movit the melle ; R 53 to the melle : 179. R Off hie revovne for 30ng desire ; R renown effray : 180. L 53 did say : 181. E quhen ewir ; R 53 neuertheles : 182. R The : 184. E forto be ; R Na for na ; 53 Nor na knitting : 187. R 53 samyn : 188. C venerall ; E R L B 53 venerabill : 190. C beld *e corrected from y* ; R 53 and with wallis : 192. R Nane of my : 194. E R 53 [in] ; L Incord and : 195. R tocum sall athir : 196. E sall leif I sall freyndschip ; R [sall] : 197. 53 [to] : 198. L 30ur werk : 203. E R L dois : 204. R 53 to the : 207. E L B And of his ; E [wonderand all] : 208. E And with : 209. E than gan : 210. E [sik] ; 53 werk : 211. R with mycht forcis ; 53 Blissit with : 213. L gadderis has : 214. L The : 215. 53 thir cieti3anis has laed : 216. E R bleiß : 217. B vpgydis : 218. E [of the] : 221. E tyrentir

scheip ; R [scheip] : 222. E thair ; R thir accorde : 223. R 53 The : 226. L thair hait :
227. R 53 Stude blunt.

XIII.vii. heading. R with latynus kene

1. E R secund schynnand : 3. 53 Ausomanis : 11. 53 only son : 12. R Iulius : 13. 53
Alethus : 14. 53 sergest : 15. 53 Serestus : 16. 53 Syas : 17. R 53 Eftir thame ; 53 went
atayne : 18. R 53 folkis : 19. E R L meyne tyme ; B [quhile] : 20. R 53 ischit out : 21.
R laude myrth in solempnite ; 53 and myche : 23. 53 in to : 29. R verray face : 33. E
contenas : 34. R [that] : 35. B ather to othir gudly : 36. R And hie wourdis : 39. 53
Latinis : 42. R dissauit the : 44. L Of : 46. R changis : 49. C that *cancelled erroneously
before* manis ; E R L B 53 [that] ; R 53 And thocht : 52. R 53 The : 55. E Full of : 59. R
it is : 63. R 53 the wikkit : 65. E [now] : 69. R in mariage : 72. E beltit : 73. R that wer
conquest : 74. E L B doun bet and kest : 76. R 53 verray age : 77. 53 [I] : 78. 53 Quhaire
in : 82. R [said] : 85. 53 O this : 86. 53 traist : 90. 53 fald : 92. R 53 That now ressauis ;
53 fra thys : 93. E chance : 95. E anchises de : 96. R to mc here in : 100. B Towart.

XIII.viii. heading. 53 that wourey gentil knycht

1. R [sikkyn] ; 53 siclike : 2. 53 wyth thet : 4. 53 and the : 6. E the wyndois : 9. 53 In
grte : 15. R compaissit as thing maist : 16. E R 53 bewtie : 18. B and gude : 21. L quhen
as : 22. E fur3et : 23. 53 ythil, aganis : 26. R lang space : 27. E R 53 Dois : 30. 53 smout,
the : 34. B and thair : 40. 53 and hie : 43. R 53 Italie : 45. E [fest] : 49. R [thar-] ; 53
chalmeris : 51. 53 Of fare ladyis : 57. R 53 dois : 58. 53 the troyane : 61. R And at . . . als
wox : 62. R In : 64. R quhen that na : 66. R sic ane : 67. R in hope : 68. E R 53 aucht
to : 69. L hand for hand : 72. 53 The : 82. B Eneas thus capys : 84. 53 reche robbis : 85.
C precyus *in margin*, prescius *cancelled* ; R 53 [the] : 86. C with *cancelled before* of :
87. E L B andromacha is hand ; R Adromachus : 89. 53 the cowar : 93. R [that] ; 53
were fare : 96. R gold weill engraif : 99. E [to] : 104. R 53 blith breistis ; R and deulie
obeysance : 105. R interteny ; L festyng enterit and ; B entertenyt ; 53 intertene : 108.
53 houris, driuand.

XIII.ix. heading. R 53 feist ; R Remembrand . . . geist ; L [ald] ; 53 and auld geist

1. E L B [it] ; 53 [the] : 2. E [fast] : 4. R 53 sit at : 7. R according to : 10. 53 hallis hicht :
13. E L B [the] : 15. R [with] masis : 17. E And quhow : 18. E *omits 18-20* : 24. E dois . . .
that large : 25. R drynking glasß ; 53 cassis : 27. 53 thare walkin : 29. 53 grete chere : 31.
R And : 33. R of his : 34. E his spech : 36. R 53 [his] : 41. R kisß : 43. R 53 declarit : 44.
R 53 bedewit : 45. R has gevin : 46. R 53 quhill : 47. E mony : 51. R Sone schape : 52.
C hard *cancelled before* Troianys ; R aventure : 55. R his mynde : 56. E L B quharby
and ; R As quhen : 57. R discumfit : 59. R dart ; R 53 swerdis : 63. E on the : 66. 53
Latynis : 67. R 53 and sufferand princis : 69. E the day is ; L B the days : 70. R B the
mychty : 71. R How quhylum : 73. L dyd in latium : 74. 53 [dwelt] : 76. R [lawys] ; 53
law : 77. E thame the grub : 78. R 3ok the carte : 81. C he *interlined* ; E And quhen :
83. R Or dardanus : 84. 53 Iosyus : 86. R se his went and with : 89. E And quhan ; 53
[And] : 94. E [the] : 97. E maneir takkin ; R 53 taking : 99. E that wanis ; R [with] :
100. R 53 hillis : 101. C sownd *cancelled before* voce : 102. R vphie the dyn vprentis ;

53 vpwenis : 103. 53 blesand orchis : 104. E R bemys : 105. E B [the] : 109. E throw thair ; R to vthir : 110. 53 futtit it : 111. R Thay haisty : 112. L neir the day ; 53 quhil sic riot nere : 114. E that nycht : 115. E to draw : 116. R 53 [sik] ; L vnknaw.

XIII.x. heading. 53 foundit

3. R spouß : 4. R [tent] : 7. R 53 make ane cirkill : 9. B foundyt : 10. R 53 dykis ; 14. 53 lychting : 16. C B Lavinia is : 17. C lyft *in margin*, lyß *cancelled* ; E L B fra hyne : 20. E be takyne ; 53 be takin : 21. R to the hevin ; 53 towart the heuyn : 22. 53 his bane : 23. E L B [euer] : 24. C baith *cancelled before* baith : 26. R and syre ; 53 or fyre : 27. E or godheid : 28. R in ony : 30. 53 ȝit, that restis : 31. 53 dois : 32. E [this] : 33. R and syne pece : 35. B warpit : 38. R carpit : 39. R out of : 40. E goldin singis ; R gudelie ; 53 godlie thingis : 41. E reiouß : 44. E R the extreme ; 53 cum : 46. E L B [vp] : 47. E 30u ; R now nocht the flamb of flambis : 48. E spowß : 51. C the ; R 53 thy douchty ; B and douchty : 52. R successioun renewe : 53. R troianis princis fra : 62. B warld : 63. 53 glorie : 67. 53 *reverses 67–68* : 71. R The : 72. R [thy] : 74. E L B [this syng] : 76. R honoure of hir [sal] : 78. E spouß : 79. C goddis *in margin*, god *cancelled* : 80. 53 [it] : 83. 53 thou gart them sone, to be : 85. C E L B Tharto ; 53 eternal : 87. E stranguly : 95. 53 fortinat : 97. E Quhair ; 53 Quham : 98. R 53 folkis : 100. 53 ydraw : 101. R 53 to the goistis in [the] : 102. E L B [dolly] ; R dayis to de : 105. B weld *cancelled*, wend *interlined* : 108. R [And] Vp to the : 110. E R 53 dois ; E L B gleid : 112. L [I want nocht] *space left* : 117. B rewlys : 118. R [the] ; R 53 Latynis : 119. E his ceptre : 121. R 53 Italiane : 122. E lordschipis : 124. R 53 reulis : 127. R 53 maner : 131. R 53 and ally.

XIII.xi. heading. E Quhen

6. E this ; R expresß : 7. R from the : 11. R 53 that quhen : 12. E onwrendly : 13. R Thy promyß : 15. 53 promyssis : 19. E blyß peax ; R bliss and : 21. 53 the estrnit : 22. 53 thy maist : 23. E R L 53 abuif the : 25. C in thy *cancelled before* rollyng ; E R 53 dois : 26. 53 dois : 27. E Eneas I the : 31. R His ; 53 Ther : 33. L knawis full stranglie : 35. R has I : 37. E and quhayr that ; R [that] oft tymes : 38. R [the] : 39. R the throw diseiß : 40. E L B haue I : 41. R All thir ; L and thar ennoy : 42. E [weill] : 46. R [that] : 49. 53 And thus I : 50. E [clenge] ; R [se] that now change ; L 53 change : 52. 53 aboue al the : 53. R And I : 55. R 53 lovingis : 56. E do : 57. R elikewise : 59. 53 The hoddis aboue : 62. 53 [the] heuin : 64. E *omits* : 66. R Nor quhare that Municus : 68. 53 Dikit : 71. C was *interlined* ; E 53 mortall and : 74. B [it] : 76. 53 the stremes : 77. 53 kinred : 78. R amang : 82. 53 [gan].

ending. E Conclusio Explicit liber decimus tertius aeneados : quod bocardo et baroco ; R *as* C *except* in eneados ; L Conclusio explicit liber decimus tertius Eneados &c. scriptum per me Iohannem mudy ; B Conclusio Explicit liber decimus tertius ; 53 Finis.

Conclusio heading. E The conclusioune of this bulk of Aeneados *twice* ; R *as* C ; L B *omit* ; 53 Conclusion.

1. E [all] ; R my buke : 3. E L B and doun ; 53 Nor trensche and swerd : 5. R [that] : 10.
R comparing : 13. R for ʒore : 14. E fixt : 16. E salbe now : 17. C solitar *cancelled after*
solitar ; E dois ; 53 solitary : 18. R 53 all is : 21. R sweand in the : 23. R Adew gladenes ;
L B *omit 23–24* ; 53 *last four lines read*

> And wyl derek my laubouris, euer moir
> Unto the commoun welth, and goddis gloir
> Adew gud readeris, god gif ʒou al gud nycht
> And eftir deth, grant vs his heueinly lycht

24. R [gentill].

ending. C Geddes *or* Geddas ; E R L B 53 *omit*.

Directioun, heading. E *as* C *except repealed* ; R Here the direkkare and translatare of
this buke direkkis it and excusis him self &c. ; L B 53 *omit*

1. 53 *omits 1–148* : 4. R in gude : 8. E Than this my : 13. E R L B will spy : 14. B bagbyte :
18. R [full] : 20. R sic spite : 21. L B [be] : 23. E [thai] ; R I haue myne honeste : 24. L B
[schute a but] *space left* : 25. R thing in threpe ; L B [heir] *space left* : 28. R of scharpe :
29. R weddir schynys : 30. R als preseruit : 37. E prophitabile : 38. E [full] : 39. R Eik
it sall : 43. R thame that wald : 47. R tharof : 48. E in ʒour ; R and skulis : 50. B my
tyme onthrifty : 51. R [For] : 52. R Euery rude rurale : 61. L B lordschip : 63. R [so] :
66. E Quhilkis : 71. R devill of : 78. E L B to ʒour : 79. R and of all : 90. E the berd
roin : 94. R termeʒ plane and : 96. R obseruit bene perfite ; L B [scant] *space left* : 97.
R [otheris] ; L B [say] *space left* : 101. E [be] : 102. E R translatit : 108. R And bruik :
110. R I said I wrate : 115. R B I haue ; R [said] be ma na : 116. R B folkis : 125. L haue
haue I : 128. R the bell : 129. E fame as blaw : 132. R ane tratour : 134. E as ʒou ; L B
[as thou art] *space left* : 135. L [dyd] : 138. R promyst.

ending. E R L B *as* C.

Exclamatioun, heading. E *as* C *except* Ane exclamatioune aganis detractouris
repeated, and crafty warkis ; R L B 53 *as* C

3. R him volume : 4. E I sowir ; R raik now : 6. E [have] ; 53 perrellis : 8. C *parentheses
in MS* ; L B [beis wyd quhar] *space left* : 9. R 53 [owr] ; L B [red in our] *space left* : 11.
R in euery : 12. R biddis thame birn : 16. R or in nuke ; 53 and nuke : 18. E lo thair ; B
thair he fenʒeis luke ; 53 lo here : 20. E [have] : 22. R 53 as sa : 24. R or than deulie : 27.
E thingis guid : 28. E R L B 53 and mote : 29. R 53 vthir : 30. R That but ; 53 to wyte :
31. R 53 so birnand hote : 32. 53 Bald thay : 33. R 53 and [to] ; R bytebyte : 41. E neid
is ; 53 thy licht : 43. E *reverses 43–44* ; R L B 53 sall : 45. B [erst] *space left*.

ending. E R B *as* C ; L Quod Gawynus Dowglaß ; 53 Finis. *ends with the riddle* To
knaw the name of the translator, *in other texts after the end of Book XII.*

Tyme, heading. E *as* C *except* [space] *and repeated* ; R L B *as* C ; 53 *this section precedes the Exclamacion* The space tyme [Heir followys]

1. 53 Compilet : 2. R Fra apoun : 5. E [gret] : 6. R 53 mony ane day : 7. R 53 neuertheles : 8. E thairto fyrst I sett my pen ; 53 [fyrst] set my pen : 9. R 53 thare : 11. E ken me : 12. R I was compilit in till ; L B 53 monethis : 13. E L B moneth ; 53 [I] : 14. R that mycht : 17. R [of] : 20. R Quharfore : 23. R 53 rede : 24. 53 nowthir mail : 26. R 53 [now] ; B [haue].

ending. E *adds* Opere finito sit laus et gloria Christo &c. I. E. m Iohannes Elphinstoun M Ioannes Elphynstoun ; L *adds* Heir endis the buke of Virgill writtin be the hand of Iohanne mudy with master thomas bellenden of auchinnovll Iustis Clerke and endit the 2 februarii anno &c. xlv *library stamp* ; B Heir endis the buke of Virgill prince of Latyn poetis in his twelf bukis of Eneados Traslatit furth of Latyne in oure scottis Langage be ane rycht nobil and wirschipfull clerk master gawane dowglas provest off Sanct Gelis kirk in Edinburgh and persoun of Lyntoun in Louthian quhilk eftir was bischope of Dunkeld And als endis the xiii buke translait as said is with the Prolougis tharof writtin be me henry aytoun notare publict and endit the twentytwa day of November the 3eir off god m vc fourtysevin 3eris &c. Finis &c. ; 53 Finis.

Epitaph, heading. E L B 53 *omit* ; R tenet me [nunc]

1–6. E L B 53 *omit* : 3. R grave I stant : 4. R notablis.

ending. C *f. 330ʳ library stamp* ; *f. 330ᵛ–flyleaf 4ʳ blank* ; *flyleaf 4ᵛ* Suntque mei vel wis In primis cui[us]que Tunc In illo tempore *at top of folio* ; R Quod Gawinus Douglas &c. ; *in later hand* Lib. Bibl. Edinensis., *followed by blank page on reverse of which are written first three stanzas of the Testament of Cresseid and the inscription* Partenet Wilhelmo / domino de Ruthven.